The Complete Stylist

Also by Sheridan Baker

The Practical Stylist, SECOND EDITION
The Essayist, SECOND EDITION
Problems in Exposition: Supplementary Exercises for The Complete Stylist *and* The Practical Stylist (WITH DWIGHT STEVENSON)

The Complete Stylist

Second Edition

SHERIDAN BAKER
The University of Michigan

THOMAS Y. CROWELL COMPANY
New York *Established 1834*

FRONT COVER ILLUSTRATION:
"Herodotus Crowned by Apollo."
Woodcut on title page of *Historiarum libri IX* (Venice, 1494), edited by Giovanni and Gregorio de Gregoriis (Bibliothèque Nationale)

DESIGNED BY ANGELA FOOTE

L.C. Card 76-165376
ISBN 0-690-20763-8 (cloth)
ISBN 0-690-20764-6 (paper)

Manufactured in the United States of America

To my father,

Preface

Several years ago, a number of teachers asked for some treatment of rhetorical problems beyond the essentials presented in THE PRACTICAL STYLIST, for a more comprehensive book that would serve as both basic text and handbook throughout the college years. In response, I wrote THE COMPLETE STYLIST, which, though more comprehensive, aimed to emulate its smaller parent by remaining thoroughly practical. Since then, many teachers, and even some students, have sent in comments about what had worked well for them and what had not, asking particularly for more examples and fuller explanations. This second edition revises the first throughout, especially in the light of these suggestions. As before, it hopes to prove practical and useful to anyone, in school and out, who must sit down before the facts of language as he faces a blank page.

Again I stress rhetoric, the art of communication and persuasion, the styling of language to attract, edify, and convince the reader. I urge the student to see that style is both personal and public, a matter of finding oneself in language—one's own personality written into reason and looking its best—a matter of rendering that self sensible and persuasive to the public at large.

Again I emphasize argument as the quickest and clearest teacher of rhetorical principles. I begin at the big end of the compositional problem, thus reversing the order traditional with many handbooks, that of beginning with simple units and gradually building upward toward the "whole essay." This process I myself have always found too slow, as it postpones the whole essay's two most essential rhetorical principles, those of outer form and inner idea, of structure and thesis. Once the student has grasped the communicative and clarifying powers in structure and thesis, he can proceed easily to the smaller and smaller units, which get more powerful as they decrease in size—to paragraphs, to sentences, and to words, those conceptual wonders where our meanings begin and end. Throughout, I have tried to encourage the student's sense of the play and wonder of language, his pleasure in mastering the ordinary by trying the extraordinary in sentence and vocabulary.

The book begins by introducing the student to rhetoric, and to the question of the writer's attitude toward his subject and his readers. It encourages him to find his own voice, his own style, as he mediates between the need to express his thoughts and the need to communicate them persuasively. The first chapter concludes with some practical advice on writing and rewriting, on materials and mechanics. Appended to each chapter are exercises to bring out the main points, particularly in short engagements of five or ten minutes in class, with one or two exercises selected from those offered.

Chapters 2, 3, 4, and 5 explain the basic principles of inner idea and outer form. The student learns to distinguish between his subject and what he intends to say about it. He learns to discover his thesis, to qualify it, and to give it the argumentative thrust that organizes his whole essay from within. He then proceeds to the concept of structure —the "outer" ordering of parts along essential psychological lines. First, the basic Beginning, Middle, and End; then the several orders that range from the temporal and spatial to the inductive and deductive—the leading in and the leading out. Chapter 5 concludes the general structural lesson by considering outlines, in their various kinds and uses.

Chapters 6 and 7 consider the paragraph. The student begins with the general rhetorical reasons for paragraphing, and sees how the paragraph follows the same structural pattern as the essay itself, repeating in smaller scale the principles he has learned in the preceding chapters. He considers the special structural demands of the beginning paragraph and the end paragraph, and how both differ from the "middle" paragraph, the standard building block of composition. He then moves to different ways to develop narrative and expository paragraphs.

Chapters 8 and 9 present the sentence, also with a structural emphasis, and with some advice on structural clarity. Chapter 8 considers compound and complex structuring, coordination and subordination, modifying and paralleling. It concludes with a short consideration of variety in sentences, and with a generous number of exercises to help the student try out various patterns and stretch his wings. Chapter 9 concentrates on correcting bad sentences, again with copious exercises. Chapter 10 reinforces Chapters 8 and 9 by considering the conventions and meanings of punctuation.

Chapter 11 deals with words, the smallest and most dynamic units, including some advice on spelling. It considers vocabulary, abstract and concrete words, metaphor, allusion, and diction. It distinguishes between meaningful words and wordiness, and shows how diction can get out of hand.

Next come "Four Excursions." The book's chief lesson of moving from big idea to small word is now complete. The student may now try other things, and perhaps even enjoy himself. First, a trip into the autobiographical essay, which brings narrative and description within the expository compass. Next, the Terrible Essay—frequently a howling success with the class—in which the student writes the worst essay he can, learning in reverse, as it were, all the things to avoid and getting them out of his system. The Ironic Essay then takes the student a step further into deriving meaning by indirection, into the wizardry of words. Finally, the Critical Review returns to regular exposition, as the student considers the questions of criticism and applies them to a short story, a novel, a play, or motion picture.

Chapter 13, "Straight and Crooked Thinking," is a logical refiner of the lessons that run through the book—that writing is itself a discovery of reasons and reason, that writing both clarifies and creates thought, of which it is the palpable substance. Some teachers use only half the chapter, omitting the final section on logical proof; others assign the whole chapter in conjunction with the chapter on "Words."

The final chapter, "The Research Paper," brings all the student's acquisitions to bear on a major project. Again he finds a subject and locates his thesis within it. He then proceeds in practical steps through the library, the techniques of research, the drafting and revising, and all the conventions of documentation, footnoting, and typing, achieving a solid foundation for his subsequent work in college, and indeed in graduate school and beyond. Examples of papers from my classroom show what can be done and how to do it.

The three appendices reinforce earlier chapters. Appendix A, "A Writer's Grammar," aims to make the student something of a family doctor for ailing sentences, a practitioner able to spot the symptom, diagnose the cause, and apply the proper treatment. Some teachers begin with this appendix; others assign it concurrently with the chapters on sentences and punctuation. Appendix B provides "A Glossary of Usage" for reference throughout the course. Appendix C, "Rhetorical Devices," is something more of a personal whim, something I have always wanted and never found, in modern print, all in one place. And I am pleased to learn that a number of other teachers use it to supplement their work on sentences and words. From these devices, the student may learn not only about rhetoric, but also about language, especially about those linguistic patterns that have proved durable these two thousand years and more.

THE COMPLETE STYLIST, then, parallels THE PRACTICAL STYLIST in amplified form, moving from the big essentials down to particulars. Two other books likewise parallel this form to make both the STYLISTS serviceable to an even wider variety of needs. THE ESSAYIST, newly revised, offers a series of parallel readings for discussion, together with further exercises. PROBLEMS IN EXPOSITION: SUPPLEMENTARY EXERCISES FOR THE COMPLETE STYLIST AND THE PRACTICAL STYLIST is a workbook in which the student systematically reinforces the lessons of the text by completing partial sentences, filling in blanks, composing short passages, correcting faulty syntax and punctuation, and the like, with pages to be torn out and handed in.

The options, indeed, are open. The instructor will find plenty of leeway for his own course, and for his own kind of class, and plenty of opportunity to sail into the book's wind, should it prove contrary. Many teachers prefer to begin with sentences and paragraphs before launching into the big ideas of composition with Chapter 2; any tack that will get the student to the essences and wonders of language is fine. The essentials are here. THE COMPLETE STYLIST aims to get at those essential powers of the essay, as they dwell in its natural psychic material—in this language of ours, the writing of which is our only steady means of getting our thinking clear and straight, and of persuading others that it is so.

I wish to acknowledge an extensive debt to a great many teachers and students whose queries, suggestions, and general encouragement have helped me to improve this book. I am also grateful to Marilyn Ferris and Tom Blaske, two good students from the same good class, who reworked their papers and permitted me to adapt them for my chapter on the research paper.

SHERIDAN BAKER

Contents

The Complete Stylist

First Considerations

1

Rhetoric is a kind of angling, a catching of the audience with choice devices. Style is the perfected casting of rhetoric. And so my title alluding to Izaak Walton's genial old *Compleat Angler* is not altogether whimsical. Walton has humor and a pleasant audacity: he well understands that no man living, nor book, can be truly complete, and yet he aims to tell his reader everything worth notice about fishing, to make him a fisherman by the end of the summer session. So if you will take *The Complete Stylist* as a general guide to the resources of the rhetorical tacklebox, you may come out in the end a stylist complete enough for most contingencies.

As it surveys the rhetorical possibilities, this book attends to the one big problem haunting every course in composition and every expository writer: how to write an essay. It shows you how to attack the problem and, step by step, how to work out the details. It hopes to give you confidence in your writing and thinking, to give you a command of your verbal resources. You have already acquired more skill than you realize. You long ago mastered the basic structures of English simply by speaking it, acquiring your native tongue as you followed your wishes and the bigger boys and girls next door. You know a good deal about its different idioms, and you have noticed the strangely automatic shift in vocabulary from the playground to the dinner table. You have learned to spell, somewhat, and to write, more or less. For about a dozen years, in fact, you have been schooled in writing your native language. You have studied a little grammar, perhaps more than a little if you have taken a foreign language and discovered that its grammatical demands clarified your understanding of English. You have compiled reports from the *Encyclopaedia Britannica* and *Life* magazine. You have written about your summer, your outside reading, racial discrimination, the mood of an autumn afternoon. You have, in short, already tried out a number of the rhetorical possibilities.

But unless especially lucky in your schooling, you probably have not worked consistently at the problem of writing an essay—how to find an interesting idea, how to get the facts straight, how to pursue them to a conclusion, how, in entering the great intellectual debate of the rights and wrongs and truths in daily life, to persuade your readers that the right is right and the true true. As you move on through college, such writing will be the recurrent task of your education. After you leave college, your mastery of thought and its expression may well mark your place in society—or place your mark on it.

Mark your place and place your mark—I have deliberately indulged in that double play to introduce you to the rhetorical devices and to the serious playfulness that rhetoric can achieve as the occasion beckons. When the late John F. Kennedy said, "Ask not what your country can do for you; ask what you can do for your country," he was using the same device, known as a *chiasmus,* a "crossing" (from the Greek letter *chi,* the cross, or X) in which two terms exchange places to emphasize a difference in meaning. Marking one's place in society suggests a much lower station (in which you perhaps mark time) than the one from which you could imprint something of your intellect and personality on society itself; and the crisscross in Kennedy's famous sentence neatly contrasts the selfish with the selfless. Appendix C contains a collection of the most useful of these rhetorical devices, among which you can browse, and find an occasional one to suit your needs as your ability to play meaningfully with language grows.

The remarkable thing is that you can find these old Greek contrivances in modern English, and in the work of people who probably never heard of them. The two languages, of course, are different. Our own language has differed from one century to the next, changing quickly or slowly as the intellectual climate has changed. But the rhetorical principles remain the same, since they are based on the psychology of perception and persuasion, and on logic. It is indeed almost breathtaking to discover that virtually everything Aristotle had to say about his Attic Greek in the *Rhetoric* and in the *Poetics* applies equally well to American English. Aristotle left many things unsaid, of course. The essay, and the printing press that made it a common literary genre, was still some centuries in the future. Nevertheless, the rhetorical principles that Aristotle discerned in language are as valid as ever, and you will meet a number of them in this book. The rhetorical approach will enable you to discern the larger principles behind the essay's form, and our general fund of rhetorical devices will provide you with a number of useful details.

You will begin, then, by learning the general organizing principles for the essay. You will learn the difference between exposition and argument. You will learn the feel of a likely subject. You will learn how to find a thesis that will, in a sense, virtually organize your essay for you from the start. Next you will see the relatively simple principles behind the structure of your essay: (1) the natural pattern of beginning, middle, and end; and (2) the natural expectancy that each new point will be better than the one just passed. Once you have grasped the essay's essentials—the thesis that starts it going, the structure that shapes it as it goes, the expectation that drives it along—you will then study its parts. You will study paragraphs in their various kinds. You will experiment with various styles of sentence, playing with length and complexity, mastering punctuation. Finally, you will get down to the rhetorical forces in words themselves, to the ultimate powers and mysteries of writing.

All this while, you will have been writing essays, keeping the whole problem in front of you as you attend to its various parts, from organization down to the individual word. Since you will have covered all the fundamentals, you will next take some excursions into special kinds of essays, to break the monotony and to limber up your language. You will also take a final look at what you have been doing all along—thinking. You will consider the ways of logic and illogic. And at the end you will see what you can do with the student's major scholarly problem: how to bring your discovered facts and your knowledge of rhetoric together in a research paper. You may then walk out into the sunshine as scholar, scientist, rhetorician, logician, and master of the art of common sense.

Grammar, Logic, and Rhetoric

Since rhetoric may be suspect and logic forbidding, perhaps we had better clarify our terms. Rhetoric is the art of persuasion. Logic is the science of reason. Add grammar—the anatomy of discourse—and you have language in its three major constituencies. Grammar, logic, and rhetoric are the first three of the seven liberal arts. They formed the *trivium* of an ancient educational system that lasted almost two thousand years, from the old Roman schools of two centuries before Christ, through the medieval universities, almost down to our own day. The trivium was obviously a kind of cognitive bedrock extending beneath seas, continents, and shifts in vernacular. Grammar gave you command of language; logic, command of thought; rhetoric, command of men. From here you went on to the other four liberal arts—geometry, arithmetic, music, and astronomy—which gave you the physical world and the heavenly spheres, revolving to inaudible music. But grammar, logic, and rhetoric were enough for the affairs of men; and today, from the statesman to his hostess, from ad man to club woman, from football coach to football fan, their essential potency is still evident, though grammar may frequently be sent to the showers, and logic to the bench.

You can check your grammar in Appendix A (especially by having a look at the fifteen ailing sentences on pages 321–322), and by consulting Appendix B, "A Glossary of Usage," for particular uncertainties. Your logic you can usually manage by common sense, and, for the time being, common sense is enough. But you can look ahead to Chapter 13, "Straight and Crooked Thinking," dipping into it if curious about fact and opinion, assumptions and fallacies, and the like, postponing a wrestle with logic itself until your writing has gained in power.

We live by the powers of language; and today, as before, rhetoric culminates those powers. When we talk, we do not really notice the words or their grammatical sequences: we grasp the idea *behind* the words, and that is enough. But rhetoric takes this natural, unnoticed flow of language and heightens it a bit by repeating and paralleling natural elements, by changing the natural order slightly, by bringing out the beauty of natural rhythms, so as to emphasize the idea by calling our attention just slightly to the wonders of the language that carries it. Rhetoric cultivates the natural shrubs and herbage of grammar, and channels logic into a coherence that moves us to admiration. Rhetoric adds emotion and art. But because our emotional and aesthetic pleasures may lose all touch with value, as when we thrill to the house afire, rhetoric too may break loose from intrinsic worth. Without worthy purpose, rhetoric may become mere hatred, or a bouquet of paper adjectives. It may be superb yet diabolical, as when the serpent sold Eve on the delights of the apple. Rhetoric, we must admit, is the manipulation of words for persuasive ends. Our responsibility is to see that the message justifies the means, that our tricks are not merely tricky, that our emotion is indeed conviction and our art the incarnation of truth.

Rhetoric at Gettysburg

Let us look at a famous, and familiar, rhetorical event to clarify our ideas about rhetoric. I mean, of course, "The Consecration of the National Cemetery at Gettysburg, Pa.," on November 19, 1863, when two very different speeches presented much the same idea. Here we may see the rhetoric of two masters, both of whom labored at their addresses, and we may see how the soul of the occasion moves into the rhetoric of Lincoln's short masterpiece, after only an occasional visit among the more roundly rhetorical sentences of Edward Everett, the Orator of the Day.

But we should not underestimate Everett, or we shall underestimate

Lincoln, too. Preacher, professor of Greek, member of the House of Representatives, governor of Massachusetts, minister to Great Britain, president of Harvard, secretary of state, and senator, Everett was the most distinguished orator of his time. With an oration on George Washington, delivered in all parts of the country, he had raised more than $100,000 to buy Mount Vernon for the nation.

Everett's two-hour analysis of the three-day battle at Gettysburg is still one of the best, but his style, alongside that of Lincoln's two-minute dedication, seems enormously puffy:

> **. . . whether this august republican Union, founded by some of the wisest statesmen that ever lived, cemented with the blood of some of the purest patriots that ever died, should perish or endure. . . .**
> **. . . those who sleep beneath our feet, and their gallant comrades who survive to serve their country on other fields of danger. . . .**

These two quotations, as you will already have noticed, were echoed by Lincoln, who followed Everett on the program. Having read the press release of Everett's oration in advance, Lincoln seems to have remembered Everett's thoughts as he wrote out his own brief dedicatory remarks:

> **. . . whether that nation . . . can long endure.**
> **The brave men, living and dead, who struggled here . . .**
> **. . . shall not perish. . . .**

Later, in Gettysburg, Lincoln reworked his address twice before the ceremony. The first version, with his subsequent alterations, is reprinted below. Lincoln, with his speech in hand, nevertheless spoke mostly from memory and followed his text almost verbatim, adding only *under God,* as his speaking moved him. You will notice that Lincoln, like Everett, elevates his language rhetorically. In one place, indeed, he may have elevated a touch too much: Matthew Arnold told friends that he could never get beyond "dedicated to the proposition." And by itself the phrase, rhyming a little slushily with "nation," does indeed sound like good old sociological jargon in full flower.

But the fault is ever so slight, and it consorts unnoticed with the general rhetorical heightening the occasion required. Note Lincoln's slightly inverted order of words in the famous opening sentence, and the alliterative tying of words beginning in *f* and *s* and *c*—all elevating the language above the ordinary. Note his repetitions, some merely emphatic, some worked for extra meaning—especially *lives-live,* and *dedicated,* which came only after revision. Note the new "fitting and proper" sentence, where the purely rhetorical need of bringing the paragraph to rest demands the redundant comfort of a cliché. Finally, notice how Lincoln dignifies and intensifies his thought by echoing the biblical "threescore years and ten"—a man's traditional span of life—to resonate his idea of the uncertain life of the nation at that moment, a nation that had perhaps already outlived its divinely appointed time in its present, ominous, internal war. "Eighty-seven years ago" would have seemed too short, too insignificant, and Lincoln would have lost not only the biblical solemnity but also the idea of the life of man, of birth, life, and death, which he beautifully elaborates in the first sentence with *fathers, brought forth,* and *conceived,* and in the last with *new birth of freedom,* as the life cycle starts again.

I have bracketed the portions Lincoln deleted as he revised, and I have underlined his additions. The phrase *who fought here* and the word *advanced* (indicated in italics) he added for publication at some time after the event.

Four score and seven years ago our fathers brought forth [,up]on this continent, a new nation, conceived in [liberty] Liberty, and dedicated to the proposition that ["]all men are created equal.["]

Now we are engaged in a great civil war, testing whether that nation, or any nation so conceived, and so dedicated, can long endure. We are met on a great battle-field of that war. We have come to dedicate a portion of [it] that field, as a final resting place for those who [died here, that the] here gave their lives that that nation might live. [This we may, in all propriety do.] It is altogether fitting and proper that we should do this.

But, in a larger sense, we can not dedicate—we can not consecrate —we can not hallow—this ground. The grave men, living and dead, who struggled here, have [hallowed] consecrated it, far above our poor power to add or detract. The world will little note, nor long remember what we say here [; while], but it can never forget what they did here. It is [rather] for us, the living [to stand here || we here be dedicated], rather, to be dedicated here to the unfinished work which they *who fought here* have thus far so nobly [carried on] *advanced.* It is rather for us to be here dedicated to the great task remaining before us—that from these honored dead we take increased devotion to that cause for which they [here] gave the last full measure of devotion—that we here highly resolve that these dead shall not have died in vain—that [the] this nation, under God, shall have a new

birth of freedom—and that government of the people, by the people, for the people, shall not perish from the earth.*

There, indeed, is rhetoric. Coming after Everett's two hours of rotundity, it has always seemed simplicity unadorned, the homespun prose of Honest Abe, the noble backwoodsman. But note again the rhetorical force accumulating behind the word *dedicated,* used (with *dedicate*) six times in the ten sentences. The whole purpose was to *dedicate* a national cemetery. The nation, which the Civil War was cruelly testing, had been *dedicated* to the equality of men. We who have come to *dedicate* a portion of that battlefield cannot match the personal *dedication* of those who died there. We must again *dedicate* ourselves to equally shared freedom. Lincoln has punned in a serious way to extract from the word its shades of meaning and to emphasize the essential democratic ideal, which requires the dedication of all. He briefly works a similar rhetorical emphasis with the word *devotion,* before his final rhetorical repetition and parallel—*of the people, by the people, for the people*—alliterating beautifully and meaningfully with the *perish* he had borrowed from Everett.

Here also we can see how a command of grammar takes its rhetorical effect. Grammar is necessary, of course, merely to steer clear of any error that would lose the audience's respect. But Lincoln uses his grammar rhetorically as well, not only in the slightly heightened inversion at the beginning (*brought forth on this continent a new nation*) but in a number of grammatical parallels: his contrast of *remember what we say here* as against *forget what they did here,* for instance. But the grammatical parallels with which he closes are the most striking; two triple parallels, one within the other, achieving a magnificent and moving finality. He puts equivalent thoughts into the same grammatical structure, again accumulating an emphasis: we are to resolve (1) that these dead shall not have died in vain, (2) that this nation shall have a new birth, (3) that democratic government shall not perish. And within this third parallel we learn, again in a triple grammatical parallel, that government of the people (any government at all) is, in a democracy, government *by* the people, but more especially *for* the people, as grammar effects the rhetorical point.

---

* *Abraham Lincoln's Gettysburg Address: The First and Second Drafts Now in the Library of Congress* (Washington, D.C.: U.S. Government Printing Office, 1950), as compared against Lincoln's final fair copy—his fifth and last holograph, known as the "Bliss" copy (Joseph Tausek, *The True Story of the Gettysburg Address* [New York: Lincoln MacVeagh, The Dial Press, 1933], facsimile fold-out facing p. 36).

And in all this is logic, since rhetoric accents the logical point, and grammar puts it in logical order. Lincoln works straight through a logical unfolding from the Liberty in which the nation began, through the war over liberty not achieved because some men were slaves and some thought themselves at liberty to own slaves, and on to the new birth of freedom that will reaffirm the original political ideal. The grammar, logic, and rhetoric are here inseparable, fused together by Lincoln's deep conviction. Perhaps the truly right message is the best rhetorical device after all, and the truth the best persuader.

But even the simple truth needs a vehicle. It cannot just gather in midair, like a disembodied glow. It must arrive in some procession, preceded by a few heralds and attended by visible evidence. Hence the rhetorical heightening, the biblical allusion and metaphor, the parallels, the repetitions, the emphases, in what is sometimes taken as Lincoln's simple, and simply moving, statement. If logic is language as pure reason, and grammar, language as pure structure, then rhetoric is language as part emotion, part reason, part accident, part precision—an array of many colors for the reader's delight and edification, and yet not so showy as to call too much attention to itself. Truth needs the devices of rhetoric to make itself known, to reveal itself in full, to make itself understood in the reader's own eyes and bones.

So, then: grammar for clarity, logic for rationality, rhetoric for conviction. The aim of rhetoric, after all, is to persuade the reader that what the writer believes interesting is in fact interesting, that what he believes amusing is in fact amusing, that what he believes true is in fact true.

Attitude

Writing well is a matter of conviction. You learn in school by exercises, of course; and exercises are best when taken as such, as body-builders, flexions and extensions for the real contests ahead. But when you are convinced that what you write has meaning, that it has meaning for you—and not in a lukewarm, hypothetical way, but truly—then your writing will stretch its wings and have the whole wide world in range. For writing is simply a graceful and articulate extension of the best that is in you. Writing well is not easy. It does not come naturally, though your natural endowments will certainly help. It takes unending practice, each essay a polished exercise for the next to come, each new trial, as T. S. Eliot says, a new "raid on the inarticulate."

In writing, you clarify your own thoughts. Indeed, you probably grasp them for the first time. All kinds of forgotten impressions, lost facts, and surprising updrafts of words and knowledge support your flight. As you test your thoughts against their opposites, as you answer the questions rising in your mind, your conviction grows. You learn as you write. In the end, after you have rewritten and rearranged for your best rhetorical effectiveness, your words will carry your readers with you to see as you see, to believe as you believe, to understand your subject as you now understand it.

Don't take yourself too seriously.

Take your subject seriously—if it is a serious subject—but take yourself with a grain of salt. Your attitude is the very center of your prose. If you take yourself too importantly, your tone will go hollow, your sentences will go moldy, your page will go fuzzy with *of*'s and *which's* and nouns clustered densely in passive constructions. In your academic career, the worst dangers lie immediately ahead. Freshmen usually learn to write tolerably well, but from the sophomore to the senior year the academic damp frequently sets in, and by graduate school you can often cut the gray mold with a cheese knife.

You must constantly guard against acquiring the heavy, sobersided attitude that makes for wordiness and its attendant vices of obscurity, dullness, and anonymity. Do not lose your personality and your voice in the monotone of official prose. Your professors will have served on committees, which too often will have lulled them into the anonymous passive voice: "It has been decided" instead of "We decided." They will have wanted to impress other zoologists, psychologists, economists, and literary critics by writing like them—again in the ponderous passive voice, with fashionable jargon added. Their modesty and their scholarly objectivity will have strengthened their wordy and passive tendencies. You will be in great danger of a thorough soaking from this linguistic fog. But although you should work like a scholar and scientist, you should write like a writer. Copy only those professors who have mastered the economy and beauty of language on paper. The classroom personality can sometimes turn out to be the dullest of writers, and only the writer gets the best out of language.

Your attitude, then, should form somewhere between a confidence in your own convictions and a humorous distrust of your own rhetoric, which can so easily carry you away. You should bear yourself as a member of the human race, knowing that we are all sinners, all redundant, and all too fond of big words. Here is an example from—I blush to admit—the pen of a professor:

> **The general problem is perhaps correctly stated as inadequacy of nursing personnel to meet demands for nursing care and services. Inadequacy, it should be noted, is both a quantitative and qualitative term and thus it can be assumed that the problem as stated could indicate insufficient numbers of nursing personnel to meet existing demands for their services; deficiencies in the competencies of those who engage in the various fields of nursing; or both.**

Too few good nurses, and a badly swollen author—that is the problem. "Nursing personnel" may mean nurses, but it also may mean "the nursing of employees." Notice that "nursing personnel to meet demands" does not say what the author intends. And the ponderous jingle of "deficiencies in the competencies" would nearly do for a musical comedy. The author is taking herself too seriously and taking her readers almost nowhere.

Consider your readers.

If you are to take your subject with all the seriousness it deserves and yourself with as much skeptical humor as you can bear, how are you to take your readers? Who are they, anyway? Hypothetically, your vocabulary and your tone would vary all the way from Skid Row to Oxford as you turn from social work to Rhodes Scholarship; and certainly the difference of audience would reflect itself somewhat in your language. Furthermore, you must indeed sense your audience's capacity, its susceptibilities and prejudices, if you are to win even a hearing. No doubt our language skids a bit when down on the Row, and we certainly speak different tongues with our friends, and with the friends of our parents.

But the notion of adjusting your writing to a whole scale of audiences, though attractive in theory, hardly works out in practice. First, you are *writing*, and the written word presupposes a literate norm that immediately eliminates all the lower ranges of mere talk. Even when you speak, you do not so lose your identity as to pass for a Dead End Kid. You stand on your own linguistic feet, in your own linguistic personality, and the only adjustment you should assiduously practice in your writing, and in your speaking as well, is the upward one toward verbal adulthood.

Consider your audience a mixed group of intelligent and reasonable adults. You want them to think of you as well informed and well educated. You wish to explain what you know and what you believe. You wish to persuade them pleasantly that what you know is important and what you believe is right. Try to imagine what they might ask you, what they might object to, what they might know already, what they might find interesting. Be simple and clear, amusing and profound, using plenty of illustration to show what you mean. But do not talk down to them. That is the great flaw in the slumming theory of communication. Bowing to your reader's supposed level, you insult him by assuming his inferiority. Thinking yourself humble, you are actually haughty. The best solution is simply to assume that your reader is as intelligent as you. Even if he is not, he will be flattered by the assumption. Your written language, in short, will be respectful toward your subject, considerate toward your readers, and somehow amiable toward human failings.

The Written Voice

Make your writing talk.

Writing has seemed magical to primitive peoples. The chiseled stone has spoken as divinity itself; the birchbark-that-talks has freed the leather-stockinged scout. That the silent page should seem to speak with the writer's voice is still remarkable, when you stop to think of it. With all gestures gone, no eyes to twinkle, no notation at all for the amazing hills and valleys of utterance, and only a handful of punctuation marks, the level line of type can yet convey the writer's voice, the tone of his personality.

To achieve this tone, to find your own voice and style, simply try to write in the language of intelligent conversation, cleared of all the stumbles and weavings of talk. Indeed, our speech, like thought, is amazingly circular. We can hardly think in a straight line if we try. We think by questions and answers, repetitions and failures; and our speech, full of *you know*'s and *I mean*'s, follows the erratic ways of the mind, circling around and around as we stitch the simplest of logical sequences. Your writing will carry the stitches, not the loopings and pauses and rethreadings. It should be literate. It should be broad enough of vocabulary and rich enough of sentence to show that you have read a book. It should not be altogether unworthy to place you in the company of those who have written well in your native tongue. But it should nevertheless retain the tone of intelligent and agreeable conversation. Good writing should have a voice, and the voice should be unmistakably your own.

Suppose your spoken voice sounded something like this (I reconstruct an actual response in one of my classes):

> Well, I don't know, I like Shakespeare really, I guess—I mean, well, like when Lear divides up his kingdom like a fairy tale or something, I thought that was kind of silly, dividing his kingdom. Anyone could see that was silly if you wanted to keep your kingdom, why divide it? But then like, something begins to happen, like a real family, I mean. Cordelia really gets griped at her older sisters, I mean, like all older sisters, if you've ever had any. There's a kind of sibling rivalry, you know. Then she's kind of griped at her father, who she really loves, but she thinks, I mean, like saying it right out spoils it. You can't really speak right out, I mean, about love, well, except sometimes, I guess, without sounding corny.

Your written voice might then emerge from this with something of the same tone, but with everything straightened out, filled in, and polished up:

> The play begins like a fairy tale. It even seems at first a little abstract and silly. A king has three daughters. The two elder ones are bad; the youngest is good. The king wishes to keep his kingdom in peace, and keep his title as king, by dividing his kingdom in a senseless and almost empty ceremonial way. But very soon the play seems like real life. The family seems real, complete with sibling rivalry. It is the king, not the play, who is foolish and senile. The older daughters are hypocrites. Cordelia, the youngest, is irritated at them, and at her father's foolishness. As a result, she remains silent, not only because she is irritated at the flattering words of her sisters, but because anything she could say about her real love for her father would now sound false.

You might wish to polish that some more. You might indeed have said it another way, one more truly your own. The point, however, is to write in a tidy, economical way that wipes up the lapses of talk and fills in the gaps of thought, and yet keeps the tone and movement of good conversation, in your own voice.

As you write your weekly assignments and find your voice, you will also be learning to groom your thoughts. Whatever their essential condition, you will want them running their best and looking splendid. You will need to check for all loose ends, lengthening an explanation here, cinching down a notion there, and tucking up every flapping phrase and dangling participle. Since the signals of writing are few compared to those of speech, with all its ranges of voice and accompanying gesture, you will also look with a critical eye for anything that might be misread. You will, in short, be rewriting.

Plan to rewrite.

Good writing comes only from rewriting. Even your happy thoughts will need resetting, as you join them to the frequently happier ones that a second look seems to call up. Even the letter-perfect paper will improve almost of itself if you simply sit down to type it through again. Sharper words, better phrases, new figures of speech, and new illustrations and ideas will appear from nowhere to replace the weedy patches not noticed before.

Allow yourself time for revision. After you have settled on something to write about, plan for at least three drafts—and try to manage four. Thinking of things to say is the hardest part at first. Even a short assignment of 500 words seems to stretch ahead like a Sahara. You have asserted your central idea in a sentence, and that leaves 490 words to go. But if you step off boldly, one foot after the other, you will make progress, find an oasis or two, and perhaps end at a run in green pastures. With longer papers you will want some kind of outline to keep you from straying, but the principle is the same: step ahead and keep moving until you've arrived. That is the first draft.

The second is a penciled correction of the first. Of course, if the first has been really haphazard, you will probably want to type it again, rearranging, dropping a few things, adding others, before you can do much detailed work with a pencil. But the second, or penciled, draft is where you refine and polish, checking your dubious spellings in the dictionary, sharpening your punctuation, clarifying your meaning, pruning away the deadwood, adding a thought here, extending an illustration there—running in a whole new paragraph on an inserted page. You will also be tuning your sentences, carefully adjusting your tone until it is clearly that of an intelligent, reasonable person at ease with his knowledge and his audience.

Here is my penciled draft of the paragraph above, as it appeared on my first typescript:

> The second is a pencil~~ing~~ *ed correction* of the first. *Of course,* ~~I~~if the first has been really haphazard, you will probably want to type it again, rearranging, dropping~~, filling out,~~ *a few things, adding others,* before you can do much detailed work with a pencil. But the second, or pencil*ed*, draft is where you refine and polish, checking your *dubious* spelling*s in a dictionary*, sharpening your punctuation, ~~clearing up~~ *clarifying* your meaning, ~~clearing out~~ *pruning away* the deadwood, adding a thought here, extending an ~~explanation~~ *illustration* there--~~you may need arrows leading you to~~ *perhaps using* the back of the page to write a whole new paragraph. You will also be tuning your sentences, ~~sophisticating~~ *carefully adjusting* your tone ~~into~~ *until it is clearly* that of the intelligent, reasonable person ~~perfectly~~ at ease with his knowledge and his audience.

Your third draft is a smoothing of all this for public appearance. Still other illustrations and better phrases will suggest themselves as you get your penciled corrections into order. My penciled paragraph, above, stood up unusually well. I chose it, in fact, because most of my other paragraphs are so crisscrossed and scarred, draft after draft, that their evolution would be too complicated to represent in any practical way. For a classroom paper, three drafts, with several rereadings of the first and the second, are usually adequate. But, if you have time, a fourth draft will do no harm. Reading aloud will frequently pick up errors, lapses in punctuation, and infelicities of phrase. You may have to retype a page of your most polished draft, as a brilliant idea hits you at last, or a terrible sentence finally rears its fuzzy head. Furthermore, your instructor will probably require revisions after he has marked your paper, as my own editor's marking is, at this very moment, requiring me to cross out half a line and to write this sentence above it and over into the crowded margin. (The editor, like your instructor, was devilishly right, of course; I had not completed my thought; and now the printer has graciously covered my awkward tracks.)

Here is a passage from a student's paper that has gone the full

First Draft and Corrections

In a college education, a person should be allowed to
choose his All the he must take
~~make their~~ own course. ~~Too many~~ requirements^ ~~are discouraging~~
discourage he
~~to~~ a person's creativity, and he cannot learn anything ~~which~~ is
R restrict
not motivated ~~for him~~ to learn. ~~With~~ ~~r~~equirements^ his freedom
and his eagerness to learn. He is only discouraged
to choose ~~what he is interested in is taken away~~ by having to
in which he can see no relevance
study dull subjects like German, ~~which he is not interested in.~~
to his interests.

The Paper, with Instructor's Markings

In a college education, a person should be allowed (can you get rid of the passive?)

to choose his own curriculum and select his own courses.

(redundant) All the requirements he must take stifle the student's

(relevant?) creativity. Moreover, he cannot learn anything he is (true?)

not motivated to learn. Requirements restrict his free-

dom to choose and his eagerness to explore the subjects

he is interested in. He is only discouraged by having (activate)

to study dull subjects like German, in which he can see

no relevance.

Revised Paper

A person should choose his own education, his own curriculum, his own courses. His education is really his alone. Every college requirement threatens to stifle the very enthusiasms upon which true education depends. A student learns best when motivated by his own interests, but, in the midst of a dozen complicated requirements, he can hardly find time for the courses he longs to take. Requirements therefore not only restrict his freedom to choose but destroy his eagerness to explore. Dull subjects like German, in which he can see no relevance anyway, take all his time and discourage him completely.

course. First you see the student's initial draft, with his own corrections on it. Next you see the passage after a second typing, as it was returned by the instructor with his marks on it. Then you see the final revision, handed in again, as this particular assignment required:

And so you are always well off resmoothing the smooth. Your writing will be better; and certainly the tidiest appearance makes the best impression—even on teachers who claim to live on ideas and essences.

Materials and Mechanics

Be a good mechanic.

When it comes to materials and mechanics, originality is no asset. Use standard paper, standard ink, and all the conventions of spacing and typography. Type on good 8½-by-11-inch bond paper, or write in your best hand on regular composition paper, also 8½ by 11, ruled with wide lines. Use one side of the paper only. Have a good black ribbon in your typewriter, and clean off your bank of type. Dig out all that black fuzz from the *o* and *e*. For longhand, use blue ink or black. Any other color may make your instructor see red; he will want to save his eyes, even if your colored ink does not interfere with his favorite system of colored markings. Similarly, a dim or difficult script of any kind will strain his eyes, and his patience, and your paper's chances for a sympathetic reading. Make your handwriting clear, distinguishing your *a*'s from your *o*'s, your *n*'s from your *u*'s and *r*'s. Try not to tangle your lines by looping your *l*'s too high or your *g*'s too low.

Your instructor will undoubtedly tell you how and where he would like your name, the name of the class, the number of the paper, and the date—whether on the outside jacket of the paper folded the long way, or in an upper corner of the first page. Papers for publication use the upper, *left* corner, so get used to this convention unless otherwise instructed:

Charles Beckman
English 123
Paper No. 6
October 12, 1984

Center your title about three inches from the top of your first page,

Emily Maddox
English 123
Paper No. 1
September 15, 1974

On Growing Up

Reading for pleasure is not considered to be popular. Young adults prefer the "boob tube," the television set with which they have spent so many childhood hours. Too many attractions beckon them away from the books ~~which~~ that the teacher recommended to the class for summer reading. One's friends come by in their automobiles to drive down for a coke. The kids go to the moving pictures, or to the beach, and the book one had intended to read remains on the shelf, or pr~~a~~obably in the library, where one has not yet been able to find the time to go. Nevertheless, a book can furnish real enjoyment.

The reader enjoys the experience of being in another world. While he reads, he forgets that he is in his own room. The book has served as a magic carpet to ~~take~~ transport him to India, or Africa, or Sweden, or even to the cities and areas of his own country where he has never been. It has also transported him into the lives of people with different experiences and problems, from which he can learn to solve his own problems of the future. The young person, in particular, can learn by the experience of reading what it is like to be a complete adult.

A book is able to help the young person to mature even further, and change his whole point of view. Growing Up in New Guinea by Margaret Mead is a valuable experience for this reason. I found the book on our shelf, after having seen Margaret Mead on TV. I was interested in her because the teacher had referred to her book entitled Coming of Age in Samoa. I was surprised to find this one about New Guinea. I thought it was a mistake. I opened it and read the first sentence:

> The way in which each human infant is transformed into the finished adult, into the complicated individual version of his city and his century, is one of the most fascinating studies open to the curious minded.

The idea that the individual is a version of his city and his century was fascinating. I started reading and was surprised when I was called to dinner to learn that two hours had passed. I could hardly eat my dinner fast enough so that I could get back to New Guinea.

From this book, I learned that different cultures have very different conceptions about what is right and wrong, in particular about the sex relations and the marriage ceremony, but that people have the same problems all over the world, namely, the problem of growing up. I also learned that books can be more enjoyable than any other form of pleasure. Books fascinate the reader because while he is learning about other people and their problems, particularly about the problem of growing up, he is also learning about his own problems.

capitalizing principal words, double-spacing and centering additional lines, using italics and quotation marks as you would in your text:

The Problem of Time in Faulkner's *The Sound and the Fury*

Heaven in Frost's "After Apple Picking"

You will notice that the names of books, as *The Sound and the Fury*, are in italics (which you indicate by underlining with the typewriter), but that the names of smaller units within books, as Frost's poem, or short stories and articles, are "quoted." Put no period after your title. But you may use question or exclamation marks.

In typing your text, leave margins of an inch and a half, especially at the left. The right-hand margin will vary to accommodate your typing, where unevenness is better than frequent hyphenations. Avoid hyphenating after only one syllable, and hyphenate only on syllables your dictionary will mark: ac·com·mo·date. Avoid breaking with a second hyphen words already hyphenated, such as *eye-opener* or *ready-witted.*

Paragraph by indenting about an inch in longhand, and about five spaces in typewriting. Double-space your typewriting; but do not double-space your longhand, unless you can find only narrow-lined paper. Do not use extra spaces between paragraphs. Run right into your text, within quotation marks, like this, "quotations that take only two or three typewritten lines." Set longer quotations apart by indenting, single-spacing, and *omitting quotation marks.* This simulates the smaller types used in books. (If you were typing your manuscript for print, you would double-space even these indented blocks of quotation, for the typesetter's convenience, and your editor would mark your manuscript for the necessary size of type.) Number your pages in the upper right-hand corner, beginning with number 2 on the second page. Check Chapter 10 for further details on the mechanics of punctuation. Proofread carefully. You may correct a word or two neatly in pencil or ink, drawing a line through the erroneous word and printing the correction immediately above. You may insert a brief addition above the line, marking a caret (∧) to show where it belongs.

On pages 18 and 19 is a paper in which you can see the mechanics of typing, spacing, quoting, and so forth. It is a little wordy. The author is a little uncertain of her language. This is her first paper, and she has not yet fully discovered her own written voice. But it is an excellent beginning. The assignment had asked for a paper of about 500 words on some book (or movie, or TV program) that had proved personally meaningful. Even a memorable experience would do—fixing a car, or building a boat, or even being arrested. The aim of the assignment was to generalize from a personally valuable experience and to explain to others how such an experience can be generally valuable.

With that as a model for a good first start and how to type it, you are now almost ready to write. You have been briefed for the mission. You know that rhetoric is a persuasive refining of language and that style is rhetoric individualized and perfected. You have learned something of the attitude from which style springs: a serious engagement with your subject, a pleasant arrangement with your audience, a humorous effacement of yourself. You know that revision is necessary and inevitable, and your mechanics are in order. Now for something to write.

Exercises

1. Consult Appendix C on pages 382 and 384, and write two examples of each of the following rhetorical devices: antithesis, chiasmus, antanaclasis.

2. Turn to Appendix A and correct the fifteen ailing sentences on pages 321–322.

3. Look up the following items in the Glossary of Usage (Appendix B) and use them correctly in a sentence apiece: *like, as, as if, none, lay, lie, laid, lain.*

4. Explain what is illogical or ambiguous, in a commonsense way, about the following statements, and explain what the writer probably meant:

a. Every seat in the house was filled to capacity.

b. Too many requirements are discouraging.

c. Going to work, the pavement was icy.

d. A porcupine was brought into the laboratory by a biologist in a moribund condition.

e. This book fills a much-needed gap.

5. Write a parody of the Gettysburg address in which you repeat some word with accumulating emphasis, as Lincoln repeats *dedicated.* You might begin like this:

Four score and seven days ago, my father brought me to this campus *committed* to study hard. Now I am committed to the study of English. . . .

6. Write five pairs of sentences, one in normal order and one with that order slightly inverted, on the pattern

a. They brought forth a new nation on this continent.

b. They brought forth on this continent a new nation.

7. Write a 500-word essay on some valuable experience or book in which you try to strike a genial attitude toward subject and reader, to write in a conversational prose that is yet slightly tightened, heightened, and dignified, and to find in the process your *written* voice.

From Subject to Thesis

2

What shall I write? That is the question, persisting from the first Christmas thank-you letter down to this very night. Here you are, an assignment due and the paper as blank as your mind. The Christmas letter may give us a clue. Your mother probably told you to write about what you had been doing. Almost anything would do—Cub Scouts, Brownies, the birthday party, skating—so long as you had been doing it. As you wrote, it grew interesting all over again. Finding a mature subject is no different: look for something you have experienced, or thought about. The more it matters to you, the more you can make it matter to your readers. It might be skiing. It might be fashions. It might be roommates, the Peloponnesian War, a sit-in, a personal discovery of racial tensions, an experience as a nurse's aide. But do not tackle a big philosophical abstraction, like Freedom, or a big subject, like the Supreme Court. They are too vast. Your time and space and knowledge are all too small. You would probably manage no more than a collection of platitudes. Start rather with something specific, like baby-sitting, and let the ideas of freedom and justice arise from there. An abstract idea is a poor beginning. To be sure, as you move ahead through this course, you will work more directly with ideas, with problems posed by literature, with questions in the great civilizing debate about what we are doing in this strange world and universe. But again, look for something within your concern. The best subjects lie nearest at hand, and nearest the heart.

Suppose we start simply with "The Teen-Ager." That, in the recent past, is certainly close enough. Moreover, it will illustrate admirably how to generalize from your own experience, and how to cut your subject down to manageable size. Your first impulse might be to describe the temptations of theft, or drugs, or first cars, and the realities of breaking the law. Were you to write this in the first person, it might be amusing, especially to your acquaintances and friends. But it would remain merely personal; it would still lack an important ingredient of adulthood. You would still be working in that bright, self-centered spotlight of consciousness in which we live before we really begin to grow up, in which the child assumes that all his experiences are unique. If you shift from "me" to "the teen-ager," however, you will be stepping into maturity: acknowledging that others have gone through exactly the same thing, that your particular experiences have illustrated once again the general dynamics of youth and the group. So you will write not "I was afraid to say anything" but "The teen-ager fears going against the group more than death itself. He keeps silent when the speedometer hits 100, though his heart is in his throat." You simply assume you are normal and fairly representative, and you then generalize with confidence, transposing your particular experiences, your particular thoughts and reactions, into statements about the general ways of the world.

But you still face wide areas of adolescence beyond your experience. You have been out of the woods only a short time yourself, and "The Teen-Ager," like any subject, is broad enough for a large number of topics. The psychologist, the historian, and the social worker would each write a different kind of report on "The Teen-Ager," and would still leave plenty of room for the doctor, the minister, and the parent. You must limit yourself to the one corner of the field you know most immediately, "The Teen-Ager at High Speed," let us say. But the subject alone will still not get you an essay. You must assert something. You must turn your subject into a thesis: "The teen-ager's high-speed ride, if it does not kill him, will probably open his eyes to the dynamics of the group." Put your proposition into one sentence. This will get you focused. And now you are ready to begin.

Where Essays Fail

You can usually blame a bad essay on a bad beginning. If your essay falls apart, it probably has no primary idea to hold it together. "What's the big idea?" we used to ask. The phrase will serve as a reminder that you must find the "big idea" behind your several smaller thoughts and musings before you start to write. In the beginning was the *logos,* says the Bible—the idea, the plan, caught in a flash as if in a single word. Find your *logos,* and you are ready to round out your essay and set it spinning.

The big idea behind our ride in the speeding car was that in adolescence, especially, the group can have a very deadly influence on the individual. If you had not focused your big idea in a thesis, you might have begun by picking up thoughts at random, something like this:

> **Everyone thinks he is a good driver. There are more accidents caused by young drivers than any other group. Driver education is a good beginning, but further practice is very necessary. People who object to driver education do not realize that modern society, with its suburban pattern of growth, is built around the automobile. The car becomes a way of life and a status symbol. When a teen-ager goes too fast he is probably only copying his own father.**

A little reconsideration, aimed at a good thesis-sentence, could turn this into a reasonably good beginning:

> **Modern society is built on the automobile. Every child looks forward to the time when he can drive; every teen-ager, to the day when his father lets him take out the car alone. Soon he is testing his skill at higher and higher speeds, especially with a group of friends along. One final test at extreme speeds usually suffices. The**

teen-ager's high-speed ride, if it does not kill him, will probably open his eyes to the deadly dynamics of the group.

Thus the central idea, or thesis, is your essay's life and spirit. If your thesis is sufficiently firm and clear, it may tell you immediately how to organize your supporting material and so obviate elaborate planning. If you do not find a thesis, your essay will be a tour through the miscellaneous. An essay replete with scaffolds and catwalks—"We have just seen this; now let us turn to this"—is an essay in which the inherent idea is weak or nonexistent. A purely expository and descriptive essay, one simply about "Cats," for instance, will have to rely on outer scaffolding alone (some orderly progression from Persia to Siam) since it really has no idea at all. It is all subject, all cats, instead of being based on an idea *about* cats.

The Argumentative Edge

Find your thesis.

The *about*-ness puts an argumentative edge on the subject. When you have something to say *about* cats, you have found your underlying idea. You have something to defend, something to fight about: not just "Cats," but "The cat is really man's best friend." Now the hackles on all dog men are rising, and you have an argument on your hands. You have something to prove. You have a thesis.

"What's the big idea, Mac?" Let the impudence in that time-honored demand remind you that the best thesis is a kind of affront to somebody. No one will be very much interested in listening to you deplete the thesis "The dog is man's best friend." Everyone knows that already. Even the dog lovers will be uninterested, convinced they know better than you. But the cat . . . .

So it is with any unpopular idea. The more unpopular the viewpoint and the stronger the push against convention, the stronger the thesis and the more energetic the essay. Compare the energy in "Democracy is good" with that in "Communism is good," for instance. The first is filled with platitudes, the second with plutonium. By the same token, if you can find the real energy in "Democracy is good," if you can get down through the sand to where the roots and water are, you will have a real essay, because the opposition against which you generate your energy is the heaviest in the world: boredom. Probably the most energetic thesis of all, the greatest inner organizer, is some tired old truth that you cause to jet with new life, making the old ground green again.

To find a thesis and to put it into one sentence is to narrow and define your subject to a workable size. Under "Cats" you must deal with all felinity from the jungle up, carefully partitioning the eons and areas, the tigers and tabbies, the sizes and shapes. The minute you proclaim the cat the friend of man, you have pared away whole categories and chapters, and need only think up the arguments sufficient to overwhelm the opposition. So, put an argumentative edge on your subject—and you will have found your thesis.

Simple exposition, to be sure, has its uses. You may want to tell someone how to build a doghouse, how to can asparagus, how to follow the outlines of relativity, or even how to write an essay. Performing a few exercises in simple exposition will no doubt sharpen your insight into the problems of finding orderly sequences, of considering how best to lead your readers through the hoops, of writing clearly and accurately. It will also illustrate how much finer and surer an argument is.

You will see that picking an argument immediately simplifies the problems so troublesome in straight exposition: the defining, the partitioning, the narrowing of the subject. Actually, you can put an argumentative edge on the flattest of expository subjects. "How to build a doghouse" might become "Building a doghouse is a thorough introduction to the building trades, including architecture and mechanical engineering." "Canning asparagus" might become "An asparagus patch is a course in economics." "Relativity" might become "Relativity is not so inscrutable as many suppose." You have simply assumed that you have a loyal opposition consisting of the uninformed, the scornful, or both. You have given your subject its edge; you have limited and organized it at a single stroke. Pick an argument, then, and you will automatically be defining and narrowing your subject, and all the partitions you don't need will fold up. Instead of dealing with things, subjects, and pieces of subjects, you will be dealing with an idea and its consequences.

Sharpen your thesis.

Come out with your subject pointed. Take a stand, make a judgment of value. Be reasonable, but don't be timid. It is helpful to think of your thesis, your main idea, as a debating question—"Resolved: Old age pensions must go"—taking out the "Resolved" when you actually write the subject down. But your resolution will be even stronger, your essay clearer and tighter, if you can sharpen your thesis even further—"Resolved: Old age pensions must go because———." Fill in that blank and your worries are practically over. The main idea is to put your whole argument into one sentence.

Try, for instance: "Old age pensions must go because they are making people irresponsible." I don't know at all if that is true, and neither will you until you write your way into it, considering probabilities and alternatives and objections, and especially the underlying assumptions. In fact, no one, no master sociologist or future historian, can tell absolutely if it is true, so multiplex are the causes in human affairs, so endless and tangled the consequences. The basic assumption—that irresponsibility is growing—may be entirely false. No one, I repeat, can tell absolutely. But by the same token, your guess may be as good as another's. At any rate, you are now ready to write. You have found your *logos*.

Now you can put your well-pointed thesis–sentence on a card on the wall in front of you to keep from drifting off target. But you will now want to dress it for the public, to burnish it and make it comely. Suppose you try:

> **Old age pensions, perhaps more than anything else, are eroding our heritage of personal and familial responsibility.**

But is this true? Perhaps you had better try something like:

> **Despite their many advantages, old age pensions may actually be eroding our heritage of personal and familial responsibility.**

This is really your thesis, and you can write that down on a scrap of paper too.

Believe in your thesis. Notice how your original assertion has mellowed. And not because you have resorted to cheap tactics, though tactics may get a man to the same place, but rather because you have brought it under critical inspection. You have asked yourself what is true in it: what can (and cannot) be assumed true, what can (and cannot) be proved true. And you have asked yourself where you stand.

You should, indeed, look for a thesis you believe in, something you can even get enthusiastic about. Arguing on both sides of a question, as debaters do, is no doubt good exercise, if one can stand it. It breaks up old ground and uncovers what you can and do believe, at least for the moment. But the argument without the belief will be hollow. You can hardly persuade anyone if you can't persuade yourself. So begin with what you believe, and explore its validities.

Conversely, you must test your belief with all the objections you can think of, just as you have already tested your first proposition about old age pensions. First, you have acknowledged the most evident objection—that the opposition's view must have some merit—by starting your final version with "Despite their many advantages . . . ." Second, you have gone a little deeper by seeing that in your bold previous version you had, with the words *are eroding*, begged the question of whether responsibility is in fact undergoing erosion; that is, you had silently assumed that responsibility *is* being eroded. This is one of the oldest fallacies and tricks of logic. To "beg the question," by error or intent, is to take for granted that which the opposition has not granted, to assume as already proved that which is yet to be proved. But you have saved yourself. You have changed *are eroding* to *may be eroding*. You have gone further in deleting the *perhaps more than anything else*. You have come closer to the truth.

Truth, for many, is something mystical and awesome; for others, something remote and impractical. And you may wonder if it is not astoundingly presumptuous to go around stating theses before you have studied your subject from all angles, made several house-to-house surveys, and read everything ever written. A natural uncertainty and feeling of ignorance, and a misunderstanding of what truth is, can well inhibit you from finding a thesis. But no one knows everything. No one would write anything if he waited until he did. To a great extent, as I have already said, the writing of a thing is the learning of it.

So, first, make a desperate thesis and get into the arena. This is probably solution enough. If it becomes increasingly clear that your thesis is untrue, no matter how hard you push it, turn it around and use the other end. If your convictions have begun to falter with:

> **Despite their many advantages, old age pensions undermine responsibility . . . .**

try it the other way around, with something like:

> **Although old age pensions may offend the rugged individualist, they relieve much want and anxiety, and they dispel much familial resentment.**

You will now have a beautiful command of all the objections to your new position. And you will have learned something about human fallibility and the nature of truth.

We *are* fallible. Furthermore, the truth about most teasing and insistent questions usually lies somewhere beyond our fingertips. You may know, or guess, the truth; you may believe that such-and-such is so. But often you can never know it or prove it in any physical way. And neither can anyone else. You can only take it on faith—as much faith as your temperament allows.

Differences of opinion, it is said, make a horse race, and we often hear that one man's opinion is as good as another's. But the race rather quickly proves that one man's opinion was wrong. There is no proof at all, however, of the opinion that Man O' War is the greatest three-year-old of all time. "All time" is a long time. All the returns are not yet in. And much of the past is beyond reach. But even this opinion, though we can never know for certain, is either right or wrong. All we can do is to weigh the probabilities, and believe.

Persuade your reader.

Once you believe in your proposition, you will discover that proving it is really a venture in persuasion. You have made a thesis, a hypothesis really—an opinion as to what the truth seems to be from where you stand, with the information you have. Oddly enough, your proof has nothing to do with *making* that opinion right or wrong. If it is right, it is right; if wrong, wrong—with or without proof. Your thesis is not "more right" after you have backed it with proof: it is merely shown to have been right all the time. Whether you got it in a flash or in a year's careful analysis makes no difference. You knew it from the moment of your conviction; now the skeptical reader must believe it too.

Trying to persuade the skeptics will strengthen your own conviction. The truth remains constant, but your conviction about it grows as you discover more and more persuasive reasons to back it. Recently, for instance, I found myself arguing with my class that colleges should continue to require a foreign language. I knew, from my own experience, that the requirement was extremely valuable. But persuading the class was another matter. I had to find reasons to back my as yet unreasoned belief.

A number of reasons came to mind: the advantages of getting around in foreign countries, of learning still other languages, having learned one, of knowing foreign people and experiencing a foreign culture in one's own person (learn a French phrase and you spontaneously throw in the gestures), of understanding great literature in its original tongue. I argued that American monolingualism was arrogant, that to become the world's only nation not to require foreign languages was unthinkable. I also argued that studying a foreign language revealed one's own language as nothing else could, that studying languages was the supreme strengthener of minds, since it exercised one's mind at the very synapses of thought, where words and meanings meet. I even mentioned some psychological experiments showing that the brains in rats who were forced to think are bigger than those in rats who were not. In short, discovering persuasive reasons strengthened my convictions as it strengthened my argument. I did not persuade the hardiest opponents, of course; but I persuaded some doubters, and I discovered the ground for my belief.

Belief does indeed contain this unfolding energy. Write what you believe. You may be wrong, of course, but you will probably discover this as you probe for reasons, and can then reverse your thesis, pointed with your new conviction. The truth remains true, and you must at least glimpse it before you can begin to persuade others to see it. So follow your convictions, and think up reasons to convince your reader. You must then give him enough evidence to persuade him that what you say is probably true, finding arguments that will stand up in the marketplace and survive the public haggle. You must find public reasons for your private convictions.

Don't apologize.

"In my opinion," the beginner will write repeatedly, until he seems to be saying "It is only *my* opinion, after all, so it can't be worth much." He has failed to realize that his whole essay represents his opinion—of what the truth of the matter is. Don't make your essay a letter to Diary, or to Mother, or to Teacher, a confidential report of what happened to you last night as you agonized upon a certain question. "*To me,* Robert Frost is a great poet"—this is really writing about yourself. You are only confessing private convictions. To find the "public reasons" often requires no more than a trick of grammar: a shift from "*To me,* Robert Frost is . . ." to "Robert Frost is . . . ," from "*I thought* the book was good" to "The book is good," from you and your room last night to your subject and what it *is.* The grammatical shift represents a whole change of viewpoint, a shift from self to subject. You become the man of reason, showing the reader around firmly, politely, and persuasively.

Once you have effaced yourself from your thesis, once you have erased *to me* and *in my opinion* and all such signs of amateur terror, you may later let yourself back into the essay for emphasis of graciousness: "Mr. Watson errs, I think, precisely at this point." You can thus ease your most tentative or violent assertions, and show that you are polite and sensible, reasonably sure of your position but aware of the possibility of error. Again: the man of reason. But it is better to omit the "I" altogether than to write a junior autobiography of your discoveries and doubts.

Now, with clear conscience, you are ready to write. Your single thesis-sentence has magically conjured up your essay. All you need now is some form to put it in.

Exercises

1. Write three short sentences arising from some personal experience, each beginning with "I": "I was afraid of the ball"; "I thought I knew all about driving." Now, convert each of these into the third person, thus generalizing it, and extend it into two or three sentences:

> The Little Leaguer is afraid of the ball at first. He stands three feet from the plate and swings timidly behind the ball. In the outfield, he hopes desperately that nobody will hit anything his way.

2. Now make a thesis-sentence for each of your generalized experiences. Your statement about the Little Leaguer might produce a thesis like "Baseball teaches a boy self-confidence," for example.

3. Now write a paragraph of four or five sentences for each of your generalized experiences, merely taking each one a little further along and ending each with its thesis.

4. Write six debating resolutions on the pattern "Resolved: Cats make better pets than dogs"; "Resolved: Old age pensions must go."

5. Convert each of these resolutions into a complete thesis-sentence by dropping the "Resolved," beginning with an "Although" or other qualification, and adding a "because" ("Despite their many advantages, old age pensions must go because they are making people irresponsible").

6. Pick something you believe in—abolishing the draft, legalizing marijuana, liberalizing abortion, or whatever. Now assert a simple thesis-sentence ("The draft should be abolished"), and list under it as many supporting reasons as you can think of.

Basic Structure

3

Beginning, Middle, and End

Build your essay in three parts. There really is no other way. As Aristotle long ago pointed out, works that spin their way along through time need a beginning, a middle, and an end to give them the stability of spatial things like paintings and statues. You need a clear beginning to give your essay character and direction, so the reader can tell where he is going and can look forward with expectation. Your beginning, of course, will set forth your thesis. You need a middle to amplify and fulfill. This will be the body of your argument. You need an end to let the reader know that he has arrived and where. This will be your final paragraph, a summation and reassertion of your theme.

Give your essay the three-part *feel* of beginning, middle, and end. The mind likes this triple order. Three has always been a magic number. The woodcutter always has three sons or three daughters; even the physical universe has three dimensions. Three has a basic psychological appeal as strong as a triangle or pyramid—especially with words and music, which the mind must pick up out of the air and assemble for itself into something like a spatial structure, a total impression. Many a freshman's essay has no structure and leaves no impression. It is all chaotic middle. It has no beginning, it just begins; it has no end, it just stops, fagged out at two in the morning.

The beginning must feel like a beginning, not like an accident. It should be a full paragraph that lets your reader gently into the subject and culminates with your thesis. The end, likewise, should be a full paragraph, one that drives the point home, pushes the implications wide, and brings the reader to rest, back on middle C, giving a sense of completion with the tonic. You have already looked at a three-part essay in Chapter 1 (pp. 18–19). In Chapter 6, you will examine the beginning paragraph and the end paragraph more closely. For the present, however, the "middle," which constitutes the bulk of your essay, needs further structural consideration.

Middle Tactics

Arrange your points in order of increasing interest.

Once your thesis has sounded the challenge, your reader's interest is probably at its highest pitch. He wants to see how you can prove so outrageous a thing, or to see what the arguments are for this thing he has always believed but never tested. Each step of the way into your demonstration, he is learning more of what you have to say. But, unfortunately, his interest may be relaxing as it becomes satisfied: the reader's normal line of attention is a progressive decline, arching down like a wintry graph. Against this decline you must oppose your forces, making each successive point more interesting, so that the vector of your reader's interest will continue at least on the horizontal, with no sag, and preferably with an upward swing:

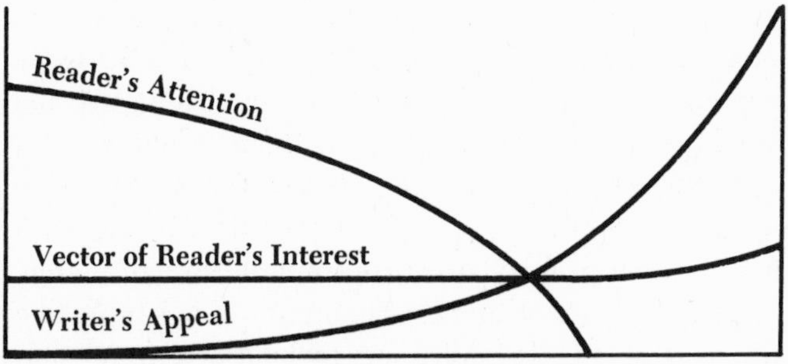

This is the basic principle for organizing the middle of your essay. Save your best till last. It is as simple as that.

Here, for example, is the middle of a short, three-paragraph essay developing the thesis that "Working your way through college is valuable." The student arranged his three points in an ascending order of interest:

> **The student who works finds that the experience is worth more than the money. First, he learns to budget his time. He now uses the time he would otherwise waste to support himself, and he studies harder in the time he has left because he knows it is limited. Second, he makes real and lasting friends on the job, as compared to the other casual acquaintances around the campus. He has shared rush hours, and nighttime cleanups with the dishes piled high, and conversation and jokes when business is slow. Finally, he gains confidence in his ability to get along with all kinds of people, and to make his own way. He sees how businesses operate, and how waitresses, for instance, can work cheerfully at a really tiring job without much hope for the future. He gains an insight into the real world, which is a good contrast to the more intellectual and idealistic world of the college student.**

Again, each successive item of your presentation should be more interesting than the last, or you will suddenly seem anticlimactic. Actually, minor regressions of interest make no difference so long as the whole tendency is uphill and your last item clearly the best. Suppose, for example, you were to undertake the cat thesis. You decide that four points would make up the case, and that you might arrange them in the following order of increasing interest: (1) cats are affectionate but make few demands; (2) cats actually look out for themselves; (3) cats have, in fact, proved extremely useful to man throughout history in controlling mice and other plaguey rodents; (4) cats satisfy some basic need in man for a touch of the jungle, savagery in repose, ferocity in silk, and have been worshiped for the exotic power they still seem to represent, even dozing on the banister. It may be, as you write, thinking of things, that you will find Number 1 developing attractive or amusing instances, and perhaps even virtually usurping the whole essay. Numbers 2, 3, and 4 should then be moved ahead as interesting but brief preliminaries. Your middle structure, thus, should range from least important to most important, from simple to complex, from narrow to broad, from pleasant to hilarious, from mundane to metaphysical—whatever "leasts" and "mosts" your subject suggests.

Acknowledge and dispose of the opposition.

Your cat essay, because it is moderately playful, can proceed rather directly, throwing only an occasional bone of concession to the dogs. But a serious controversial argument demands one organizational consideration beyond the simple structure of ascending interest. Although you have taken your stand firmly as a *pro,* you will have to allow scope to the *con*'s, or you will seem not to have thought much about your subject. The more opposition you can manage as you carry your point, the more triumphant you will seem, like a man on a high wire daring the impossible.

The basic organizing principle here is to get rid of the opposition first, and to end on your own side. Probably you will have already organized your thesis sentence in a perfect pattern for your *con-pro* argument:

Despite their many advantages, old age pensions . . . .
Although dogs are fine pets, cats . . . .

The subordinate clause states the subordinate part of your argument, which is your concession to the *con* viewpoint; your main clause states your main argument. As the subordinate clause comes first in your thesis-sentence, so with the subordinate argument in your essay. Sentence and essay both reflect a natural psychological principle. You want, and the reader wants, to get the boys off the street so the men can have room. And you want to end on your best foot. (You might try putting the opposition last, just to see how peculiarly the last word insists on seeming best, and how, when stated last by you, the opposition's case seems to be your own.)

Get rid of the opposition first. This is the essential middle tactic of argumentation. You have introduced and stated your thesis in your beginning paragraph. Now start your Middle with a paragraph of concession to the *con's*:

> **Dog-lovers, of course, have tradition on their side. Dogs are indeed affectionate and faithful . . . .**

And with that paragraph out of the way, go to bat for the cats, showing their superiority to dogs in every point. In a very brief essay, you can even use the opposition at the very beginning of your Beginning, using it to introduce your thesis itself and really getting rid of it right at the start, as in the essay at the end of this chapter (p. 000). But usually your beginning paragraph will lead up to your thesis more or less neutrally, and you will attack your opposition head-on in paragraph two, as you launch into your Middle.

Compare point by point.

Introducing the opposition inevitably invokes a comparison—and one final principle. Run your comparisons point by point. Compare your dogs and your cats, or your sheep and your goats, item by item. Your defense of cats would follow the order of your concessions to the dogs—affection, faithfulness, and so forth, right down the line. You will thus help your reader to see the contrast, perhaps reinforcing his assent with pure gratitude. In extended contrasts, you would alternate your equal time, *pro* and *con:* a paragraph for one, then a paragraph for the other; a sentence or two for one, then a sentence or two for the other. We shall look at this dialectic order more closely in the next chapter.

But for the present, keep the principle in mind: run your comparisons point by point. Don't write all about sheep for three pages, then all about goats. Every time you say something about a sheep, say something comparable about a goat, pelt for pelt, horn for horn, beard for beard. Otherwise, your essay will fall in two, and you will have to repeat any sheep's points you want to develop among the goats. The tendency to organize comparisons by halves is so strong that you will probably find you have fallen into it unawares, and in rewriting you will have to reorganize everything point for point—still arranging your pairs of points from least important to most. Finally, the only comparison worth making is one that aims to demonstrate a superiority, one, that is, with a thesis—"Resolved: Sheep are more useful than goats."

To summarize, the essential middle tactics are three: (1) follow the order of ascending interest, (2) get rid of the opposition first, and (3) run your comparisons point by point.

Now you have almost finished your essay. You have found a thesis. You have worked it into a decent beginning. You have then worked out a convincing middle, with your arguments presented in a sequence of ascending interest; you have used up all your points and said your say. You and your argument are both exhausted. But don't stop. You need an end, or the whole thing will unravel in your reader's mind. You need to buttonhole him in a final paragraph, to imply "I told you so" without saying it, to hint at the whole round experience he has just had, and to leave him convinced, satisfied, and admiring. One more paragraph will do it: beginning, middle, *and* end.

Structure: Classical and Modern

You now have the essential structure well in mind—the inevitable beginning-middle-and-end, the internal principles of the argumentative edge, of ascending interest, of dialectic order, and of comparison. Actually, these structural points have evolved from the classical pattern for oratory, an early summary of the nearly changeless structural dynamics of communication. Consequently, the classical form is still visible not only in the modern essay, but even in the modern scientific paper, which reproduces in most of its details the ancient Greek oratorical form that Cicero (first century B.C.) polished in his orations and outlined in his *De Oratore*.

You can detect this classic oratorical form almost anywhere you look in the literature and exposition of the Middle Ages and the Renaissance. Sir Philip Sidney turned to it automatically when he wrote *An Apologie for Poetrie*, as did John Milton for his famous *Areopagitica*. The great formal essayists, like John Henry Newman, followed it in more recent times. And today, as I have said, it appears universally behind the structure of the essay and the scientific report.

The form was adjustable; parts were sometimes omitted, and subdivisions added. But the usual form, as set forth by Cicero, Quintilian, and their followers, with the first three items matching our "beginning," and the last one our "end," was more or less like this, under the traditional Latin headings:

1. *Exordium* (or *Proem*). The introduction.

2. *Narratio*. General description of subject and background.

3. *Propositio*. The thesis, the statement of what is to be demonstrated or proved.

4. *Partitio*. Statement of how the thesis is to be divided and handled.

5. *Confirmatio* (or *Argumentatio*, or *Explicatio*). The chief evidence in support of the thesis; the body, the longest part, of the oration. Roughly, our "middle."

6. *Reprehensio*. The knocking-out of the opposition. Although the ancients, with somewhat more leisure than we, saved their merriment until after their own case was firmly established, the *reprehensio* contained exactly the refutations that must always accompany an enumeration of the opposition's claims. The structure of the *reprehensio* was exactly that recommended in our discussion of *pro*'s and *con*'s: setting up the opposition only to knock it flat.

7. *Digressio*. The name speaks for itself. The "digression" was intended to lighten the load. It could come anywhere between *exordium* and *peroratio*, with matters related, but not essential, to the subject.

8. *Peroratio*. The conclusion, summarizing the discussion and urging the thesis with greater eagerness and enthusiasm.

Shorter orations sometimes dropped the *reprehensio*, if no opposition had to be refuted, and absorbed the *propositio* and *partitio*, the statements of thesis and method, into the *narratio*, coming very near to what we have described as our "beginning." *Digressio*, which is largely decoration or relief anyway, was also frequently dropped, or inserted at some different place. Since these parts were movable, we have in the ancient form the larger framework of beginning-middle-end, of assertion and refutation, that we have already outlined for the modern essay in general. Here is how the modern scientific paper, or lab report, reflects the form of classical oration:

Classical	*Scientific*
Exordium *Narratio*	Introduction
Propositio	Purpose (thesis)
Partitio	Materials and methods
Confirmatio	Results
Peroratio	Discussion Summary

The modern essayist has simply streamlined the classical form a little further than has the systematic scientist. The classical orator stated his case, faced the opposition, then stated his case again—and at some length—in his summative peroration. The essayist's only real alteration is in putting the *reprehensio,* the managing of the opposition, before his own argument rather than after it, for simple economy. By hitting the opposition first, he need state his case but once, repeating only a little in his conclusion, which immediately follows.

Classical Oration	*Modern Essay*
Exordium *Narratio* *Propositio*	Beginning (with thesis)
Confirmatio *Reprehensio*	Middle (*reprehensio* followed by *confirmatio*)
Peroratio	End

Here is a short essay of three paragraphs (Beginning, Middle, End), in which you may detect, by way of structural exercise, something of the old classical divisions. You will notice that the writer has stated the opposition (*reprehensio*) to introduce his thesis itself, an excellent beginning for the three-paragraph essay. In an essay of four or five paragraphs, he would have begun more neutrally ("Chance plays a large role in our lives. We bump into an old friend in Paris. We lose our keys, or find a good restaurant.") And he would have put the world's disasters—the *con*-side, the *reprehensio*—in the second paragraph.

Happy Accidents

Every morning the newspaper brings us the world's most recent disasters. An earthquake in Turkey vies for horror with a landslide in Peru or a burning liner at sea. Planes crash, mines cave in, and wreckage strews the expressway. Among the usual robberies and murders are always a few bizarre accidents: deaths from stray bullets, falling hammers, or slipping ladders. Yet accidents can be happy.

The blessing in disguise has indeed become proverbial. The Grayton *Globe* recently ran an article about a woman who had been paralyzed from the waist down by a fall in her kitchen. She realized for the first time that cripples needed to feel useful, and frequently had skills for which they could find no employment. She organized

a small company employing only cripples, taking contracts from larger companies for work that handicapped people could do, frequently in their homes, like assembling small parts for radio and television manufacturers. Seated in her wheelchair at her telephone, she discovered work for many handicapped people, depending on their capacities. Her accident had changed her life into something valuable both for herself and for others.

So accidents are not always bad. A personal tragedy may make one aware of human suffering, and transform his life. He may understand people better, and he may become kinder to his fellow men. Or he might dedicate his whole life to alleviating human suffering. The loss of some physical ability may add to his inner strength. The disaster that had seemed to crush him may prove the blessing in disguise—the accident that fulfilled his life and made him truly happy.

Exercises

1. Write five *con*-and-*pro* thesis-sentences, beginning "Although . . . ."

2. Write a 500-word description of a process you know well—how to plan a vacation, how to play winning croquet, how an internal combustion engine works. This is straight exposition. It will introduce you to the fine dry air of objectivity; to the problem of laying out in orderly sequence, for the reader's gathering comprehension, details that are in fact simultaneous; and to the difficulty of finding the clear, accurate, and descriptive phrase.

3. Now find a thesis-sentence that will change this description into an argument making some statement *about* the subject: the best-planned vacations can be disastrous; winning croquet is no child's play; what's under the hood is really no mystery. Rewrite the first paper using your new thesis-sentence and using, in some way, everything you said before.

4. Write a three-paragraph argumentative essay, conveying a thorough sense of Beginning, Middle, and End. (One of the best stylists I know, a German whose command of English is a living rebuke to American education, told me that his grasp of organization comes from having had to write, through a number of grammar-school years, nothing but three-paragraph essays. The treatment appears to have been excellent.)

5. Take a conventional proposition, like "Democracy is good" or "The dog is man's best friend," and write down as many unusual and

interesting supporting arguments as you can think of, ones that would really stick. Arrange your items in order of increasing interest.

6. Arrange the following points in order of ascending interest, and in a *pro-con* structure, adding necessary *but*'s and *of course*'s, and intermediate points of your own:

The United Nations has not prevented war.

The United Nations provides a safety valve for international pressures.

The United Nations gives small nations a necessary sense of prestige.

The United Nations should include Red China.

The large nations dominate the United Nations.

7. Write an outline of a comparative argument. State your thesis; then simply list your points in order of increasing interest, phrasing them in the general pattern of "Football is good, but baseball is better."

The Middle: Other Arrangements

4

In the last chapter, you made the acquaintance of what is usually called the deductive order of presentation: first, the thesis, then a "leading away from" it (*de-ducere*), as you take your reader through an explanation of it, point by point. This is indeed the basic structure of argument: beginning assertion, middle demonstration, and ending reassertion. In this structure, you have seen the simple and complex *con*'s and *pro*'s of your middle tactics, and the one psychological principle that underlies all possible arrangements of your middle points—the order of ascending interest, the saving of best for last. Since ascending interest is obviously not limited to argument alone, we shall now look at some of those other possibilities. There are orders other than *con*-and-*pro,* and climaxes other than those of battle. The less pugnacious your subject, the less need for assertion and opposition. Your subject may indeed demand, or quietly suggest, other ways of arranging your entire middle section. The possibilities, inherited more or less with the universe around us, seem to be these several orders: space, time, cause and effect, problem and solution, natural divisions, induction, deduction, and deduction-induction.

The Order of Space

Arranging details in some kind of tour through space is as natural as walking. When your subject dwells upon physical space—the layout of a campus, for instance—you literally take your reader with you. You simply organize your entire middle section by starting at the gate and conducting him in an orderly progress down the mall or around the quadrangle. Or you show him a rooming house floor by floor, from the apartment by the entry to the garret four flights up, where the graduate student lives on books and cheese. A city's slum or its crowded parking, a river's pollution, a mountain's trees from valley to timberline—any spatial subject will suggest a convenient route, from bottom to top, or top to bottom, left to right, east to west, center to periphery. You will instinctively use a series of spatial signals: *on the right, above, next, across, down the slope.* Your concern is to keep your progress orderly, to help your reader see what you are talking about.

This is exactly the way that Oliver Statler, in his *Japanese Inn,* takes us to the place he loves:

> **On this day, I have already progressed along the old Tokaido Road to the village of Yui. A new highway has been built a few hundred yards inland to avoid the congested main street of the village, but leaving Yui it swings back to the shore and runs between the sea wall on my left and the sheer face of Satta Mountain on my right.**
>
> **It is here, as I drive almost into the sea, that my spirits always quicken, for only Satta Mountain divides Yui from Okitsu, the next village, where my inn lies. . . . I notice men and women diving around the off-shore rocks, sharp knives in hand, hunting for abalone. Beyond them, fishing boats dot Suruga Bay. . . .**

At the highest point of the pass, where the path breaks out of the pines and into the open, there is a breath-taking view, and anyone who finds himself there must turn to drink it in. He faces the great sweep of Suruga Bay and the open Pacific beyond, while waves break into flowers on the rocks far beneath his feet. Yui lies on the shore at his left and Okitsu at his right. Beyond Yui, bathed in mist far off on the left, looms the mountainous coast of Izu. Beyond Okitsu, on the right, is one of the loveliest sights in Japan, for the harbor that lies there is protected by a long arm of curving black sand, covered with ancient and twisted pines. This is the fabled beach of Miho. . . .*

The Order of Time

Like space, time is a natural organizer, ancient and simple. Hour follows hour, day follows day, year follows year, life follows life. Again, you simply take your reader along the natural sequence of what happens—to us, or to nations, or to any items in experience or experiment. We understand processes most clearly by tracking the way they move through time, even processes complicated by other, simultaneous events:

And when this wheel turns, that lever tips the food into the trough.

While this conveyor moves into the oven, the other one is bringing the chassis to point *B*.

And all the time he talked, his hands were moving the shells and flicking the invisible pea.

Any event, whether a football game or the inauguration of a president, can be best perceived as you have perceived it—through time—and you can bring your reader to perceive it by following the sequence of things as they happened, stepping aside as necessary to explain background and simultaneous events, guiding your reader along with temporal signposts: *at the same time, now, when, while, then, before, after, next, all the time.*

As Audubon, the nineteenth-century naturalist, describes in his *Orinithological Biography* the passenger pigeon and its astounding flights in masses a mile wide and 180 miles long, he naturally presents his observations through the order of time. I have underlined the temporal words in one of his paragraphs:

---

* Oliver Statler, *Japanese Inn* (New York: Pyramid Books, Random House, 1962), pp. 14–16. Copyright © 1961, Oliver Statler.

> **As soon as the pigeons discover a sufficiency of food to entice them to alight, they fly round in circles, reviewing the country below. During their evolutions, on such occasions, the dense mass which they form exhibits a beautiful appearance, as it changes direction, now displaying a glistening sheet of azure, when the backs of the birds come simultaneously into view, and anon, suddenly presenting a mass of rich deep purple. They then pass lower, over the woods, and for a moment are lost among the foliage, but again emerge, and are seen gliding aloft. They now alight, but the next moment, as if suddenly alarmed, they take to wing, producing by the flappings of their wings a noise like the roar of distant thunder, and sweep through the forests to see if danger is near. Hunger, however, soon brings them to the ground. When alighted, they are seen industriously throwing up the withered leaves . . . .**

You can most clearly explain any kind of development or decline—the civil rights movement, the decay of a neighborhood—by taking your reader up or down the path of time. Following the natural order of events, from past to present, is most usual and probably best. You can sometimes gain dramatic effect, however, by beginning with the present and moving back to former insignificance or splendor, as in describing a battered tenement that was once the mayor's mansion. But you will do your reader a favor by keeping to your order, whether forward or backward, and not reversing it inadvertently somewhere along the way.

Time and space, as the physicists tell us, are functions of one another. You need space to represent time; you need time to cover space. Since your aim is to bring your reader to see what you have seen, you will frequently feel the need to mix the orders of time and space in your presentation, stopping your local history to show your reader a building floor by floor, for example.

Here is a remarkable passage from the concluding chapter of D. H. Lawrence's *The Plumed Serpent,* in which you may profitably observe the orders of space and time blended to perfection. Lawrence first describes his dreamlike Mexican scene in spatial terms, as if it were a spacious and timeless Grecian frieze. Then he moves through time, bringing us to see and feel its stately process. Notice how the implied *now,* the *then,* and the *and at last* fall into natural sequence in the second paragraph, the "timed" paragraph:

> **A black boat with a red-painted roof and a tall mast was moored to the low breakwater-wall, which rose about a yard high, from the**

shallow water. On the wall stood loose little groups of white-clad men, looking into the black belly of the ship. And perched immobile in silhouette against the lake, was a black-and-white cow, and a huge monolithic black-and-white bull. The whole silhouette frieze motionless, against the far water that was coloured brown like turtle doves.

It was near, yet seemed strange and remote. Two peons fixed a plank gangway up to the side of the boat. Then they began to shove the cow towards it. She pawed the new broad planks tentatively, then, with that slow Mexican indifference, she lumbered unwillingly on to the gangway. They edged her slowly to the end, where she looked down into the boat. And at last, she dropped neatly into the hold.*

This passage continues with undiminished magic for several pages, until the enchanted boat moves slowly off across the lake—"across the waters, with her massive, star-spangled cargo of life invisible." And Lawrence has in fact organized his entire chapter on a span of spaciously slackened time, entitling it "Here!" and implying the somehow static "and now" of deep experience. He has done what you yourself can do. He has taken his reader along the natural orders of both space and time, as his own perception of his subject has suggested them, simply keeping the orders orderly for his reader.

The Order of Cause and Effect

In the order of cause and effect, sequence has moved from a merely physical unfolding of space or time into the human domain of the rational. The *what* of space and time has become the *why* of existence —or rather, some of our answers to the *why*. *Because* is the impulse of your thinking here: "Such and such is so *because* . . . ." You think back through a train of causes, each one the effect of something prior; or you think your way into the future, speculating about the possible effects of some present cause. In other words, you organize your explanation in one of two ways:

I. You state a general effect, then deal with its several causes.
II. You state a general cause, then deal with its possible effects.

In Arrangement I, you know the effect (a lost football game, or the solar system, let us say), and you speculate as to causes. In Arrangement II, you know the cause (a new restriction, or admitting Red China to the United Nations, let us say), and you speculate as to the effects. Arrangement I concerns the past, as you look back for causes; Arrangement II concerns the future, as you look ahead for effects. Within each arrangement your proportions will vary, depending on where you want your reader's concern—with causes or with effects.

Arrangement I: Look for general conditions and immediate causes.

In Arrangement I, you look over the past for possible causes of the event you are trying to explain, but you need not, of course, go back to the beginning of time. You need not trace the quarterback's bad pass clear back to Newton and the laws of motion and gravity. You will find that causes separate into, first, several *conditions*—a weak defense, strong opponents, a wet field, a series of disheartening breaks—and, second, one or two *immediate causes*—an unblocked tackler, a slip in the mud. Your thesis from such an analysis would probably be: "Not quarterback Smith, but an unusual concentration of bad luck, lost us the game." Now, since your introductory paragraph and thesis have told the reader all he will care to know about the dismal *effect* (the lost game), you will give your middle over entirely to *immediate causes* and *conditions*. The best plan is probably to write a descriptive paragraph that lets your reader see the *immediate causes* (the unblocked tackler, the slip, the bad pass, the interception), and then to organize the *conditions* partly by chronology, partly by ascending order of interest, something like this:

1. The bad weather (of least interest)
2. The breaking of the star's arm during practice early in the season
3. The previous games unexpectedly lost
4. The other side's unusually strong team
5. The train's delay, which further tired and disheartened the players

Your concluding paragraph would return again to your thesis ("unusual bad luck") and some reminder of *immediate causes* (the bad pass).

You will probably notice, as you try to explain causes and effects, that they do not always run in a simple linear sequence, one thing following another, like a row of falling dominoes. Indeed, mere sequence is so famously untrustworthy in tracing causes that one of the classical errors of thought has been named *post hoc, ergo propter hoc* ("after this, therefore because of this"). It is wrong, in other words, to suppose that *A* caused *B* because *A* preceded *B*. The two may have been entirely unrelated. But the greatest danger in identifying causes is to fasten upon a single cause while ignoring others of equal significance. Both your thinking and your persuasiveness will be better if you do not insist, to the exclusion of all else, that Jones's failure to block the tackler lost the game.

In the lost ball game, you were interested in explaining causes, and you organized your middle entirely around *causes,* handling *effects* only in your beginning and end. But sometimes your interest will lie with *effects.* When describing a slum problem, for instance, you might in a single sentence set aside the causes as irrelevant, as water over the dam, as so much spilt milk: "perhaps caused by inefficiency, perhaps by avarice, perhaps by the indifference of Mayor Richman." Your interests, as I have said, will dictate your proportions of cause and effect. You might well write an essay that balances the slum's causes and effects in equal proportions: a paragraph each on inefficiency, avarice, and the mayor's indifference, then a paragraph each on ill health, poor education, and hopelessness.

In the following example, in three paragraphs, I have begun and ended with the *effect* (the peculiar layout of a town). First, I located the *immediate cause* (cattle) as my thesis, and then, in the middle paragraph, I moved through the cause and its *conditions* up to the *effect* again—the town as it stands today:

North of the Tracks

If you drive out west from Chicago, you will notice something happening to the towns. After the country levels into Nebraska, the smaller towns are built only on one side of the road. When you stop for a rest, and look south across the broad main street, you will see the railroad immediately beyond. All of these towns spread northward from the tracks. Why? As you munch your hamburger and look at the restaurant's murals, you will realize that the answer is cattle.

These towns were the destinations of the great cattle-drives from Texas. They probably had begun at the scattered watering places in the dry land. Then the wagon-trails and, finally, the transcontinental railroad had strung them together. Once the railroad came, the whole southwest could raise cattle for the slaughterhouses of Chicago. The droves of cattle came up from the south, and all of these towns re-

flect the traffic: corrals beside the tracks to the south, the road for passengers and wagons paralleling the tracks on the northern side, then, across the road, the row of hotels, saloons, and businesses, with the town spreading northward behind the businesses.

The cattle-business itself shaped these one-sided Nebraska towns. The conditions in which this immediate cause took root were the growing population in the East and the railroad that connected the plains of the West, and Southwest, with the tables of New York. The towns took their hopeful being north of the rails, on the leeward side of the vast cattle drives from the south. The trade in cattle has now changed, all the way from Miami to Sacramento. But the great herds of the old Southwest, together with the transcontinental railroad and man's need to make a living, plotted these Western towns north of the tracks.

Arrangement II: Look for future effects, but be reasonable.

Arrangement II is rarer, and more tenuous. Your order of presenting cause and effect is reversed. You are looking to the future. You state a known cause (a new restriction on dormitory hours) or a hypothetical cause ("If this restriction is passed"), and then you speculate about the possible, or probable, effects. Your procedure will then be much the same as before. But for maximum persuasiveness, try to keep your supposed effects, which no one can really foresee, as nearly probable as you can. Occasionally, of course, you may put an improbable hypothetical cause to good use in a satiric essay, reducing some proposal to absurdity: "If all restrictions were abolished . . . ." "If no one wore clothes . . . ." Or the improbable *if* may even help clarify a straightforward explanation of real relationships, as in the following excerpt from *Time* magazine's report on Fred Hoyle, the British astronomer and mathematician who has been modifying Newton's gravity and Einstein's relativity. The paragraph states the general condition, proposes its hypothetical cause with an *if*, then moves to the effects, first in temporal order and then in order of human interest:

The masses, and therefore the gravity, of the sun and the earth are partly due to each other, partly to more distant objects such as the stars and galaxies. According to Hoyle, if the universe were to be cut in half, local solar-system gravitation would double, drawing the earth

closer to the sun. The pressure in the sun's center would increase, thus raising its temperature, its generation of energy, and its brightness. Before being seared into a lump of charcoal, a man on earth would find his weight increasing from 150 to 300 lbs.

The Order of Problem and Solution

In the order of problem and solution, again, you are exploiting a natural order. You describe the problem for your reader; you then suggest solutions. This order serves well even for historical subjects. The Panama Canal, for instance, posed problems of politics, geology, and human survival. Your thesis would state the threefold problem; your middle would show its three solutions, one by one. Or you might choose a more obviously balanced approach, making your thesis "The Canal posed three major problems," and then organizing your middle in two equal parts:

I. The problems
- **A. Difficulties of agreement between a small government and a large one**
- **B. Difficulties with variations in terrain and differing sea levels**
- **C. Yellow fever**

II. The solutions
- **A. The Canal Zone, sovereignty, payments**
- **B. Distance, lakes, and locks**
- **C. General Gorgas and the mosquito**

This topic could expand into a considerable essay, complete with footnotes, but it also might turn out nicely in three paragraphs, based on articles in the *Encyclopaedia Britannica:*

Digging the Panama Canal

Dig this! The idea of the Panama Canal is almost as old as Columbus. When the Spanish explorers finally conceded that any passage westward to China, which Columbus had sought, was blocked by two continents and a thin isthmus, the idea of a canal was born. In 1550, Antonio Galvão began the long argument for a canal through Nicaragua, Panama, or Darien. When the United States opened the canal on August 15, 1914, the dreams of almost four centuries came true, and mountainous problems had been solved. Ultimately, the canal had posed three major problems.

Politics, geology, and human survival had confronted canal-planners from the beginning. A French company, organized in 1880 to dig the canal, repeatedly had to extend its treaties at higher and higher prices as the work dragged on. Uneasy about the French, the United States made treaties with Nicaragua and Costa Rica to dig along the other most feasible route. This political threat, together with the failure of the French and the revolt of Panama from Colombia, finally enabled the United States to buy the French rights and negotiate new treaties, which, nevertheless, continue to cause political trouble to this day. Geology also posed its ancient problems: how to manage torrential rivers and inland lakes; whether to build a longer but more enduring canal at sea level, or a shorter, cheaper, and safer canal with locks. Economy eventually won, but the problem of yellow fever and malaria, which had plagued the French, remained. By detecting and combating the fever-carrying mosquito, William Gorgas solved these ancient tropical problems. Without him, the political and geological solutions would have come to nothing.

In the end, of course, all three problems are human, as the canal answered the ancient human dream of a westward passage to China. Political tensions are nothing but human competition, and geology succumbs to human drives. And to dig a canal through the jungle, man had to triumph over the mosquito.

Any problem and its solutions can produce an essay along these lines—choosing a college, or something to wear (if you want to be light-hearted), making an apartment or a commune work, building the Eiffel Tower or the pyramids.

The Order of Comparison and Contrast

Comparison and contrast is another basic order of thought, another natural means of organizing the middle of your essay, or the whole of it, or an occasional muscular paragraph. I have already mentioned the essential tactics, with the sheep and the goats, in Chapter 3, and we shall look at these tactics again when we talk about ways to develop paragraphs in Chapter 7. The process is indeed recurrent. It may be the very basis of thought itself, or at least one of the primary elements. All knowledge involves comparing things for their similarities and noticing their contrasting differences. We group all men together as Men, and then tell them apart as individuals.

We instinctively know our friends in this way, for instance. Two of them drift side by side in our thoughts. We are comparing them. They are both boys; they are the same age and stature; we like them both. But one bubbles up like a mountain spring, and the other runs deep. Their appearances, mannerisms, and tastes match their contrasting personalities. One's room is messy; the other's is neat. One races his car; the other collects stamps. We compare the similar categories—looks, habits, hobbies, goals—and contrast the differences. In the process, we have come to know both friends more completely.

Your thoughts will intuitively pair the items and contrast them. You simply organize your comparing-contrasting essay along this pattern of thought. Let me repeat. Make your comparisons point by point, nose for nose, hobby for hobby, to keep your reader comfortably in touch with the similarities and differences. Do not write all about sheep and then all about goats. The reader cannot see the contrasting points unless they are side by side.

Of course, when writing about people or other familiar things—houses, towns, stadiums—you can risk writing a complete sketch of one for a paragraph or so, followed by an equivalent sketch of the other, because we are accustomed to thinking in these terms, and your reader can keep the details easily in mind:

> **My father is tall, blond, and outgoing. He works hard and plays hard. He does everything at a cheerful run, whether he is off to a sales conference or off to the golf course with his usual foursome on Saturday mornings. As a boy . . . .**
>
> **My mother is almost completely the opposite. She is small and quiet. Even her dark brown hair, which is naturally wavy, has a certain repose about it. She has a pleasant smile, and bursts into laughter at my father's jokes, but she never stirs up fun on her own. She never seems to hurry. She hums at her work, and the house seems to slip into order without effort. She likes to play bridge with a few close friends, but she is just as happy with a book. As a girl . . . .**

On less familiar ground, however, the principle of contrasting point by point is imperative. If you were to compare and contrast two short stories—Hemingway's "My Old Man" and Sherwood Anderson's "I Want to Know Why," for instance—you would be tempted to follow your first impulse, describing Hemingway's story for a page or two, then turning to Anderson with Hemingway comfortably behind you, and your reader wondering where you are. Don't fall into this familiar trap. Establish in your Beginning that the stories are similar, and therefore worthy of comparison: both are about horse racing; both are about young boys who painfully discover the ways of the world. Now make a thesis-sentence asserting that one is better than the other, perhaps "But Hemingway's story ultimately proves deeper than Anderson's." Now work your way through the Middle, point by point, contrasting the differences. Though both boys are young, Anderson's is somewhat older and more independent. In both stories, horse racing is corrupt, but Hemingway's gamblers are much more cynical. And so on, item by item, with brief illustrations of each in turn.

These are the underlying principles in comparing and contrasting: (1) contrasting point by point, (2) choosing a side, so that your comparison takes on meaning and an argumentative edge—

Sheep are more useful than goats.
Tom is really a better person than Bill.
Hemingway's story is deeper than Anderson's.
Zuñi society was superior to that of the more powerful Apaches.

Dialectic Order

All the while, we have been pursuing one of the most fundamental orders of thought: the dialectic order, which is the order of argument, one side pitted against the other. Our minds naturally swing from side to side as we think. In dialectics, we simply give one side an argumentative edge, producing a thesis that cuts a clear line through any subject: "This is better than that." We have already seen the essential principle: get rid of the opposition first. Hit it head on, in the first sentence of your Middle, as you pick up the concessive subordinate part of your thesis-sentence:

Despite their many advantages, old age pensions . . . .
Although dogs are fine pets, cats . . . .

If the opposing arguments seem relatively slight and brief, you can get rid of them all together in one paragraph before you get down to your case. Immediately after your Beginning, which has stated your thesis, you will write a paragraph of concession: "Of course, security is a good thing. No one wants old people begging." And so on to the end of the paragraph, deflating every conceivable objection. Then back to the main line: "But the price in moral fiber is too great." The structure might be diagramed as shown in the first diagram:

Diagram I

PRO	CON
Thesis: "This is so." →	
	"Of course, that is so, too."
"But that is unimportant in view of . . . . ←	
↓ "And	
↓ "Moreover, ...	
↓ ". . . and so forth.	
↓ "Therefore, ..."	

If the opposition is more considerable, demolish it point by point, using a series of *con*'s and *pro*'s. Each paragraph can be a small argument that presents the opposition, then knocks it flat—a kind of Punch-and-Judy show in series: "It must be admitted that . . . . But . . . ." And down goes the poor old opposition again. Or you can alternate by complete paragraphs—a paragraph for the opposition, a paragraph demolishing it and advancing your own argument, another paragraph for the opposition, and so on. The structural line might look like Diagram II (p. 56).

The bare bones of an actual controversial essay (which omits some of the turns in Diagram II) would look like Diagram III (p. 57).

Most of the subjects you undertake will not require this kind of persistent swinging back and forth. But writing one or two dialectic swingers will give you confidence in handling any argument, and it will also give you a sense of the transitional words and phrases that move you from one side to the other and ease the flow of your sentences. In the structural outlines above, you will notice that *But* and *however* are always guides for the *pro*'s, serving as switches back to the main line. You will do well to make yourself two lists of these switching words and phrases, one for the *pro*'s and one for the *con*'s, adding to those I have used above, to get the feel of the argumentative turn and to have them handy. *But, however,* and *Nevertheless* are the basic *pro*'s. *But* (not followed by a comma) always heads its turning sentence; *Nevertheless* usually does (followed by a comma). I am

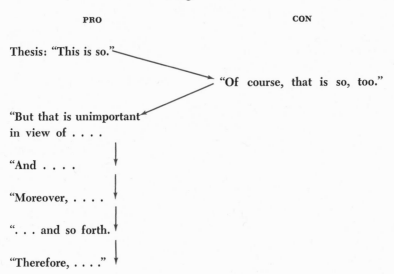

Diagram II

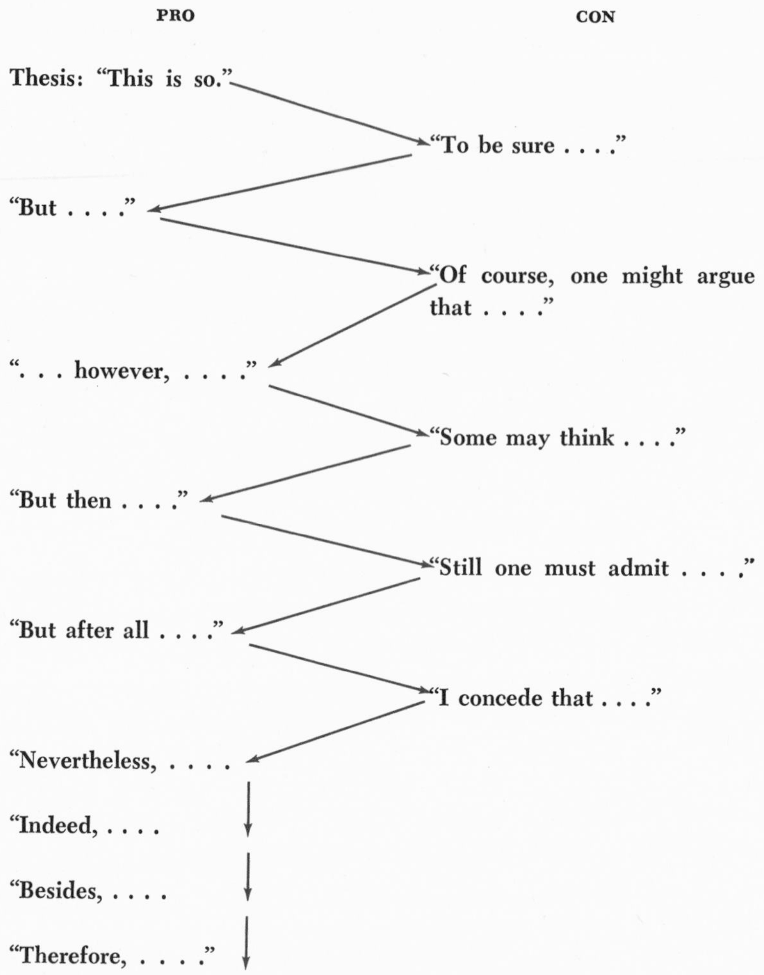

---

sure, however, that *however* is always better buried in the sentence between commas: *But* for the quick turn; the inlaid *however* for the more elegant sweep. These turning words simply follow the natural swings of the mind from side to side as we think, and they naturally guide our arguments as we organize them, *pro* and *con,* for dialectic persuasion.

The Order of Natural Divisions

Many subjects fall into natural or customary partitions, which supply you with a kind of dialectic contrast not necessarily hostile, and even

Diagram III

PRO **CON**

Thesis: "Marijuana should be legalized."

To be sure, soft drugs can lead to hard drugs. . . .

But most users of marijuana seek only mild pleasures among a group of friends. . . .

Of course, one might argue that marijuana only prolongs the groupiness of adolescence. . . .

People at every age, however, seek support from their peers. . . .

I concede that legalizing marijuana invites certain serious risks. . . .

Nevertheless, the present punishment and its social consequences far exceed these risks. . . .

Indeed, the law could eliminate many dangers by controlling quality. . . .

Besides, legality would eliminate the criminal profiteers. . . .

Therefore, legalizing marijuana would solve more problems than its illegality now creates. . . .

---

blandly jointed, like a good roast of pork, ready for carving: freshman, sophomore, junior, senior; Republicans, Democrats; right, middle, left;

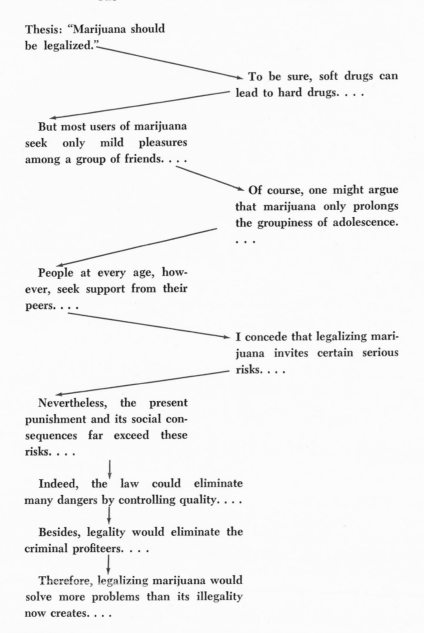

legislative, executive, judicial. Similarly, any manufacturing process, or any machine, will already have distinct steps and parts. These customary divisions will help your reader, since he knows something of them already. Describe the Democratic position on foreign aid, and he will naturally expect your description of the Republican position to follow. If no other divisions suggest themselves, you can often divide your essay into a consistent series of parallel answers, or "reasons for," or "reasons against"—something like this:

> A broad liberal education is best:
> I. It prepares you for a world of changing employment.
> II. It enables you to function well as a citizen.
> III. It enables you to make the most of your life.

Inductive Order

Induct means "to lead in"; *deduct* means "to lead away from." With inductive order, you simply lead your reader in—by successive questions and their dismissal, or partial answers—to your main and conclusive point. "Is it this? Well, no." "Then may it be this? No, not exactly this either." "Then how about this? Ah, yes, this seems to be it." The deductive order, beginning with your thesis and then explaining it, is much more usual, and usually clearer. But the inductive order has suspense, a kind of intellectual excitement, if you can keep your answer from slipping out.

Inductive order probably works best for short essays, since you must keep the cat in the bag, and you can't keep him in too long. You simply use a question for your thesis-sentence and then simulate for your reader the train of thought by which you arrived at a conclusion, as I did in the following passage:

> . . . What does Walt Whitman mean when he says "I celebrate myself"?
>
> Can he be simply an egotist? The pronoun "I" dominates his writing. "I will effuse egotism, and show it underlying all," he writes. He speaks of generations of Americans passing with "faces turned sideways or backward toward me to listen,/With eyes retrospective toward me." He loves to see the smoke of his own breath, and to hear the beating of his own heart. Yet this egotism is somehow not offensive. He is something more than a simple egotist.
>
> Perhaps he takes himself as the common man, since his "I" represents others as well as himself: "I am of old and young, of the foolish

as much as the wise,/ . . . Maternal as well as paternal, a child as well as a man." All men and women are his equals, his brothers and sisters, and he says a great deal about democracy. We soon realize that Whitman could not have done many of the things the "I" claims to have done. The "I" has been at sea with John Paul Jones; he is an artillery man in a bombarded fort; he has been a trapper, a fisherman off Newfoundland. The "I," then, is both the actual Whitman and his imaginative identification of himself with all walks of American life.

But the "I" seems even more than this. The "I" has slept for ages, has evolved upward through the eons, has been carried in a dinosaur's mouth. He has subsumed in himself all the ideas of God: "Taking myself the exact dimensions of Jehovah,/Lithographing Kronos, Zeus his son, and Hercules his grandson . . . ." Like the hawk, he sounds his "barbaric yawp over the roofs of the world." He dissolves into the next fold of the future, and waits for us somewhere up ahead. The "I" is now the spirit of life itself. So when Whitman celebrates himself, he is also celebrating the spirit of democracy and the Life Force, which are evident to him no less in geological history than in the men and women and blades of grass around him, and in his own present breathing and heartbeat.

This will give you an idea of inductive order. You may well use a short inductive section in a longer essay, especially for dismissing the opposition's arguments by putting them as questions ("Do we want unlimited freedom?") and then reducing them to absurdities. But, as I say, a wholly inductive essay is usually short, and you won't even find many of these.

Deductive Order

Deductive is the opposite of inductive, of course—a leading *away* from your general proposition. Like its inductive counterpart, deductive order is the writer's imitation of a way of thought. Inductively, putting two and two together, we think our way into a general truth: "four." Deductively, we think out the consequences of a general truth, thinking *away* from the idea of four to find its relevance for this or that particular two or one. Deductive logic, as we shall see in Chapter 13, has become a specialized procedure of thought. But, for the present, the large-to-small order of deduction will help to fix in mind the most common, useful, and dependable way of arranging an essay, as I have indicated from the beginning. You set down your thesis, your general proposition, then *explain* it in detail and at length. The mode of induction is question and partial answer; the mode of deduction is assertion and explanation. As we have seen, however, the usual deductive order does not simply begin with your Big Idea and then dwindle down to nothing. You start with your thesis, then jump down to your smallest small and work progressively uphill until you again reach your thesis, which is now restated as your conclusion and rounded off in a concluding paragraph.

In short, the deductive order of presentation is the normal one we have been talking about all along. To change your little inductive essay on Whitman into a deductive one, you would simply make your thesis an assertion to be demonstrated rather than a question to be answered: "Whitman's 'I' represents not only Whitman himself, but also the spirit of democracy and the Life Force." You would then proceed with the same evidence, and in the same general order, from actual Whitman, through democracy, to the great force of life itself. Rather than the question that opened your second paragraph, you would assert: "At first, Whitman may strike the reader as a simple egotist." Rather than the tentative "Perhaps" that opened your third paragraph, you would assert: "We soon discover that Whitman's 'I' represents others, as well as himself."

Deductive-Inductive Order

Actually, you can write a good essay about halfway between the inductive and deductive modes. The basic framework is deductive, a general thesis followed by its successive explanations in ascending order of interest and importance. But the inner movement is mostly inductive, a fairly large number of questions replacing the assertions that would otherwise guide the progress, section by section. You may set the mode very easily by putting your thesis as a broadly general question.

The more direct the question, the more purely inductive the essay. You launch a completely inductive essay when your questioning thesis asks for one specific answer among the several possibilities you will entertain and reject before letting the reader know your answer: "Is Whitman an egotist?" ("Not really"); "Should we have old age pensions?" ("Yes"). The more your question suggests your answer, the more deductive you become: "Is Whitman something more universal than a mere egotist?"; "Are old age pensions really the socialistic and bureaucratic evil they are so often said to be?"

Virginia Woolf's famous essay "How Should One Read a Book?" is an almost perfect example of the deductive-inductive mode, as both her title and her thesis suggest. Even her questioning title implies an unstated deductive assertion: "One should read a book, and read it the right way." Her thesis, also a question, likewise implies an unstated deductive assertion, which her essay proceeds to illustrate: "How are we to bring order into this multitudinous chaos and so get the deepest and widest pleasure from what we read?" Her thesis-question does not say exactly *how*—her essay proceeds to fill in the answer somewhat inductively—but the question clearly suggests that we must bring order from chaos to achieve the deep and wide pleasure she sees as the purpose of reading. A thesis-question similar to Mrs. Woolf's may get you a very nice deductive-inductive essay:

How should one plan a vacation?
What is the greatest reward in sports?
What makes an effective teacher?

You may also set the deductive-inductive mode by trimming a fully explicit thesis to get something of the open-endedness of a question. You simply trim the full-blown thesis at both ends, cutting away from the beginning the concessive "Although . . ." and from the end the explanatory "because . . . ." Your most completely stated thesis might be:

Although old age pensions may offend the rugged individualist, we should nevertheless have a system of old age pensions because they relieve much want and anxiety, and they dispel much familial resentment.

To remake this a thesis for a partially inductive essay, you simply trim it to something like: "All in all, we need some system of pensions." You then proceed with a series of questions, or open-ended assertions, supplying the answers and *because*'s as you go:

a. **But what about the threat to our ideal of self-sufficiency?**
b. **Industries and other organizations already provide a number of private pension plans.**
c. **But what about the actual needs of old people?**
d. **Can our affluent society care for its elders?**

And so on, as you jot down general headings by way of an outline, or proceed to one of the more thorough systems of outlining, which you will discover in the next chapter.

Exercises

1. Looking out of your window, write a description of the scene organized spatially: left, right, and middle distance.

2. Imagine a stage set of your own devising; then describe for your reader what he would see were he seated in the theater as the curtain goes up. Put the most striking details first, and then, in the order of their being noticed, the lesser touches. Make your reader see a clear spatial picture, so he will know exactly what is where. (Note: this is not a conventional "stage direction," which is put down from the actor's viewpoint, *left* meaning "actor's left." Your description is the other way around: the view from the audience.)

3. Describe an event that runs directly through time—a tennis match, a rock concert, a tea for the oldest living alumna. You will notice how you absorb long segments of time in a sentence ("The first five innings were deadlocked and dull") and then need a paragraph for the brilliant instant.

4. Describe something like a circus, or a track meet, in which several things happen at once, guiding the reader with directions like "while," "in the meantime," "at the same time," and so forth.

5. Write an essay explaining why your favorite team lost, or why your favorite miss is Miss America, going carefully into conditions, causes, and effects.

6. Write a three-paragraph essay in deductive order; then write a note explaining how you would rephrase the thesis and change the essay to present it in inductive order.

7. Write five thesis-sentences, as complete as possible, accompanying each with two versions that would serve for a deductive-inductive essay: (1) an abbreviated form of the complete thesis, (2) a question so derived from the complete thesis as to point the way while leaving the answers unspecified.

Outlines

5

The first thing to grasp about outlines is that they seldom work out to the letter. The second is that they always help. The third is that the headings do not represent equal space in the finished essay: one heading may represent two paragraphs and the next only two sentences, depending on how much each idea needs to be explained and illustrated. Making an outline may seem fruitless exactly because the fluid pressure of writing will always force revision of your best-laid plans. An incidental sentence may swell into an entire section; a scheduled section may end up as just a sentence. But without an outline, your first draft could be formless and your final paper incoherent, requiring an agony of unscrambling with scissors and paste.

Outline to set your thoughts in order. Outlining is not easy. It takes time, effort, and practice. But the more you do it, the easier and more helpful it becomes. An outline helps you to spot gaps in your own argument and in the arguments of others, to test the relationships of parts, to certify a thesis, to validate an assertion. Outline your reading and you will really grasp it. Outline the plan of your essay, and you straighten out your thinking for your reader to grasp.

We think and write largely by free association, following the drift of thought as it comes, picking up some of our best ideas from below the logical surface. But to explain these thoughts fully to your reader, and to yourself, you need to discover and outline their logical pattern. Once you get the logic down on paper and out of the way, you can let yourself go, writing from heading to heading, sure of your direction, and sure of your order of ascending interest. You can push aside without worry the good ideas constantly crowding in for your notice: your outline has already scheduled them, each in its most logical and effective place.

Establish your thesis and estimate your needs. Finding a firm, assertive thesis has already won much of your battle with logic. Beyond the thesis, your essay's length and its structural demands will suggest your choice from among the four kinds of outlines: (1) the jotted outline, (2) the topic outline, (3) the sentence outline, and (4) the paragraph outline. Argument, of course, demands more planning than descriptive exposition. A *pro-con* structure demands more outlining than do the orders of time and space. A short paper of five hundred or a thousand words will need but the simplest of outlines: a thesis, and three or four headings arranged in any reasonable order of ascending interest, human, logical, or chronological. Longer papers require the most detailed planning: exactly how much, you will eventually learn from experience, as you work your way past peaks of inspiration and step over the dry bones of outlines that never reached prose.

Revise your outline.

Whatever the kind of outline you choose, your best procedure is to sketch the whole thing out in rough form first, aligning and refining your points later. After setting down your thesis, and declaring your title boldly above it, rough out your main points, not bothering yet with the minor ones. Next, rearrange your main headings in some systematic sequence of ascending interest. Try to fix firmly on your main headings, or you may waste much time on subheadings that will vanish if your main heads shift. Then sketch in and arrange your subpoints under each of your main headings. Now check through your whole draft of major and minor headings to be sure your argument amply covers and develops your thesis. Finally, rephrase your headings, keeping them concise, grammatically parallel, and properly coordinated and subordinated. If you do not word your headings in grammatical parallel, the logical relations between them will be unclear. Keep your headings brief and trenchant, favoring the active voice; your outline will condition the language of your paper.

The Jotted Outline

The jotted outline is the simplest of outlines—perhaps all you will need for a short paper. Even with these jotted headings, parallel phrasing helps keep your thinking straight and strong. Here is a jotted outline for a paper against smoking:

The Wicked Cigarette

THESIS: Despite certain hazy benefits, we must admit that cigarettes are bad for us.

1. **Social benefits—put you "in," give you something to do and say, make you feel mature (in charge of your own life).**
2. **Economic benefits—support a tremendous industrial network, from farmer to company to advertising agency to magazines and newspapers, providing thousands of livelihoods.**
3. **But moral hazards—become a habit controlling you, defeating your personal autonomy, making you "follow the pack."**
4. **Physical hazards—pose an unnecessary risk to the only heart and lungs you have.**

Notice how easily you may now convert this outline into an essay. The subordinate clause in your thesis has set aside the concessions you must make to the opposition, and the main clause has asserted the main point. The jotted main headings fall neatly into place, each parallel grammatically, each a noun with its adjective ("social benefits"), each structurally equal, and the four effectively balanced—two for opposition, two for affirmation. The lesser elements of your explanation are also in parallel—*put, give, make,* for example—to indicate equivalent treatment. Your paper's structure firmly before you, now you are free to write it out.

The Topic Outline

The topic outline is the most common kind of outline, an arranging of your jotted thoughts into heads and subheads, each rank in parallel phrasing. Here you will notice two opposite currents: an inductive, uphill one, which carries your major headings upward toward your conclusion in tiers of ascending importance; and a deductive, downhill one, which partitions each major heading into smaller and smaller components. You mark heads and subheads by alternating numbers and letters as you proceed downhill from Roman numeral *I* through capital *A* to Arabic *1* and little *a,* until you reach, if you need them, parenthesized (*1*) and (*a*). You indent equal heads equally, so that they fall in the same column, Roman under Roman, capital under capital, and so on, like this:

```
I. ________________________________________
   A. _____________________________________
      1. __________________________________
      2. __________________________________
   B. _____________________________________
      1. __________________________________
         a. _______________________________
            (1) ___________________________
                (a) _______________________
                (b) _______________________
            (2) ___________________________
         b. _______________________________
      2. __________________________________
II. _______________________________________
```

Check your outline for balance.

Ideally every *I* should have its *II*, every *A* its *B*, every *1* its *2*, since an unpaired heading suggests that it is a detail too small for separate treatment, one really part of the larger heading above. For instance:

Poor	*Good*
II. Value of cats	**II. Value of cats as pets**
A. As pets	
III. Kinds of cats	**III. Kinds of cats**
A.______	**A.______**
B.______	**B.______**

One of your first revisions should be to absorb any such unpaired heading into its related major heading. Then see that each heading is a noun (or noun phrase), with or without modifiers, as necessary: "Benefits," for instance, or "Benefits to the individual." This will keep your outline neatly parallel. You can signal your major turns by adding a *But* or *Nevertheless.*

Now for a topic outline of your projected essay on cigarettes. You have already read Thackeray's *Vanity Fair,* and you remember that Dobbin took out a cigar "and amused himself for half an hour with the pernicious vegetable." The phrase suggests a title that catches the subject exactly as you mean to treat it, squarely but humorously. You will work in Thackeray himself later on, letting your reader in on the secret of your title as you cite an eminent man who apparently liked a cigar himself but knew the awful truth.

The Pernicious Vegetable

THESIS: Although cigarettes have brought certain benefits to man, we must ultimately judge them harmful.

- **I. Beneficial effects**
  - **A. Benefits to society**
    - **1. Income for the tobacco industry**
      - **a. Farmers**
      - **b. Wholesalers**
      - **c. Retailers**
    - **2. Income for the communications industry**
      - **a. Advertising agencies**
      - **b. Advertising media**

- 3. **Income for the government**
  - a. **National tax revenues**
  - b. **State and local tax revenues**
- B. **Benefits to the individual**
  - 1. **Feeling of social ease and acceptance**
  - 2. **Feeling of self-responsibility**
  - 3. **Feeling of maturity**

II. But: harmful effects

- A. **Income for criminal elements**
  - 1. **Vending-machine racketeers**
  - 2. **Narcotics and gambling racketeers**
- B. **Physical harm to the individual**
  - 1. **Historical opinions**
    - a. **James I's condemnation of tobacco**
    - b. **Thackeray's characterization of the cigar**
    - c. **Edison's refusal to hire smokers**
  - 2. **Modern findings**
    - a. **Impairment of physical stamina**
      - (1) **Views of athletes and coaches**
      - (2) **Personal experience in sports**
    - b. **Relation to heart disease**
    - c. **Relation to cancer**
      - (1) **Laboratory findings with animals**
      - (2) **Laboratory findings with human beings**
        - (a) **Lip cancer**
        - (b) **Laryngeal cancer**
        - (c) **Lung cancer**
- C. **Moral harm to the individual**
  - 1. **Surrender of one's individuality to the group**
  - 2. **Surrender of one's destiny to the habit**

Notice two things about this outline. First, section II.B on "physical harm to the individual," itself in logical order, can freely organize its subordinate parts in chronological order: historical opinions, then modern findings. Moreover, the historical opinions themselves fall into chronological order, but the subheads under "modern findings" then revert effectively to the order of ascending interest. The point is this: each heading and subheading is parallel to its co-equals—*A* matches *B*, *1* matches *2*, *a* matches *b*.

Second, notice that we have ended rather more with character than with cancer—an order opposite from that of our jotted outline back on page 65. Why? Strangely but inevitably, sheer length has changed the dynamics of our argument. For the shorter essay, "the only heart and lungs you have" seemed stronger than the equivalent business about losing individuality in habit. But in the plan for the longer essay, the laboratory details are now too extensive for a single climactic point. They have indeed moved to subordinate rank—*(1)* not *1*, and not even *a*. Now the moral argument stands in higher rank, simpler and more lofty, a fitting climax before the concluding summation.

The Sentence Outline

Single sentences are the very planks of writing, and all practice in their carpentry is to your benefit. In the sentence outline, you phrase each heading as a complete sentence. Such an outline lays out the plan of your essay as no other can, giving the fullest statement of your ideas, and showing clearly and explicitly the logical relation of parts. Often a required procedure in the assigned research paper, the sentence outline is useful for leading you through organizational intricacies and saving you from logical snares. Because it forces you to think out your plan so thoroughly beforehand, a good sentence outline can speed the actual writing of any essay that depends greatly on logical structure. But outlining in sentences consumes your time—and therein lies the danger. The outlining may leave too little time for the writing. A few experiments in the form, however, should help you decide when to use it to your advantage.

A sentence outline for your cigarette essay would begin like this:

The Pernicious Vegetable

THESIS: Although cigarettes have brought certain benefits to man, we must ultimately judge them harmful.

1. These benefits are both social and personal.

- **A. The most evident social benefit is the tremendous income generated from tobacco.**
  - **1. A wide variety of people make a living in the tobacco industry.**
    - **a. The growing, transplanting, and curing of tobacco supports thousands of farmers and farm workers in the United States alone.**
    - **b. The wholesaling of tobacco is virtually an industry of its own.**
    - **c. From cigarette stand to supermarket, money from cigarettes flows steadily into the cash register.**

Remember, each heading, whether in a jotted, topic, or sentence outline, will require widely differing amounts of space as you write out your essay. Heading *I* would probably also absorb heading *A*, as you started your paragraph:

> These benefits are both social and personal, most evidently in the tremendous income generated from tobacco. Annual retail sales of cigarettes alone are estimated at . . . .

Your next paragraph would probably also use headings *1* and *a* consecutively:

> A wide variety of people make a living in the tobacco industry. The growing, transplanting, and curing of tobacco . . . .

And then your next paragraph would probably begin with the wholesaling, run on through its associated trucking and railroading, and end with sentence *c* and the cash register.

Outlines for Reading

Outlining by sentences is additionally useful in analyzing the logical structure of a printed essay to exercise and strengthen your own structural grasp. Having first read for the meaning, you outline for the structure. Your finished outline should convey the essence of both. Here is part of an essay by George Santayana on one of the world's great books, followed by an analytical sentence outline of it:

Cervantes

Cervantes is known to the world as the author of *Don Quixote,* and although his other works are numerous and creditable, and his pathetic life is carefully recorded, yet it is as the author of *Don Quixote* alone that he deserves to be generally known or considered. Had his wit not come by chance on the idea of the Ingenious Hidalgo, Cervantes would never have attained his universal renown, even if his other works and the interest of his career should have sufficed to give him a place in the literary history of his country. Here, then, where our task is to present in miniature only what has the greatest and most universal value, we may treat our author as playwrights are advised to treat their heroes, saying of him only what is necessary to the understanding of the single action with which we are concerned. This single action is the writing of *Don Quixote;* and what we shall try to understand is what there was in the life and environment of Cervantes that enabled him to compose that great book, and that remained imbedded in its characters, its episodes, and its moral.

There was in vogue in the Spain of the sixteenth century a species of romance called books of chivalry. They were developments of the legends dealing with King Arthur and the Knights of the Table Round, and their numerous descendants and emulators. These stories had appealed in the first place to what we should still think of as the spirit of chivalry: they were full of tourneys and single combats, desperate adventures and romantic loves. The setting was in the same vague and wonderful region as the Coast of Bohemia, where to the known mountains, seas, and cities that have poetic names, was added a prodigious number of caverns, castles, islands, and forests of the romancer's invention. With time and popularity this kind of story had naturally intensified its characteristics until it had reached the greatest extravagance and absurdity, and combined in a way the unreality of the fairy tale with the bombast of the melodrama.

Cervantes had apparently read these books with avidity, and was not without a great sympathy with the kind of imagination they embodied. His own last and most carefully written book, the *Travails of Persiles and Sigismunda,* is in many respects an imitation of them; it abounds in savage islands, furious tyrants, prodigous feats of arms, disguised maidens whose discretion is as marvelous as their beauty, and happy deliverances from intricate and hopeless situations. His first book also, the *Galatea,* was an embodiment of a kind of pastoral idealism: sentimental verses being interspersed with euphuistic prose, the whole describing the lovelorn shepherds and heartless shepherdesses of Arcadia.

But while these books, which were the author's favorites among his own works, expressed perhaps Cervantes's natural taste and ambition, the events of his life and the real bent of his talent, which in time he came himself to recognize, drove him to a very different sort of composition. His family was ancient but impoverished, and he was forced throughout his life to turn his hand to anything that could promise him a livelihood. His existence was a continuous series of experiments, vexations, and disappointments. He adopted at first the profession of arms, and followed his colors as a private soldier upon several foreign expeditions. He was long quartered in Italy; he fought at Lepanto against the Turks, where among other wounds he received one that maimed his left hand, to the greater glory, as he tells us, of his right; he was captured by Barbary pirates and remained for five years a slave in Algiers; he was ransomed, and returned to Spain only to find official favors and recognitions denied him; and finally, at the age of thirty-seven, he abandoned the army for literature.

His first thought as a writer does not seem to have been to make direct use of his rich experience and varied observation; he was rather possessed by an obstinate longing for that poetic gift which, as he confesses in one place, Heaven had denied him. He began with the idyllic romance, the *Galatea,* already mentioned, and at various times during the rest of his life wrote poems, plays, and stories of a romantic and sentimental type. In the course of these labors, however, he struck one vein of much richer promise. It was what the Spanish call the *picaresque;* that is, the description of the life and character of rogues, pickpockets, vagabonds, and all those wretches and sorry wits that might be found about the highways, in the country inns, or in the slums of cities. Of this kind is much of what is best in his collected stories, the *Novelas Exemplares.* The talent and the experience which he betrays in these amusing narratives were to be invaluable to him later as the author of *Don Quixote,* where they enabled him to supply a foil to the fine world of his poor hero's imagination.

We have now mentioned what were perhaps the chief elements of the preparation of Cervantes for his great task. They were a great familiarity with the romances of chivalry, and a natural liking for them; a life of honorable but unrewarded endeavor both in war and in the higher literature; and much experience of Vagabondia, with the art of taking down and reproducing in amusing profusion the typical scenes and languages of low life. Out of these elements a single spark, which we may attribute to genius, to chance, or to inspiration, was enough to produce a new and happy conception: that of a parody on the romances of chivalry, in which the extravagances of the fables of knighthood should be contrasted with the sordid realities of life. This is done by the ingenious device of representing a country gentleman whose naturally generous mind, unhinged by much reading of the books of chivalry, should lead him to undertake the office of knight-errant, and induce him to ride about the country clad in ancient armor, to right wrongs, to succor defenseless maidens, to kill giants, and to win empires at least as vast as that of Alexander.

This is the subject of *Don Quixote.* But happy as the conception is, it could not have produced a book of enduring charm and well-seasoned wisdom, had it not been filled in with a great number of amusing and lifelike episodes, and verified by two admirable figures, Don Quixote and Sancho Panza, characters at once intimately individual and truly universal.*

This I would outline in sentences as follows, sharpening and spelling out the implications of Santayana's deductive-inductive thesis, gathered from reading the entire essay, making a completely deductive assertion, for clarity:

Cervantes

THESIS: Cervantes's chivalric idealism and realistic experience combined to produce his masterpiece, *Don Quixote*, which laughs at idealism only to endorse its realistic application.

I. Cervantes's chivalric romanticism was natural to him.
  A. He grew up when romances were in vogue.
  B. His own family, though poor, was ancient and presumably noble.
  C. He read romances avidly.
  D. His first and last writings were serious attempts at idealistic romance.

II. But, being poor, he led a harshly realistic and disappointing life.
  A. He experienced the hardships of a soldier abroad.
    1. As a private who saw service in several foreign campaigns, he was long stationed in Italy.
    2. He fought the Turks at Lepanto, suffering a wound that crippled his left hand.
    3. He was a captive of Algerian pirates for five years.
    4. Ransomed, he returned to Spain at the age of thirty-five to find neither recognition nor pay awaiting him.
  B. He turned to writing for his livelihood.
    1. He began with an idealistic romance, a kind of writing he continued throughout his life with little success.
    2. He tried the picaresque tale, the story of rogues and vagabonds.

III. From these two strains, the high and the low, came the idea for *Don Quixote*—a parodying of high chivalric romances through low situations.

IV. Cervantes's genius made this simple contrast great: he created two great characters to represent the two sides of the contrast.

Making a sentence outline really masters an essay for you. You discover the essay's parts; you summarize them into clear sentences; you work out their logical relations. You may indeed discover some logical lapses (Santayana, a professional philosopher, seems neatly coherent). You will certainly bring some of your author's points to sharper clarity as I have done with Santayana's thesis, for instance, to put the essay in a nutshell, and to make my outline clear.

To outline your reading, you first boil the essay down to its true thesis, in one sentence. Then you simply go through the essay, typing out a series of sentences that summarize the key ideas as they come along. Sometimes you use the author's very words, but usually you compress them into a sentence of your own. The next step is to grade and group your sentences into what seem their major and minor hierarchies, and this may take considerable recasting, and reassigning of *A*'s for *I*'s, of *I*'s for *A*'s, and so forth. You may need to rearrange the order of sentences for a better flow of logic, so that you can see how the essay ought to have been, in its best possible form. Such an outline gets you into a man's essay as nothing else will. You have made his thoughts and their relationships your own, and you may glow with added satisfaction from discovering that even a professional is seldom perfect.

The Paragraph Outline

The value of the paragraph outline is in strengthening your ability to organize paragraphs by topic sentences. You write a topic sentence for each paragraph in some published essay, and simply number your topic sentences consecutively. Or you may mark your larger structural divisions with a few strategically placed general headings. Since your paragraphs are many and your hierarchies few, a combination of Roman and Arabic is most convenient for numbering. A paragraph outline of the Middle of Santayana's essay would begin like this:

I. Cervantes's chivalric romanticism was natural to him. [This is a general heading, not a paragraph.]

1. There was in vogue in the Spain of the sixteenth century a species of romance called books of chivalry.

2. Cervantes had apparently read these books avidly, and was not without a great sympathy for the kind of imagination they embodied.

3. But the events of his life and the real bent of his talent drove him to a very different sort of composition.

4. His first thought as a writer was not to use his rich experience but to pursue his romantic longing.

5. We have now mentioned what were perhaps the chief elements of Cervantes's preparation for his great task.

This is the first section of Santayana's Middle. You will notice that our paragraph outline has covered in one section, as does the essay, what our sentence outline covers in two, as it makes the logic clear. I have used Santayana's own topic sentences, condensing only a little here and there. The last paragraph, as its topic sentence indicates, summarizes the points of the preceding four before moving on to describe the spark that animated the elements into a single work of genius. As you study paragraphing in the next chapter, you will discover more about the value of the topic sentence.

The Conventions of Outlining

Most of the outline's formal conventions have emerged during our survey, but some further details and reminders will be useful in summary.

(1) *Title.* Keep your title independent of the text of your outline. Do not number it in with the text; do not use it as a heading for subheads; do not refer to it by pronouns. Do not do this:

I. The Advantages of the Bikini

A. Its convenience in packing

(2) *Thesis.* To keep your logical structure straight, make as explicit a deductive thesis as you can, even when you intend to write a more inductive essay, with less explicit thesis. In outlining a printed essay, do the same, using verbatim only a thesis already clearly deductive and explicit.

(3) *Capitalization.* Capitalize only the first word of each heading (and other words normally capitalized).

(4) *Punctuation.* Put periods after headings that are complete sentences, but not after merely phrasal headings.

(5) *Headings.* For the topic outline, use all nouns (or noun phrases), with modifiers accompanying them, as needed. Do not mix kinds of headings: some single nouns, some sentences, some fragments. Checking your headings for equivalent nouns (or noun phrases) to express equivalent points is your best assurance of a tight and logical outline, and a good essay to come:

A. Benefits to society
B. Benefits to the individual
1. Feeling of social ease

2. Feeling of self-responsibility
  a. James I's condemnation
  b. Thackeray's characterization
  c. Edison's refusal

Now you have pretty well covered the general structure of the essay. You have become familiar with the thesis and its organizing power. You have acquired some feel for Beginning, Middle, and End. You have considered the ways of arranging the middle, and you have seen the advantage of outlining a good logical structure. Now you will move on to paragraphing, and to the art of bringing the logical structure to full and agreeable expression.

Exercises

1. Make a jotted outline for an essay about: (1) not deciding on a career, (2) entering political movements, (3) going out for sports, (4) volunteering for social work, (5) studying off-beat subjects, (6) eschewing conformity, or (7) any similarly controversial subject.

2. Expand your jotted outline into a topic outline.

3. Make a thorough sentence outline of a printed essay of recognized worth, beginning with the true thesis, boiled down and clearly asserted in one sentence (see pp. 24–28). Then write a brief critique of the essay's logical structure, suggesting what, if anything, might have been improved, and evaluating how well the writer supported his thesis.

4. Make a paragraph outline of the same essay.

Paragraphs
6

The Standard Paragraph

A paragraph is a structural convenience—a building-block to get firmly in mind. I mean the standard, central paragraph, setting aside for the moment the peculiarly shaped beginning paragraph and ending paragraph. You build the bulk of your essay with standard paragraphs, with blocks of concrete ideas, and they must fit smoothly. But they must also remain as perceptible parts, to rest your reader's eye and mind. Indeed, the paragraph originated, among the Greeks, as a resting place and place-finder, being first a mere mark (*graphos*) in the margin alongside (*para*) an unbroken sheet of handwriting—the proofreader's familiar ¶. You have heard that a paragraph is a single idea, and this is true. But so is a word, usually; and so is a sentence, sometimes. It seems best, after all, to think of a paragraph as something you use for your reader's convenience, rather than as some granitic form laid down by logic.

The writing medium determines the size of the paragraph. Your average longhand paragraph may look the same size to you as a typewritten one, and both may seem the same size as a paragraph in a book. But the printed page might show your handwritten paragraph so short as to be embarrassing, and your typewritten paragraph barely long enough for decency. Handwriting plus typewriting plus insecurity equals inadequate paragraphs. Your first impulse may be to write little paragraphs, often only a sentence to each. If so, you are not yet writing in any medium at all.

Journalists, of course, are habitually one-sentence paragraphers. The narrowness of the newspaper column makes a sentence look like a paragraph, and narrow columns and short paragraphs serve the rapid transit for which newspapers are designed. A paragraph from a book might fill a whole newspaper column with solid lead. It would have to be broken—paragraphed—for the reader's convenience. On the other hand, a news story printed on the page of a book would look like a gap-toothed comb, and would have to be consolidated for the reader's comfort.

Plan for the big paragraph.

Imagine yourself writing for print, but in a book, not a newspaper. Force yourself to four or five sentences at least, visualizing your paragraphs as about all of a size. Think of them as identical rectangular frames to be filled. This will allow you to build with orderly blocks, to strengthen your feel for structure. Since the beginner's problem is usually one of thinking of things to say rather than of trimming the overgrowth, you can do your filling-out a unit at a time, always thinking up one or two sentences more to fill the customary space. You will probably be repetitive and wordy at first—this is our universal failing—but you will soon learn to fill your paragraph with clean and interesting details. You will get to feel a kind of constructional rhythm as you find yourself coming to a resting place at the end of your customary paragraphic frame. Once accustomed to a five-sentence frame, say, you can then begin to vary the length for structural and rhetorical emphasis, letting a good idea swell out beyond the norm, or bringing a particular point home in a paragraph short and sharp.

Find a topic sentence.

Looked at as a convenient structural frame, the paragraph reveals a further advantage. Like the essay itself, it has a beginning, a middle, and an end. The beginning and the end are usually each one sentence long, and the middle gets you smoothly from one to the other. Since, like the essay, the paragraph flows through time, its last sentence is the most emphatic. This is your home punch. The first sentence holds the next most emphatic place. It will normally be your *topic sentence,* stating the small thesis of a miniature essay, something like this:

> ***Jefferson believed in democracy because of his fearless belief in reason.*** **He knew that reason is far from perfect, but he also knew that it is the best faculty we have. He knew that it is better than all the frightened and angry intolerances with which we fence off our own back yards at the cost of injustice. Thought must be free. Discussion must be free. Reason must be free to range among the widest possibilities. Even the opinion we hate, and have reasons for believing wrong, we must leave free so that reason can operate on it, so that we advertise our belief in reason and demonstrate a faith unafraid of the consequences—because we know that the consequences will be right. Freedom is really not the end and aim of Jeffersonian democracy: freedom is the means by which democracy can rationally choose justice for all.**

If your topic sentence covers everything within your paragraph, you are using your paragraphs with maximum effect, leading your reader into your community block by block. If your end sentences bring him briefly to rest, he will know where he is and appreciate it.

Beginning Paragraphs: The Funnel

State your thesis at the end of your beginning paragraph.

Your beginning paragraph must contain your main idea, and present it to best advantage. Its topic sentence is also the *thesis-sentence* of your entire essay. The clearest and most emphatic place for your thesis-sentence is at the *end*—not at the beginning—of the beginning paragraph. If you put it first, you will have to repeat some version of it as you bring your beginning paragraph to a close. If you put it in the middle, the reader will very likely take something else as your main point, probably whatever the last sentence contains. The inevitable psychology of interest, as you move your reader through your first paragraph and into your essay, urges you to put your thesis last—in the last sentence of your beginning paragraph.

Think of your beginning paragraph, then, not as a frame to be filled, but as a funnel. Start wide and end narrow:

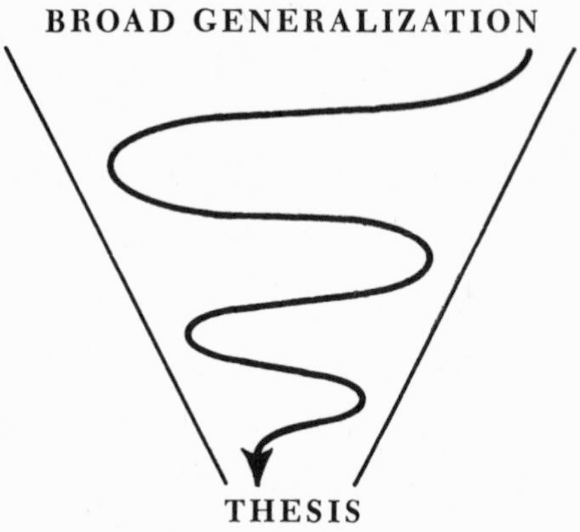

If, for instance, you wished to show that Mozart's superiority lay in putting musical commonplaces to new uses, you would want to start at some small distance back from that point. You could start almost anywhere, but you should certainly start with some innocuous and peaceable proposition: "Mozart is one of the great names in music" or "Everyone likes the familiar" or "Music undoubtedly has charms for everyone." Your opening line, in other words, should be innocent, acceptable, and inoffensive, something to which all readers would agree without a rise in blood pressure. (Antagonize and startle if you wish, but beware of losing your friends and of making your thesis an anticlimax.) Therefore: broad and genial. From the opening pleasant generalization you move progressively down to particulars. You narrow down: from all music, to eighteenth-century music, to eighteenth-century musical commonplaces, to Haydn and Mozart, to Mozart, to "the surprising turn and depth Mozart gives to the most conventional of musical phrases" (your thesis). Your paragraph might run, from broad to narrow, something like this:

All people, even the tone-deaf, like some kind of music, and the old and familiar is usually the most appealing. For modern listeners, the eighteenth century usually represents this kind of comfortable familiarity—undemanding, pleasant, and commonplace. Indeed, eighteenth-century music developed and used a number of musical commonplaces. Composers were all working in the same style, tonality, and phraseology, and they often sound very much alike. Many people will say, for instance, that Haydn and his musical heir, Mozart, are as like as two peas. But Mozart far outdid his master. He used Haydn's conventions, but in those very conventions he found new expressive power. Indeed, Mozart's genius may be said to lie in his ability to use the commonplace but to make it continually surprising, fresh, and deep. We get the old with the ever surprisingly new.

Now, that paragraph turned out a little different from what I anticipated. I even found myself violating my rule of placing the thesis last. I went one sentence further for emphasis and for coherence with the first sentence. But it illustrates the funnel, from the broad and general to the one particular point, which is the main idea, the thesis. Here is another example:

Everyone likes a garden, even if for nothing more than a look in driving by. As man put down paving stones and discovered cement, he also discovered that he needed a little space for something green and growing. However much he may like the comfort of a house and the security of a city, he cannot completely cut himself off from nature. Even the tenement dweller will devise his window box. And suburbia represents a kind of mass movement into the lawns and shrubbery. But few of the onlookers ever realize how much work a garden can be.

Middle Paragraphs

Make your middle paragraphs full, and use transitions.

The middle paragraph is the standard paragraph, the little essay in itself, with its own little beginning and little end. But it must also declare its allegiance to the paragraphs immediately before and after it. Each topic sentence must somehow hook onto the paragraph above it, must include some kind of transitional word or phrase. You may simply repeat a word from the sentence that ended the paragraph just above. You may bring down a thought left slightly hanging in air:

"His ideas are different" might be a tremendously economical kind of topic sentence with automatic transition. Or you may get from one paragraph to the next by the usual steppingstones, like *but, however, nevertheless, therefore, indeed, of course.* One brief transitional touch in your topic sentence is usually sufficient.

The topic sentences in each of the following three paragraphs by Louis J. Halle contain neat transitions. I have just used an old stand-by myself: repeating the words *topic sentence* from the close of the preceding paragraph. Mr. Halle is explaining that the current revolt of students continues the students' nihilism of the nineteenth century. *This* is his transitional word (referring to man's progress upward from the jungle). In the next paragraph, *Men . . . think* does the trick; in the last, *however.* The paragraphs are nearly the same length, all cogent, clear, and full. No one-sentence paragraphing here, no gaps, but all a lively, orderly, and well-illustrated progression:

> This is a view for which abundant evidence could be adduced, but it is not a view that can gain a hearing today because it is, for the depressing reasons I have already cited, so unwelcome to those who represent the intellectual fashions of our day. If I should write a book showing that man, like the great carnivores, is predatory by his unchangeable nature, I could be sure that it would be widely read and acclaimed; but if I wrote a book that took an optimistic and teleological view of man's evolution, regarding it as an ascent from the level of the beasts to something ethically and spiritually higher, it would hardly be well received, and few would read it. The burden of living up to a high standard is something men can do without. I do not think that this situation will change in what remains of this century, for we seem to be in one of those long periods when civilization, in decline, produces the kind of thinking appropriate to such decline. But if the Phoenix ever rises again, its rise will be accompanied by the general optimism that periods of progress always produce.
>
> Men tend to be what they think they are. If they accept a view of themselves as self-indulgent, they will tend to be self-indulgent; if they accept a view of themselves as morally responsible beings, they will tend to be morally responsible. I do not think that the widespread denial of social inhibitions on human behavior, which we call permissiveness, is altogether unrelated to the prevalent view of what our human nature really is. Here is a logic that does, in fact, associate the two trends of our time: the hopeless view of our human nature and the assault on social inhibitions. If we are really pigs, rather than fine

ladies and gentlemen, then we should not be asked to behave like fine ladies and gentlemen. We should be free to use language regarded as obscene, and there should be no restrictions on theatrical exhibitions of sexual and sadistic practices, no matter how sickening some of them may be. (Whatever may be said in favor of freedom for obscenity, I submit that it is not on the same level of importance as the freedoms guaranteed by the first ten amendments of our Constitution.)

I do not offer this, however, as the primary explanation of how it is that those who regard man as fundamentally bestial are, nevertheless, the advocates of permissiveness. A further explanation is that they are not really interested in the maintenance or enlargement of a régime of freedom that, on the one hand, they tend to take for granted (having never experienced anything else), and that, on the other, does not in itself cure the intractable problems of our societies. The causes they nominally espouse are not necessarily causes they believe in, but mere pretexts for action that has other ends than their success. Any number of activist students admit in private that when they shout for Marx, or Mao, or Castro, that does not mean they care anything about what these figures stand for. They do not carry intellectual responsibility that far.*

Reassert your thesis.

If the beginning paragraph is a funnel, the end paragraph is a funnel upside down: the thought starts moderately narrow—it is more or less the thesis you have had all the time—and then pours out broader and broader implications and finer emphases. The end paragraph reiterates, summarizes, and emphasizes with decorous fervor. This is your last chance. This is what your reader will carry away—and if you can carry *him* away, so much the better. All within decent intellectual bounds, of course. You are the man of reason still, but the man of reason supercharged with conviction, sure of his idea and sure of its importance.

The last paragraph conveys a sense of assurance and repose, of business completed. Its topic sentence should be some version of your original thesis-sentence, since the end paragraph is the exact structural

* From "The Student Drive to Destruction," *The New Republic*, October 19, 1968, pp. 10–13. Reprinted by permission of *The New Republic* © 1968, Harrison-Blaine of New Jersey, Inc.

opposite and complement of the beginning one. Its transitional word or phrase is often one of finality or summary—*then, finally, thus, and so:*

> **Mozart's commonplaces, then, are like proverbs—old truths in surprisingly new situations.**
>
> **And so the beautiful garden grew more problems than roses.**

The paragraph would then proceed to expand and elaborate this revived thesis. We would get an earnest epitome of Mozart's particular beauty, and of his ultimate quality and value; we would get an amusing sense of the gardener's endless buying of spray and fertilizer, his despair in trying to sweep back the waves of weeds. One rule of thumb: the longer the paper, the more specific the summary of the points you have made. A short paper will need no specific summary of your points at all; the renewed thesis and its widening of implications are sufficient.

Here is an end paragraph by Sir James Jeans. His transitional phrase is *for a similar reason.* His thesis was that previous concepts of physical reality had mistaken surfaces for depths:

> **The purely mechanical picture of visible nature fails for a similar reason. It proclaims that the ripples themselves direct the workings of the universe instead of being mere symptoms of occurrences below; in brief, it makes the mistake of thinking that the weather-vane determines the direction from which the wind shall blow, or that the thermometer keeps the room hot.***

Here is an end paragraph by Charles Wyzanski, Jr. His transitional phrase is *Each generation,* since he has been talking of the perpetual gap. His thesis was that differences, including those between generations, have stimulated life to higher modes:

> **Each generation is faced with a challenge of making some kind of sense out of its existence. In advance, it knows from the Book of Job and the Book of Ecclesiastes and the Greek drama that there will be no right answer. But there will be forms of answer. There will be a style. As ancient Greece had the vision of *arete* (the noble warrior), as Dante and the Medievalists had the vision of the great and universal Catholic Church, even as the founding fathers of the American Republic had the vision of the new order which they began, so for the young the question is to devise a style—not one that will be good**

* *The New Background of Science* (Cambridge: at the University Press, 1933), p. 261.

> ***semper et ubique*, but one for our place and our time, one that will be a challenge to the very best that is within our power of reach, and one that will make us realize, in Whitehead's immortal terms, that for us the only reality is the process.***

Here is an end paragraph of Professor Richard Hofstadter's. His transitional word is *intellectuals*, carried over from the preceding paragraphs. His thesis was that intellectuals should not abandon their defense of intellectual and spiritual freedom, as they have tended to do, under pressure to conform:

> **This world will never be governed by intellectuals—it may rest assured. But *we* must be assured, too, that intellectuals will not be altogether governed by this world, that they maintain their piety, their longstanding allegiance to the world of spiritual values to which they should belong. Otherwise there will be no intellectuals, at least not above ground. And societies in which the intellectuals have been driven underground, as we have had occasion to see in our own time, are societies in which even the anti-intellectuals are unhappy.†**

The Whole Essay

You have now discovered the main ingredients of a good essay. You have learned to find and to sharpen your thesis in one sentence, to give your essay that all-important argumentative edge. You have learned to arrange your points in order of increasing interest, and you have practiced disposing of the opposition in a *pro-con* structure. You have seen that your beginning paragraph should look like a funnel, working from broad generalization to thesis. You have tried your hand at middle paragraphs, which are almost like little essays with their own beginnings and ends. And finally, you have learned that your last paragraph should work like an inverted funnel, broadening and embellishing your thesis. You are ready to open the door to good writing; the Keyhole‡ on page 86 will provide you with a picture of the way your completed essay should look.

---

* "A Federal Judge Digs the Young," *Saturday Review*, July 20, 1968, p. 62.

† "Democracy and Anti-intellectualism in America," *The Michigan Quarterly Review*, LIX (1953), p. 295.

‡ Mrs. Fran Measley of Santa Barbara, California, has devised for her students of writing a mimeographed sheet to accompany my discussion of structure and paragraphing—to help them to visualize my points, through a keyhole, as it were. I am grateful to Mrs. Measley to be able to include it here.

THE KEYHOLE

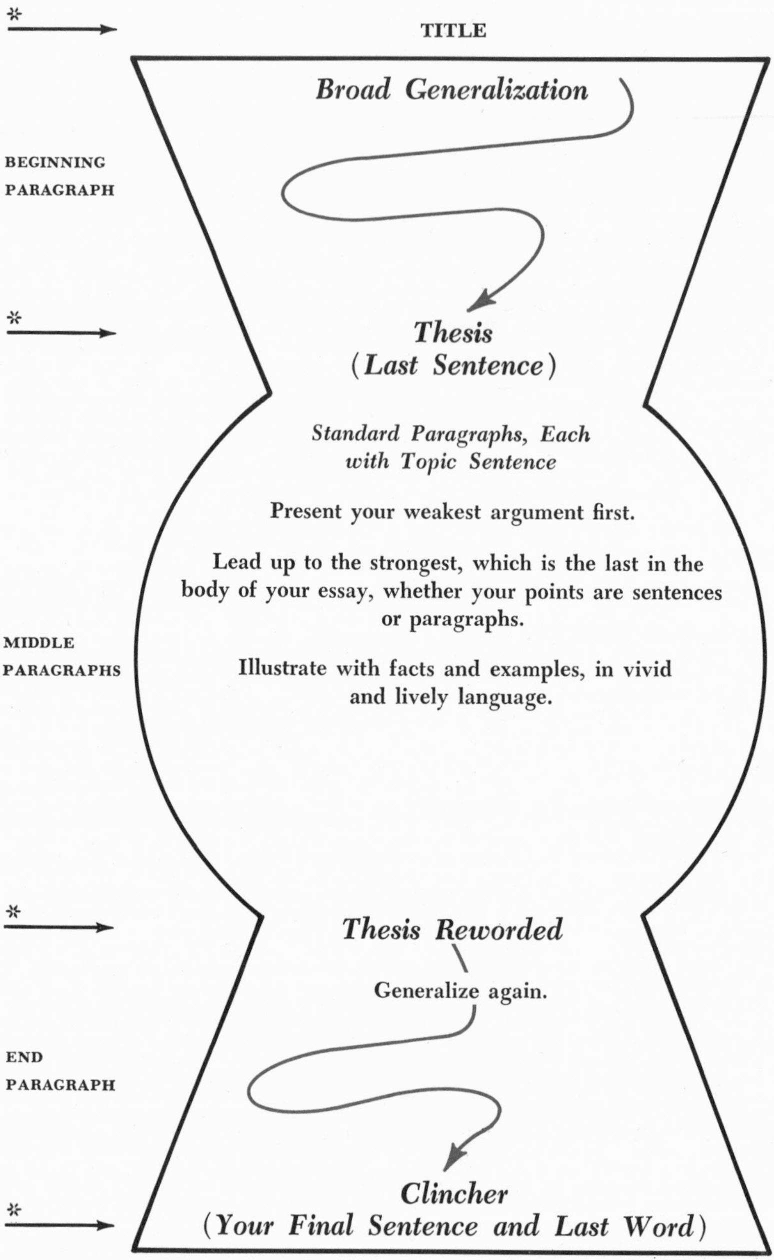
*
TITLE
Broad Generalization
BEGINNING
PARAGRAPH
*
Thesis
(Last Sentence)
Standard Paragraphs, Each
with Topic Sentence
Present your weakest argument first.
Lead up to the strongest, which is the last in the
body of your essay, whether your points are sentences
or paragraphs.
MIDDLE
PARAGRAPHS
Illustrate with facts and examples, in vivid
and lively language.
*
Thesis Reworded
Generalize again.
END
PARAGRAPH
Clincher
*
(Your Final Sentence and Last Word)

* Focal points

Exercises

1. Write three beginning paragraphs of five or six sentences each, working down in each to some such terse thesis as one of these: "Without health there is nothing." "Reason is best." "Everything is relative." "Always prepare for the worst." "Live for the day." "Worry is good."

2. Write ten topic sentences for end paragraphs, each with a different transitional tag, as in these examples: "Ill health, *then,* darkens every prospect and discolors every thought." "It is clear, *therefore,* that ill health has produced more truth and more beauty—more art, more literature, more music, and a good share of philosophy, history, invention, and scientific insight—than have all the muscles in all outdoors." "One can, *in the last analysis,* live only the present moment."

3. Write three unrelated middle paragraphs, about 200 words each. Make the topic sentences cover the contents, and give each topic sentence some transitional touch: "Fly fishing *is different.*" "*But* Judaism acknowledges man as a social being." "Kennedy *also* had his blind side."

4. Write an essay with uniform paragraphs, each about 125 words long, each, after a good beginning paragraph with a thesis, having a good sharp topic sentence—and don't forget the end.

5. Write a three-paragraph essay, then expand it into a five-paragraph essay, keeping the same beginning paragraph and end paragraph, and hand in both versions.

The Paragraph: Further Developments

7

Now you have the general idea of paragraphing. You have seen the funel of the beginning paragraph and the inverted funnel of your essay's end. You have the idea of the paragraph as a standard frame—to be filled, and to be adjusted as needed—with its little thesis at the beginning and little conclusion at the end. But since the ways of filling a paragraph are infinite, some further rhetorical considerations may be helpful.

Coherence

Check your writing for clarity and coherence.

Coherence is essential to all writing. Finding your voice and keeping your reader in mind starts the coherent journey from its beginning to its end. Your tone of voice should be coherently yours; your ideas and examples should lead the reader, without a joggle or a jump, each step of the way you are taking him. Each paragraph should lead to the next, like a stepping-stone; and the paragraph within itself (small essay that it is) should also move smoothly and coherently.

Does your paragraph really run smoothly from first sentence to last? The *topic sentence* is your best assurance that subsequent sentences will indeed fall into line, and it is the first point to check when you look back to see if they really do. Many a jumbled and misty paragraph can be unified and cleared by writing a broader topic sentence. Consider this disjointed specimen:

> **Swimming is healthful. The first dive into the pool is always cold. Tennis takes a great deal of energy, especially under a hot sun. Team sports, like basketball, baseball, and volleyball, always make the awkward player miserable. Character and health go hand in hand.**

What is all that about? From the last sentence, we can surmise something of what the writer intended. But his first sentence about swimming in no way covers his paragraph, which treats several sports not in the least like swimming, and seems to be driving at something other than health. The primary remedy, as always, is to find the paragraph's thesis and to devise a topic sentence that will state it, thus covering everything in the paragraph. Think of your topic sentence as a roof—covering your paragraph and pulling its lines and contents together.

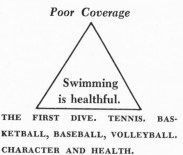

Poor Coverage

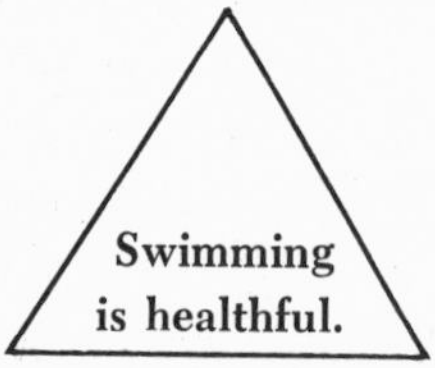
Swimming
is healthful.

THE FIRST DIVE. TENNIS. BASKETBALL, BASEBALL, VOLLEYBALL. CHARACTER AND HEALTH.

Good Coverage

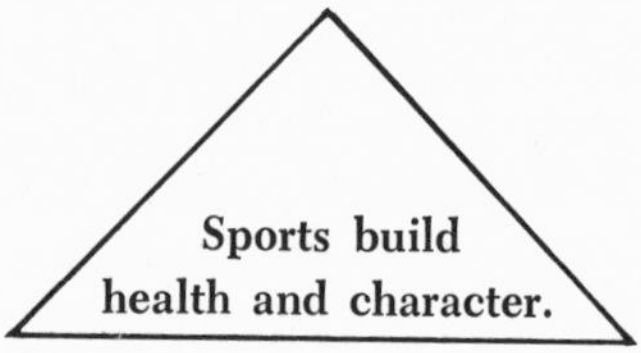
Sports build
health and character.

SWIMMING. THE FIRST DIVE. TENNIS. BASKETBALL, BASEBALL, VOLLEYBALL. CHARACTER AND HEALTH.

Suppose we leave the paragraph unchanged for the moment, adding only a topic sentence suggested by our right-hand diagram. It will indeed pull things together:

> ***Sports demand an effort of will and muscle that is healthful for the soul as well as the body.*** **Swimming is healthful. The first dive into the pool is always cold. Tennis takes a great deal of energy, especially under a hot sun. Team sports, like basketball, baseball, and volleyball, always make the awkward player miserable. Character and health go hand in hand.**

But the paragraph is still far from an agreeable coherence. The islands of thought still need some bridges. Gaining coherence is primarily a filling in, or a spelling out, of submerged connections. You may fill in with (1) thought and (2) illustrative detail; you may spell out by tying your sentences together with (3) transitional tags and (4) repeated words or syntactical patterns. Let us see what we can do with our sample paragraph.

From the first, you probably noticed that the writer was thinking in pairs: the pleasure of sports is balanced off against their difficulty; the difficulty is physical as well as moral; character and health go hand in hand. We have already indicated this doubleness of idea in our topic sentence. Now to fill out the thought, we need merely expand each sentence so as to give each half of the double idea its due expression. We need also to qualify the thought here and there with *perhaps, often, some, sometimes, frequently, all in all,* and the like. As we work through the possibilities, more detail will come to mind. We shall add a touch or two of illustration, almost automatically, as our imagination becomes more stimulated by the subject. We shall add a number of transitional ties like *but, and, of course, nevertheless,* and *similarly.* We shall look for chances to repeat key words, like *will,* if we can do so gracefully; and to repeat syntactical patterns, if we can emphasize similar thoughts by doing so, as with *no matter how patient his teammates . . . no matter how heavy his heart,* toward the end of our revision below:

> **Sports demand an effort of will and muscle that is healthful for the soul as well as the body. *Swimming is* physically *healthful,* of course, although it may seem undemanding and highly conducive to lying for hours inert in the sun. But *the first dive into the pool is always cold:* taking the plunge always requires some effort of will. And the swimmer soon summons his will to compete, against himself or others, for**

greater distances and greater speed. Similarly, *tennis takes* quantities *of energy,* physical and moral, *especially* when the competition stiffens *under a hot sun. Team sports, like basketball, baseball, and volleyball,* perhaps demand even more of the amateur. *The awkward player* is *miserable,* no matter how patient his teammates. He must drive himself to keep on trying, no matter how heavy his heart. Whatever the sport, a little determination can eventually conquer one's awkwardness and timidity, and the reward will be more than physical. *Character and health* frequently *go hand in hand.*

Accustom yourself to the transitional tags.

Our student's first paragraph well illustrates the beginner's innocence of transitional words and phrases. They are not in his vocabulary. They belong to the rhetoric of public persuasion, oral or written, in which he has had little practice. His sentences come out like independent declarations, with gaps of silence between. He needs some transitions, some bridges from assertion to assertion. We have already looked at some of the transitional bridges, first those that take you from the *pro* side of your argument to the *con* and back, and then those that, paragraph by paragraph, connect the paths of your thought from start to finish. Now let us simply summarize the common transitional possibilities, since any and all contribute importantly to the inner coherence of your paragraphs.

TRANSITIONS		USES
1. and or, nor also moreover	furthermore indeed in fact first, second . . .	You are adding something. *And* can be a good sentence-opener, when used with care.
2. for instance for example for one thing	similarly likewise	Again you are adding, and illustrating or expanding your point.
3. therefore thus so and so hence consequently	finally on the whole all in all in other words in short	You are adding up consequences, summarizing minor points to emphasize a major point.

4. frequently occasionally in particular in general	specifically especially usually	You are adding a qualifying point or illustration.
5. of course no doubt doubtless	to be sure granted (that) certainly	Now you are conceding a point to the opposition, or recognizing a point just off your main line.
6. but however yet on the contrary	not at all surely no	Now you are reversing or deflecting the line of thought, usually back to your own side.
7. still nevertheless notwithstanding		Again you return the thought to your own side after a concession.
8. although though whereas		You are attaching a concession to one of your points. Do not use *while* for *whereas; while* means "during the time that."
9. because since for		You are connecting a *reason* to an assertion.
10. if provided in case	unless lest when	You are qualifying and restricting a more general idea.
11. as if as though even if		You are glancing at tentative or hypothetical conditions that strengthen and clarify your point.
12. this that these those who whom he she	it they all of them few many most several	These relative and demonstrative words (adjectives and pronouns) tie things together, pointing back as they carry the reference ahead. But be sure there can be no mistaking the specific word to which each refers.

You may add to these tags considerably, and you should. You should also use them economically, vary them, and avoid switching your argument back and forth so frequently that you spoil your paragraph's coherence. The more various the transitional tags at your command, the more flexible your resources. Keep an eye open for unusual ones. A rare *contrariwise, mind you,* or *egad* may give you just the right turn of humor or irony. And think what you might do, perhaps once in a lifetime, with *Ods bodkins!* But remember, these tags may easily become wordy. Make them work, or retire them with your revising pencil.

Lead your reader with specific details.

Transitional tags help the reader around the turns, but specific details give him solid footing. He needs to step from detail to detail, or his progress will not be coherent. Your topic sentences are generalizations. Your reader now needs to feel the support of facts, the specific items, numbers, quotations, men, and women, that illustrate your general points. Mr. George Ramsey of Sacramento, California, likes to give his classes his Ramsey Test of Specifics. "Look at your paragraph, class," he says, "and score one point for each capital letter on a name of a person or place; score one point for each direct quotation; score one point for any numbers; and score one point for each example or illustration." Scores are frequently zero. All generalization. No specific details whatsoever. The reader has nothing under his feet at all.

The following paragraph by Loren Eiseley would score about 10 or so. He has been writing of Alfred Russel Wallace's and Charles Darwin's conflicting views as to the evolution of man's brain, and has just referred to the small-brained humanoid apes:

> **These apes are not all similar in type or appearance. They are men and yet not men. Some are frailer-bodied, some have great, bone-cracking jaws and massive gorilloid crests atop their skulls. This fact leads us to another of Wallace's remarkable perceptions of long ago. With the rise of the truly human brain, Wallace saw that man had transferred to his machines and tools many of the alterations of parts that in animals take place through evolution of the body. Unwittingly, man had assigned to his machines the selective evolution which in the animal changes the nature of its bodily structure through the ages.**

Man of today, the atomic manipulator, the aeronaut who flies faster than sound, has precisely the same brain and body as his ancestors of twenty thousand years ago who painted the last Ice Age mammoths on the walls of caves in France.*

Write about what you know and feel.

In the end, the coherence of your paragraphs and your essay comes from your own coherence of thought, your knowledge warmed by your own conviction, your own gaiety or sadness, admiration or scorn, enthusiasm or distaste—together with a sympathetic sense of the details your reader needs to know as you lead him to see things as you see them. The mature writer often produces such coherence by second nature. His topic sentences are frequently oblique, covering only part of his thought, but catching his total mood to perfection. His paragraphs, brimming with his subject, as he is, flow in effortless coherence. Nothing seems out of place, or out of order. We could easily sum up his paragraph in one topic sentence, because the effect is single and coherent; but he himself, in the full mood of his knowledge, has not found it necessary to spell his meaning out all at once, in a single sentence. Consider the topic sentences and the coherence of these two paragraphs by Katherine Anne Porter, the first with topic sentence, the second without, but both perfectly coherent. She is writing about Sylvia Beach of Shakespeare and Company, Miss Beach's Paris bookshop, famous in the twenties as the gathering place for such notables as James Joyce and Ernest Hemingway.

The bookshop at 12 Rue de l'Odéon has been closed ever since the German occupation, but her rooms have been kept piously intact by a faithful friend, more or less as she left them, except for a filmlike cobweb on the objects, a grayness in the air, for Sylvia is gone, and has taken her ghost with her. All sorts of things were there, her walls of books in every room, the bushels of papers, hundreds of photographs, portraits, odd bits of funny toys, even her flimsy scraps of underwear and stockings left to dry near the kitchen window; a coffee cup and small coffeepot as she left them on the table; in her bedroom, her looking glass, her modest entirely incidental vanities, face powder, beauty cream, lipstick. . . .

* "The Real Secret of Piltdown," in *The Immense Journey* (New York: Random House, Inc., 1955). © Copyright 1955 by Loren C. Eiseley.

Oh, no. She was not there. And someone had taken away the tiger skin from her bed—narrow as an army cot. If it was not a tiger, then some large savage cat with good markings; real fur, I remember, spotted or streaked, a wild woodland touch shining out in the midst of the pure, spontaneous, persevering austerity of Sylvia's life: maybe a humorous hint of some hidden streak in Sylvia, this preacher's daughter of a Baltimore family brought up in unexampled highmindedness, gentle company, and polite learning; this nervous, witty girl whose only expressed ambition in life was to have a bookshop of her own. Anywhere would do, but Paris for choice. God knows modesty could hardly take denser cover, and this she did at incredible expense of hard work and spare living and yet with the help of quite dozens of devoted souls one after the other; the financial and personal help of her two delightful sisters and the lifetime savings of her mother, a phoenix of a mother who consumed herself to ashes time and again in aid of her wild daughter.*

Certainly these two paragraphs are filled coherently with Miss Porter's impression of the living personality, now dead. In spite of its length, the first sentence serves perfectly as topic sentence, especially in its final, subordinate clause: "Sylvia is gone, and has taken her ghost with her." She is indeed gone, though somehow the gray shreds of her ghost seem still to hang about hauntingly. After the topic sentence, the details fall into spatial place as the visitor walks through the apartment and we walk with her: first the living room, it seems, lined with its books, then the books in every room, then the kitchen, then the bedroom. The ellipsis (. . .) is Miss Porter's own, not the editor's, as the meditation drifts off from details to some general impression of Sylvia Beach and of the strange vanity into which death turns all personal vanities.

The next paragraph has no topic sentence, rationally formulated, but it continues the general idea of life's oddly pathetic efforts, as, with a dramatic transition, Miss Porter's mind comes back from its elliptical drift into the mystery of personality: "Oh, no. She was not there." And then a detail that perfectly represents the softness, wildness, and austerity of Miss Beach's spirit: a tiger skin on an army cot of a bed. A complete topic sentence for the paragraph would be something like: "All that strange compound of modesty, femininity, wildness, and au-

* "Paris: A Little Incident in the Rue de l'Odéon," *Ladies' Home Journal,* August 1964, p. 54.

sterity, all the unusual power that commanded a lifetime of sacrifices from herself and others, is gone."

Miss Porter's way is simpler—the quiet exclamation, the repeated fact of absence, the tiger skin, the narrow bed—and the paragraph proceeds with perfect coherence. Try an occasional topic-sentenceless paragraph yourself, for dramatic effect, if your subject moves you. But if you suspect that your paragraph is not coherent, make for it the best topic sentence you can, and then pull your sentences into line with transitions, filling in details, and perhaps throwing out a few things too. In sum, all paragraphs, like all writing, should be smoothly coherent, as you lead your reader along. Now we shall look at particular kinds of paragraphs, all of which must sustain the same coherent flow.

Descriptive Paragraphs

Put your perceptions into words.

Description is essentially spatial. When your subject concerns a campus, or a failing business district, you may want to write your middle as some orderly progress through space, and your paragraphs virtually as units of space: one paragraph for the intersection, one for the first building, one for the second, one for the tattered cigar store at the end of the block. Within a paragraph, you simply take your reader from one detail to the next in order. Your topic sentence summarizes the total effect: "The Whistler Building was once elegant, three stories of brick with carved stone pediments." Then your paragraph proceeds with noteworthy details in any convenient spatial order: first the sagging front door, then the windows to the left, then those to the right, then the second floor's windows, with their suggestion of dingy apartments, then those of the third, which suggest only emptiness.

The best spatial description follows the perceptions of a person entering or looking at the space described, as with the imaginary visitor in this description by R. Prawer Jhabvala of a modern house in India:

> **Our foreign visitor stands agape at the wonderful residence his second host has built for himself. No expense has been spared here, no decoration suggested by a vivid taste omitted. There are little Moorish balconies and Indian domes and squiggly lattice work and an air-conditioner in every window. Inside, all is marble flooring, and in**

the entrance hall there is a fountain lit up with green, yellow, and red bulbs. The curtains on the windows and in the doorways are of silk, the vast sofa-suites are upholstered in velvet, the telephone is red, and huge vases are filled with plastic flowers.*

This procedure may be seen in elaborate extension, paragraph after paragraph, at the beginning of Thomas Hardy's *The Return of the Native,* in which we are moved into the setting from a great distance, as if, years before moving pictures, we are riding a cameraman's dolly.

Description frequently blends space and time, with the observer's perceptions unifying the two as he moves through them, and takes his readers with him. You pick out the striking features, showing the reader what would strike him first, as it did you, then proceeding to more minute but no less significant details. This is the usual way of describing people, as in this paragraph (by the anonymous reporter for the *New Yorker*'s "Talk of the Town") about an actual Englishman, whose odd occupation is mending the broken eggs brought to him by bird's-egg collectors:

Colonel Prynne, who is sixty-seven, lives and carries on his singular pursuit in a rambling, thatch-roofed, five-hundred-year-old cottage in the tiny village of Spaxton, Somerset, and there, on a recent sunny afternoon, he received us. A man of medium build who retains a military carriage, he was sprucely turned out in a brown suit, a tan jersey vest, a green shirt and tie, and tan oxfords. He has a bald, distinctly egg-shaped head, wears a close-cropped mustache and black shell-rimmed glasses, and seems always to have his nose tilted slightly upward and the nostrils faintly distended, as if he were sniffing the air. After taking us on a rather cursory tour of his garden, which is as neat and well tended as its owner, he remarked crisply that it was time to get cracking, and we followed him indoors, past an enormous fireplace, which burns five-foot logs, and up a flight of stairs to a room that he calls his studio.†

You may use a descriptive paragraph to good effect in almost any kind of essay, as you illustrate by a detailed picture—the face of a town, the face of a drifter—the physical grounds for your convictions. For this, the paragraph makes an extremely convenient and coherent unit.

---

* *Encounter,* May 1964, pp. 42–43.
† *The New Yorker,* May 23, 1964, p. 37.

Narrative Paragraphs

Narrate to illustrate.

Time is the essence of narrative. The narrative paragraph merely exploits convenient units of time. Narrative is the primary business of fiction, of course, but occasionally an expository essay will give over its entire middle to a narrative account of some event that illustrates its thesis. Of this kind is George Orwell's great essay "Shooting an Elephant." Orwell's thesis is that imperialism tyrannizes over the rulers as well as the ruled. To illustrate it, he tells of an incident during his career as a young police officer in Burma, when he was compelled, by the expectations of the watching crowd, to shoot a renegade elephant. Here is a narrative paragraph in which Orwell reports a crucial moment; notice how he mixes external events and snippets of conversation with his inner thoughts, pegging all perfectly with a topic sentence:

> **But I did not want to shoot the elephant. I watched him beating his bunch of grass against his knees, with that preoccupied grandmotherly air that elephants have. It seemed to me that it would be murder to shoot him. At that age I was not squeamish about killing animals, but I had never shot an elephant and never wanted to. (Somehow it always seems worse to kill a *large* animal.) Besides, there was the beast's owner to be considered. Alive, the elephant was worth at least a hundred pounds; dead, he would only be worth the value of his tusks, five pounds, possibly. But I had got to act quickly. I turned to some experienced-looking Burmans who had been there when we arrived, and asked them how the elephant had been behaving. They all said the same thing: he took no notice of you if you left him alone, but he might charge if you went too close to him.***

Orwell is simply giving us an account of events, and of his inner thoughts, as they happened, one after the other. Almost any kind of essay could use a similar paragraph of narrative to illustrate a point.

But to select details and get them in order is not so simple as it may seem. Here are four of the most common flaws in narrative paragraphs, against which you may check your own first drafts:

---

* From "Shooting an Elephant," in *Shooting an Elephant and Other Essays* by George Orwell, copyright 1945, 1946, 1949, 1950 by Sonia Brownell Orwell. Reprinted by permission of Harcourt Brace Jovanovich, Inc., and Martin Secker & Warburg Limited.

Insufficient detail. A few words, of course, can tell what happened: "I saw an accident." But if the reader is to feel the whole sequence of the experience, he needs details, and many of them. He also needs in the first sentence or two some orientation to the general scene—a topic sentence of setting and mood. The following is the opening of a narrative paragraph from an essay that has already logically discussed its thesis that "haste makes waste." It is not a bad beginning, but a few more details, as we shall see in a moment, would help us know where we are, and at what time of day or night:

> **The sky was very dark. People were walking quickly in all directions . . . .**

Details out of order. The writer of the dark-sky paragraph went on in her next two sentences with additional detail.

> **The sky was very dark. People were walking quickly in all directions. The trees were tossing and swaying about. The air felt heavy, and lightning flickered here and there behind the gray sky.**

But, clearly, the further details are out of order. Although she has said the trees were moving, the air seems to have remained still. She eventually rearranged these details, but not before committing another error.

Comments breaking into the narrative flow. Our dark-sky student went on to intrude an editorializing comment, and a clever one at that. But she would have been better off letting her details *imply* the moral of the story. Here is her paragraph, revised after conference, with the opening details of setting filled and rearranged, but with the intruding comment, which she actually deleted, left in italics to illustrate the fault:

> **One day, going home from school, I came to understand for the first time how costly haste can be. The sky was very dark, and people were walking quickly across the streets through the afternoon traffic. The air was heavy, and lightning flickered here and there behind the overcast. Suddenly a soft wind moved through the trees, setting them tossing and swaying; and then came a great gust, sending leaves and papers scurrying, and rattling shop signs. Wet splotches the size of quarters began to dapple the sidewalk; and then it started to pour. Everyone began to run in a frenzied scramble for shelter.** ***People should not lose their heads at the very time they need them most.*** **At the street corner ahead of me, two girls, running from different directions, crashed together. A boy riding a bicycle slammed on his brakes to avoid them, and he went skidding, out of control, into the middle**

of the street. A car caught him squarely. That night, still stunned, I read in the paper that he had died on the way to the hospital.

Shifting viewpoint. The effect of a shift of viewpoint is about the same as that of the intruding comment. The narrative flow is broken. The author seems to have jumped out of his original assumptions, from one location to another:

My boys of Tent Five were suddenly all piling on top of me on the shaky bunk. I didn't feel much like a counselor, but at least I was keeping them amused. The giggling heap on top of me seemed happy enough. It was organized recreation time, and they seemed pretty well organized. *The Chief hurried across the camp ground, wondering what was going on over there, and issuing a silent death warrant for the counselor of Five.* I looked out through a wiggly chink in the heap and saw the Chief in the doorway, with his face growing redder and redder.

The writer of this paragraph has let his imagination shift from his recollected location on the bunk, beneath the heap of boys, to his reconstruction of what must have been going on in the Chief's head, out on the campground. Similar unwarranted shifts occur when you have been writing *he,* and suddenly shift to *they,* or when you unwittingly shift your tenses from present to past, or past to present.

Expository Paragraphs

Develop most paragraphs by illustration.

The standard way of developing paragraphs, as I have already suggested in Chapter 6, is by illustration. You begin with your topical assertion. You follow with three or four sentences of illustration. You round off with some concluding sentence or phrase. After your topic sentence, you may well fill your whole paragraph with a single illustration, as does Albert Schweitzer in this paragraph from his "The Evolution of Ethics":

For the primitive man the circle of solidarity is limited to those whom he can look upon as his blood relatives—that is to say, the members of his tribe, who are to him his family. I am speaking from experience. In my hospital I have primitives. When I happen to ask a hospitalized tribesman, who is not himself bedridden, to render little services to a bedridden patient, he will consent only if the latter belongs to his tribe. If not, he will answer me candidly: "This, no brother

> for me," and neither attempts to persuade him nor threats will make him do this favor for a stranger.*

Or you may illustrate your topical assertion with several parallel examples:

> The undercurrent of admiration in hatred manifests itself in the inclination to imitate those we hate. Thus every mass movement shapes itself after its specific devil. Christianity at its height realized the image of the antichrist. The Jacobins practiced all the evils of the tyranny they had risen against. Soviet Russia is realizing the purest and most colossal example of monopolistic capitalism. Hitler took the Protocols of the Wise Men of Zion for his guide and textbook; he followed them "down to the veriest detail."†

Your illustration may also be hypothetical, as it frequently is in scientific explanation. "Suppose you are riding along in a car," the scientist will say, as he tries to convey the idea of relative motion; "You drop a baseball straight down from your hand to the floor between your feet." And he continues by explaining that this vertical drop describes a long slanting line in relation to the line of the rapidly receding highway beneath the car. After this paragraph, he might have an additional one for each new aspect of relativity, illustrating each by the same dropped ball in its relation to curves in the road, the earth itself, the sun, and to whatever hypothetical platforms he may wish to put into orbit. You may also use a hypothetical illustration, as we have already seen in discussing cause and effect, to reduce to absurdity an opponent's hidden implications. Suppose someone has proposed enhancing the democratic process by installing "Yes-No" switches on our TV sets, all to be recorded by computer in Washington. You could develop a sarcastic paragraph of suppositions, somewhat along these lines: "This would mean that any child could vote, and we could put little pictures, cleverly devised, on the tiny voting machines."

Develop by citing authority.

Of course, citing authorities has certain pitfalls, as we shall see when we consider straight and crooked thinking in Chapter 13. Dishonesty here is all too easy. Mention no more than "science" or "doctors," and you have already persuaded your reader unfairly, unless you go on to bring in the evidence and make the connection clear. "Science"

---

* *The Atlantic Monthly*, November 1958, p. 69.

† Eric Hoffer, *The True Believer* (New York: Harper & Row, Publishers, 1951), pp. 94–95.

and "doctors" are very persuasive authorities. The TV actor in the laboratory coat who intones his claims for soaps and gasoline is all too familiar. To avoid unfair persuasion, cite your authorities as specifically as possible, and in the area of their authoritative competence. Citing Einstein to support a point of grammar, for example, would be inevitably persuasive, but certainly unfair, since Einstein was no grammarian.

Make your appeal to authority honest, and your citation explicit, quoting directly, for your reader's benefit, when the quotation is sharp and not too long. In the following paragraph, W. T. Stace cites Alfred North Whitehead, one of the twentieth century's most noted philosophers, to support his point, and he does so by epitomizing a number of Whitehead's writings in one telling quotation:

> **For . . . the past three hundred years there has been growing up in men's minds, dominated as they are by science, a new imaginative picture of the world. The world, according to this new picture, is purposeless, senseless, meaningless. Nature is nothing but matter in motion. The motions of matter are governed, not by any purpose, but by blind forces and laws. Nature on this view, says Whitehead—to whose writings I am indebted in this part of my paper—is "merely the hurrying of material, endlessly, meaninglessly." You can draw a sharp line across the history of Europe dividing it into two epochs of very unequal length. The line passes through the lifetime of Galileo. European man before Galileo—whether ancient pagan or more recent Christian—thought of the world as controlled by plan and purpose. After Galileo, European man thinks of it as utterly purposeless.****

Develop by comparisons.

With a comparison, you help your reader grasp your subject by showing how it is like something familiar. Your topic sentence asserts the comparison, and then your paragraph unfolds the comparison in detail:

> **School spirit is like patriotism. A student takes his school's fortunes as his own, defending and promoting them against those of another school, as a man champions his country, right or wrong. Like the soldier, he will do battle on the football field for both personal glory and the greater glory of the domain he represents; as for the girls—they will mourn at defeat as if dragged in chains through the streets of Rome.**

* "Man Against Darkness," *The Atlantic Monthly,* September 1948, p. 54..

Here is E. B. White describing Thoreau's *Walden* by analogy, a form of comparison that is really an extended metaphor:

> **Thoreau's assault on the Concord society of the mid-nineteenth century has the quality of a modern Western: he rides into the subject at top speed, shooting in all directions. Many of his shots ricochet and nick him on the rebound, and throughout the melee there is a horrendous cloud of inconsistencies and contradictions, and when the shooting dies down and the air clears, one is impressed chiefly by the courage of the rider and by how splendid it was that somebody should have ridden in there and raised all that ruckus.***

That is probably as long as an analogy can effectively run. One paragraph is about the limit. Beyond that, the reader may tire of it.

Develop by contrasts.

Your comparisons present helpful illustrations of your subject by emphasizing similarities. Contrasts, on the other hand, compare similar things to emphasize their differences—West Germany as against East Germany, for example—usually to persuade your reader that one is in some or most ways better than the other.

The problem in paragraphing such "comparative contrasts" is exactly what we have already seen with the sheep and goats in Chapter 3 and the more extended discussion in Chapter 4 (pp. 52–57): the problem of keeping both sides before the reader, of not talking so long about West Germany that your reader forgets all about East Germany. Again, the rule is to run your contrasts point by point, and this you may do in one of two ways: (1) by making a topic sentence to cover one point —agriculture, let us say—and then continuing your paragraph in paired sentences, one for the West, one for the East, another for the West, another for the East, and so on; or (2) by writing your paragraphs in pairs, one paragraph for the West, one for the East, using the topic sentence of the first paragraph to govern the second, something like this:

> **West Germany's agriculture is far ahead of the East's. Everywhere about the countryside, one sees signs of prosperity. Trucks and tractors are shiny. Fences are mended and in order. Buildings all seem newly**

* "A Slight Sound at Evening," in *The Points of My Compass* (New York: Harper & Row, Publishers, 1962), p. 17.

> **painted, as if on exhibit for a fair. New Volkswagens buzz along the country roads. The annual statistics spell out the prosperous details . . . .**
>
> **East Germany, on the other hand, seems to be dropping progressively behind. The countryside is drab and empty. On one huge commune, everything from buildings to equipment seems to be creaking from rusty hinges . . . . The statistics are equally depressing . . . .**

In an extended contrast, you will probably want to contrast some things sentence against sentence, within single paragraphs, and to contrast others by giving a paragraph to each. Remember only to keep your reader sufficiently in touch with both sides.

Here is a paragraph in which the writer illustrates his point (a seaman's sense of the weather) by contrasting it to something more familiar (the landsman's inattention to the weather):

> **This was a sullen, dripping morning with wet, woolly clouds smothering the land and sea. Every few minutes, Mike or I would go up on deck and peer at the sky, wondering whether it would clear later and give us a decent day. In New York, I am like most people, only marginally aware of the weather. Before going out of my apartment, I want to know what the temperature is and whether it is raining, but I don't experience weather in any real sense; it is only an interim sensation, a transient state, known briefly between the enduring reality of interiors—living room, subway, stores, offices, the library. On the Sound, the situation is reversed; the sky and the air and the things they contain are the real world, and the interiors of boats and buildings are only burrows that one crawls into for brief periods to comfort oneself. The sailor is forever intensely aware of the sky, immense and enveloping. On the Sound, as on the open sea, one is in, under, and of the sky; one's eyes constantly search its vastness to know whether it means well or ill. When the sky changes, the man under it finds that his mood changes accordingly. Yet the moment he steps ashore, he becomes detached. The sky is now a thing apart.***

Develop by definition.

I concede that definition may sometimes unduly oppress your reader by telling him what he already knows, or what he can easily gather from your context. I know to my despair that a definition

---

* Morton M. Hunt, "The Inland Sea," *The New Yorker,* September 5, 1964, pp. 57–58.

from a dictionary, especially to get an essay started, has been a device most dismally hackneyed by generations of desperate students. I know that you should, if possible, avoid the necessity of definition, and the big subjects that demand it. Nevertheless, an occasional bout with a big subject is good for the sinews, and you will certainly need to clarify for your reader your particular emphasis in dealing with the likes of "Love," "Loyalty," or "Happiness."

Richard Hofstadter, for instance, found it necessary in his essay "Democracy and Anti-intellectualism in America" to devote a number of paragraphs to defining both *democracy* and *intellectual,* each paragraph clarifying one aspect of his term. Coming early in his essay, after he has set his thesis and surveyed his subject, his section of definition begins with the following paragraph:

> **But what is an intellectual, really? This is a problem of definition that I found, when I came to it, far more elusive than I had anticipated. A great deal of what might be called the journeyman's work of our culture—the work of engineers, physicians, newspapermen, and indeed of most professors—does not strike me as distinctively intellectual, although it is certainly work based in an important sense on ideas. The distinction that we must recognize, then, is one originally made by Max Weber between living *for* ideas and living *off* ideas. The intellectual lives for ideas; the journeyman lives off them. The engineer or the physician—I don't mean here to be invidious—needs to have a pretty considerable capital stock in frozen ideas to do his work; but they serve for him a purely instrumental purpose: he lives off them, not for them. Of course he may also be, in his private role and his personal ways of thought, an intellectual, but it is not necessary for him to be one in order to work at his profession. There is in fact no profession which demands that one be an intellectual. There do seem to be vocations, however, which almost demand that one be an anti-intellectual, in which those who live off ideas seem to have an implacable hatred for those who live for them. The marginal intellectual workers and the unfrocked intellectuals who work in journalism, advertising, and mass communication are the bitterest and most powerful among those who work at such vocations.***

Try different kinds of definition.

Your subject will prompt you in one of two ways, toward inclusiveness or toward exclusiveness. Hofstadter found that he needed to be inclusive about the several essentials in *democracy* and *intellec-*

---

* *The Michigan Quarterly Review,* LIX (1953), p. 282.

tual—terms used commonly, and often loosely. Inclusiveness is the usual need, as you will find in trying to define *love* or *loyalty* or *education*. But you may sometimes need to move in the opposite direction, toward exclusiveness, as in sociological, philosophical, or scientific discussion, when you need to nail your terms firmly to single meanings: "By *reality*, I mean only that which exists in the physical world, excluding our ideas about it."

Such exclusive defining is called *stipulative*, since you stipulate the precise meaning you want. But you should avoid the danger of trying to exclude more than the word will allow. If you try to limit the meaning of the term *course* to "three hours per week per semester," your discussion will soon encounter courses of different hourage; or you may find yourself inadvertently drifting to another meaning, as you mention something about graduating from an "engineering course." At any rate, if you can avoid the sound of dogmatism in your stipulation, so much the better. You may well practice some disguise, as with *properly speaking* and *only* in the following stipulative definition: "Properly speaking, the *structure* of any literary work is only that framelike quality we can picture in two, or three, dimensions."

Definitions frequently seem to develop into paragraphs, almost by second nature. A sentence of definition is usually short and crisp, seeming to demand some explanation, some illustration and sociability. The definition, in other words, is a natural topic sentence. Here are three classic single-sentence kinds of definition that will serve well as topics for your paragraphs:

(*1*) *Definition by synonym.* A quick way to stipulate the single meaning you want: "Virtue means moral rectitude."

(*2*) *Definition by function.* "A barometer measures atmospheric pressure"—"A social barometer measures human pressures"—"A good quarterback calls the signals and sparks the spirits of the whole team."

(*3*) *Definition by synthesis.* A placing of your term in striking (and not necessarily logical) relationship to its whole class, usually for the purposes of wit: "The fox is the craftiest of beasts"—"A sheep is a friendlier form of goat"—"A lexicographer is a harmless drudge"—"A sophomore is a sophisticated moron."

Here are three more of the classic kinds of definition, of broader dimensions than the single-sentence kinds above, but also ready-made for a paragraph apiece, or for several. Actually, in making paragraphs from your single-sentence definitions, you have undoubtedly used at least one of these three kinds, or a mixture of them all. They are no more than the natural ways we go in trying to define our meanings.

(4) *Definition by example.* The opposite of *definition by synthesis.* You start with the class ("crafty beasts") and then give an example of a member or two ("fox"—plus monkey and raccoon). But of course you would go on to give further examples or illustrations—accounts of how the bacon was snatched through the screen—that broaden your definition beyond the mere naming of class and members.

(5) *Definition by comparison.* You just use a paragraph of comparison (which we have already considered on pages 103–104) to expand and explain your definition. Begin with a topic sentence something like: "Love is like the sun." Then extend your comparison on to the end of the paragraph (or even separate it, if your cup runneth over, into several paragraphs), as you develop the idea: love is like the sun because it too gives out warmth, makes everything bright, shines even when it is not seen, and is indeed the center of our lives.

(6) *Definition by analysis.* This is Hofstadter's way, a searching out and explaining of the essentials in terms used generally, loosely (and often in ways that emphasize incidentals for biased reasons), as when it is said that an *intellectual* is a manipulator of ideas.

Cover all the angles.

You may find that in a defining paragraph—or a defining essay—you have said all you wish to say as you clarified what a thing *is.* Nevertheless, in your preliminary sketching, try jotting down also what it *is not.* You can indeed build some good paragraphs (or parts of paragraphs, or parts of essays) by spelling out the *not*'s, especially if you can thus set aside or qualify (as Hofstadter does) such popular misconceptions as "the intellectual is a manipulator of ideas." You might come up with something like: "Love is not greed. It is no mere lust for gold or beefsteak or people of the opposite sex, although some component of greed has caused the popular misconception. We all declare, on occasion, that we love a good steak, and we mean it. But certainly this usage is only incidental to the real meaning of love as most of us understand it, fundamentally and seriously."

Here are four good steps to take in reaching a thorough definition of something, assuring that you have covered all the angles. Consider:

1. What it *is not like.*
2. What it *is like.*
3. What it *is not.*
4. What it *is.*

This program can produce a good paragraph of definition:

> **Love may be many things to many people, but, all in all, we agree on its essentials. Love is not like a rummage sale, in which everyone tries to grab what he wants. It is more like a Christmas, in which gifts and thoughtfulness come just a little unexpectedly, even from routine directions. Love, in short, is not a matter of seeking self-satisfaction; it is first a matter of giving and then discovering, as an unexpected gift, the deepest satisfaction one can know.**

The four steps above can also furnish four effective paragraphs, which you would present in the same order of ascending interest and climax.

Beware of cracks in your logic.

Defining is, of course, a way of classifying your concepts and of keeping your headings straight. Elucidation is your major concern; rigorous logical precision is not always necessary (although rhetorical precision, the subject of the next chapter, is). Nevertheless, you should be aware of some pitfalls, and some standard precautions:

(1) Avoid echoing the term you are defining. Do not write "Courtesy is being courteous" or "Freedom is feeling free." Look around for synonyms: "Courtesy is being polite, being attentive to another's needs, making him feel at ease, using what society accepts as good manners." You can go against this rule to great advantage, however, if you repeat the *root* of the word meaningfully: "Courtesy is treating your girl like a princess in her *court*."

(2) Don't make your definitions too narrow—except for humor ("professors are only disappointed students"). Do not write: "Communism is subversive totalitarianism." Obviously, your definition needs more breadth, something about sharing property, and so forth.

(3) Don't make your definition too broad. Do not go uphill in your terms, as in "Vanity is pride" or "Affection is love." Bring the definers down to the same level: "Vanity is a kind of frivolous personal pride"—"Affection is a mild and chronic case of love."

Exercises

1. Write down the first four sentences that come to mind on any convenient topic: ice-skating, careers for girls, early marriage, dieting. Then make a topic sentence for them that will assert a covering attitude or precept. Next make a full paragraph by filling the gaps with sentences, phrases, transitions, and qualifiers—rearranging where you can gain clarity or achieve ascending interest. Hand in both your original group of four sentences and your finished paragraph.

2. Write a paragraph in which you take your reader from the outside to the interior of some house or building; your own home will do very well.

3. Write two descriptive paragraphs on the model of those by Katherine Ann Porter (pp. 95–96), providing the first with a complete topic sentence and the second with an oblique, dramatic one, like "Ah, yes." "Too late." "Well."

4. Write a one-paragraph description of a person, blending space and time (see pp. 96–98), including details of appearance, as well as surroundings.

5. Write a paragraph in which you blend the incidents and thoughts of a crucial moment (see p. 99).

6. Develop two paragraphs by illustration, using the same topic sentence for both. In the first paragraph, illustrate by one extended example; in the second, by a series of examples.

7. Develop a paragraph by some humorous but apt comparison like E. B. White's on p. 104.

8. Write a paragraph of comparative contrast, using pairs of contrasted sentences (and paired clauses and phrases).

9. Write two paragraphs contrasting something like high school and college, home and dorm, or small town and city—the first paragraph describing one, the second the other, the two using parallel contrasting terms (see pp. 104–105).

10. Write a paragraph defining something by telling: (1) what it is not like, (2) what it is like, (3) what it is not, (4) and, finally, what it is (see pp. 108–109).

11. Write an essay defining something like education, friendship, sincerity, loyalty, love, or hate.

Writing Good Sentences

8

All this time you have been writing sentences, as naturally as breathing, and perhaps with as little variation. Now for a close look at the varieties of the sentence. Some varieties can be shaggy and tangled indeed. But they are all offshoots of the simple active sentence, the basic English genus *John hit Joe,* with action moving straight from subject through verb to object.

This subject-verb-object sentence can be infinitely grafted and contorted, but there are really only two general varieties of it: (1) the "loose, or strung-along," in Aristotle's phrase, and (2) the periodic. English naturally runs "loose." Our thoughts are by nature strung along from subject through verb to object, with whatever comes to mind simply added as it comes—a word order happily acquired from French as a result of the Norman Conquest. But we can also use the periodic sentence characteristic of our German and Latin ancestry, a sentence in which ideas hang in the air like girders until all interconnections are locked by the final word: *John, the best student in the class, the tallest and most handsome, hit Joe.*

So we have two varieties of the English sentence, partly because its old Germanic oak was first limbered by French and then cured by Latin, but mostly because (as Aristotle observed of Greek) the piece-by-piece and the periodic species simply represent two ways of thought: the first, the natural stringing of thoughts as they come; the second, the more careful contrivance of emphasis and suspense.

The Simple Sentence

Use the simple active sentence, loosely periodic.

Your best sentences will be hybrids of the loose and the periodic. First, learn to use active verbs (*John* HIT *Joe*), which will keep you within the simple active pattern with all parts showing (subject-verb-object), as opposed to verbs in the passive voice (*Joe* WAS HIT *by John*), which throw your sentences into the shade. Then learn to give your native strung-along sentence a touch of periodicity and suspense.

Any change in normal order can give you unusual emphasis, as when you move the object ahead of the subject:

That I like.
The house itself she hated, but the yard was grand.
Nature I loved; and next to Nature, Art.
The manuscript, especially, he treasured.

You can vary the subject-verb-object pattern more gently by interruptive words and phrases, so that the meaning gathers excitement from the delay. The *especially* does more for the manuscript than the words themselves could manage: the phrase postpones the already postponed subject and predicate. Put the phrase last, and the emphasis fades considerably; the speaker grows a little remote: "The manuscript he treasured, especially." Put the sentence in normal order—"He especially treasured the manuscript"—and we are, in fact, back to normal.

We expect our ideas one at a time, in normal succession—*John hit Joe*—and with anything further added, in proper sequence, at the end —*a real haymaker.* Change this fixed way of thinking, and you immediately put your reader on the alert for something unusual. Consequently, some of your best sentences will be simple active ones sprung wide with phrases coloring subject, verb, object, or all three, in various ways. You may, for instance, effectively complicate the subject:

King Lear, proud, old, and childish, probably aware that his grip on the kingdom is beginning to slip, devises a foolish plan.

To come all this way, to arrive after dark, and then to find the place locked and black as ink was almost unbearable.

Or the verb:

He made his way, carefully at first, then confidently, then with reckless steps, along the peak of the smoldering roof.

A good speech usually begins quietly, proceeds sensibly, gathers momentum, and finally moves even the most indifferent audience.

Or the object:

She finally wrote the paper, a long desperate perambulation, without beginning or end, without any guiding idea—without, in fact, much of an idea at all.

His notebooks contain marvelous comments on the turtle in his back yard, the flowers and weeds, the great elm by the drive, the road, the earth, the stars, and the men and women of the village.

These are some of the infinite possibilities in the simple active sentence as it delays and stretches and heightens the ordinary expectations of subject-verb-object.

Compound and Complex Sentences

Learn the difference between compound and complex sentences.

You make a compound sentence by linking together simple sentences with a coordinating conjunction (*and, but, or, nor, yet*) or with a colon or a semicolon. You make a complex one by hooking lesser sentences onto the main sentence with *that, which, who,* or one of the many other subordinating connectives like *although, because, where, when, after, if*. The compound sentence *coordinates,* treating everything on the same level; the complex *subordinates,* putting everything else somewhere below its one main self-sufficient idea. The compound links ideas one after the other, as in the basic simple sentence; the complex is a simple sentence delayed and elaborated by clauses instead of merely by phrases. The compound represents the strung-along way of thinking; the complex represents the periodic.

Avoid simple-minded compounds.

Essentially the compound sentence *is* simple-minded, a set of clauses on a string—a child's description of a birthday party, for instance: "We got paper hats and we pinned the tail on the donkey and we had chocolate ice cream and Randy sat on a piece of cake and I won third prize." *And . . . and . . . and.*

But this way of thinking is necessary, even in postgraduate regions. It is always useful simply for pacing off related thoughts, and for breaking the staccato of simple statement. It often briskly connects cause and effect: "The clock struck one, and down he run." "The solipsist relates all knowledge to his own being, and the demonstrable commonwealth of human nature dissolves before his dogged timidity." The *and* can link causes with all sorts of different effects and speed, can bring in the next clause as a happy afterthought or a momentous consequence. Since the compound sentence is built on the most enduring of colloquial patterns—the simple sequence of things said as they occur to the mind—it has the pace, the immediacy, and the dramatic effect of talk. Hemingway, for instance, often gets all the numb tension of a shell-shocked mind by reducing his character's thoughts all to one level, in sentences something like this: "It was a good night and I sat at a table and . . . and . . . and . . . ."

With *but* and *or,* the compound sentence becomes more thoughtful. The mind is at work, turning its thought first one way then another, meeting the reader's objections by stating them. With semicolon and colon (or, if the clauses are very short, with comma), the compound grows more sophisticated still:

John demands the most from himself; Pete demands.

I came, I saw, I conquered.

Economic theorists assume a common man: he commonly wants more than he can supply.

Think of the compound sentence in terms of its conjunctions—the words that yoke its clauses—and of the accompanying punctuation. Here are three basic groups of conjunctions that will help you sort out and punctuate your compound thoughts.

Group I. The three common coordinating conjunctions: and, but, *and* or (nor). *Put a comma before each.*

I like her, and I don't mind saying so.
Art is long, but life is short.
Win this point, or the game is lost.

Group II. Conjunctive adverbs: therefore, moreover, however, nevertheless, consequently, furthermore. *Put a semicolon before, a comma after, each.*

Nations indeed seem to have a kind of biological span like the ages of man himself, from rebellious youth, through caution, to decay; consequently, predictions of doom are not uncommon.

Group III. Some in-betweeners—yet, still, so—*which sometimes take a comma, sometimes a semicolon, depending on your pace and emphasis.*

We long for the good old days, yet we never include the disadvantages.
Man longs for the good old days; yet he rarely takes into account the inaccuracy of human memory.
The preparation had been halfhearted and hasty, so the meeting was wretched.
Rome declined into the pleasures of its circuses and couches; so the tough barbarians conquered.

Learn to subordinate.

You probably write compound sentences almost without thinking. But the subordinations of the complex usually require some thought. Indeed, you are ranking closely related thoughts, arranging the lesser ones so that they bear effectively on your main thought and clarify their connections to it. You must first pick your most important idea. You must then change the thoughtless coordination of mere sequence into various forms of subordination—ordering your lesser thoughts "sub," or below, the main idea. The childish birthday sentence, then, might come out something like this:

After paper hats and chocolate ice cream, after Randy's sitting on a piece of cake and everyone's pinning the tail on the donkey, I WON THIRD PRIZE.

You do the trick with connectives—with any word, like *after* in the sentence above, indicating time, place, cause, or other qualification:

***If* he tries, *if* he fails, HE IS STILL GREAT because his spirit is unbeaten.**

You daily achieve subtler levels of subordination with the three relative pronouns *that, which, who,* and with the conjunction *that. That, which,* and *who* connect thoughts so closely related as to seem almost equal, but actually each tucks a clause (subject-and-verb) into some larger idea:

The car, *which* runs perfectly, is not worth selling.
The car *that* runs perfectly is worth keeping.
He thought *that* the car would run forever.
He thought [*that* omitted but understood] the car would run forever.

But the subordinating conjunctions and adverbs (*although, if, because, since, until, where, when, as if, so that*) really put subordinates in their places. Look at *when* in this sentence of E. B. White's from *Charlotte's Web:*

Next morning *when* the first light came into the sky and the sparrows stirred in the trees, *when* the cows rattled their chains and the rooster crowed and the early automobiles went whispering along the road, Wilbur awoke and looked for Charlotte.

Here the simple *when,* used only twice, has regimented five subordinate clauses, all of equal rank, into their proper station below that of the main clause, "Wilbur awoke and looked for Charlotte." You can vary the ranking intricately and still keep it straight:

***Although* some claim *that* time is an illusion, *because* we have no absolute chronometer, *although* the mind cannot effectively grasp time, *because* the mind itself is a kind of timeless presence almost oblivious to seconds and hours, *although* the time of our solar system may be only an instant in the universe at large, WE STILL CANNOT QUITE DENY *that* some progression of universal time is passing over us, *if* only we could measure it.**

Complex sentences are at their best really simple sentences gloriously delayed and elaborated with subordinate thoughts. The following beautiful and elaborate sentence from the Book of Common Prayer is all built on the simple sentence "draw near":

> **Ye who do truly and earnestly repent you of your sins, and are in love and charity with your neighbors, and intend to lead a new life, following the commandments of God, and walking from henceforth in his holy ways, draw near with faith, and take this holy sacrament to your comfort, and make your humble confession to Almighty God, devoutly kneeling.**

Even a short sentence may be complex, attaining a remarkably varied suspense. Notice how the simple statement "I allowed myself" is skillfully elaborated in this sentence by the late Wolcott Gibbs of the *New Yorker:*

> **Twice in my life, for reasons that escape me now, though I'm sure they were discreditable, I allowed myself to be persuaded that I ought to take a hand in turning out a musical comedy.**

Once you glimpse the complex choreography possible within the dimensions of the simple sentence, you are on your way to developing a prose capable of turns and graceful leaps, one with a kind of intellectual health that, no matter what the subject or mood, is always on its toes.

Try for still closer connections: modify.

Your subordinating *if*'s and *when*'s have really been modifying—that is, limiting—the things you have attached them to. But there is a smoother way. It is an adjectival sort of thing, a shoulder-to-shoulder operation, a neat trick with no need for shouting, a stone to a stone with no need for mortar. You simply put clauses and phrases up against a noun, instead of attaching them with a subordinator. This sort of modification includes the following constructions, all using the same close masonry: (1) appositives, (2) relatives understood, (3) adjectives-with-phrase, (4) participles, (5) absolutes.

Appositives. Those phrases about shoulders and tricks and stones, above, are all in apposition with *sort of thing,* and they are grammatically subordinate to it. The phrases are nevertheless nearly coordinate and interchangeable. They are compressions of a series of sentences ("It is an adjectival sort of thing. It is a neat trick . . . ," and so forth) set side by side, "stone to stone." Mere contact does the work of the verb *is* and its subject *it*. English often does the same with subordinate clauses, omitting the *who is* or *which is* and putting the rest directly into apposition. "The William who is the Conqueror" becomes "William the Conqueror." "The Jack who is the heavy hitter" becomes "Jack the heavy hitter." These, incidentally, are called "restrictive" appositions, because they restrict to a particular designation the nouns they modify, setting this William and this Jack apart from all others (with no separating commas). Similarly, you can make nonrestrictive appositives from nonrestrictive clauses, clauses that simply add information (between commas). "Smith, who is a man to be reckoned with, . . . " becomes "Smith, a man to be reckoned with, ..." "Jones, who is our man in Liverpool, . . ." becomes "Jones, our man in Liverpool, ..." Restrictive or nonrestrictive, close contact makes your point. You glow with the pleasures of economy and fitness.

Relatives understood. You can often achieve the same economy, as I have already hinted, by omitting any kind of relative and its verb, thus gaining a compression both colloquial and classic:

A compression [that is] both colloquial and classic . . . .
The specimens [that] he had collected . . . .
The girl [whom] he [had] left behind . . . .

But be careful after verbs of feeling and seeing; omitting *that* may lead to confusion: "She felt his ears were too big." "He saw her nose was too small."

Adjectives-with-phrase. This construction is also appositive and adjectival. It is elegant, neat, and useful:

The law was passed, *thick with provisions and codicils, heavy with implications.*

There was the lake, *smooth in the early air.*

Participles. Participles—verbs acting as adjectives—are extremely supple subordinators. Consider these three coordinate sentences:

He finally reached home. He discovered how tired he was. He went to bed without reading his mail.

Change the main verbs into present participles, and you can subordinate any two of the sentences to the other (so long as you still make sense), economizing on excess *He*'s, balancing incidentals, and emphasizing the main point. You simply use the participles as adjectives to modify the subject *he:*

Finally *reaching* home, *discovering* how tired he was, he went to bed . . . .

The past participle has the same adjectival power:

> **Dead to the world, *wrapped* in sweet dreams, *untroubled* by bills, he slept till noon.**

You will appreciate how like the adjective is the participle when you notice that *dead,* in the sentence above, is in fact an adjective, and that the participles operate exactly as it does.

Beware of dangling participles. They may trip you, as they have tripped others. The participle, with its adjectival urge, may grab the first noun that comes along, with shocking results:

> **Bowing to the crowd, the bull caught him unawares.**
> **Observing quietly from the bank, the beavers committed several errors in judgment.**
> **Squandering everything on beer, the money was never paid.**
> **By bending low, the snipers could not see the retreating squad.**
> **Tired and discouraged, half the lawn was still uncut.**
> **What we need is a list of teachers broken down alphabetically.**

Simply move the participle next to its intended noun or pronoun; you will have to supply this word if inadvertence or the passive voice has omitted it entirely. You may also save the day by changing a present participle to a past:

> **Observed quietly from the bank, the beavers . . . .**
> **Squandered on beer, the money . . . .**

Or you may move to ultimate sophistication by giving your participle a subject of its own within the phrase:

> **Every cent squandered on beer, the money was never paid.**

Here is a sentence from Jane Austen's *Persuasion* that illustrates the adjectival and subordinating power of the participle—*delighted* twice modifying *She* and subordinating everything to the one basic four-word clause that begins the sentence:

> **She always watched them as long as she could, delighted to fancy she understood what they might be talking of, as they walked along in happy independence, or equally delighted to see the Admiral's hearty shake of the hand when he encountered an old friend, and observe their eagerness of conversation when occasionally forming into a little knot of the navy, Mrs. Croft looking as intelligent and keen as any of the officers around her.**

This sentence ends so gracefully because, with the phrase *Mrs. Croft looking,* it achieves the ultimate in participial perfection—the ablative absolute.

Absolutes. The absolute phrase has a great potential of polished economy. Many an absolute is simply a prepositional phrase with the preposition dropped:

He ran up the stairs, [with] *a bouquet of roses under his arm,* and rang the bell.

He walked slowly, [with] *his gun at the ready.*

But the ablative absolute is the supreme sophisticate of subordination. *Ablative* means "removed," and the ablative absolute is absolutely removed from grammatical connection with the main clause, modifying only by proximity. If you have suffered the rudiments of Latin, you will probably remember this construction as some kind of brusque condensation, something like "*The road completed,* Caesar moved his camp." But it survives in the best of circles. Somewhere E. B. White admits to feeling particularly good one morning, just having brought off an especially fine ablative absolute. The construction does have tone. And it is actually more common than you may suppose. A recent newspaper article stated that "the Prince has fled the country, *his hopes of a negotiated peace shattered.*" The *hopes shattered* pattern (noun plus participle) marks the ablative absolute. The idea might have been more conventionally subordinated: "since his hopes were shattered" or "with his hopes shattered." But the ablative absolute accomplishes the subordination with economy and style.

Take a regular subordinate clause: "*When* the road *was* completed." Cut the subordinator and the finite verb. You now have an ablative absolute, a phrase that stands absolutely alone, shorn of both its connective *when* and its full predication *was*: "*The road completed,* Caesar moved his camp." Basically a noun and a participle, or noun and adjective, it is a kind of grammatical shorthand, a telegram: *ROAD COMPLETED CAESAR MOVED*—most said in fewest words, speed with high compression. This is its appeal and its power.

The cat stopped, its *back arched,* its *eyes frantic.*

The whole economy, *God willing,* soon will return to normal.

***All things considered,* the plan would work.**

The *dishes washed,* the *baby bathed* and *asleep,* the last *ashtray emptied,* she could at last relax.

It is certainly a construction you should use with caution. It can sound exactly like a bad translation. But able writers come to it sooner or later, whether knowingly or through discovering for themselves the horsepower in a subordinate clause milled down to its absolute minimum of noun and participle, or noun and adjective, or even noun and noun. Hemingway uses it frequently. Here is one of the noun-noun variety at the end of a sentence about pistols in *To Have and Have Not:* ". . . their only *drawback the mess* they leave for relatives to clean up." And here are two noun-participle ones (*he playing* and *the death administered*), in a passage that will serve as a closing illustration of how a complex sentence can subordinate as many as 164 words to the 7 of its one main clause ("They will put up with mediocre work"):

> **If the spectators know the matador is capable of executing a complete, consecutive series of passes with the muleta in which there will be valor, art, understanding and, above all, beauty and great emotion, THEY WILL PUT UP WITH MEDIOCRE WORK, cowardly work, disastrous work because they have the hope sooner or later of seeing the complete faena; the faena that takes a man out of himself and makes him feel immortal while it is proceeding, that gives him an ecstasy, that is, while momentary, as profound as any religious ecstasy; moving all the people in the ring together and increasing in emotional intensity as it proceeds, carrying the bullfighter with it, he playing on the crowd through the bull and being moved as it responds in a growing ecstasy of ordered, formal, passionate, increasing disregard for death that leaves you, when it is over, and the death administered to the animal that has made it possible, as empty, as changed, and as sad as any major emotion will leave you.***

Parallel Construction

Use parallels wherever you can.

Hemingway's 171-word sentence could not have held together without parallel construction, the masonry of syntax. No complex sentence can sustain a very long arch without it. Actually, Hemingway's "that is" after "ecstasy" makes a false parallel, throwing his arch briefly out of line (he should have used "which is" or something like "an ecstasy as profound, though momentary, as any . . ."). You have also seen examples of parallel ranking in White's *when* sentence (p. 116) and in the sentence that followed, dealing with

---

* Reprinted by permission of Charles Scribner's Sons from *Death in the Afternoon*, pp. 206–207. Copyright 1932 Charles Scribner's Sons; renewal copyright © 1960 Ernest Hemingway.

time. The sentence about the cat and the one about the relaxing housewife (p. 120) have shown you ablative absolutes laid parallel.

Parallel masonry can be very simple. Any word will seek its own kind, noun to noun, adjective to adjective, infinitive to infinitive. The simplest series of things automatically runs parallel:

> shoes and ships and sealing wax
> I came, I saw, I conquered
> to be or not to be
> a dull, dark, and soundless day
> mediocre work, cowardly work, disastrous work

But they very easily run out of parallel too, and this you must learn to prevent. The last item especially may slip out of line, as in this series: "friendly, kind, unobtrusive, and *a bore*" (boring). Your paralleling articles and prepositions should govern a series as a whole, or should accompany *every* item:

> a hat, a cane, a pair of gloves, and a mustache
> a hat, cane, pair of gloves, and mustache
> by land, by sea, or by air
> by land, sea, or air

Repeat your paralleling connectives.

When your series consists of phrases or of clauses, you should repeat the preposition or conjunction introducing them, to ensure clarity:

> *By* weeks of careful planning, *by* intelligence, *by* thorough training, and *by* a great deal of luck . . . .
>
> *Since* all things are not equal, *since* consequences cannot be foreseen, *since* we live but a moment . . . .
>
> He looked *for* clean fingernails and polished shoes, *for* an air of composure and a quick wit.

Watch the paralleling of pairs.

Pairs should be pairs, not odds and ends. Notice how the faulty pairs in these sentences have been corrected:

> She liked *the lawn and gardening* (the lawn and the garden).
>
> They were all *athletic or big men on campus* (athletes or big men on campus).

He wanted *peace without being disgraced* (peace without dishonor).
He liked *to play well and winning before a crowd* (to play well and to win; playing well and winning).
She was *shy but an attractive girl* (shy but attractive).

Check your terms on both sides of your coordinating conjunctions (*and, but, or*) and see that they match:

Orientation week seems both worthwhile [adjective] and ~~a necessity~~ necessary [noun].

He prayed that they would leave and ∧ that the telephone would not ring.

Learn to use paralleling coordinators.

The first sentence above has used one of a number of useful (and tricky) parallel constructions: *Both/and; either/or; not only/but also; not/but; first/second/third; as well as.* This last one is similar to *and,* a simple link between two equivalents, but it often causes trouble:

A person should take care of his physical self [noun] *as well as* being [participle] able to read and write.

Again, the pair should be matched: "his physical self as well as his intellectual self," or "his physical self as well as his ability to read and write"—though this second is still slightly unbalanced, in rhetoric if not in grammar. The best cure would probably extend the underlying antithesis, the basic parallel:

A person should take care of his physical self as well as his intellectual self, of his ability to survive as well as to read and write.

With the *either/or*'s and the *not only/but also*'s you continue the principle of pairing. The *either* and the *not only* are merely signposts of what is coming: two equivalents linked by a coordinating conjunction (*or* or *but*). Beware of putting the signs in the wrong place—too soon for the turn.

Either he is an absolute piker or a fool.

Neither in time nor space . . . .

He not only likes the girl, but the family, too.

In these examples, the thought got ahead of itself, as in talk. Just make sure that the word following each of the two coordinators is of the same kind, preposition for preposition, article for article, adjective for adjective—for even with signs well placed, the parallel can skid:

> The students are not only organizing [present participle] social activi-
> discussing
> ties, but also are ~~interested~~ [passive construction] ~~in~~ political questions.

Put identical parts in parallel places; fill in the blanks with the same parts of speech: "not only ______, but also ______." You similarly parallel the words following numerical coordinators:

> However variously he expressed himself, he unquestionably thought, first, *that* everyone could get ahead; second, *that* workers generally were paid more than they earned; and, third, *that* laws enforcing a minimum wage were positively undemocratic.
>
> For a number of reasons he decided (1) that he did not like it, (2) that she would not like it, (3) that they would be better off without it. [Note that the parentheses around the numbers operate exactly as any parentheses, and need no additional punctuation.]
>
> My objections are obvious: (1) it is unnecessary, (2) it costs too much, and (3) it won't work.

In parallels of this kind, *that* is usually the problem, since you may easily, and properly, omit it when there is only one clause and no confusion:

> . . . he unquestionably thought everyone could get ahead.

If second and third clauses occur, as your thought moves along, you may have to go back and put up the first signpost:

> that
> . . . he unquestionably thought ^ everyone could get ahead, that workers . . . , and that laws . . . .

Enough of *that.* Remember simply that equivalent thoughts demand parallel constructions. Notice the clear and massive strategy in the following sentence from the concluding chapter of Freud's last book, *An Outline of Psychoanalysis.* Freud is not only summing up the previous discussion, but also expressing the quintessence of his life's work. He is pulling everything together in a single sentence. Each of the parallel *which* clauses gathers up, in proper order, an entire chapter of his book (notice the parallel force in repeating *picture,* and the summarizing dash):

> **The picture of an ego which mediates between the id and the external world, which takes over the instinctual demands of the former in order to bring them to satisfaction, which perceives things in the latter and uses them as memories, which, intent upon its self-preservation, is on guard against excessive claims from both directions, and which is governed in all its decisions by the injunctions of a modified pleasure principle—this picture actually applies to the ego only up to the end of the first period of childhood, till about the age of five.**

Such precision is hard to match. This is what parallel thinking brings—balance and control and an eye for sentences that seem intellectual totalities, as if struck out all at once from the uncut rock. Francis Bacon also can seem like this (notice how he drops the verb after establishing his pattern):

> **For a crowd is not company, and faces are but a gallery of pictures, and talk but a tinkling cymbal, where there is no love.**
>
> **Reading maketh a full man; conference a ready man; and writing an exact man.**

And the balance can run from sentence to sentence through an entire passage, controlled not only by connectives repeated in parallel, but by whole phrases and sentences so repeated, as in this passage by Macaulay:

> **To sum up the whole: we should say that the aim of the Platonic philosophy was to exalt man into a god. The aim of the Baconian philosophy was to provide man with what he requires while he continues to be man. The aim of the Platonic philosophy was to raise us far above vulgar wants. The aim of the Baconian philosophy was to supply our vulgar wants. The former aim was noble; but the latter was attainable.**

The Long and Short of It

Your style will emerge once you can manage some length of sentence, some intricacy of subordination, some vigor of parallel, and some play of long against short, of amplitude against brevity. Try the very long sentence, and the very short. The best short sentences are meatiest:

To be awake is to be alive.
A stitch in time saves nine.
The mass of men lead lives of quiet desperation.
The more selfish the man, the more anguished the failure.

Experiment, too, with the fragment. The fragment is close to conversation. It is the laconic reply, the pointed afterthought, the quiet exclamation, the telling question. Try to cut and place it clearly (usually at beginnings and ends of paragraphs) so as not to lead your reader to expect a full sentence, or to suspect a poor writer:

But no more.
First, a look behind the scenes.
Again: the man of reason.
No, not really.
Enough of that.

The conversational flow between long and short makes a passage move. Study the subordinations, the parallels, and the play of short and long in this elegant passage of Virginia Woolf's—after you have read it once for sheer enjoyment. She is writing of Lord Chesterfield's famous letters to Philip Stanhope, his illegitimate son:

But while we amuse ourselves with this brilliant nobleman and his views on life we are aware, and the letters owe much of their fascination to this consciousness, of a dumb yet substantial figure on the farther side of the page. Philip Stanhope is always there. It is true that he says nothing, but we feel his presence in Dresden, in Berlin, in Paris, opening the letters and poring over them and looking dolefully at the thick packets which have been accumulating year after year since he was a child of seven. He had grown into a rather serious, rather stout, rather short young man. He had a taste for foreign politics. A little serious reading was rather to his liking. And by every post the letters came—urbane, polished, brilliant, imploring and commanding him to learn to dance, to learn to carve, to consider the management of his legs, and to seduce a lady of fashion. He did his best. He worked very hard in the school of the Graces, but their service was too exacting. He sat down half-way up the steep stairs which lead to the glittering hall with all the mirrors. He could not do it. He failed in the House of Commons; he subsided into some small post in Ratisbon; he died untimely. He left it to his widow to break the news which he had lacked the heart or the courage to tell his father—that he had been married all these years to a lady of low birth, who had borne him children.

The Earl took the blow like a gentleman. His letter to his daughter-in-law is a model of urbanity. He began the education of his grandsons . . . .*

Those are some sentences to copy. We immediately feel the rhythmic play of periodic and loose, parallel and simple, long and short. Such orchestration takes years of practice, but you can always begin.

Exercises

1. Write five short sentences that invert normal order for emphasis: "That I like."

2. Write nine simple sentences (make sure you have no subordinate clauses), three complicating the subject, three the verb, and three the object.

3. Write nine compound sentences, three with *and,* three with *but,* three with *or* (*nor*). Try to get as grand a feeling of consequence as possible: "Empires fall, and the saints come marching in."

4. Write five compound sentences using conjunctive adverbs, on the pattern: "______; therefore, ______"—punctuated carefully with semicolon and comma.

5. List all the subordinators you can think of (*since, if, before,* etc.).

6. Write five sequences of three simple sentences on the pattern: "He finally reached home. He was tired. He went to bed." Then, changing verbs to participles, subordinate two of the sentences to the remaining one in each sequence.

7. To appreciate participial subordination, rewrite each of the following as a series of simple coordinate sentences, changing the participles into finite verbs and the principal adjectives into predicate adjectives ("They danced. They swayed . . . . Some were intense."):

> They danced, swaying in dim light, dreaming happily, some laughing, some intense, some even embarrassed and awkward, wishing but failing to join the dream completely.
>
> Fishing, hiking, playing cribbage, sometimes talking seriously, sometimes merely sitting together in silence, they spent the last of summer.

---

* *The Second Common Reader,* p. 81. Copyright, 1932, by Harcourt Brace Jovanovich, Inc.; renewed, 1960, by Leonard Woolf. Reprinted by permission of Harcourt Brace Jovanovich, Inc., and The Hogarth Press, Ltd.

He was every inch a soldier, clipped, tailored, polished, as if straight from a musical comedy.

His train already late, his money stolen, his hat gone, his plans upset from start to finish, he hoped desperately that he still had time.

Complicated, misleading, inadequate, and distorted by special interests, the bill deserved defeat.

8. Review the discussion of parallel coordinators on pages 123–125. Then write two sentences apiece for each of the following sets of coordinators. Try different parts of speech, but keep your parallels true by filling the blanks in any one sentence with the same parts of speech.

both _____ and _____
either _____ or _____
not only _____ but also _____
(1) _____, (2) _____, (3) _____
_____ as well as _____

9. Write five sentences with dangling participles, with a remedy for each.

10. Write five sentences with ablative absolutes, some using present participles, some using past.

11. Now, write a 100-word sentence *with only one independent clause* in each, and with everything else subordinated. You can get started with a string of parallel clauses: "When I get up in the morning, when I look at my bleary eyes in the mirror, when I think of the paper still to be done . . . ," or "After . . . , after . . . , after . . . ." See how far you can run on before you must bring in your main subject and verb.

12. Adjust or clarify the parallels in the following (taken from freshman papers):

These men are not only cheating themselves, but also are banded together into crime syndicates which help to lower the character of the entire nation.

He stated two ways in which man could hope to continue survival. (1) World citizenship, or (2) destroying most of the inventions that man is uncertain of and go back to where we can understand ourselves and progress.

In this way not only the teacher needs to be concerned with the poorest student, but every class member helped.

A student follows not only a special course of training, but among his studies and social activities finds a liberal education.

Education is something that can't be taken for granted but instead requires serious thought.

When they go to church, it is only because they have to go and not of their own desire.

Many people argue that the so-called virtues of man belong to the age of chivalry, and they do not apply to the present.

This is not only the case with the young voters of the United States but also of the adult ones.

. . . an education which will not only embarrass her but also is dangerous to a self-governing people.

Certain things are not actually taught in the classroom. They are learning how to get along with others, to depend on oneself, and managing one's own affairs.

Every time I sit down and attempt to read one of those interesting essays, or else studying German . . . .

Knowing Greek and Roman antiquity is not just learning to speak their language but also their culture.

I think fraternities are sociable as well as the dormitories.

All the girls now intend to get married as well as having families of three or four.

13. (a) In the following famous sentence of Bacon's straighten the faulty parallels and fill out all the phrasing implied by them:

Histories make men wise; poets witty; the mathematics subtle; natural philosophy deep; moral grave; logic and rhetoric able to contend.

(b) Now write five sentences on the Baconian pattern: "Jack would eat no fat; his wife no lean; the old dog only soup . . . ; the young . . . ."

14. Write an imitation, or a parody, of the following passage from Samuel Johnson, matching him sentence for sentence and phrase for phrase ("Of genius, that power which constitutes a ball player . . . ." "Of glamour, that power which constitutes an actress . . . ."):

Of genius, that power which constitutes a poet; that quality without which judgement is cold and knowledge is inert; that energy which collects, combines, amplifies, and animates—the superiority must, with some hesitation, be allowed to Dryden. It is not to be inferred that of this poetical vigour Pope had only a little, because Dryden had more, for every other writer since Milton must give place to Pope; and even of Dryden it must be said that if he has brighter paragraphs, he has not better poems. Dryden's performances were always hasty, either excited by some external occasion, or extorted by domestick necessity; he composed without consideration, and published without correction. What his mind could supply at call, or gather in one excursion, was all that he sought, and all that he gave. The dilatory caution of Pope enabled him to condense his sentiments, to multiply his images, and to accumulate all that study might produce, or chance might supply. If the flights of Dryden therefore are higher, Pope continues longer on the wing. If of Dryden's fire the blaze is brighter, of Pope's the heat is more regular and constant. Dryden often surpasses expectation, and Pope never falls below it. Dryden is read with frequent astonishment, and Pope with perpetual delight.

15. Write an imitation of the passage from Virginia Woolf on pages 126–127, aiming toward effective rhythms of short and long.

Correcting Bad Sentences

9

Now let us contemplate evil—or at least the innocently awful, the bad habits that waste our words, fog our thoughts, and wreck our delivery. Our thoughts are naturally roundabout, our phrases naturally secondhand. Our satisfaction in merely getting something down on paper naturally blinds us to our errors and ineptitudes. Writing is devilish. It hypnotizes us into believing we have said what we meant, when our words actually say something else: "Every seat in the house was filled to capacity." Good sentences therefore come from constant practice in correcting the bad.

Count your words.

The general sin is wordiness. We put down the first thought that comes, we miss the best order, and we then need lengths of *is*'s, *of*'s, *by*'s and *which*'s—words virtually meaningless in themselves—to wire our meaningful words together again. Look for the two or three words that carry your meaning; then see if you can rearrange them to speak for themselves, cutting out all the little useless wirings:

> **This is the young man who was elected to be president by the class. [The class elected this young man president. *7 words for 14*]**

See if you can't promote a noun into a verb, and cut overlaps in meaning:

> **Last week, the gold stampede in Europe reached near panic proportions. [Europe's gold rush almost *stampeded* last week. *7 words for 11*]**

When you convert the noun, *stampede,* into a verb, *stampeded,* you suddenly discover that you have already said "near panic proportions" and you can drop it entirely: stampedes *are* panics. The ungrammatical *near* (which, incidentally, should be either *nearly* or *almost*) is usually a symptom of wordiness, probably because it reveals a general inattention to meanings: the writer is not, as his word seems to say, visualizing a hand reaching around near something called "panic."

The basic cure for wordiness is to count the words in any suspected sentence—and to make each word count. If you can rephrase to save even one word, your sentence will be clearer. And seek the active verb: *John* HIT *Joe.*

Avoid the passive voice.

The passive voice drones like nothing under the sun, bringing active English to a standstill. Of course, it can, in a string of active sentences, give mere variety, although phrasal and clausal variations are better. It can also vary the emphasis; it too depends on inverting normal order. *Joe was hit by John* throws selective light on Joe, by inverting regular consequences and distinguishing him from all other unfortunates, and it gives John a certain dubious distinction too. The passive voice can also, if need be, eliminate the doer altogether: *Joe was hit.* ("I was sunk." "It was done.")

In fact, your meaning sometimes demands the passive voice; the agent may be better under cover—insignificant, or unknown, or mysterious. The active "Shrapnel hit him" seems to belie the uncanny impersonality of "He was hit by shrapnel." The broad forces of history similarly demand the passive: "The West was opened in 1848." Moreover, you may sometimes need the passive voice to place your true subject, the hero of the piece, where you can modify him conveniently: *Joe was hit by John, who, in spite of all* . . . . And sometimes it simply is more convenient: "This subject-verb-object sentence can be infinitely contorted." You can, of course, find a number of passive constructions in this book, which preaches against them, because they can also space out a thought that comes too fast and thick. In trying to describe periodic sentences, for instance (p. 112), I changed "until all interconnections lock in the final word" (active) to ". . . are locked by the final word" (passive). The *lock* seemed too tight, especially with *in,* and the locking seemed contrary to the way buildings *are built.* Yes, the passive has its uses.

But avoid it if you can. It is wordy and unclear. It liquidates and buries the active individual. Our massed and scientific society is so addicted to the passive voice that the individual writer must constantly alert himself against its drowsy, soporific pomp. The simple English sentence is active; it *moves* from subject through verb to object: "Smith laid the cornerstone on April 1." But because we must sound important, because the impersonal institution must be bigger than Smith, the historian writes "The cornerstone was laid on April 1," and Smith vanishes from the earth. The doer and the writer both—all traces of individuality, all human interest—disappear behind the elongated passive verb: *was laid* instead of *laid.* Committees always write this way, and the effect on academic writing, as the professor goes from committee to desk to classroom, is astounding. "It was moved that a meeting would be held," the secretary writes, to avoid pinning the rap on anybody. So writes the professor, so writes the student.

The passive voice puts excess words in a sentence. Its dullness derives as much from its extra wordage as from its impersonality. *Joe was hit by John* says no more than *John hit Joe,* but takes 66 percent more words! The passive's inevitable *was* and *by* do nothing but connect; worse, all the *was*'s and *by*'s and *has been*'s actually get in the way of the words carrying the meaning, like underbrush slowing you down and hiding what you want to see.

The best way to prune is with the active voice, cutting the passive and its fungus as you go. Notice the effect on the following typical, and actual, samples:

Public concern *has* also *been given* a tremendous impetus *by* the findings of the Hoover Commission on the federal government, and "little Hoover" commissions to survey the organizational structure and functions of many state governments *have been established.* [In the federal government, the findings of the Hoover Commission *have* also greatly stimulated public concern, and many states *have established* "little Hoover" commissions to survey their governments. *28 words for 38*]

The algal mats *are made up of* the interwoven filaments of several genera. [The interwoven filaments of several genera *make up* the algal mats. *11 words for 13*]

Many of the remedies *would* probably *be shown to be* faith cures. [Many of the remedies *are* probably faith cures. *8 words for 12*]

Anxiety and emotional conflict *are lessened* when latency sets in. The total personality *is oriented* in a repressive, inhibitory fashion so as to maintain the barriers, and what Freud has called "psychic dams," against psychosexual impulses. [When latency sets in, anxiety and emotional conflict *subside.* The personality *inhibits* itself, maintaining its barriers—Freud's "psychic dams"—against psychosexual impulses. *22 words for 36*]

The passive voice, simply in its wordiness, is always a bit unclear even on the surface; but, if it eliminates the real subject of the verb, as it usually does, it is intrinsically unclear as well. "This passage has been selected because . . . ," the student will write, and the reader cannot tell who did the selecting. Does he mean that he, the writer, has picked it, or does he describe some process of natural or popular selection? We surmise he means himself, of course; but why doesn't he say so, and save a word, and avoid confusion? "I selected this passage because . . . ."

Any form of the verb *is* may reveal that you have a passive construction. Our language must use some form of *is* so frequently in stating that things *are* and in forming its compound verbs (*is falling, were playing*) that you should drop as many *is*'s and *was*'s as possible, simply to avoid monotony. But when they are—as they often are—signs of the passive voice, you can also avoid rigor mortis by replacing your *is*'s with active verbs, along with their true subjects, the real doers of the action.

To be, itself, frequently ought not to be:

He seems [to be] upset about something.
She considered him [to be] perfect.
This appears [to be] difficult.

Similarly, in restrictive clauses (p. 154), many an improper *which,* and many a *that, who,* and *whom* as well, may depart, and good riddance:

The rule [which] the committee favors . . . .
I think [that] he should go.
The man [whom] I respect . . . .

Above all, keep your sentences awake by not putting them into those favorite stretchers of the passivists, *There is . . . which, It is . . . that,* and the like:

Moreover, [there is] one segment of the population [which] never seeks employment.
[There are] many women [who] never marry.
[There] is nothing wrong with it.
[It is] his last book [that] shows his genius best.
[It is] this [that] is important.

The bracketed words can disappear without a ripple. Furthermore, *It is* frequently misleads your reader by seeming to mean something specific (*beer,* in the following example):

Several members voted for beer. *It is* hard to get *it* through some people's heads that minors can't buy it. [Some people never learn that minors can't buy it.]

Cut every *it* not referring to something. Next to activating your passives, and cutting the passivistic *there is*'s and *it is*'s, perhaps nothing so improves your prose as to go through it systematically deleting every *to be,* every *which, that, who,* and *whom* not needed for utter clarity or for spacing out a thought. All your sentences will feel better.

Beware the of-*and*-which *disease.*

The passive sentence also breaks out in a rash of *of*'s and *which*'s, and even the active sentence may suffer. Diagnosis: something like sleeping sickness. *With*'s, *in*'s, *to*'s, and *by*'s also inflamed. Surgery imperative. Here is a typical, and actual, case:

> **Many biological journals, especially those *which* regularly publish new scientific names, now state *in* each issue the exact date *of* publication *of* the preceding issue. *In* dealing *with* journals *which* do not follow this practice, or *with* volumes *which* are issued individually, the biologist often needs *to* resort *to* indexes . . . *in order to* determine the actual date *of* publication *of* a particular name.**

Note *of publication of* twice over, and the three *which*'s. The passage is a sleeping beauty. The longer you look at it the more useless little attendants you see. Note the inevitable passive voice (*which are issued*) in spite of the author's active efforts. The *of*'s accompany extra nouns, *publication* repeating *publish*, for instance. Remedy: (1) eliminate *of*'s and their nouns, (2) change *which* clauses into participles, (3) change nouns into verbs. You can cut more than a third of this passage without touching the sense (using 39 words instead of 63):

> **Many biological journals, especially those regularly *publishing* new scientific names, now give the date of each preceding issue. With journals not *following* this practice, and with some books, the biologist must turn to indexes . . . *to date* a particular name.**

I repeat: you can cut most *which*'s, one way or another, with no loss of blood. Participles can modify their antecedents directly, since they are verbal adjectives, without an intervening *which:* "a car *which was* going south" is "a car going south"; "a train *which is* moving" is "a moving train." Similarly with the adjective itself: "a song *which was* popular last year" is "a song popular last year"; "a person *who is* attractive" is "an attractive person." Beware of this whole crowd: *who are, that was, which are.*

If you need a relative clause, remember *that. Which* has almost completely displaced it in labored writing. *That* is still best for restrictive clauses, those necessary to definition: "A house that faces north is cool" (a participle would save a word: "A house facing north is cool"). *That* is tolerable; *which* is downright oppressive. *Which* should signal the nonrestrictive clause (the afterthought): "The house, which faces north, is a good buy." Here you need *which.* Even restrictive clauses must turn to *which* when complicated parallels arise. "He preaches the brotherhood of man *that* everyone affirms" elaborates like this: "He preaches the brotherhood of man *which* everyone affirms, *which* all the great philosophies support, but *for which* few can make any immediate concession." Nevertheless, if you need relatives, a *that* will often ease your sentences and save you from the *which*'s.

Verbs and their derivatives, especially present participles and gerunds, can also help to cure a string of *of*'s. Alfred North Whitehead, usually of clear mind, once produced this linked sausage: "Education is the acquisition *of* the art *of* the utilization *of* knowedge." Anything to get around the three *of*'s and the three heavy nouns would have been better: "Education instils the art of using knowledge"—"Education teaches us to use knowledge well." Find an active verb for *is the acquisition of,* and shift *the utilization of* into some verbal form: the gerund *using,* or the infinitive *to use.* Shun the *-tion*'s! Simply change your surplus *-tion*'s and *of*'s—along with your *which* phrases—into verbs, or verbals (*to use, learning*). You will save words, and activate your sentences.

Beware the use of.

In fact, both *use,* as a noun, and *use,* as a verb, are dangerously wordy words. Since *using* is one of our most basic concepts, other words in your sentence will already contain it:

He uses rationalization. [He rationalizes.]
He uses the device of foreshadowing. [He foreshadows.]
Through [the use of] logic, he persuades.
His [use of] dialogue is effective.

The utilization of and *utilize* are only horrendous extremes of the same pestilence, to be stamped out completely.

Break the noun habit.

Passive writing adores the noun, modifying nouns with nouns in pairs, and even in denser clusters—which then become official jargon. Break up these logjams, let the language flow, make one noun of the pair an adjective:

***Teacher militancy* is not as marked in Pittsburgh. [*Teachers* are not so *militant* in Pittsburgh. *7 words for 8*]**

Or convert one noun to a verb:

***Teacher power* is less in evidence in Pittsburgh. [*Teachers demand* less in Pittsburgh. *5 words for 8*]**

Of course, nouns have long served English as adjectives, as in "*rail*road," "*railroad* station," "*court*house," and "*noun* habit." But modern prose has aggravated the tendency beyond belief; and we get such monstrosities as *child sex education course*, whole strings of nothing but nouns. Professors of education, sociology, and psychology are the worst noun-stringers, the hardest for you not to copy if you take their courses. But we have all caught the habit. The nouns *level* and *quality* have produced a rash of redundancies. A meeting of "high officials" has now unfortunately become a meeting of "high-*level* officials." The "finest cloth" these days is always "finest *quality* cloth." Drop those two redundant nouns and you will make a good start, and will sound surprisingly original. You can drop many an excess noun:

WORDY	DIRECT
advance notice	notice
long in size	long
puzzling in nature	puzzling
of an indefinite nature	indefinite
of a peculiar kind	peculiar
in order to	to
by means of	by
in relation to	with
in connection with	with
1974-model car	1974 car

Wherever possible, find the equivalent adjective:

of great importance	important
highest significance level	highest significant level
government spending	governmental spending
reaction fixation	reactional fixation
teaching excellence	excellent teaching
encourage teaching quality	encourage good teaching

Or change the noun to its related participle:

advance placement	advanced placement
charter flight	chartered flight
uniform police	uniformed police
poison arrow	poisoned arrow

Or make the noun possessive:

reader interest	reader's interest
factory worker wage	factory worker's wage
veterans insurance	veterans' insurance

Or try a cautious *of:*

WRONG	RIGHT
color lipstick	**color of lipstick**
teaching science	**science of teaching**
production quality	**quality of production**
high quality program	**program of high quality**
significance level	**level of significance**
a Marxist-type program	**a Marxist program** *or* **a Marxist type of program**

Of all our misused nouns, *type* has become peculiarly pestilential and trite. Advertisers talk of *detergent-type cleansers* instead of *detergents;* educators, of *apprentice-type situations* instead of *apprenticeships;* newspapermen, of *fascist-type organizations* instead of *fascistic organizations.* Don't copy your seniors; write boldly. We have become a nation of hairsplitters, afraid of saying *Czechoslovakia's Russian tanks* for fear that the reader will think they really belong to Russia. So the reporter writes *Russian-type tanks,* making an unnecessary distinction, and cluttering the page with one more *type-type* expression. We have forgotten that making the individual stand for the type is the simplest and oldest of metaphors: "Give us this day our daily bread." A twentieth-century man might have written "bread-type food."

The simple active sentence transmits the message by putting each word unmistakably in its place, a noun as a noun, an adjective as an adjective, with the verb—no stationary *is*—really carrying the mail. Recently, after a flood, a newspaper produced this apparently succinct and dramatic sentence: **Dead animals cause water pollution.** (The word *cause,* incidentally, indicates wasted words.) That noun *water* as an adjective throws the meaning off and takes 25 percent more words than the essential active message: **Dead animals pollute water.** As you read your way into the sentence, it seems to say *dead animals cause water* (which is true enough), and then you must readjust your thoughts to accommodate *pollution.* The simplest change is from *water pollution* (noun-noun) to *polluted water* (adjective-noun), clarifying each word's function. But the supreme solution is to make *pollute* the verb it is, and the sentence a simply active message in which no word misspeaks itself. Here are the possibilities, in a scale from most active and clearest to most passive and wordiest, which may serve to chart your troubles if you get tangled in causes and nouns:

Dead animals pollute water.
Dead animals cause polluted water.

Dead animals cause water pollution.

Dead animals are a factor in causing the pollution of water.

Dead animals are a serious factor in causing the water pollution situation.

Dead farm-type animals are a danger factor in causing the post-flood clearance and water pollution situation.

So the message should now be clear. Write simple active sentences, outmaneuvering all passive eddies, all shallow *is*'s, *of*'s, *which*'s, and *that*'s, all overlappings, all rocky clusters of nouns: they take you off your course, delay your delivery, and wreck many a straight and gallant thought.

Exercises

1. Write five sentences in the passive voice, and change each to its active equivalent.

2. Pick five obese and passive sentences from your textbooks (including this one, if I have slipped). Change them to clean active sentences, indicating the number of words saved in each.

3. Find in your textbooks two or three passages suffering from the *of*-and-*which* disease, the *the-use-of* contagion, and the noun habit ("which shows the effect of age and intelligence level upon the use of the reflexes and the emergence of child behavior difficulties") and rewrite them in clear English.

4. Following the examples on pages 134–137, recast these sentences in the active voice, clearing out all passive constructions, saving as many words as you can, and indicating the number saved:

The particular topic chosen by the instructor for study in his section of English 2 must be approved by the Steering Committee. [Start with "The Steering Committee," and don't forget the economy of an apostrophe *s*. I managed 16 words for 22.]

Avoidance of such blunders should not be considered a virtue for which the student is to be commended, any more than he would be praised for not wiping his hands on the tablecloth or polishing his shoes with the guest towels. [Begin "We should not"; try *avoiding* for *avoidance*. I dropped *virtue* as redundant and scored 34 for 41.]

The first respect in which too much variation seems to exist is in the care with which writing assignments are made. ["First, care in assigning"—8 for 21.]

The remaining variations that will be mentioned are concerned not with the assignment of papers but with the marking and grading of them. ["Finally, I shall mention"—16 for 23.]

The difference between restrictives and nonrestrictives can also be better approached through a study of the different contours that mark the utterance of the two kinds of element than through confusing attempts to differentiate the two by meaning. ["One can differentiate restrictives" —I managed 13 for 38.]

5. Here are seven more to prune, especially of *that*'s, *which*'s, *who*'s, *of*'s, and *there is . . . which*'s (my figures again are merely guides; other solutions are equally good):

There is a certain tendency to defend one's own position *which* will cause the opponent's argument to be ignored. [14 for 19]

It is the other requirements *that* present obstacles, some *of which* may prove insurmountable in the teaching of certain subjects. [13 for 20]

In the sort of literature-centered course being discussed here, *there is* usually a general understanding *that* themes will be based on the various literary works *that* are studied, the theory being *that* both the instruction in literature and *that* in writing will be made more effective by this interrelationship. [26 for 50]

The person *whom* he met was an expert *who was* able to teach the fundamentals quickly. [13 for 16]

They will take a pride *which is* wholly justifiable in being able to command a prose style *that is* lucid and supple. [13 for 22]

The work *which is* reported *in this* study *is* an investigation *of* language *within* the social context *of* the community *in which it is spoken. It is* a study *of* a linguistic structure *which is* unusually complex, but no more than the social structure *of* the city *in which it* functions. [I tried two versions, as I chased out the *which's;* 29 for 52, and 22 for 52.]

Methods *which are* unique to the historian *are illustrated* throughout the volume *in order to* show how history *is written* and how historians work. The historian's approach to his subject, *which* leads to the asking of provocative questions and to a new understanding of complex events, situations, and personalities *is probed.* The manner *in which* the historian reduces masses of chaotic fact—and occasional fancy—to reliable meaning, and the way *in which* he formulates explanations and tests them *is examined and clarified* for the student. *It is its* emphasis on historical method *which* distinguishes this book from other source readings in western civilization. The problems *which are examined* concern *themselves with* subjects *which are dealt with by* most courses in western civilization. [82 for 123]

Punctuation

10

Punctuation gives the silent page some of the breath of life. It marks the pauses and emphases a speaker uses to point his meaning. Loose punctuators forget what every good writer knows: that even silent reading produces an articulate murmur in our heads, that language springs from the breathing human voice, that the beauty and meaning of language depend on what the written word makes us *hear*, on the sentence's tuning of emphasis and pause. Commas and semicolons and periods do what they can to transcribe our meaningful pauses to the printed page.

The Period: Sentences and Fragments

Learn what a sentence is.

Having used sentences all our lives, we all think we know what one is. But commas still appear where periods should be, and the reader blunders ahead when he should have stopped. Think of a *sentence* as a subject completed in its verb and tacked home with a period. We rarely mistake a *phrase* for a sentence, since, having no verb, it cries for completion. But a *clause,* which does have subject and verb, is indeed a complete sentence—unless it looks to the main sentence for fulfillment:

After the ball, the sweepers come. [phrase]
After the ball is over, the sweepers come. [clause]

Your sentence is complete if the first part clearly looks ahead toward the period, and if the end clearly looks back toward its beginning. If you find the first part of your sentence looking back, or looking ahead in vain, you have no sentence: you have a fragment that should be hooked, with a comma, to its governing sentence:

He dropped his teeth. _Which had cost two hundred dollars._

A good example is Hawthorne. _A writer who could dramatize abstract moral theories._

Cleopatra is the stronger. _Trying to create Antony in her own Egyptian image._

The accidental fragment is almost invariably found *after* its governing sentence.

But try an occasional rhetorical fragment.

Nothing so firmly demonstrates your command over the sentence as a judicious fragment, as I have already suggested (p. 126). Make it stand alone, and no mistake. Fragments are safest and most effective, exerting all their transitional force, at the head of a paragraph. Such fragments are especially dramatic, economical, and close to speech:

First, a word to the wise.
Another point.
Of course.
Not at all.
Expert within limits, that is.

Notice that all these fragments—condensations, afterthoughts, answers, quiet exclamations—usually omit some hypothetical form of *is*, with its subject:

First, [here is] a word to the wise.
Of course [it is *or* he did].
[It is] not at all [so].

This kind of dramatic fragment, in other words, is talking about existences, about what *is*, letting the words assert their own being—exactly the kind of streamlining the Latin writers liked, and still swift and racy. But be careful.

Use a period after a declarative sentence.

This, of course, is the everyday period, the one ending the sentences and fragments we have been discussing. It ends a declaration and makes it independent. It concludes each thought you complete with subject, verb, and other attachments, even when you only imply both subject and verb, as in the fragment *Of course.* Notice that you may change your declarations to questions and exclamations merely by switching from the declarative period to a question mark or exclamation point: *Of course? Of course!*

Use a period after an indirect question.

The following are not really questions, but declarations of what the question was; hence the period.

She asked me when I was going to finish college.
I wonder if you could come tomorrow.
He wanted to know how I found it and why I hadn't told him.

Use a period after a polite command or request.

The exclamation point shouts a little, and the question mark can grow a little shrill. My page would startle you had I written: "Use a period after a polite command or request!" Similarly, the question mark may seem too insistent: "Will you kindly remit?"

But be careful.
Come when you can.
Will you kindly give this matter your earliest attention.
May the council please have your comments at your convenience.

Use them after standard abbreviations (Colo., Ave.), and after initials used as abbreviations (A.D., D.C., U.S.A.). This is the rule, but exceptions are many. Use your dictionary to determine accepted forms. Alphabetical titles and acronyms ("tip-names" made from the initials or "tips" of longer titles, as in CORE or UNESCO) usually go without periods. Radio and television stations (WQXR-FM, NBC-TV) and tuberculosis (TB) are other common exceptions. MS. and MSS. (manuscript, manuscripts) are curious hybrids. Here are some special problems:

(a) An abbreviation at the end of a declarative sentence. End the sentence with the final abbreviating period.

He asked her to mail it C.O.D. [not C.O.D..]

(b) An abbreviation at the end of a question or exclamation. Add the question mark or exclamation point after the abbreviating period.

C.O.D.? Yes—but not to Washington, D.C.!

(c) An abbreviation inside a sentence. Let the abbreviating period stand as it comes, and add other punctuation as necessary.

All prices are F.O.B. at our nearest warehouse.
I hope my MS., which I mailed Tuesday, reached you in time.
The joy of his life, i.e., his mother-in-law, arrived.

Note that common abbreviations like *i.e., etc., viz.,* and the like, are enclosed in commas, since they are parenthetical remarks. But, except for heavy irony, as with the *i.e.* before *mother-in-law,* your phrase will be smoother if you omit these abbreviations completely, or use *that is, and so on,* and *namely.*

(d) Abbreviations like *Mr., Mrs., Mlle., Mme., Dr., St.* (Saint), *Co.,* and *Ltd.* occur without the period in some British papers and books. Follow U.S. usage, which requires the period. Note that the abbreviation *U.S.* may be used *only* as an adjective: "U.S. Postal Service," but not "life in the U.S." This should read "life in the United States."

Use periods in designating parts of literary works.

Separate act, scene, and line (or book, chapter, and page, and the like) by intervening periods and *no intervening spaces*: II.iii.22; Sam. xviii.33; *Iliad* IX.93; *Julius Caesar* III.ii.187.

The Comma

You need only four rules to use the comma expertly, and the last two share a single principle. Use a comma:

I. Before the coordinator—*and-but-or-nor-yet-still-for*—when joining independent clauses.
II. Between all terms in a series, *including the last two.*
III. To set off parenthetical openers and afterthoughts.
IV. Before and after parenthetical insertions (use a *pair* of commas).

Use a comma before conjunctions like and, but, *and* for *when joining independent clauses* (RULE I).

You have perhaps been told that you omit the comma when your two clauses are short: "He hunted and she fished." You certainly can get away with it, and in the best of publications. But it is the first tiny slip toward utter abandon. Your clauses will grow longer. You will begin to touch in a comma only now and then, still leaving the main gap between clauses unplugged. You will omit commas before *but* and *for* and really throw your reader off. Nothing is wrong with "He hunted, and she fished." With the comma, in fact, it shows the slight pause you make when you say it. Stick to the rule, and you can't go wrong. And you will greatly improve your sense of style.

Think of the "comma-and" (**, and**) as a unit equivalent to the period. The period, the semicolon, and the "comma-and" (**, and**) all designate independent clauses, but with different emphases:

.	**He was tired. He went home.**
;	**He was tired; he went home.**
, and	**He was tired, and he went home.**

If you can just think of the **, and** or the **, but** as a unit, perfectly equivalent to the **.** and the **;** as a buffer between independent clauses, you will have mastered the basic problem in punctuation, the cause of most trouble.

What you need is a firm rule to follow. You may find exceptions—or what seem exceptions until you see the underlying reasons, since good punctuation is based on reason and meaning. Look again at E. B. White's *when* sentence (p. 116):

Next morning when the first light came into the sky and the sparrows stirred in the trees, when the cows rattled their chains and the rooster

crowed and the early automobiles went whispering along the road, Wilbur awoke . . . .

White omits several commas before *and,* but the reason is dazzlingly clear. He is regimenting short coordinate clauses under one subordinator, *when.* A comma after *sky,* for instance, would block the *when* from the *sparrows* and throw the clauses out of rank. For reasons of rank, he also omits the "introductory" comma after *Next morning.* A comma here, since only two other commas control the whole long sentence, would have thrown *Next morning* into sudden prominence, into unjustified equality with the long *when* elements.

Your punctuation, or lack of it, signals your meaning as it comes in, word by word. The "comma-and" (**, and**) tells your reader that a whole new predication is coming; just-plain-**and** tells him to expect only a smaller unit:

He hunted the hills and . . . .

brings an entirely different expectation from:

He hunted the hills, and . . . .

In the first you expect something like *dales,* something parallel to *hills.* In the second you expect another subject and predicate: "and he found . . . ," or "and they were . . . ."

Omitting the comma between independent clauses joined by *and* really makes a false parallel, and the silence of print often encourages the error. When you *say* "hills and dales," you do not pause. When you *say* ". . . hills, and he found . . . ," you do pause. English invariably expresses this difference in meaning by pausing or not. Modern linguists, who call this pause a "double-bar juncture," have reminded us that commas signify meaning.

The same may be seen with *but, or,* and *yet*:

She was naughty but nice.
She was naughty, but that is not our business.
Wear your jacket or coat.
Wear your jacket, or you will catch cold.
It was strong yet sweet.
It was strong, yet it was not unpleasant.

Of course, you may use a comma in *all* the examples above if your sense demands it. The contrast set by *but, or,* and *yet* often urges a comma, whether or not full predication follows: "It was strong, yet sweet." Notice that the commas always signal where you would pause in speaking.

The meaningful pause also urges an occasional comma in compound predicates, usually not separated by comma:

He granted the usual permission and walked away.
He granted the usual permission, and walked away.

Both are correct. In the first sentence, however, the granting and walking are perfectly routine, and the temper unruffled. In the second, some kind of emotion has forced a pause, and a comma, after *permission.* Similarly, meaning itself may demand a comma between the two verbs:

He turned and dropped the ball.
He turned, and dropped the ball.

In the first sentence, he turned the ball; in the second, himself. Your **, and** in compound predicates suggests some touch of drama, some meaningful distinction, or afterthought.

You need a comma before *for* and *still* even more urgently. Without the comma, their conjunctive meaning changes; they assume their ordinary roles, *for* as a preposition, *still* as an adjective or adverb:

She liked him still . . . . [that is, either *yet* or *quiet!*]
She liked him, still she could not marry him.
She liked him for his money.
She liked him, for a good man is hard to find.

An observation: *for* is the weakest of all the coordinators. Almost a subordinator, it is perilously close to *because. For* can seem moronic if cause and effect are fairly obvious: "She liked him, for he was kind." Either make a point of the cause by full subordination—"She liked him *because* he was kind"—or flatter the reader with a semicolon: "She liked him; he was kind." *For* is effective only when the cause is somewhat hard to find: "Blessed are the meek, for they shall inherit the earth."

To summarize the basic point (RULE I): put a comma before the coordinator (*and-but-or-nor-yet-still-for*) when joining independent clauses, and add others necessary for emphasis or clarity.

Use commas between all terms in a series, including the last two (RULE II).

Again, the meaningful pause demands a comma. Items in series are equal, and they silently wait for equal treatment:

words, phrases, or clauses in a series

to hunt, to fish, and to hike
He went home, he went upstairs, and he could remember nothing.
He liked oysters, soup, roast beef, wine, and women.

The linguists' recordings will show a pause between the last two items of a series as well as between any other two: not *wine-and-women,* but *wine,* and *women.* The good punctuator would drop the last comma only if he meant *wine and women* as a unit equivalent to *oysters.* Since the last element will always have some climactic or anticlimactic effect, solemn or humorous, don't blur it into the one preceding. Keep *wine* and *women* separate.

By carefully separating all elements in a series, you keep alive a final distinction long ago lost in the daily press, the distinction Mrs. Woolf makes (see page 126): "urbane, polished, brilliant, imploring and commanding him . . . ." *Imploring and commanding* is syntactically equal to each one of the other modifiers in the series. If Mrs. Woolf customarily omitted the last comma, as she does not, she could not have reached for that double apposition. The muscle would have been dead. These other examples of double apposition will give you an idea of its effectiveness:

They cut out his idea, root and branch.
He lost all his holdings, houses and lands.
He loved to tramp the woods, to fish and to hunt.

A comma makes a great deal of difference, of sense and distinction.

But adjectives in series, as distinct from nouns in series, change the game a bit. Notice the difference between the following two strings of adjectives:

a good, unexpected, natural rhyme
a good old battered hat

With adjectives in series, only your sense can guide you. If each seems to modify the noun directly, as in the first example above, use commas. If each seems to modify the total accumulation of adjectives and noun, as with *good* and *old* in the second phrase, do not use commas. Say your phrases aloud, and put your commas in the pauses that distinguish your meaning.

Finally, a special case. Dramatic intensity sometimes allows you to join clauses with commas instead of conjunctions:

She sighed, she cried, she almost died.
I couldn't do it, I tried, I let them all get away.

It passed, it triumphed, it was a good bill.
I came, I saw, I conquered.

The rhetorical intensity of this construction—the Greeks called it *asyndeton*—is obvious. The language is breathless, or grandly emphatic. As Aristotle once said, it is a person trying to say many things at once. The subjects repeat themselves, the verbs overlap, the idea accumulates a climax. By some psychological magic, the clauses of this construction usually come in three's. The comma is its sign. But unless you have a stylistic reason for such a flurry of clauses, go back to the normal comma and conjunction, the semicolon, or the period.

Set off parenthetical openers and afterthoughts with a comma (RULE III).

Again, note the preliminary pause that expresses your meaning:

Besides, she hated it.
However, she liked him.
Inside, everything was snug.

Stunned, he opened the telegram.
Thoroughly disgruntled, he left.
Green with envy, she smiled weakly.

For several reasons, they stayed home.
Being of stout heart, he dieted.
A good man at poker, he still failed at bridge.

Although his listeners looked bored, he kept on talking.
Because it never gets cold, they wear few clothes.
If it is not too much trouble, punctuate accurately.

First observation: a comma often makes considerable difference in meaning:

However she tried, she could not do it.
However, she tried.
However she tried. [??]

You can usually avoid the danger of forgetting the comma and spoiling the sense by substituting *but* for your initial *however*'s: "But she tried." Put your *however*'s within the sentence between commas: "She tried, however, a little longer."

With afterthoughts, the rule still holds: ordinarily you should set them off with a comma. But close sequences of cause and effect (even in openers) often make the comma optional with *for, because,* and *if,* and occasionally with others.

They stayed home for several reasons.
For several reasons they stayed home.
Everything was snug inside.
They wear few clothes because it never gets cold.
Punctuate accurately if you can.

Emphasis makes the difference. A comma would have damaged none of them (when in doubt, follow the rule); it would merely have changed their rhetoric.

Second observation: what looks like an introductory phrase or clause may actually be the subject of the sentence *and should take no comma.* A comma can break up a good marriage of subject and verb. The comma in each of these is an interloper, and should be removed:

That handsome man in the ascot tie, is the groom.
The idea that you should report every observation, is wrong.
The realization that we must be slightly dishonest to be truly kind, comes to all of us sooner or later.

If your clause-as-subject is unusually long, or confusing, you may relieve the pressure by inserting some qualifying remark after it, between two commas:

The idea that you should report every observation, *however insignificant,* is wrong.
The realization that we must be slightly dishonest to be truly kind, *which is obviously the higher motive,* comes to all of us sooner or later.

Third and final observation: our Rule III will comfortably manage the following kinds of preliminaries, afterthoughts, and additions.

(a) When adding a contrasting phrase or clause:

Use a fork, not a knife.
He is ten, not eleven.
The more he earns, the less he has.
Take your subject seriously, yourself with a grain of salt.

(b) When streamlining parallel clauses by omitting the repeated idea:

Jack would eat no fat; his wife, no lean; the dog, only soup.
The Romans lived in marble halls; the British, in mud huts.
On this side of town you will find green suburbs; on that, nothing but salt flats.

(c) In place of the usual colon or dash, when adding informal explanations:

He found what he expected, nothing.
His aim was simple, to win a Volkswagen.

(d) For direct address:

Goodbye, Mr. Chips.
John, please come here.
Really, Mary, you should have known.

(e) When adding a conversational question:

He really can't win, can he?
You're a fine one, aren't you.

(In the second example, since the voice neither rises nor shouts in this kind of question-as-exclamation, you use a properly urbane period.)

(f) When reporting inner thought:

How do they know, he wondered.
She never could leave, she thought.

Notice that these last are the way an author suggests the swiftness and quietness of thought only halfway verbalized. Compare:

"I never could leave," she thought.

Now our heroine is thinking explicitly in words, as if imagining herself speaking aloud.

(g) When identifying the speaker in dialogue:

"You never could leave," she said.
He said, "I want to go home," and began to cry.

Note that in dialogue the question and exclamation marks replace the comma:

"What have I done now?" she said.
"Nothing!" he said.

Enclose parenthetical insertions with a pair of commas (RULE IV).

Here you are cutting a sentence in two and inserting something necessary. But if you do not tie off both ends, your sentence will die on the table:

When he packs his bag, however he goes.
The car, an ancient Packard is still running.
April 10, 1980 is agreeable as a date for final payment.
John Jones, Jr. is wrong.

You do not mean that 1980 is agreeable, or that Junior is wrong. As the rule indicates, parenthetical insertions need a *pair* of commas:

The case, *nevertheless,* was closed.
She will see, *if she has any sense at all,* that he is right.
Sam, *on the other hand,* may be wrong.
Note, *for example,* the excellent brushwork.
John Jones, *M.D.,* and Bill Jones, *Ph.D.,* doctored the punch to perfection.
He stopped at Kansas City, *Missouri,* for two hours.

The same rule applies, of course, to *nonrestrictive* remarks, phrases, and clauses—all elements simply additive, explanatory, and hence parenthetical:

John, *my friend,* will do what he can.
Andy, *his project sunk, his hopes shattered,* was speechless.
The taxes, *which are reasonable,* will be paid.
That man, *who knows,* is not talking.

Think of *nonrestrictive* as "nonessential" to your meaning, hence set off by commas. Think of *restrictive* as essential and "restricting" your meaning, hence not set off at all (use *which* for nonrestrictives, *that* for restrictives; see p. 136):

The taxes that are reasonable will be paid.
Southpaws who are superstitious will not pitch on Friday nights.
The man who knows is not talking.

Commas are often optional. The difference between a restrictive and a nonrestrictive meaning may be very slight. For example, you may take our recent bridegroom either way (but not halfway):

That handsome man, in the ascot tie, is the groom. [nonrestrictive]
That handsome man in the ascot tie is the groom. [restrictive]

Your meaning will dictate your choice. But use *pairs* of commas or none at all. Never separate subject and verb, or verb and object, with just one comma.

Some finer points. One comma of a pair enclosing an inserted remark may coincide with, and, in a sense, overlay, a comma "already there":

In each box, a bottle was broken.
In each box, however, a bottle was broken.

The team lost, and the school was sick.
The team lost, in spite of all, and the school was sick.

The program will work, but the cost is high.
The program will work, of course, but the cost is high.

Between the coordinate clauses, however, a semicolon might have been clearer:

The team lost, in spite of all; and the school was sick.
The program will work, of course; but the cost is high.

Beware: *however,* between commas, cannot substitute for *but,* as in the perfectly good sentence: "He wore a hat, *but* it looked terrible." You would be using a comma where a full stop (period or semicolon) should be.

WRONG:
He wore a hat, however, it looked terrible.

RIGHT (*notice the two meanings*):
He wore a hat; however, it looked terrible.
He wore a hat, however; it looked terrible.

But a simple **, but** avoids both the ambiguity of the floating *however* and the ponderosity of anchoring it with a semicolon, fore or aft: "He wore a hat, but it looked terrible."

Another point. *But* may absorb the first comma of a pair enclosing an introductory remark (although it need not do so):

At any rate, he went.
But, at any rate, he went.
But at any rate, he went.
But [,] if we want another party, we had better clean up.

The party was a success, but [,] if we want another one, we had better clean up.

Treat the "he said" and "she said" of dialogue as a regular parenthetical insertion, within commas, and without capitalizing, unless a new sentence begins.

"I'm going," he said, "whenever I get up enough nerve."
"I'm going," he said. "Whenever I get up enough nerve, I'm really going."

And of course you should put the comma *inside* ALL quotation marks:

"He is a nut," she said.
She called him a "nut," and walked away.

The Semicolon

Use the semicolon only where you could also use a period, unless desperate.

The dogmatic formula that heads this section, which I shall loosen up in a moment, has saved many a punctuator from both despair and a reckless fling of semicolons. Confusion comes from the belief that the semicolon is either a weak colon or a strong comma. It is most effective as neither. It is best as a kind of tight period, a separator of contrasts. Used sparingly, it retains its tight-lipped emphasis; used recklessly, it merely clutters your page. *Never* use it as a colon: its effect is exactly opposite. A colon, as in the preceding sentence, is a green light; a semicolon, as in this sentence, is a stop sign.

Of course, you may occasionally need to unscramble a long line of phrases and clauses, especially those in series and containing internal commas:

You should see that the thought is full, the words well cleaned, the points adjusted; and then your sentence will be ready to go. [*Note that the period rule would still guide you here:* ". . . adjusted. And then . . . ."]

Composition is hard because we often must discover our ideas by writing them out, clarifying them on paper; because we must also find a clear and reasonable order for ideas the mind presents simultaneously; and because we must find, by trial and error, exactly the right words to convey our ideas and our feelings about them.

But the semicolon is better when it pulls related sentences together, replacing the period (or the comma-plus-conjunction) for some unusual emphasis:

She liked him; he was good to her; he had money in the bank.

And better still when it pivots a contrast:

Work when you work; play when you play.
The semicolon is a stop sign; the colon, a green light.

Notice that the semicolon (like the colon) goes *outside* quotation marks:

This was no "stitch in time"; it was complete reconstruction.

The Colon

Use a colon as a green light, or arrow.

The semicolon, as we have seen, makes a full stop; the colon waves the traffic on through the intersection: "Go right ahead," it says, "and you will find what you are looking for." The colon is like one of those huge arrows that says HERE IT IS after you have been following the signs for half a continent. It emphatically and precisely introduces the clarifying detail, the illustrative example, the itemized series, the formal quotation:

Pierpont lived for only one thing: money.
In the end, it was useless: Adams really was too green.
Now he speaks in the romantic mode: "Hasten, O damsel" (I.ii.24).
The Lord helps those who help themselves: Jasper helped himself.
Several things were missing: the silver service, his gold watch, Beth's pearls, and the moonstone.
The committee considered three things: (1) how to reduce expenditures, (2) how to raise more money, and (3) how to handle Smith's unfortunate laxity.
The point is precisely this: no one can win.
He thought not only of home: he thought of grandmother's oatmeal cookies.

Use the colon to introduce quotations.

You naturally introduce long quotations with a colon, indenting them and setting them apart from your own words. Do the same with short quotations within your running text, when they need your sentence but are not part of its grammar:

We remember Sherman's words: "War is hell."

You may use a comma informally:

We remember Sherman's words, "War is hell."

When a quotation is an integral part of your sentence, punctuate as necessary, but do not use a colon:

As Sherman implied, "war is hell" for all concerned.
We remember, as Sherman said, that "war is hell."

Notice that here you do not capitalize "war," although you would capitalize in the most careful scholarly writing, to preserve exactly all the details of your quotation.

Do not use a colon immediately after a verb, a preposition, or the conjunction *that,* where it would break up grammatical connections:

WRONG:
The trouble was: he never listened.
The trouble was that: he never listened.
She liked the simple things, like: swimming pools, diamonds, and unadorned mink.
She was fond of: swimming pools, diamonds, and unadorned mink.

Do not capitalize after a colon, unless what follows is normally capitalized, as with a proper name, a quotation beginning with a capital, or, occasionally, a sequence of several sentences.

RIGHT:
All effort is painful: pleasure comes with achievement.
Again we may say with Churchill: "Never have so many owed so much to so few."
But several major considerations remain: Unending leisure is no blessing for the ordinary mortal. We must be occupied, and yet we cannot forever occupy ourselves. Furthermore, ... [I still prefer a period after *remain,* since the colon tends to tie the first two sentences too closely.]

Parenthesis and Dash

The dash says aloud what the parenthesis whispers. Both enclose interruptions too extravagant for a pair of commas to hold. The dash is the more useful—since whispering tends to annoy—and will remain useful only if not overused. Overdone, it can be a sign of ignorance or laziness. But a well-cultivated dash will give you the ultimate in urbane control. It can serve as a conversational colon. It can set off a concluding phrase—for emphasis. It can bring long introductory matters to focus, as in Freud's sentence on page 125. It can insert a full sentence—a clause is really an incorporated sentence—directly next to a key word. The dash allows you to insert—with a kind of shout!—an occasional exclamation. You may even insert—and who would blame you?—an occasional question. The dash affords a structural complexity with all the tone and alacrity of talk.

With care, you can get much the same power from a parenthesis:

Many philosophers have despaired (somewhat unphilosophically) of discovering any certainties whatsoever.

Thus did Innocent III (I shall return to him shortly) inaugurate an age of horrors.

But in such circumstances (see page 34), be cautious.

Delay had doubled the costs (a stitch in time!), so the plans were shelved.

But dashes seem more generally useful, and here are some special points. When one of a pair of dashes falls where a comma would be, it absorbs the comma:

If one wanted to go, he certainly could.

If one wanted to go—whether invited or not—he certainly could.

Not so with the semicolon:

He wanted to go—whether he was invited or not; she had more sense.

To indicate the dash, type two hyphens (--) flush against the words they separate—not one hyphen between two spaces, nor a hyphen spaced to look exactly like a hyphen.

Put commas and periods *outside* a parenthetical group of words (like this one). (But if you make an entire sentence parenthetical, put the period inside.)

Brackets

Brackets indicate your own words inserted or substituted within a quotation from someone else: "Byron had already suggested that [they] had killed John Keats." You have substituted "they" for "the gentlemen of the *Quarterly Review*" to suit your own context; you do the same when you interpolate a word of explanation: "Byron had already suggested that the gentlemen of the *Quarterly Review* [especially Croker] had killed John Keats." *Do not use parentheses*: they mark the enclosed words as part of the original quotation. Don't claim innocence because your typewriter lacks brackets. Just leave spaces and draw them in later, or type slant lines and tip them with pencil or with the underscore key:

[. . .]

In the example below, you are pointing out with a *sic* (Latin for "so" or "thus"), which you should not italicize, that you are reproducing an error exactly as it appears in the text you are quoting:

"On no occassion [sic] could we trust them."

Similarly you may give a correction after reproducing the error:

"On the twenty-fourth [twenty-third] we broke camp."
"In not one instance [actually, Baldwin reports several instances] did our men run under fire."

Use brackets when you need a parenthesis within a parenthesis:

(see Donald Allenberg, *The Future of Television* [New York, 1973], pp. 15–16)

Your instructor will probably put brackets around the wordy parts of your sentences, indicating what you should cut:

In fact, [the reason] he liked it [was] because it was different.

Quotation Marks and Italics

Put quotation marks around quotations that "run directly into your text" (like this), but *not* around quotations set off from the text and indented. Put periods and commas *inside* quotation marks; put semicolons and colons *outside*:

Now we understand the full meaning of "give me liberty, or give me death."
"This strange disease of modern life," in Arnold's words, remains uncured.
In Greece it was "know thyself"; in America it is "know thy neighbor."
He left after "Hail to the Chief": he could do nothing more.

Although logic often seems to demand the period or comma outside the quotation marks, convention has put them inside for the sake of appearance, even when the sentence ends in a single quoted word or letter:

Clara Bow was said to have "It."
Mark it with "T."

If you have seen the periods and commas outside, you were reading a British book or a freshman's paper.

If you are quoting a phrase that already contains quotation marks reduce the original double marks (") to single ones ('):

ORIGINAL	YOUR QUOTATION
Hamlet's "are you honest?" is easily explained.	**He writes that "Hamlet's 'are you honest?' is easily explained."**

Notice what happens when the quotation within your quotation falls at the end:

A majority of the informants thought *infer* meant "imply."	**Kirk reports that "a majority of the informants thought *infer* meant 'imply.' "**

And notice that a question mark or exclamation point falls between the single and the double quotation marks at the end of a quotation containing a quotation:

"Why do they call it 'the Hippocratic oath'?" she asked.
"Everything can't be 'cool'!" he said.

But heed the following exception:

"I heard someone say, 'Is anyone home?' " she declared.

Do not use *single* quotation marks for your own stylistic flourishes; use *double* quotation marks or, preferably, none:

It was indeed an "affair," but the passion was hardly "grand."
It was indeed an affair, but the passion was hardly grand.

Some "cool" pianists use the twelve-tone scale. [Once you have thus established this slang meaning of *cool,* you may repeat the word without quotation marks.]

In general, of course, you should favor that slang your style can absorb without quotation marks.

Do not use quotation marks for calling attention to words as words. Use italics (an underscore when typing) for the words, quotation marks for their meanings.

This is taking *tergiversation* too literally.
The word *struthious* means "like an ostrich."

Use quotation marks for titles *within* books and magazines: titles of chapters, articles, short stories, songs, and poems; use them also for titles of statues and paintings. But use italics for titles of books, plays, movies, long poems, ships, trains, and airplanes.

Poe's description of how he wrote "The Raven" was attacked in the *Atlantic Monthly* [or: the *Atlantic*].
We saw Michelangelo's "Pietà," a remarkable statue in white marble.
We took the Santa Fe *Chief* from Chicago to Los Angeles.
He read all of Frazer's *The Golden Bough.*
His great-grandfather went down with the *Titanic.*

Italicize foreign words and phrases, unless they have been assimilated into English through usage (your dictionary should have a method for noting the distinction; if it does not, consult one that does):

The statement contained two clichés and one *non sequitur.*
The author of this naïve exposé suffers from an *idée fixe.*

Use neither quotation marks nor italics for the Bible, for its books or parts (Genesis, Old Testament), for other sacred books (Koran, Talmud, Upanishad), and for famous documents like the Magna Carta, the Declaration of Independence, the Communist Manifesto, and the Gettysburg Address.

Ellipsis

(1) Use three spaced periods . . . (the ellipsis mark) when you omit something from a quotation. Do *not* use them in your own text in place of a dash, or in mere insouciance. (2) If you omit the end of a sentence, add the period . . . ✓ (3) If your omission falls after a completed sentence, add the three ellipsis marks to the period already there✓. . . I have put a check over the periods. Notice the difference in spacing. Note that each placement of the ellipsis means something different.

Here is an uncut passage, followed by a shortened version that shows in succession the three kinds of ellipsis, with the third appearing in two variations.

To learn a language, learn as thoroughly as possible a few everyday sentences. This will educate your ear for all future pronunciations. It will give you a fundamental grasp of structure. Some of the details of grammar will begin to appear. It will give you confidence. If you

go abroad, you can buy a newspaper and find your way back to the hotel.

To learn a language, learn (1) . . . a few everyday sentences. This will educate your ear (2) . . . . It will give you a fundamental grasp of structure. (3) . . . It will give you confidence. (3) . . . you can buy a newspaper and find your way back to the hotel.

The three spaced dots of the ellipsis may fall on either side of other punctuation, to indicate exactly where you have omitted something from the text you are quoting:

In many instances . . . , our careful words are superfluous.
In many instances of human crisis, . . . words are superfluous.
We have the bombs . . . ; it looks as if they have the troops.
Eighteenth-century prisons were vicious: . . . the people no less than the rats and the fevers.
Alas, poor Yorick! . . . a fellow of infinite jest.
In this sonnet, Shakespeare is well aware of the foolishness of self-pity: "And trouble deaf heaven with my bootless cries,/ . . . and curse my fate, ..."

If you omit a line or more of poetry, or a paragraph or more of prose, and *if the omission is significant,* use a whole line of elliptical dots:

When in disgrace with Fortune and men's eyes,
I all alone beweep my outcast state,
And trouble deaf heaven with my bootless cries,
. . . . .
Yet in these thoughts myself almost despising,
Haply I think on thee, ...

If the omission had not been significant, the ellipsis would have followed *cries*:

And trouble deaf heaven with my bootless cries, . . .
Yet in these thoughts . . . .

Be sure that your omissions do not distort your author's meaning. And remember this: *the shorter your quotation, the better.* A short quotation puts your purpose into sharpest focus for your reader's attention. A long quotation may require you to requote or paraphrase to make your point.

If you begin to quote in the middle of a sentence, place three elliptical dots before the first quoted word:

> **. . . whether this august republican Union, founded by some of the wisest statesmen that ever lived, cemented with the blood of some of the purest patriots that ever died, should perish or endure. . . .**

But if you quote a full sentence that falls in the middle of a paragraph, omit the initial elliptical dots:

> **We have come to dedicate a portion of that field as a final resting place for those who here gave their lives that that nation might live. It is altogether fitting and proper that we should do this.**
>
> **But, in a larger sense . . . .**

When you use a short partial quotation within a sentence, you can omit the beginning and ending ellipses:

> **Lincoln was determined that the Union, "cemented with the blood of . . . the purest patriots," would not fail.**

Use the ellipsis in quoted material only. If you use it in your own text, you will seem to drift like a girl on the summer moor, which is precisely what it means in a novel: the passage of time, or the drifting of thought. Only most rarely can you work it into expository prose, as in Katherine Anne Porter's description of Sylvia Beach. The ellipsis following the first sentence is a part of the passage:

> **. . . her modest entirely incidental vanities, face powder, beauty cream, lipstick. . . .**
>
> **Oh, no. She was not there. And someone had taken away the tiger skin from her bed—narrow as an army cot.**

It is dramatic, and risky. You risk seeming affected. I have used it only once in this entire book (p. 26), and I do not recall ever having used it before:

> **Even the dog-lovers will be uninterested, convinced they know better than you. But the cat . . . .**
>
> **So it is with any unpopular idea. The more unpopular the viewpoint and the stronger the push against convention, the stronger the thesis and the more energetic the essay.**

As I threw the cat in after the dogs to emphasize a point already made, the ellipsis seemed right. But the exception does not overturn the rule: use ellipsis marks in quoted material only.

Apostrophe

Add *'s* to form the singular possessive (*dog's life, man's world, horse's mouth, Marx's ideas*)—and even with words already ending in *s* (*Yeats's poems, Charles's crown, Leavis's error, Moses's law, Pericles's Athens, Vassilikos's work*). A few plurals also form the possessive by adding *'s* (*children's hour, men's attitudes, women's rights, mice's hole, sheep's bellwether*). But most plurals take the apostrophe after the *s* already there (*witches' sabbath, ten cents' worth, citizens' rights, the Joneses' possessions,* and similarly, *The Beaux' Strategem*).

I repeat, the rule for making singulars possessive is to add *'s*, regardless of length and previous ending. Of course, many people will merely add the apostrophe to names already ending in *s* (*Dickens' novels, Adams' horse*). Indeed, we can make possessives of some French words in no other way: *Camus' works, Marivaux' life, Berlioz' Requiem.* And certainly there is colloquial and auditory cause for so handling the longest names, as with *Themistocles' death* and *Aristophanes' wit.*

But *Sis' plans* and *the boss' daughter* are not what we say, and, even with long words, I myself find the added *s* an improvement in euphony as well as in sense: *ThemIStoCLESes DEATH, ArisTOPHanESes WIT.* The same is true for *Horace's satires, Catullus's villa, Cummings's style, Dickens's Pip.* The extra *s* makes no mistake, and you may prefer to distinguish Dickens from Dicken and Adams from Adam. If your page grows too thick with double *s*'s, substitute a few pronouns for the proper names, or rephrase: *the death of Themistocles, the Dickens character, Pip.*

The apostrophe can help to clarify clusters of nouns. These I have actually seen: *Alistair Jones Renown Combo, the church barbecue chicken sale, the uniform policeman training program, the members charter plane.* And of course, *teachers meeting* and *veterans insurance* are so common as to seem almost normal. But an apostrophe chips one more noun out of the block. It makes your meaning one word clearer, marking *teachers'* as a modifier, and distinguishing *teacher* from *teachers.* Inflections are helpful, and the written word needs all the help it can get: *Jones's Renowned, church's barbecued, uniformed policeman's, members' chartered.* Distinguish your modifiers, and keep your possessions.

Don't forget the *'s* in the possessive before a gerund:

She objected to Bill's smoking.
The teacher's leaving upset our plans.
He didn't like anyone's working overtime.

Your *'s* makes clear that she is not objecting to Bill and that "He" is not disliking anyone: the smoking and the working are being disliked.

Compound words take the *'s* on the last word only: *mother-in-law's hat, the brothers-in-law's attitude* (all the brothers-in-law have the same attitude), *somebody else's problem, Governor Cass of Michigan's proposal.* Joint ownerships may similarly take the *'s* only on the last word (*Bill and Mary's house*), but *Bill's and Mary's* house is more precise, and preferable.

Possessive pronouns have no apostrophe: *hers, its, theirs, yours, whose, oneself* (but *one's self,* if you are emphasizing the self). Note that *it's* means *it is,* and that *who's* means *who is;* for possession, use *its* and *whose.*

The double possessive uses both an *of* and an *'s*: *a friend of my mother's, a book of the teacher's, a son of the Joneses', an old hat of Mary's.* Note that the double possessive indicates one possession among several of the same kind: mother has several friends; the teacher, several books.

Use the apostrophe to indicate omissions: *the Spirit of '76, the Class of '02, can't, won't, don't.* Finally, use the apostrophe when adding a grammatical ending to a number, letter, sign, or abbreviation: *1920's;* his *3's* look like *8's; p's* and *q's;* he got four *A's;* too many *of's* and *and's;* she *X'd* each box; *K.O.'d* in the first round.

Hyphen

"*Time* abhors the hyphen," someone once said, and, ever since James Joyce's *hoofirons* and *steelyringing,* modern print has tended to compound the work of time and *Time* by squeezing the hyphens out of compounds. But the unfamiliar compound is hard on the eye, and the hyphens come back in—until another burst of editorial housekeeping.

The oldest and most useful compounds have coalesced from their original two words, first through hyphenation, then into one solid compound. *Housekeeping,* with the *housekeeper,* has scrubbed out the hyphen entirely. But many very common compounds live happily separated: *horse racing, Adam's apple, all right, blood pressure, stock market, girl friend.* And many very common compounds go steadily hyphenated, and go no further: *blue-pencil, clear-cut, deep-freeze, good-bye, mother-in-law.* Check your dictionary.

But one rule remains solid: hyphenate two or more words serving together as an adjective. Unhyphenated words acquire hyphens when moved to an adjectival position:

She teaches in high school.
She is a high-school teacher.

He was sick of olive drab.
He was sick of his olive-drab uniform.

He was well known.
He was a well-known drifter.

His serve is red hot.
He has a red-hot serve.

It was never to be forgotten.
It was a never-to-be-forgotten gesture.

You will have to check the hyphenation of prefixes and suffixes in your dictionary, but you can be sure of hyphenating prefixes to proper names:

anti-Semitism	**trans-Russian**
post-Crimean War	**un-American**

Similarly, hyphenate suffixes to single capital initials:

F-sharp	**U-turn**
I-beam	**V-neck**
T-shirt	**X-ray**

Hyphenate *ex-*, meaning former, and *self-* (except *selfhood, selfless,* and *selfsame*):

ex-champion	**self-reliance**
ex-president	**self-respect**

Hyphenate to distinguish meanings:

co-op from coop	**re-collect from recollect**
re-cover from recover	**re-creation from recreation**

Hyphenate to avoid doubling *i*'s and tripling consonants:

anti-intellectual	**bell-like**
semi-invalid	**wall-less**

Hyphenate compound words expressing numbers:

twenty-one	**three-fourths**
ninety-nine	**one ten-thousandth**
three hundred twenty-four	**twenty-one forty-fourths**

Use the "suspensive" hyphen for hyphenated words in series:

We have ten-, twenty-five-, and fifty-pound sizes.
He still prefers the six- to the eight-cylinder job.

Or, with only two items, you can avoid the truncated look by using a few more words:

He still prefers the six-cylinder job to the eight-cylinder one.

Diacritical Marks

Many foreign words, though very common in English, retain their native markings, as in *naïveté*. Diacritical marks occasionally appear on native words, as when a writer wishes to distinguish the *learnèd man* from what he has learned. Here are some specifics:

Diaeresis (*coöperation, coördinate, naïve, Chloë, Danaë*). Let your dictionary be your guide. Newspapers tend to omit the diaerisis, and some very common doubles go unmarked in the most meticulous print, as with *coordination* in this book, and with *cooperation* and *zoology*. But *coördination, coöperation,* and *zoölogy* are perfectly acceptable. You also use the diaeresis to indicate the umlaut in German words: *über, Fräulein, Götterdämmerung.*

Acute accent. For certain words borrowed from French. The *é* sounds like the *a* in *hay*:

attaché	**fiancé, fiancée**
blasé	**habitué**
café	**naïveté**
cliché	**outré**
communiqué	**passé**
décor	**précis**
décolleté	**protégé, protégée**
éclat	**résumé**
exposé	**séance**

Grave accent. For words from French. The *à* sounds like *a* in *ah;* the *è* like the *e* in *bet.*

à la carte	***mise en scène***
à la mode	**Molière**
crème de la crème	***pièce de résistance***

Circumflex accent. Also for words from French. The *â* sounds like *ah;* the *ê* like the *e* in *bet;* the *ô,* like the *o* in *holes*:

bête noire	***raison d'être***
coup de grâce	**table d'hôte**
papier-mâché	**tête-à-tête**

Cedilla. For words from French, the ç being pronounced *s*:

aperçu	***garçon***
façade	**Provençal**
français	**soupçon**

Tilde. For Spanish words pronouncing *n* like the *ny* in *canyon*: *doña, mañana, señor, vicuña.*

Virgule

Spare this "little rod" (/), and don't spoil your work with the legalistic *and/or.* Don't write "bacon and/or eggs"; write "bacon or eggs, or both." But you should learn to use the virgule when quoting poetry in your running text: "That time of year thou mayst in me behold/When yellow leaves, or none, or few, do hang/Upon those boughs which shake against the cold,/Bare ruin'd choirs where late the sweet birds sang."

Exercises

1. Write five fragments that are unmistakable accidents, crying out for attachment to some governing sentence. Then write five complete sentences with these fragments properly attached.

2. Write three groups of three or four sentences, each group containing a *rhetorical* fragment that cannot be mistaken for a mistake.

3. Write five sentences containing indirect questions, ending them properly with periods.

4. Write six pairs of sentences, using the six conjunctions *and, but, for, or, yet, still,* on the pattern:

He hunted the hills and . . . .
He hunted the hills, and . . . .

5. Write five pairs of sentences with compound predicates, each pair identical except that the second sentence contains a dramatic comma between the verbs:

He dropped the ball and walked away.
He dropped the ball, and walked away.

6. Write five pairs of sentences with compound predicates showing how a comma changes verbal meaning, briefly explaining the difference in meaning after each:

He turned and dropped the ball.
He turned, and dropped the ball.

(In the first sentence he could be turning the ball; in the second, he himself turns around, which makes him drop the ball.)

7. Write five sentences with concluding double appositives which might look like parts of a simple series but which are not: "He loved to tramp the woods, to hunt and to fish."

8. Write five asyndetic sentences (see p. 151), each with three clauses.

9. Master *however* by writing two groups of three sentences on the following pattern:

However she tried, she could not do it.
She tried, however, a very long time.
She tried; however, she could not do it.

10. Write three sentences with long clauses as subjects, avoiding the temptation of putting a comma after the clause. Then repeat each of these sentences, but after each subject-clause insert a qualifying remark, between commas, thus setting the subject apart from its verb for clearer distinction (see p. 152).

11. Write five pairs of sentences to practice enclosing parenthetical insertions within a pair of commas:

April 10 is agreeable.
April 10, 1980, is agreeable.

The taxes will be paid.
The taxes, which are reasonable, will be paid.

12. Do the same with dashes and with parentheses.

13. Write five pairs of sentences showing the difference between nonrestrictive and restrictive clauses on the pattern:

The taxes, which are reasonable, will be paid.
The taxes that are reasonable will be paid.

14. Write five compound sentences, using a semicolon between two contrasting independent clauses.

15. Write five sentences on the pattern:

The semicolon is a stop sign; the colon, a green light.

16. Write five sentences using the colon to introduce a complete clarifying "sentence"—that is, write your sentence so that the colon is clearly more meaningful than a period and new capitalization would have been:

In the end, it was useless: he really was too green.
The point is precisely this: no one can win.

17. Think up, or collect from observation, five strings of nouns an *'s* would help clarify; then clarify each string:

the church barbecue chicken sale
the church's barbecued chicken sale
[They were not cooking the church.]

the sophomore cheesecake rally
the sophomores' cheesecake rally
[The cheesecake was no sophomore.]

18. To strengthen your perception of the possessive before a gerund, write five pairs of sentences on the following pattern, explaining after each pair the difference in meaning:

He didn't like anyone working overtime.
He didn't like anyone's working overtime.

19. Write five pairs of sentences demonstrating your control of the hyphen:

She teaches in high school.
She is a high-school teacher.

It was never to be forgotten.
It was a never-to-be-forgotten gesture.

Words

11

Here is the word. Sesquipedalian or short, magniloquent or low, Latin or Anglo-Saxon, Celtic, Danish, French, Spanish, Indian, Hindustani, Dutch, Italian, Portuguese, Chinese, Hebrew, Turkish, Greek—English contains them all, a million words at our disposal, if we are disposed to use them. Although no language is richer than English, our expository vocabularies average probably fewer than 8,000 words. We could all increase our active vocabularies; we all have a way to go to possess our inheritance.

Vocabulary

If you can increase your hoard, you increase your chances of finding the right word, *le mot juste,* when you need it. Read as widely as you can, and look words up the second or third time you meet them. I once knew a man who swore he learned three new words a day from his reading by using each at least once in conversation. I didn't ask him about *polyphiloprogenitive* or *antidisestablishmentarianism.* It depends a little on the crowd. But the idea is sound. The bigger the vocabulary, the more various the ideas one can get across with it—the more the shades and intensities of meaning.

The big vocabulary also needs the little word. The vocabularian often stands himself on a Roman cloud and forgets the Anglo-Saxon ground—the common ground between him and his audience. So do not forget the little things, the *stuff, lint, get, twig, snap, go, mud, coax.* Hundreds of small words not in immediate vogue can refresh your vocabulary. The Norse and Anglo-Saxon adjectives in *-y* (*muggy, scrawny, drowsy*), for instance, rarely appear in sober print. The minute the beginner tries to sound dignified, in comes a misty layer of words a few feet off the ground and nowhere near heaven, the same two dozen or so, most of them verbs. One or two will do no harm, but any accumulation is fatal—words like *depart* instead of *go:*

accompany—go with
appeared—looked *or* seemed
arrive—come
attempt—try
become—get
cause—make
cease—stop
complete—finish
continue—keep on
delve—dig
discover—find
locate—find
place—put
possess—have
prepare—get ready
questioned—asked
receive—get
relate—tell
remain—stay
remove—take off
retire—go to bed
return—go back
secure—get
transform—change

I add one treasured noun: *manner—way.* The question, as always, is one of meaning. *Manner* is something with a flourish; *way* is the usual way. But the beginner makes no distinction, losing the normal *way,* and meaning, in a false flourish of *manners.* Similarly, "she *placed* her cigarettes on the table" is usually not what the writer means. *Delve* is something that happens only when students begin to meditate. *Get* and *got* may be too colloquial for constant use in writing, but a discreet one or two can limber many a stiff sentence. Therefore, use the elegant Latin and the commonplace Anglo-Saxon, tastefully fitted; but shun the frayed gentility of *secure* and *place* and *remain,* whose shades of meaning you can find in your dictionary.

Abraham Lincoln read the dictionary from cover to cover, and you really can browse it with pleasure, looking at the pictures and finding out about aardvarks and axolotyles, jerboas and jerkins. You can amaze yourself at the number of things *set* can mean. Best of all, you can look at a word's derivation and get a quick sense of our linguistic history, of families of words and ideas, of how some meanings have changed and some others have persisted through centuries and across continents. *Mid,* for instance, is still what it has been for the last 5,000 years, persisting in most of the Indo-European languages all the way from Old Norse to Sanskrit and giving English a whole family of words from *middle* to *intermezzo.* Acquaintance with a family can make you feel at home. You can know and use a *ramp,* or a *rampage,* or a lion *rampant* familiarly, once you see the Old French for *climb* in all three. You can cut your meaning close to the old root, as in "He was *enduring* and *hard* as nails," where the Latin *durus* ("hard") has suggested its Anglo-Saxon synonym and given you a phrase your readers will like, though most of them won't know why.

Through the centuries, English has added Latin derivatives alongside the Anglo-Saxon words already there, keeping the old with the new: after the Anglo-Saxon *deor* (now *deer*) came the *beast* and then the *brute,* both from Latin through French, and the *animal* straight from Rome. Although we use more Anglo-Saxon in assembling our sentences (*to, by, with, though, is*), well over half our total vocabulary comes one way or another from Latin. The things of this world tend to be Anglo-Saxon (*man, house, stone, wind, rain*): the abstract qualities, Latin and French (*value, duty, contemplation*).

Our big words are Latin and Greek. Your reading acquaints you with them; your dictionary will show you their prefixes and roots. Learn the common prefixes and roots (see Exercises, this chapter), and you can handle all kinds of foreigners at first encounter: *concession* (going along with), *ex-clude* (lock out), *pre-fer* (carry before), *sub-version* (turning under), *trans-late* (carry across), *claustro-*

phobia (dread of being locked in), *hydro-phobia* (dread of water), *ailuro-philia* (love of cats), *megalo-cephalic* (big-headed), *micro-meter* (little-measurer). You can even, for fun, coin a word to suit the occasion: *megalopede* (big-footed). You can remember that *intramural* means "within the (college) walls," and that "intermural sports," which is the frequent mispronunciation and misspelling, would mean something like "wall battling wall," a physical absurdity.

Besides a good dictionary, you should own Roget's *Thesaurus,* the treasury of synonyms ("together-names"), in which you can find the word you couldn't think of, and all the shades of good and bad you want, from *pants* through *trousers* to *galligaskins.* Peter Roget's great work of 1852, compiled for fifty years and since augmented and refined, is indeed a treasury. Any one word will open the door. And once the writer sees all the resources, all the related words, "an instinctive tact," as Roget says, "will rarely fail to lead him to the proper choice." Checking for meaning in a dictionary will assure that your instincts are sound.

Learn to spell the words you use.

The dictionary is your best friend as you face the inevitable anxieties of spelling, but three underlying principles and some tricks of the trade can help immeasurably:

Principle I. Letters represent sounds: proNUNciation can help you spell. No one proNOUNcing his words correctly would make the familiar errors of "similiar" and "enviorment." You can even improve your social standing by learning to say *envIRONment* and *goverNment* and *FebRUary* and *intRAmural.* Simply sound out the letters. You can even say "convert*i*ble" and "indel*i*ble" and "plaus*i*ble" without sounding like a fool, and you can silently stress the *able* in words like "prob*able*" and "immov*able*" to remember the difficult distinction between words ending in *-ible,* and *-able.*

Consonants reliably represent their sounds. Remember that *c* and *g* go soft before *i* and *e.* Consequently you must add a *k* when extending words like *picnic* and *mimic—picnicKing, mimicKing*—to keep them from rhyming with *slicing* or *dicing.* Conversely, you just keep the *e* (where you would normally drop it) when making *peace* into *peacE-able* and *change* into *changEable,* to keep the *c* and *g* soft.

Single *s* is pronounced *zh* in words like *vision, occasion, pleasure.* Knowing that *ss* hushes ("sh-h-h") will keep you from errors like *occassion,* which would sound like *passion.*

Vowels sound short and light before single consonants: *hat, pet, mit(t), hop, mut(t).* When you add any vowel (including *y*) the first vowel will say its name: *hate, Pete, mite, hoping, mutable.* Notice how the *a* in *-able* keeps the main vowel saying its name in words like *unmistakable, likable,* and *notable.* Therefore, to keep a vowel short, protect it with a double consonant: *petting, hopping.* This explains the troublesome *rr* in *occuRRence*: a single *r* would make it say *cure* in the middle. *Putting* a golf ball and *putting* something on paper must both use *tt* to keep from being pronounced *pewting.* Compare *stony* with *sonny* and *bony* with *bonny.* The *y* is replacing the *e* in *stone* and *bone,* and the rule is working perfectly. It works in any syllable that is accented: compare *forgeTTable* as against *markeTing, begiNNing* as against *buttoNing,* and *compeLLing* as against *traveLing.*

Likewise, when *full* combines and loses its stress, it also loses an *l.* Note the single and double *l* in *fulFILLment.* Similarly, *SOULful, GRATEful, AWful*—even *SPOONful.*

Principle II. This is the old rule of *i* before *e,* and its famous exceptions.

I before *e*
Except after *c*,
Or when sounded like *a*
As in *neighbor* and *weigh*.

It works like a charm (*achieve, believe, receive, conceive*). Note that *c* needs an *e* to make it sound like *s.* Remember also that *leisure* was once pronounced "lay-sure," and *foreign,* "forayn." Memorize these important exceptions: *seize, weird, either, sheik, forfeit, counterfeit.* Note that all are pronounced "ee" (with a little crowding) and that the *e* comes first. Then note that another small group goes the opposite way, having a long *i* sound as in German "Heil"; *height, sleight, seismograph, kaleidoscope. Financier,* another exception, follows its French origin and its original sound.

Principle III. Most big words, following the Latin or French from which they came, spell their sounds letter for letter. Look up the derivations of the words you misspell (note that double *s*, and explain it). You will never again have trouble with *desperate* and *separate* once you discover that the first comes from *de-spero,* "without hope," and that sePARate divides equals, the PAR values in stocks or golf. Nor with *definite* or *definitive,* once you see the kinship of both with *finite* and *finish.* Derivations can also help you a little with the devilment of *-able* and *-ible,* since, except for a few ringers, the *i* remains from Latin, and the *-ables* are either French (*ami-able*) or Anglo-Saxon copies (*workable*). Knowing origins can help at crucial points: *resemblAnce* comes from Latin *simulAre,* "to copy"; *existEnce* comes from Latin *existEre,* "to stand forth."

The biggest help comes from learning the common Latin prefixes, which, by a process of assimilation (*ad-similis,* "like to like"), account for the double consonants at the first syLLabic joint of so many of our words:

AD- (toward, to): *abbreviate* (shorten down), *accept* (grasp to).
CON- (with): *collapse* (fall with), *commit* (send with).
DIS- (apart): *dissect* (cut apart), *dissolve* (loosen apart).
IN- (into): *illuminate* (shine into), *illusion* (playing into).
IN- (not): *illegal* (not lawful), *immature* (not ripe).
INTER- (between): *interrupt* (break between), *interrogate* (ask between).
OB- (toward, to): *occupy* (take in), *oppose* (put to), *offer* (carry to).
SUB- (under): *suffer* (bear under), *suppose* (put down).
SYN- ("together"—this one is Greek): *symmetry* (measuring together), *syllogism* (logic together).

Spelling takes a will, an eye, and an ear. And a dictionary. Keep a list of your favorite enemies. Memorize one or two a day. Write them in the air in longhand. Visualize them. Imagine a blinking neon sign, with the wicked letters red and tall—d e f i n I t e—d e f i n I t e. Then print them once, write them twice, and blink them a few times more as you go to sleep. But best of all, make up whatever devices you can—the crazier the better—to remember the tricky parts:

DANCE attenDANCE.
EXISTENCE is TENSE.
There's IRON in this enVIRONment.
The resisTANCE took its STANCE.
There's an ANT on the defendANT.
LOOSE as a goose.
LOSE loses an O.
ALLOT isn't A LOT.
Already isn't ALL RIGHT.
I for gaIety.
The LL in paraLLel gives me *el.*
PURR in PURsuit.

Here are some of the perpetual headaches:

accept—except
accommodate
acknowledgment—judgment
advice—advise
affect—effect
allusion—illusion—disillusion
analysis—analyzing—annual
apologize—Apollo
arrangement—argument
businessman
capital—capitol
careful—successful—fulfillment
challenge
cite—site—insight
committee
complement—compliment
council—counsel—consul
curriculum—career—occurrence
decide—divide—devices
desert—dessert
despair—desperate—separate
detrimental—dealt
dilemma—condemn
disastrous
embarrassment—harassment
eminent—imminent—immanent
exaggerate
explanation
forward—foreword
genius—ingenious
height—eighth
hypocrisy—democracy
irritable
lonely—loneliness
Negroes—heroes—tomatoes
obstacle
operate (opus, opera)
possession
primitive
principal—principle
proceed—precede—procedure
until—till

Check your capitals.

You know about sentences and names, certainly; but the following points are troublesome. Capitalize:

1. Names of races and languages—Negro, Indian, French, English.
2. North, south, east, and west *only when they are regions*—the mysterious East, the new Southwest.
3. The *complete* names of churches, rivers, hotels, and the like—the First Baptist Church, the Mark Hopkins Hotel, the Suwannee River (not First Baptist church, Mark Hopkins hotel, Suwannee river).
4. All words in titles, except prepositions, articles, and conjunctions. But capitalize even these if they come first or last, or if they are longer than five letters—"I'm Through with Love," *Gone with the Wind,* "I'll Stand By," *In Darkest Africa.* Capitalize nouns, adjectives, and prefixes in hyphenated compounds—*The Eighteenth-Century Background, The Anti-Idealist* (but *The Antislavery Movement*). But when referring to magazines and newspapers in sentences, drop the *The* as part of the

title (the *Saturday Evening Post,* the Kansas City *Star*—note that only *Star,* or *Tribune,* or *Times* is treated as the newspaper's proper title).

5. References to a specific section of a work—the Index, his Preface, Chapter 1, Act II, Scene iii, Volume IV.

6. Abstract nouns, when you want emphasis, serious or humorous—". . . the truths contradict, so what is Truth?"; Very Important Person; the Ideal.

Do not capitalize the seasons—spring, winter, midsummer.

Do not capitalize after a colon, unless what follows is normally capitalized (see p. 158).

Abstract and Concrete

An understanding of the distinction between abstract and concrete words lies at the center of any style. Tangible things—things we can touch—are "concrete"; their qualities, along with all our emotional, intellectual, and spiritual states, are "abstract." The rule for a good style is to be as concrete as you can, to illustrate tangibly your general propositions, to use *shoes* and *ships* and *sealing wax* instead of *commercial concomitants.* But this requires constant effort: our minds so crave abstraction we can hardly pin them down to specifics.

Abstraction, a "drawing out from," is the very nature of thought. Thought moves from concrete to abstract. In fact, *all* words are abstractions. *Stick* is a generalization of all sticks, the crooked and the straight, the long and the short, the peeled and the shaggy. No word fits its object like a glove, because words are not things: words represent ideas of things. They are the means by which we class eggs and tents and trees so that we can handle them as ideas—not as actual things but as *kinds* of things. A man can hold an egg in his hand, but he cannot think about it, or talk about it, unless he has some larger idea with which his mind, too, can grasp it, some idea like *thing,* or *throwing thing,* or *egg*—which classes this one white ellipsoid with all the eggs he has known, from ostrich to hummingbird, with the *idea* of egg. One word per item would be useless; it would be no idea at all, since ideas represent not items, but *classes* of items.

In fact, abstract words can attain a power of their own, as the rhetorician heightens attention to their meanings. This ability, of course, does not come easily or soon. First, and for the present, I repeat, you need to be as concrete as you can, to illustrate tangibly, to pin your abstractions down to specifics. But once you have learned this, you can move on to the rhetoric of abstraction, which is, indeed, a kind of squeezing of abstract words for their specific juice.

Lincoln does exactly this, as we have seen, when he concentrates on *dedication* six times within ten sentences—in his dedication at Gettysburg. Similarly, Eliot refers to "faces / Distracted from distraction by distraction" (*Four Quartets*). Actually, most of the rhetorical devices in Appendix C likewise concentrate on abstract essences:

> **. . . tribulation works patience, and patience experience, and experience hope. (Rom. v.3–4.)**
> **The humble are proud of their humility.**
> **Care in your youth so you may live without care.**

An able writer like Samuel Johnson can make a virtual poetry of abstractions, as he alliterates and balances them against each other (I have capitalized the alliterations and italicized the balances):

> **Dryden's performances were always hasty, either *Excited* by some *External occasion*, or *Extorted* by some *domestic necessity;* he *ComPosed without Consideration*, and *Published without Correction.***

Notice especially how *excited* ("called forth") and *extorted* ("twisted out"), so alike in sound and form, so alike in making Dryden write, nevertheless contrast their opposite essential meanings. Johnson thus extorts the specific juice of each abstract word.

So before we disparage abstraction, we should acknowledge its rhetorical power; and we should understand that it is an essential distillation, a primary and natural and continual mental process. We cannot do without it. We could not make four of two and two. So we make abstractions of abstractions to handle bigger and bigger groups of ideas. *Egg* becomes *food*, and *food* becomes *nourishment*. We also classify all the psychic and physical qualities we can recognize: *candor, truth, anger, beauty, negligence, temperament.* But because our thoughts drift upward, we need always to look for the word that will bring them nearer earth, that will make our abstractions seem visible and tangible, that will make them graspable—mentioning a *handle*, or a *pin*, or an *egg*, alongside our abstraction, for instance. We have to pull our abstractions down within reach of our reader's own busily abstracting headpiece.

In short, we must pin our abstractions down with constant comparisons to the concrete eggs from which they sprang. I might have written that sentence—as I found myself starting to do: "Abstractions should be actualized by a process of constant comparisons with the concrete objects which they represent." But note what I have done to pull this down within reach. First, I have used *we*—that is, you and me, real people—and I have cut the inhuman passive voice to put us in the act. Then I have changed *actualize* to *pin down,* a visible action that, being commonplace and proverbial, makes us feel at home among the abstractions. I have replaced the abstract *by a process of* with its simpler abstract equivalent *with.* More important, I have made *eggs* stand for all objects—and note how easily our abstracters take this in. Furthermore, I have punned on *concrete,* making it, for a fleeting instant, into cement. How? By choosing *egg,* something that could really be made out of concrete, instead of *stick* (which I had first put there): a concrete stick is not much as a physical possibility. Finally, I have gone on to use *egg* also as a real egg by having the abstract ideas spring from it. Later, I almost changed *sprang* to *hatched,* but decided that this was too vivid. It would make the concrete egg too nearly real, and the picture of broken cement with fluffy abstractions peeping forth would have gotten in the way of the idea—that is, the disembodied abstract concept—I was trying to convey.

The writer's ultimate skill perhaps lies in making a single object represent its whole abstract class. I have paired each abstraction below with its concrete translation:

***Friendliness* is the salesman's best asset.**
***A smile* is the salesman's best asset.**

A *proper protein diet* might have save John Keats.
A *good steak* might have saved John Keats.

To *understand* the world by *observing all of its geological details* . . . .
To *see* the world in *a grain of sand* . . . .

Metaphor

As you have probably noticed, I have been using metaphors—the most useful way of making our abstractions concrete. The word is Greek for "transfer" (*meta* equals *trans* equals *across; phor* equals *fer* equals *ferry*). The idea is that of representing something as if it were something else, objects as if all of them were eggs, abstractions as if they were chickens that are also vaguely like flowers springing, thought as if it were rising steam. Metaphors illustrate, in a word, our general ideas. I might have written at length about how an idea is like an egg. I did, in fact, follow each declaration with an example, and I illustrated the point with a man holding an egg. But the metaphor makes the comparison at a stroke. I used our common word *grasp* for "understanding," comparing the mind to something with hands, *transferring* the physical picture of the clutching hand to the invisible mental act.

Almost all our words are metaphors, usually with the physical picture faded. *Transfer* itself pictures a physical portage. When the company *transfers* its men, it is sending them about the country as if by piggyback, or raft, or whatever. But mercifully the physical facts have faded—*transfer* has become a "dead metaphor"—and we can use the word in comfortable abstraction. Now, precisely because we are constantly abstracting, constantly letting the picture fade, you can use metaphor to great advantage—or disastrously, if your eyes aren't sharp. With metaphors, you avoid the nonpictorial quality of most of our writing; you make your writing both vivid and unique. As Aristotle said, the metaphor is clear, agreeable, and strange; like a solved riddle, it is the most delightful of teachers.

It seems to me that there are four levels of metaphor, each with a different clarity and force (and, as you will see, we must here distinguish between the general idea of "metaphor" as the whole process of transfer, and that specific thing called "a metaphor"). Suppose you wrote "She snorted, and tossed the red mane of her hair." You have transferred to a woman the qualities of a horse to make her appearance and personality vivid. You have chosen one of the four ways to make this transfer, which I shall simplify for clarity, and then discuss:

Simile:	**She was *like* a horse.**	**(I)**
	She stopped *as* a horse stops.	
	She stopped *as if* she were a horse.	
Metaphor:	**She was a horse.**	**(II)**
Implied metaphor:	**She snorted and tossed her mane.**	**(III)**
Dead metaphor:	**She bridled.**	**(IV)**

I. *Simile.* The simile is the most obvious form the metaphor can take, and hence would seem elementary. But it has powers of its own, particularly where the writer seems to be trying urgently to express the inexpressible, comparing his subject to several different possibilities, no one wholly adequate. In *The Sound and the Fury,* Faulkner thus describes two jaybirds (my italics):

> **[they] whirled up on the blast *like gaudy scraps of cloth or paper* and lodged in the mulberries, . . . screaming into the wind that ripped their harsh cries onward and away *like scraps of paper or of cloth* in turn.**

The simile has a high poetic energy. D. H. Lawrence uses it frequently, as here in *The Plumed Serpent* (my italics):

> **The lake was quite black, *like a great pit.* The wind suddenly blew with violence, with a strange ripping sound in the mango trees, *as if some membrane in the air were being ripped.***

II. *Metaphor.* The plain metaphor makes its comparison in one imaginative leap. It is shorthand for "as if she were a horse"; it pretends, by exaggeration (*hyperbole*), that she *is* a horse. We move instinctively to this kind of exaggerated comparison as we try to convey our impressions with all their emotional impact. "He was a maniac at Frisbee," we might say, "a dynamo, a computer." The metaphor is probably our most common figure of speech: *the pigs, the swine, a plum, a gem, a phantom of delight, a shot in the arm.* It may be humorous or bitter; it may be simply and aptly visual: "The road was a ribbon of silver." Thoreau extends a metaphor through several sentences in one of his most famous passages:

> **Time is but the stream I go a-fishing in. I drink at it; but while I drink I see the sandy bottom and detect how shallow it is. Its thin current slides away, but eternity remains. I would drink deeper; fish in the sky, whose bottom is pebbly with stars.**

III. *Implied Metaphor.* The implied metaphor is even more widely useful. It operates most often among the verbs, as in *snorted* and *tossed,* the horsy verbs suggesting "horse." Most ideas can suggest analogues of physical processes or natural history. Give your television system *tentacles* reaching into every home, and you have compared TV to an octopus, with all its lethal and wiry suggestions. You can have your school spirit *fall below zero,* and you have implied that your school spirit is like temperature, registered on a thermometer in a sudden chill. In the following passage about Hawthorne's style, Malcolm Cowley develops his explicit analogy first into a direct simile (*like a footprint*) and then into the implied metaphor that phrases are people, walking at different speeds:

> **He dreamed in words, while walking along the seashore or under the pines, till the words fitted themselves to his stride. The result was that his eighteenth-century English developed into a natural, a *walked*, style, with a phrase for every step and a comma after every phrase like a footprint in the sand. Sometimes the phrases hurry, sometimes they loiter, sometimes they march to drums.***

Cowley's implied metaphor about hurrying and loitering phrases is in fact a kind of extended pun, to illustrate the *walked* style he italicizes. You can even pun on the physical Latin components in our abstract words, turning them back into their original suggestions of physical acts, as in "The *enterprise* grabbed everything" (some beast or army is rushing in), for *enterprise* means in Latin something like "to rush in and grab." Too subtle? No, the contrast between *enterprise* and *grabbed* will please anyone, and the few who see it all will be delighted.

IV. *Dead Metaphor.* *Enterprise* is really a dead metaphor, and the art of resuscitation is the metaphorist's finest skill. It comes from liking words, and paying attention to what they say. The punster makes the writer, if he can restrain himself. Simply add onto the dead metaphor enough implied metaphors to get the circulation going again: *She bridled, snorting and tossing her mane. She bridled* means, by itself, in our usual nonpictorial parlance, nothing more than "reacted disdainfully." By bringing the metaphor back to life, we keep the general meaning but also restore the physical picture of a horse lifting its head and arching its neck against the bridle. This is exhilarating. We recognize *bridle* concretely and truly for the first time. We know the word, and we know the woman. We have an image of her, a posture vaguely suggestive of a horse.

Perhaps the best dead metaphors to revive are those in proverbial clichés. See what Thoreau does (in his journal) with *spur of the moment:*

> **I feel the spur of the moment thrust deep into my side. The present is an inexorable rider.**

Or again, when in *Walden* he speaks of wanting "to improve the nick of time, and notch it on my stick too," and of not being *thrown off the track* "by every nutshell and mosquito's wing that falls on the rails." In each case, he takes the proverbial phrase literally and physically, adding an attribute or two to bring the old metaphor back alive.

---

* *The Portable Hawthorne* (New York: The Viking Press, 1948).

You can go too far, of course. Your metaphors can be too thick and vivid, and the obvious pun brings a howl of protest. Jane Austen disliked metaphors, as Mary Laselles notes (*Jane Austen and Her Art*, pp. 111–112), and reserved them for her hollow characters. I myself have advised scholars not to use them because they are so often overworked and so often tangled in physical impossibilities. "The violent population explosion has paved the way for new intellectual growth" looks pretty good—until you realize that explosions do not pave, and that new vegetation does not grow up through pavement. The metaphor, then, is your most potent device. It makes your thought concrete and your writing vivid. It tells in an instant how your subject looks to you. But it is dangerous. It should be quiet, almost unnoticed, with all details agreeing and all absolutely consistent with the natural universe.

Allusion

Allusions also illustrate your general idea by referring it to something else, making it take your reader as Grant took Richmond, making you the Mickey Mantle of the essay, or the Mickey Mouse. Allusions depend on common knowledge. Like the metaphor, they illustrate the remote with the familiar—a familiar place, or event, or personage. "He looked . . . like a Japanese Humphrey Bogart," writes William Bittner of French author Albert Camus, and we instantly see a face like the one we know so well (a glance at Camus' picture confirms how accurate this unusual allusion is). Perhaps the most effective allusions depend on a knowledge of literature. When Thoreau writes that "the winter of man's discontent was thawing as well as the earth," we get a secret pleasure from recognizing this as an allusive borrowing from the opening lines of Shakespeare's *Richard III*: "Now is the winter of our discontent/Made glorious summer by this sun of York." Thoreau flatters us by assuming we are as well read as he. We need not catch the allusion to enjoy his point, but if we catch it, we feel a sudden fellowship of knowledge with him. We now see the full metaphorical force, Thoreau's and Shakespeare's both, heightened as it is by our remembrance of Richard Crookback's twisted discontent, an allusive illustration of all our pitiful resentments now thawing with the spring.

Allusion can also be humorous. The hero of Peter De Vries's *The Vale of Laughter*,* for instance, contemplating adultery for a moment, decides on the path toward home and honor:

---

* Copyright © 1953, 1962, 1964, 1967 by Peter De Vries. The two following excerpts are reprinted by permission of Little, Brown and Co.

> **If you look back, you turn into a pillar of salt. If you look ahead, you turn into a pillar of society.**

He alludes, of course, to Lot's wife, who looked back on the adulterous city of Sodom, against orders, and was turned into a pillar of salt (Gen. xix.26). De Vries begins his book with a wildly amusing allusion to Melville's already allusive beginning of *Moby Dick*, the archetypal whale-hunt. Melville's narrator says to call him "Ishmael," the Biblical outcast (Gen. xvi.11–12). De Vries throws a devilish comma into Melville's opening sentence, then turns allusion into metaphor:

> **Call me, Ishmael. Feel absolutely free to. Call me any hour of the day or night at the office or at home, and I'll be glad to give you the latest quotation with price-earnings ratio and estimated dividend of any security traded in those tirelessly tossing, deceptively shaded waters in which we pursue the elusive whale of Wealth, but from which we come away at last content to have hooked the twitching bluegill, solvency. And having got me, call me anything you want, Ish baby. Tickled to death to be of service.**

Diction

"What we need is a mixed diction," said Aristotle, and his point remains true twenty-three centuries and several languages later. The aim of style, he says, is to be clear but distinguished. For clarity, we need common, current words; but used alone, these are commonplace, and as ephemeral as everyday talk. For distinction, we need words not heard every minute, unusual words, strange words, foreign words, metaphors; but used alone, these become gibberish. What we need is a diction that weds the popular with the dignified, the clear current with the sedgy margins of language and thought.

Not too low, not too high; not too simple, not too hard—an easy breadth of idea and vocabulary. English is peculiarly well endowed for this Aristotelian mixture. The long abstract Latin words and the short concrete Anglo-Saxon ones give you all the range you need. For most of your ideas you can find Latin and Anglo-Saxon partners. In fact, for many ideas you can find a whole spectrum of synonyms from Latin through French to Anglo-Saxon, from general to specific—from *intrepidity* to *fortitude* to *valor* to *courage* to *bravery* to *pluck* to *guts*. You can choose the high word for high effect, or you can get tough with Anglo-Saxon specifics. But you do not want all Anglo-Saxon, and you must especially guard against sobriety's luring you into all Latin. Tune your diction agreeably between the two extremes.

Indeed, the two extremes generate incomparable zip when tumbled side by side, as in *incomparable zip, inconsequential snip, megalocephalic creep,* and the like. Rhythm and surprise conspire to set up the huge adjective first, then to add the small noun, like a monumental kick. Here is a passage from Edward Dahlberg's *Can These Bones Live,** which I opened completely at random to see how the large fell with the small (my italics):

> Christ walks on a *visionary sea;* Myshkin . . . has his ecstatic premonition of infinity when he has an *epileptic fit.* We know the inward size of an artist by his *dimensional thirsts* . . . .

This mixing of large Latin and small Anglo-Saxon, as John Crowe Ransom has noted, is what gives Shakespeare much of his power:

> This my hand will rather
> The multitudinous seas incarnadine,
> Making the green one red.

The short Anglo-Saxon *seas* works sharply between the two magnificent Latin words, as do the three short Anglo-Saxons that bring the big passage to rest, contrasting the Anglo-Saxon *red* with its big Latin synonym, *incarnadine.* William Faulkner, who soaked himself in Shakespeare, gets much the same power from the same mixture. He is describing a very old Negro woman in *The Sound and the Fury* (the title itself comes from Shakespeare's *Macbeth,* the source of the *multitudinous seas* passage). She has been fat, but now she is wrinkled and completely shrunken except for her stomach:

> . . . a paunch almost dropsical, as though muscle and tissue had been courage or fortitude which the days or the years had consumed until only the indomitable skeleton was left rising like a ruin or a landmark above the somnolent and impervious guts . . . .

The impact of that short, ugly Anglo-Saxon word, with its slang metaphorical pun, is almost unbearably moving. And the impact would be nothing, the effect slurring, without the grand Latin preparation. "What we need is a mixed diction."

---

* Ann Arbor: University of Michigan Press, Ann Arbor Paperbacks, 1967, p. 80.

Beware of wordiness.

Verbosity is a disease. Symptoms: severe inflation of the language, difficulty in following the point, extreme drowsiness. Cause: too much Latin and the passive voice (see pages 132–135). Cure: making words count, and administering moderate doses of Anglo-Saxon. In speaking of sentences earlier, I commended elaboration. But I also recommended deletion. A fully worded sentence, each word in place and pulling its weight, is a joy to see. But a sentence full of words is not. Words should count, I say again. And the best way to make them count is to count the words in each suspicious case. Any shorter version will be clearer. I once counted the words, sentence by sentence, in a thirty-page manuscript rejected as "too loose." In some sentences I cut no more than one or two words. I rephrased many, but I think I cut no entire sentence. In fact, I added a considerable paragraph; and I still had five pages fewer, and a better essay.

Sentences can be too short and dense, of course. Many thoughts need explanation and an example or two. Many need the airing of *and*'s and *of*'s. Many simply need some loosening of phrase. In fact, colloquial phrasing, which is as clear and unnoticed as a clean window, is usually longer than its formal equivalent: *something to eat* as compared to *dinner*. By all counts, *dinner* should be better. It is shorter. It is more precise. Yet *something to eat* has social delicacy (at least as I am imagining the party). "Shall we have something to eat?" is more friendly than the more economical "Shall we have dinner?" We don't want to push our friends around with precise and economical suggestions. We want them at their ease, with the choices slightly vague. Consequently, when we write *what we are after* for *object* and *how it is done* for *method*, we give our all-too-chilly prose some social warmth. These colloquial phrases use more words, but they are not wordy if they pull with the rest of the sentence.

It all comes down to redundancy, the clutter of useless words and tangential ideas—"the accumulation of words that add nothing to the sense and cloud up what clarity there is," as Aristotle says. What we write should be easy to read. Too many distinctions, too many nouns, and too much Latin can be pea soup:

> **Reading is a processing skill of symbolic reasoning sustained by the interfacilitation of an intricate hierarchy of substrata factors that have been mobilized as a psychological working system and pressed into service in accordance with the purpose of the reader.**

This comes from an educator, with the wrong kind of education. He is saying:

> **Reading is a process of symbolic reasoning aided by an intricate network of ideas and motives.**

Try *not* to define your terms. If you do, you are probably either evading the toil of finding the right word, or defining the obvious:

> **Let us agree to use the word signal as an abbreviation for the phrase "the simplest kind of sign." (This agrees fairly well with the customary meaning of the word "signal.")**

Now, really! That came from a renowned semanticist, a student of the meanings of words. The customary meaning of a word *is* its meaning, and uncustomary meanings come only from careful punning. Don't underestimate your readers, as this semanticist did.

The definer of words is usually a bad writer. Our semanticist continues, trying to get his signals straight and grinding out about three parts sawdust to every one of meat. In the following excerpt, I have bracketed his sawdust. Read the sentence first as it was written; then read it again, omitting the bracketed words:

> **The moral of such examples is that all intelligent criticism [of any instance] of language [in use] must begin with understanding [of] the motives [and purposes] of the speaker [in that situation].**

Here, each of the bracketed phrases is already implied in the others. Attempting to be precise, the writer has beclouded himself. Naturally the speaker would be "in that situation"; naturally a sampling of language would be "an instance" of language "in use." *Motives* may not be *purposes*, but the difference here is insignificant. Our semanticist's next sentence deserves some kind of immortality. He means "Muddy language makes trouble":

> **Unfortunately, the type of case that causes trouble in practice is that in which the kind of use made of language is not transparently clear . . . .**

Clearly, transparency is hard. Writing is hard. It requires constant attention to meanings, and constant pruning. It requires a diction a cut above the commonplace, a cut above the inaccuracies and circumlocutions of speech, yet within easy reach. Clarity is the first aim; economy, the second; grace, the third; dignity, the fourth. Our writing should be a little strange, a little out of the ordinary, a little beautiful, with words and phrases not met every day but seeming as right and natural as grass. A good diction takes care and cultivation.

It can be overcultivated. It may seem to call attention to itself rather than to its subject. Suddenly we are aware of the writer at work, and a little too pleased with himself, reaching for the elegant cliché and the showy phrase. In the following passage, I have italicized elements that individually may have a certain effectiveness, but that cumulatively become mannerism, as if the writer were watching himself gesture in a mirror. Some of his phrases are redundant; some are trite. Everything is somehow cozy and grandiose, and a little too nautical. Note the final, glorious fragment.

> **_There's_ little excitement _ashore_ when merchant ships from _far-away_ India, Nationalist China, or Egypt _knife through_ the _gentle swells_ of Virginia's Hampton Roads. This _unconcern_ may simply reflect the _nonchalance_ of people who live by _one of the world's great seaports._ Or perhaps _it's just_ that _folk_ who _dwell_ in the _home towns_ of atomic submarines and Mercury astronauts are not likely to be impressed by a visiting freighter, _from however distant a realm._ An apprentice seaman aboard one of these _vessels soon learns_ that he is entering _no sleepy southern harbor._ Around him in _the Roads_ itself _ride_ naval vessels of many nations, _perhaps including his own._ The big gray warships _dwarf_ the _tiny_ sailing _craft_ and motor boats that _dart_ around the water _on a good day. Off to port lies_ Norfolk, _home_ of the largest naval operating base _on this globe,_ NATO's North Atlantic headquarters. _Upstream a bit_ and also _to port,_ the mouth of the Elizabeth River leads to Portsmouth and a major naval shipyard. _To starboard lies_ Hampton, where at Langley Air Force Base the National Aeronautics and Space Administration prepares to send a man _into the heavens._ Just beyond Hampton _looms_ the _huge_ steel framework of the Newport News Shipbuilding and Dry Dock Company, _from whose ways slide_ the atom-powered surface and underseas warships _of tomorrow. All this and more_ form today's _metropolitan complex_ surrounding Hampton Roads—four large, booming cities _peopled_ by more than a million _souls. It's a huge, sprawling_ urban area, _engaged_ more than ever in world commerce and _deeply involved_ in the nation's defense. _Here is the resurgent south, making instead of awaiting its destiny,_ a hundred years and _a world away_ from the _day_ when the Monitor and the Merrimac _battled clumsily_ in Hampton Roads. And still further away in time, _if not entirely in temper,_ from the _geographically nearby restored_ Colonial Capital at Williamsburg, from Captain John Smith's Jamestown Island, from the Yorktown battlefield on which George Washington _accepted the sword of surrender_ from Cornwallis.***

---

* Robert Damron, "Hampton Roads," *Voyager,* July-August 1960, p. 124.

Exercises

1. Browse your dictionary and find half a dozen families of words, like *ramp-rampage-rampant*. Give the root-idea of each family, and a word or two in definition of each word.

2. Make a permanent reference list by looking up in your dictionary each of the Latin and Greek prefixes and constituents listed below. Illustrate each with several English derivatives closely translated, as in these two examples: *con-* (*with*)—convince (conquer with), conclude (shut with), concur (run with); *gyne-* (*woman*)—gynephobia (fear of women), gynecocracy (government by women), gynecology (female physiology).

LATIN: *a-* (*ab-*), *ad-*, *ante-*, *bene-*, *bi-*, *circum-*, *con-*, *contra-*, *di-* (*dis*), *e-* (*ex-*), *in-* (*two meanings*), *inter-*, *intra-*, *mal-*, *multi-*, *ob-*, *per-*, *post-*, *pre-*, *pro-*, *retro-*, *semi-*, *sub-* (*sur-*), *super-*, *trans-*, *ultra-*.

GREEK: *a-* (*an-*), *-agogue*, *allo-*, *anthropo-*, *anti-*, *apo-*, *arch-*, *auto-*, *batho-*, *bio-*, *cata-*, *cephalo-*, *chron-*, *-cracy*, *demo-*, *dia-*, *dyna-*, *dys-*, *ecto-*, *epi-*, *eu-*, *-gen*, *geo-*, *-gon*, *-gony*, *graph-*, *gyn-*, *hemi-*, *hepta-*, *hetero-*, *hexa-*, *homo-*, *hydr-*, *hyper-*, *hypo-*, *log-*, *mega-*, *-meter*, *micro-*, *mono-*, *morph-*, *-nomy*, *-nym*, *-pathy*, *penta-* *-phag*, *phil-*, *-phobe* (*ia*), *-phone*, *poly-*, *pseudo-*, *psyche-*, *-scope*, *soph-*, *stero-*, *sym-* (*syn-*), *tele-*, *tetra-*, *theo-*, *thermo-*, *tri-*, *zoo-*.

3. Think up and look up eight or nine words built on each of the following Latin verbs and their past participles:

agere, actus **(do)—agent, act**
audire, auditus **(hear)—audit**
capere, captus **(seize)—capable**
cedere, cessus **(go)—concede**
claudere, clausus **(shut)—close, include**
currere, cursus **(run)—recur, course**
dicere, dictus **(say)—dictate**
ducere, ductus **(lead)—produce**
facere, factus **(make)—infect**
ferre, latus **(carry)—infer, relate**
fidere, fisus **(trust)—confide, Fido**
fundere, fusus **(pour)—refuse, refund**
gradi, gressus **(step)—grade, digressions**
ire, itus **(go)—exit, tradition**
jacere, jactus **(throw)—reject**
legere, lectus **(choose, read)—legible, elect**
loqui, locutus **(speak)—circumlocution**
mittere, missus **(send)—permit, mission**
pellere, pulsus **(drive)—impel, repulse**
pendere, pensus **(hang)—depend, pension**
plicare, plicatus **(fold)—implication, complex**
ponere, positus **(put)—response, position**

portare, portatus **(carry)—import**

rumpere, ruptus **(break)—rumpus, erupt**

scribere, scriptus **(write)—scribble, script**

sedere, sessus **(sit)—sedentary, assess**

sentire, sensus **(feel)—sense**

specere, spectus **(look)—speculate**

tendere, tensus **(stretch)—tend, tense**

tenere, tentus **(hold)—content**

trahere, tractus **(drag)—tractor**

venire, ventus **(come)—convene, invent**

vertere, versus **(turn)—diverting, verse**

videre, visus **(see)—divide, visible**

vocare, vocatus **(call)—vocation**

4. Capitalize the following and italicize where necessary:

go west, young man.
the east side of town
east side, west side
the tall negro spoke french.
she loved the spring.
health within seconds (book)
the methodist episcopal church
the missouri river
the new york public library
the neo-positivistic approach (book)
the country gentleman (magazine)
the st. louis post-dispatch

5. Make five series of words running from particular to general, as in *ripe peach, peach, drupaceous fruit, fruit, dessert, food, nourishment.*

6. Make five series of words running from low connotations to high (see p. 187), drawing a line (when possible) where the Anglo-Saxon gives way to French or Latin. Start with *swine* and *stuck-up* (meaning *conceited*). The abstract ideas will work best, and Roget's *Thesaurus* can be most helpful.

7. Write five sentences in which you use a concrete object to represent an entire abstract class, each sentence paired with its abstracted translation:

> A *good steak* might have saved John Keats.
> A *proper protein diet* might have saved John Keats.

8. Write five sentences in which you extend the metaphorical picture in common phrases such as *pin down, stick to, outline, count your chickens* ("She pinned him down methodically, each question sticking in a different place, until he couldn't wriggle out of it").

9. In your next essay, use a tactful *sweet as a nut, sharp as a tack,* and so forth, once on every page (see "Clichés," p. 358).

10. Write five sets of sentences illustrating the four levels of metaphor (see pp. 183–186).

11. Write five sentences in which you revive a dead metaphor.

12. Write five sentences in which you pun metaphorically on a Latin word: "The *enterprise grabbed* everything"; "His *introspection looked in* too keenly." Browsing your dictionary will help you here.

13. Write five sentences in which you couple a Latin adjective and an Anglo-Saxon noun, as in the phrase *inconsequential snip*.

Four Excursions

12

The semester is now perhaps half over. Very likely you have been writing an essay a week, with exercises in between. You and your instructor are running out of ideas. Now is the time for greener pastures, before the harvest of the research paper. I propose four vacations without leaving the expository area. Each will tone up different linguistic muscles.

The Autobiographical Essay

The problem in this autobiographical excursion will be twofold: first, to demonstrate a point; second, to describe accurately and vividly a personal experience. You will find yourself writing metaphorically as you try to bring to the reader exactly what your adventure was like. The aim of the exercise is to refresh your language with a dip into the descriptive, that stream of specific sights, sounds, feelings, and figurative comparisons into which regular expository writing rarely ventures.

You will be telling an anecdote. And it must be interesting. Anecdotes are interesting only when they demonstrate some old truth about existence, when they offer an example of "they'll do it every time," sharpened to philosophical precision. Your tale may be comic or tragic. Look for the kind you would tell about yourself, or *on* yourself, to the young lady on your right at dinner. It must have a point, or her smile will be thin. For your essay, *cherchez la pointe*.

Suppose this is your proposition: "Pride goeth before a fall." You have in mind the time you were skating—capering and swooping for admiration, farther and farther, till the ice broke. With no thought at all, you would have known that it would make good conversation. In using it for your essay, you need more thought, more clarity, and more structure. You need a thesis. You need a beginning, a middle, and an end.

As always, devise your thesis first: "The old saying about pride's going before a fall can prove disastrously true." Now, as always, crank back for your opening sentence. Keep *yourself* out of the beginning paragraph, at least until just before the thesis. You are not really writing about yourself. You are writing an essay about something generally true: you will be illustrating the general proposition with a personal experience, but the general truth is your point. Your beginning paragraph might look like this:

> **No one believes that his parents know much. We are all sure that we know better, that all the old warnings are plots to curtail enjoyment, that all the old sayings are relics of the Puritans. The parental warning, moreover, seems a gross underestimation of our powers and maturity. We are insulted; we have been treated as children. This resentful pride, these illusions of manhood, are woefully normal, and undoubtedly behind most of the evening paper's reports of catastro-**

phes befalling the young. In this petulant image, it seems, we are made, and all of us are lucky if we escape bodily harm from our own arrogance. The old saying about pride's going before a fall can prove disastrously true.

Now for the middle. This tells the story. Your entire episode comes in to illustrate your thesis:

I learned this one sunny winter afternoon. Five of us, close friends since first grade, had eaten lunch at my house, three blocks from the Willawee River. We had been obstreperous. My mother had been harried and amused as she made more sandwiches, more hot chocolate, and scraped out the last of the pudding. "Now, be careful," she had said as we started to get our things together on the porch. "Now, be careful," I mimicked to the others, feeling too good for thought. She called me into the hall and dressed me down. "Just remember that pride goes before a fall," she said. How I hated that old saying. My grandmother always managed to work it in at least once a visit. As I turned to go, my mother added in a completely different tone: "Please don't go out too far, John. Remember the Simmons boy."

I remembered nothing as I walked away with my grinning companions—except my resentment, a small dull twist in my stomach even after the bright afternoon had lifted all of us again to our lunchtime heights. The air was like alcohol on the skin. Everything sparkled in the clear air; everything seemed closer than normal. The river looked like frosting, but down the middle a dull green vein straggled.

And so on, to the climax, which now threatens to be tragic. You, of course, would know how it ended, because your experience, unlike the one above, would have been real.

The value of the exercise depends on your using a real experience. This demands of your powers something more than logical progressions. This asks you not to think up a subject and think out its consequences, but to render as truly and particularly as possible a subject already there, something you experienced but perhaps have never put into words, have never fully conveyed to someone else. It asks you to gather the half-remembered circumstances into a picture very like what they were, a picture that will show your readers how it was. You could tell the whole thing in three sentences: "I dared Bill to follow. We fell in. He froze and drowned." But you need to do what every storyteller must do: keep from telling the story, keep it from ending, while neither losing your reader's interest nor trying his patience. You need detail and detail and detail, simile after simile after metaphor, to postpone the climax and to let us see and feel how it was.

The ending may be no more than a sentence, or it may be a ruminative paragraph, generalizing upward and outward from the particulars to mirror the beginning paragraph, as in a regular essay. The dramatic curve of your incident will tell you what to do. It may be well to end when the story has told itself out, and made its point starkly: "The four of us walked numbly up the street toward home."

The Terrible Essay

Now that you have made an extended excursion into figurative language, and have seen what concrete words can do, you will go on a treasure hunt for the horrendously abstract. Nothing can be more salutary. You will work out all the fever. Again we follow the essay's form, this time in parody not only of the form itself, but especially of that abstract lint the bad essay uses for language. You write the worst essay you can think of.

First, some rules:

1. Use no other verb but *is*. Rule 2 will then be easy.
2. Put EVERYTHING in the passive voice.
3. Use no adjectives; use nouns instead. An *excellent idea* becomes *the excellence of conception of program.* Do not say *governmental spending;* say *government spending.*
4. Use no participles; use verbs with *which:* not *dripping,* but *which drip.*
5. Use only one adverb, frequently repeated, and pick a good big cloudy one like *considerably* or *indubitably*—nothing like *sharply,* or *painfully,* or *crazily,* or *happily.*
6. Use only big abstract nouns—as many *-tion*'s as possible.
7. Use plenty of *which*'s.
8. String out your sentences in festoons of three or more prepositional phrases, each with the same preposition—especially *of.*
9. Use as many words as possible to say the least. Say "It has been considerably in evidence for a considerable period of time that something is in a state of putrefaction in one of the most time-honored and revered of Nordic commonwealths and principalities" instead of "Something is rotten in the state of Denmark" (even Shakespeare could use a few words too many).

10. Work in as many trite expressions as possible: *needless to say, all things being equal, in the foreseeable future, a better world in which to live, due to the fact that, in terms of, various and sundry*.
11. Sprinkle heavily with *-wise*-type and *-type*-type expressions.
12. Say *hopefully* every three or four sentences.
13. Compile a basic vocabulary: *situation, aspect, function, factor, phase, utilize, the use of, -type, -wise,* and so on. The class may well cooperate in this.

As with all rules, you can sometimes break these to good effect. Were you to follow them meticulously you would be unintelligible. What you want is a parody of badness, with enough goodness to make it fun. Your project will be an ultraserious study of trivia. I propose: *A Report of a Study of the Person Sociology and Night Loss Cost Economics of the Faucets Which Drip in the Second Floor North Corner Woman Dormitory Lavatory.*

Now write a good bad beginning paragraph:

> **The necessity of cleanliness is considerably in evidence to every individual who is concerned in the creation of a better world in which to live. Water is necessary to be utilized as a maintenance factor in the health functioning of all human-type beings. Hopefully, it will not be denied that young women which are classified as beings of the college-type category should not be excluded from consideration in this connection. As a consequence of this nature-life principle, which is a major aspect of the situation, every dormitory situated on the property of the campus of the University of Blank has been provided with a number of examples of lavatories which are of a tile-chromium nature. They have the appearance of being adequate, hopefully, and of being the finalized result of an investment utility program of an economy-necessity nature. However, careful investigation of the science objective type has disclosed a large number of factors operative phasewise, the chief of which is that of a number of chromium fixture lavatory faucets which function in a manner not in accordance with economy or utility. All things being equal, they drip. The present study is hopefully an examination of lavatation in terms of a representative example, and features the inclusion of conclusions in regard to confusion between a water waste compulsion type individual and a drip.**

With ingenuity you can keep this going throughout your essay, filling out a sober middle with statistics and an elegant end with pomp.

The Ironic Essay

Your Terrible Essay has, of course, been ironic. In it, you have feigned an appearance contrary to reality. To spoof the errors of earnest professionalism, you have pretended to be an earnest professional. You have practiced one kind of verbal irony, making your words mean the opposite of what they say. They have appeared to say "This is serious and important"; they have really said that all of it—with the whole mode of vanity it represents—is nonsense. You have proceeded, moreover, with a perfect understanding that your reader sees the pose and is enjoying it with you.

The first requirement for irony, then, is an understanding shared between author and reader. It is like Pig Latin, or any other secret language, in which two can talk and circumvent a third. It is, in William Empson's words, a way of getting by the censor. The pleasure in irony is the smuggler's pleasure. I can say, "It was a fine day"; the uninitiated will think it really was, but you and I will know that it was not. The pleasure in the secret, furthermore, gives the truth an emphasis beyond that of bald statement. Alongside irony, plain statement seems uncouth. "It was a terrible day" seems young and petulant. "It was a fine day" is the voice of refined experience, a suggestion of tweed and teacups, Tobruk to El Alamein, tigers in Bengal, and never a hair turned. A few of the guests might think the day's shooting had been good, but the speaker and you and I would know—and enjoy the unperturbed secret, even secretly enjoy the disappointment because it made irony possible—that the day had been terrible.

For your ironic essay, therefore, pick something that is common knowledge. The ironist does not write to one alone, but he writes to all his readers as if each were the only one, complimenting each on his perspicacity. If his subject is not generally and publicly important, he will be talking in riddles. He takes something of public interest—a proposal to raise taxes, for instance. He pretends to be pompous and nearsighted, as if he narrowly misconceives the issue and cannot see the full implications of his words. His pose will be much like yours in the "terrible essay." He makes his pose the opposite of his true standpoint, at the same time making his true standpoint clear. He writes:

> **The popular clamor against the proposed raise in taxes is as shortsighted as it is unfounded. Purging the purse is good for the spleen.**

> **What does it matter that the present Drain Commissioner has wasted exactly a half-million dollars on a poorly conceived plan? What does it matter that our fine city council now finds it necessary to ask for a new bond and a new assessment to overhaul a drainage system just four years old? It matters not. The moral discipline of digging deeper into the pocket so that the Commissioner may dig a deeper drain is good for the soul, even if we must all skip a meal now and then and take out a second mortgage. There is nothing like good drainage.**

Or he writes:

> **The public has again expressed its infinite wisdom in voting down the recent bond issue. Niggardliness is next to godliness, as my great-uncle used to say. It really does not matter that classrooms built for twenty are desperately trying to hold forty; or that our best teachers are leaving for Southfield and Adams and Middlebranch, and even Potfield, simply because they can no longer teach the numbers of students pouring into our beautiful Smith School—one of our most revered landmarks, by the way, and certainly the oldest. If we can save enough for our beer and TV tubes, our children's education really does not matter. We're keeping them off the streets, aren't we?**

This mixing of fact and irony exacts careful wording. The two examples above seek to keep clear the line between straight statement and ironic inversion. It does matter, the writer implies, that the local classrooms are crowded. It is true that they are crowded to almost twice their effective capacity; it is true that at least three good teachers have left for positions in Southfield, Adams, and Middlebranch, and that a fourth has even been lured away to dumpy Potfield. The writer calls the public wise and means foolish; yet he calls them niggardly and means niggardly. How does he do it?

The first clue is overstatement: *expressed its infinite wisdom* is a rotund circumlocution for *wise,* and *infinite wisdom* is a cliché. Then the language goes straight, and we know that the bond issue was, in fact, defeated. The tactics change in the next sentence. Here the writer calls a spade a spade but uses it as an argument for the opposition, making it a poor argument by the harshness of *niggardliness* and the absurdity of its new setting in the old proverb. He implies that the opposing arguments are just that poorly founded. The next sentence makes its irony clear when the facts of two-for-one crowding controvert the opening phrase, making it pure verbal irony: *it does not matter* means *it does matter*. And so on. *Beautiful* means *ugly;* the building is old and it is a landmark, all right, but if it is revered it is wrongly revered.

Now, the writer did not (as I think I can testify) ask himself "Is this an overstatement?" or "Is this an understatement?" or "Is this a cliché?" He simply had his point in mind, took the ironic stance, and struck the ironic tone. He allowed his language to inflate or to belittle (*it really does not matter*) as he went along, assuming the ironic pose, the ignorant pose, and dropping it when he wanted to go straight. He knows that his audience is with him, or that the secret appeal of irony will make them wish they were.

Your first step then, in writing an ironic essay, is to take some current campus issue, for which you will have a supporting audience. A topic that works well, because of its simplicity and perennial currency, is the state of dormitory food. Actually, dormitory food is not bad, but then it is not what mother used to make either. You can probably think of enough amusing detail to make you glad of the chance for irony its mediocrity affords. So: your real thesis is that dormitory food is horrible. Your ironic thesis, obviously, will be: "Dormitory food is absolutely delicious." Now, put on the blinkers; narrow your vision down to that one point. You cannot possibly understand how anyone can complain of such a splendid cuisine. Your first paragraph will go something like this:

The Delicacies of the Smith Hall Steam Table

One of man's perversities is to complain. Give him a new suit, and he complains that his neckties do not match. Give him a new car, and he complains about the size of his garage. Give a child wholesome food, and he complains that he does not like it. Food, in fact, is one of man's oldest complaints. Adam and Eve wearied of the bill of fare even in Paradise, and nothing in this world is better roughage than fruit and raw vegetables. We hear the same old story in Smith Hall. Give students paradise, and they want steak. Give them steak even as frequently as once a year, and they complain that it is thin or cold or dried out. The cuisine at the Smith Hall steam table, as any educated palate can tell, is delicious; and though to a handful of dyspeptic latecomers it may seem cold and dry and unappetizing, it is nonetheless extremely well balanced: in fact, it never changes.

Now, if you wish, take this as your beginning paragraph, adjust it to your needs, and write on—through the satisfactions of cold mashed potatoes, plastic whipped cream, and gravied busboys, not forgetting to fashion a rich and impassioned peroration as your end paragraph. Any other convenient local topic will do. The trick is to find the ironic stance and tone, and through irony to learn the dynamics in even the commonest words.

The Critical Review

In a critical review, instead of starting with an idea and then finding ways to illustrate it, you should start with the grand illustration—a literary work—and then find the underlying idea and all its ramifications. Short story, novel, play, or motion picture, each acts out in its particular way some general idea that remains unstated. Each demonstrates something about life, but does not tell us exactly what. These are the *mimetic* arts—actions imitating life, grand mimickings of the human animal. They are like games in pantomime, charades in which the silent actors do strange things, as we, the onlookers, piece together the meaning with our shouted guesses until we have it summarized in our minds.

The characters in a play, novel, or movie do say things, of course, and one or another may even state the play's thesis explicitly. Even so, the critic must select the stated thesis from all the other things said, and then he must interpret it in the light of the entire play's action. When Hamlet says "the readiness is all," we know we have a thesis. Hamlet has found an important answer to both his brooding inaction and his impetuosity. Yet, is it *the* thesis? Perhaps—but certainly we need to qualify it with something about murderous ambitions, about thinking too little and too much, about appearance and reality, about the strange, dark web of thought and circumstance in which all life in this play seems caught beyond control.

The critic's first step, then, is to find the action's thesis, even though —and precisely because—the writer will have bent his best efforts to avoid stating a thesis or seeming to have one. The writer has wanted to *dramatize* his problem, not to state it; to display it in action, not to describe it. He has not wanted to tack a moral to his tale. That is the critic's job: to find the one idea toward which these moral and immoral actions point.

For this exercise, then, you are the critic facing a new novel. (And the process for a play or movie is essentially the same.) You are the reviewer—he who views the work again, to describe it for his readers. First, remove yourself from the market. Do not think of your review as an advertisement, but as an effort to describe a work's aesthetic, emotional, and intellectual content. A good review is like a good scholarly essay. The chief difference is that the review, treating a new work, tries to leave a few surprises and discoveries for the reader's (viewer's) enjoyment. The reviewer gives the general idea and a few illustrations —leaving the grand illustration, the work itself, for the reader's full possession.

Next, collect your thoughts, and lay your plans. You will organize your review like any essay, around a thesis and within a three-part frame of beginning-middle-end. But you will take one step beyond the ordinary essay: you will make a thesis about a thesis. Your review's thesis, in other words, will contain (1) an assertion of the novel's hidden thesis, and (2) your evaluation of that thesis. To discover your novel's thesis and what you think about it, you will address yourself to the four essential critical questions:

What?
How?
How well?
So what?

The first two take you into the area of description, the last two into evaluation. As you make notes toward answering these questions, you will develop not only your thesis, but also all the evidence you need to illustrate it. As you jot down your answers to *What?*, you describe, as a scientist might, what is *there* by way of setting, characters, and plot. Where does the story take place? When? What are the people like? What happens? Most important of all—what does it add up to? What is the thesis? The *How?* is a lesser question, a technical and aesthetic question. Is the book long or short? Fast or slow? Has it much or little dialogue? Is its structure balanced or unbalanced?

The first of your two evaluative questions—*How well?*—is also a lesser one, being, like the *How?*, a question of technique and aesthetic effect, of means rather than ends. You may in fact not need to answer it, unless the means—the style, organization, and general management of the book—contribute noticeably to the end, to the book's final power and meaning. Most books are reasonably well written, and you will need little beyond a sentence observing the fact. The *How well?* becomes important only when technique makes an unusual contribution, or when it is noticeably at odds with content, as with a book that is skillfully written but empty, like a clever advertisement for raincoats or lipstick. On the other hand, you will occasionally find a book whose lack of art is forgivable because it has something to say. Although Defoe's *Moll Flanders,* for example, is an awkward and cluttered book, its moral vitality has enabled it to endure these two centuries and a half. If you know *Moll Flanders* at all, you understand that by *moral vitality* I do not mean simply "goodness," but any instructive and vital display of the various heavens and hells of existence.

The ultimate evaluative question, *So what?*, is one we like to ask but hate to answer. Evaluation is extremely hard, and it is dangerous. When it applies inappropriate standards to something new, it may go badly wrong, as when the critics decried Beethoven's dissonance. But warmth of judgment, even though wrong, is better than an eternal freeze of indecision. A mind gathered firmly around a reasoned conviction is better than no mind at all. Try to reach a judgment. Is it a good book (or movie) or a poor one? What does it amount to? What do its particulars tell you about life in general? Here is a film that takes place in three hours in Hoboken, as two characters search for a lost train and relive their lives, seem to fall in love, but then move off on different tracks, both richer for the experience. It is ably done, perfectly believable, and the characters look and speak like real people. It seems to say that we are all on trains that pass in the night. Well—so what? You know it is good. But to explain to your readers *why* it is good, you must go beyond the movie to what man seems to value in life itself—love over hate, compassion over vindictiveness, sympathy over selfishness—to some perception of the whole agony and wonder of being human.

Here is a book. It has held your attention and moved you, and you feel that it is good. But what has it said, what has it amounted to? What, in short, is its thesis and the worth of its thesis? The story is about a boy in prep school who has run away to the city because everything at school has suddenly turned to ashes in his mouth. Everyone and everything—the whole system—seems false, as if they would turn to dust when touched. He finds the same in the city's more devious ways. But he also comes to see that life, at its center, can sustain its false surfaces if one can give something of himself to others equally lost, if one can find some mutual support in the family. He may not have a stable center himself, but he sees that life does have this center, whereas he formerly saw only a void.

You have been describing, of course, Salinger's amusing and moving *The Catcher in the Rye*. You have summarized *what is there* until you have come to a statement of the novel's thesis. Although moving unseen among the details, the thesis also has been *there* for you to find and state, if you are to grasp the novel as anything more than a series of seriocomic episodes. Now you can write your first paragraph:

J. D. Salinger's *The Catcher in the Rye* at first seems no more than a humorous, slangy tale about an adolescent boy in a hunting cap, which he wears turned backward for some obscure adolescent reason. We follow Holden Caulfield's escapades in New York City with amusement, and we listen to his wild, earnest slang with delight. How can anyone resist such good entertainment? But as we read on, we discover that the story is not simply funny; it is also pathetic. For all his distraught immaturity, Holden is a very decent person. We soon find ourselves believing he is right and the world is wrong, until finally we discover, with him, that the wrong, empty world can have a center after all, that the center consists in helping the still more helpless, in an act of protective love much like a parent's for a child. In short, at the center of the sham and chaos is a simple affection and understanding that begins at home, in the family.

Your middle may now well begin by summarizing the *What,* describing the story and the people, in more detail.

The story begins at Holden's prep school, on a Saturday night, when ends are especially loose . . . .

You tell just enough to establish the book for your reader without telling him everything. Do not assume that he has read the book, or you will seem to be mumbling conundrums.

Next you will probably want to say something about the *How,* since the book's language is not only striking but important. Holden's improper idiom carries us to the truth, which the proper world has apparently lost. Proper speech seems a sham, and the only true language left is Holden's yearning, vivid, inaccurate slang. So you give an example or two of this. Another important *How* about the book, one that immediately moves into the question of *How well,* arises at the end. There we discover that Holden's entire story has been a monologue addressed to his psychiatrist. His telling of his story has presumably straightened out his perspectives. You would certainly point out this unusual technical feature to your reader, and comment on whether it works. Perhaps you think it a bit too much the gimmick to come off with complete conviction. Nonetheless, you think the book stands up under the sudden strain of its ending. Explaining the strain and the survival will lead you to the heart of the book's value. You will have come from describing contents and technique to answering the question *So what?*, to which your thesis had addressed itself, though briefly, at the start.

Here you are, then, at the last section of your middle and just before your conclusion, ready to answer the question that will give your thesis its fullest explanation: how, exactly, does the book assert its thesis that familial affection triumphs over social chaos? Here you explain the title: Holden's hunting cap symbolizes his role as "catcher" in the rye; he wears it backward, like a baseball catcher's cap, though he does not know why he likes it that way. You explain his curious misunderstanding of the song "Coming Through the Rye"; his seeing the little boy on a Sunday walk with his father and mother, happily walking the gutter's edge; his imaginary waiting in the rye, the savior of little children, ready to catch them just before they fall over cliffs. Then, of course, you describe his little sister, "old Phoebe," and tell how he gives her his hunting cap, and how *she* saves *him.*

Notice that you have not needed to answer directly the devastating final question of value. You have implied its answer. From the very first, everything you have said has implied, "This book is valuable." You have asserted the grounds for its value: its thesis that love, and family love, can hold the world together. Few would think to dispute that assertion very strenuously. Furthermore, your paper has shown, without directly saying so, that this valid thesis is convincingly acted out, in Salinger's superb mimesis.

There is your working model for a critical review. Of course, you can write as well about a bad book (or movie, or play) as a good one. You can profitably analyze a valueless book, especially a popular one that seems good, but that proves to be built on moral sand. The solid reasons for liking what we like (and the reasons we ought to dislike some of the things we like)—these are what the critical review should look for, as it examines the particular book or play or moving picture that acts out some judgment upon our lives.

Suggestions for Topics

1. *The Autobiographical Essay.* An automobile accident, a harrowing experience as camp counselor, a family picnic, a party that flopped, the big date, a new friend who clung, a disappointing trip, a first week at college.

2. *The Terrible Essay.* Book borrowers, the habits of smokers, the way professors enter the classroom, library daydreamers, freshman composition, fashions in make-up, creaking doors.

3. *The Ironic Essay.* The joys of learning languages by tape, Chinese made easy, happy college days, the beloved roommate, the eight o'clock class, our courteous age, chivalry is not dead, the joys of cooking, college—the home away from home.

4. *The Critical Review.* (a) Following the pattern suggested in this chapter, write a critical review of a novel or short story you have recently read, or of a movie you have recently seen.

(b) Try one of the variations of the critical review. Compare a movie with its original book, or a story in a popular magazine with a similar story by some acknowledged master, asserting as your thesis that one is better than the other because ———.

(c) Write one or more single-paragraph reviews—of books, stories, movies, plays—for practice in quickly getting at the meat and in concisely expressing a judgment.

(d) Following the same program of description and evaluation that you would apply to a novel, review some work of nonfiction—a book of ideas, political, sociological, philosophical; an autobiography; a history.

Straight and Crooked Thinking

13

By now you have written more than a little. You have gone through the forms and have taken some excursions. You have been thinking and feeling your way into writing, and writing your way into feeling and thought. Now let us consider how writing can keep your thinking straight.

In fact, we can think straight only on paper. Our thinking is really not logical, but psychological: instant zigzags from murky clouds, or a drifting over the lawn, sometimes with almost no words at all.

Louisa May Alcott once recorded her morning's activities as "having fun with my mind." This sounds attractive, but it probably involved no thinking—in any straight and logical way. Straight thinking is work, and our minds are really not built for it; or, rather, they are built too well for it.

These humming computers called minds, in which we spend our beings, awake and asleep, are really too quick and complex for words. The murmuring voice with which we read, or dream of telling off the boss, is reporting just a fraction of all our tumbling, wordless impressions. You can occasionally catch an extraneous thought distinctly apart from the inner murmur. You can read with the mind's voice, or even read aloud to a child, while the rest of your mind is a mile away, perhaps even "saying" something else. The mind really is a wonder; from the data it has stored away, mostly on its own initiative, it will snap out an answer you can verify, and support with evidence, only after much careful work on paper. The answer may be wrong, because storage has been partial, wrongly weighted, or distorted by your subsurface yearnings and fears; or remembrance has simply faded away. Again, only on paper, which holds your thoughts steady enough to look at them, can you work out the fallacies.

The mind *is* a wonder; and much of its activity is, indeed, *wondering,* which is the beginning of thought. We actually think by a series of questions. What you finally produce on paper as an essay, an effort in straight thinking, is far different from the swinging pendulum of questions and answers that produced it. Nevertheless, your finished essay is an idealized analogue of your mental electronics. Your thesis is the answer your computer flashed in the beginning. Your reasoning and illustration are the stored mental data uncoiled and laid out reasonably straight, so we can see them.

So we can see them—here is the key to the power of written words. We want to see them as well as hear them; we want Space to collaborate with Time—so we may have time and space to think. The ancient world designated sight as the chief of the five senses—superior to hearing, smell, taste, and touch. And certainly most of us would still agree. We would probably rather be deaf than blind, and *light* is our commanding metaphor for intelligence (*illumination, enlightenment, throw light on the subject*). Because the spoken word, or the mind's idea, spins away as soon as it comes, we want to get it down on paper where it will stay put, where, by seeing it, we come to understand. Writing, then, is our basic straightener of thought.

Words and Things

Learn the multiple meanings of words.

The first step to straight thinking is to understand the nature of words. Speech, in a sense, is virtually "wordless," since our meaningful utterances are words blended together in a fluid sweep of sound, with their meanings selected for us by their position and emphasis and pitch. You have probably heard about the difference between "HEzaLIGHThousekeeper" and "HEzalightHOUSEkeeper," and about the subtle differences in stress, pitch, and pause by which we select from a word's several meanings the one we want. When conversing, we enjoy a total context of understanding, complete with shrugs and *you know*'s, that makes individual words and sentences of minimal importance. We actually speak as much in fragments as in sentences, and we constantly repeat and circle, even after we know we have been understood. In a sense, the other person doesn't hear a word we say: he gets the meaning without necessarily noticing the words at all.

But on the silent printed page, you must place your words with care: the pitch, the stress, the general context of understanding—all the elements that free our speech from care—are gone. And the visible presence of words heightens our awareness of them *as* words. So much so, indeed, that we sometimes think them physical things, confusing them with the actual sticks and stones of this world.

Words are not things, nor are they symbols of things: words are symbols of our *ideas* of things. The primary fact about words, as I have already suggested (p. 180), is that they are the abstractions or generalizations by which we pick up the particular sticks of this world. A written word is a symbol for a generalization in our heads. Since we like our words to be as concrete as possible, the idea of generalization may bother us. But a word's function is to name a general class of things, or states, or thoughts, or whatever, and we want a word's limits no narrower. When I say *bed,* I mean the general idea of "bed." The physical bed you may picture will be different from mine, but we will understand each other perfectly. You will get the general idea, and you will also know that I do not specifically mean your little bunk at the dorm, though I mean something like it.

So: words are symbols for our general ideas of things. They are classifiers not only of the sticks and stones of the physical world, but of all the qualities, movements, functions, and conditions we know—*cold, grateful, walk, marry, mother, president, slow, exactly.* Many words refer to nothing in the physical world, though we may infer the entity by its effects—*anger, confidence, peace,* for example; and many words seem to symbolize a kind of mental gesture, the grammar with which we connect our thoughts or describe the connections of the physical world, as with *of, by, in, with, when.*

Words, like other symbols, usually represent a multiplicity of things, not all closely related to each other. A *log* is something for cabins or hearths, a gadget towed behind a ship, or a book on its bridge. A *bridge* may be not only on a ship, but in someone's mouth, or across the Golden Gate (which has neither gold nor hinges). The skipper could take out his bridge while sailing under the bridge and playing bridge on the bridge. Context is usually sufficient to select the wanted meanings automatically from the unwanted. That words have varieties of meanings bothers no one but the theoreticians—or your readers, if you are careless.

Try a little punning.

To master words you must keep alert to all their possibilities of meaning. Hence the punster usually makes the good writer: he forestalls any diabolical misreading because he has already seen the possibility himself. He would never accidentally write: "The situation was explosive, and he was no match for it." Nor: "The girls were barely attractive." A certain devilish eye for meanings will keep your thinking straight, and save you from innocent damnation.

Words are full of deviltry. *Pale* means bloodless of complexion (from Latin *pallidus*); and *pale* means a region staked out for one's reign (from Latin *palus,* or stake). Add such homophones ("same-sounders") as *rain* and *reign* to *pail* (bucket) and *pale* (bloodless; region), and you can see what Shakespeare, that prince of punsters and master of meanings, could do when full of springtime, as in this, the best of all his songs, from *The Winter's Tale*:

When daffodils begin to peer,
With heigh! the doxie over the dale—
Why, then comes in the sweet o' the year,
For the red blood reigns in the winter's pale.

A good writer revels in multiple meanings, letting the ones he doesn't want just linger around the edge of the fun, to show that he knows them but decrees them temporarily insignificant.

A word acquires multiple meanings as it drifts into a new general usage and its specific meaning fades. A circle is a circle, but in expressions like *well known in artistic circles* the word has faded until it means little more than "group." It is a dead metaphor, ready for the touch of the good writer's pencil. The first user was making a metaphor (a *metonymy*, in fact; see Appendix C), in which he pictured admirers literally standing around an artist in a ring; he called them not people but a *circle*, naming them by something logically similar. In ordinary thoughtless parlance, we certainly do not see the circle; the physical, literal origin has faded. But the good writer will turn up the color a little, will bring the physical origin back for the reader to see: "The artist found in his circle a charmed protection from the world." Or he will at least prevent any unwanted physical or literal meanings, never writing, for instance, "The artist painted his circle." The writer's best control of a word's multiple meanings lies in respecting the essentially physical thing it says, and in keeping an impudent eye open for all transferred and metaphorical meanings.

Facts, and Degrees of Belief

Write as close to the facts as possible.

Words may radiate several meanings, but they are your only means of lighting the facts for your reader. You cannot really present him the "hard facts" themselves. You cannot reach through the page to hand him actual lumps of coal and bags of wheat. You can only tell him *about* these things, and then persuade him to see them as you believe they should be seen. Let us now look briefly at the nature of fact, and of belief, opinion, and preference—all matters of concern in keeping your thinking straight, and in convincing your reader that you know what you are about.

Facts are the firmest kind of thought, but they are *thoughts* nevertheless—verifiable thoughts about the coal and wheat and other entities of our experience. The whole question of fact comes down to verifiability: things not susceptible of verification leave the realm of factuality. Fact is limited, therefore, to the kinds of things that can be tested by the senses (verified empirically, as the philosophers say) or by inferences from physical data so strong as to allow no other explanation. "Statements of fact" are assertions of a kind provable by referring to experience. The simplest physical facts—that a stone is a stone and that it exists—are so bound into our elementary perceptions of the world that we never think to verify them, and indeed could not verify them beyond gathering testimonials from the group. With less simple and tangible facts, verification is simply doing enough to persuade any reasonable man that the assertion of fact is true, beginning with what our senses can in some way check.

Measuring, weighing, and counting are the strongest empirical verifiers; assertions capable of such verification are the most firmly and quickly demonstrated as factual:

Smith is five feet high and four feet wide.
The car weighs 2,300 pounds.
Three members voted for beer.

In the last assertion, we have moved from what we call physical fact to historical fact—that which can be verified by its signs: we have the ballots. Events in history are verified in the same way, although the evidence is scarcer the farther back we go.

Facts, then, are those things, states, or events of a kind susceptible of verification. Notice: *of a kind* susceptible of verification. Some perfectly solid facts we may never be able to verify. The place, date, and manner of Catullus's death; whether a man is guilty as accused or innocent as claimed—these may never be known to us, may never be established as "facts," because we lack the evidence to verify them. But we would not want to remove them from the realm of factuality; they are the *kind* of thing that could be verified, if only we could get at the evidence.

Believe what you write—but learn the nature of belief.

Facts, then, are things susceptible of verification. Belief presents an entirely different kind of knowledge: things believed true but yet beyond the reach of sensory verification—a belief in God, for instance. We may infer a Creator from the creation, a Beginning from the beginnings we see in Nature. But a doubting Thomas will have nothing to touch or see; judging our inferences wrongly drawn, he may prefer to believe in a physical accident, or in a flux with neither beginning nor end. The point is that although beliefs are unprovable, they are not necessarily untrue, and they are not unusable as you discourse with your reader. You can certainly assert beliefs in your writing, establishing their validity in a tentative and partially probable way, so long as you do not assume you have *proved* them. State your convictions; support them with the best reasons you can find; and don't apologize. But, for both politeness and persuasion, you may wish to qualify your least demonstrable convictions with "I believe," "it seems reasonable to suppose," "perhaps," "from one point of view," and the like—unless the power of your conviction moves you beyond the gentilities, and you are writing heart to heart.

Don't mistake opinion for fact.

Halfway between fact and belief is opinion. An opinion is a candidate for fact, something you believe true but about whose verification you are still uncertain. All the facts are not in, you are not sure of the tests, and you may not be sure that there are tests; but you can at least present tentative verification. The difference between fact and opinion, then, is simply a difference in verifiableness. One man's opinion may eventually prove true, and another's false; an opinion may strengthen, through verifying tests, into accepted fact, as with Galileo's opinion that the earth moved.

The testing of opinions to discover the facts is, indeed, the central business of straight thinking. When you assert something as fact, you indicate (1) that you assume it true and easily verified, and (2) that its truth is generally acknowledged. When you assert something as opinion, you imply some uncertainty about both these things. Here are two common opinions that will probably remain opinions exactly because of such uncertainty:

Girls are brighter than boys.
Men are superior to women.

Although these statements are in *kind* susceptible of verification, we know we will probably never verify them satisfactorily. We know that the necessary tests are difficult, not merely to administer and control, but to agree upon, and we know that the terms *brighter* and *superior* have a range of meaning hard to pin down. Even when agreeing upon the tests for numerical and verbal abilities, and for memory and ingenuity, we cannot be sure that we will not miss other kinds of brightness and superiority, or that our tests will measure these things in any thorough way. The range of meaning in our four other terms, moreover, is so wide as virtually to defy verification. We need only ask "At what age?" to illustrate how broad and slippery the terms *girls, boys, men,* and *women* really are.

Dispute your preferences with care.

Preferences are something else again. They are farther from proof than opinions—indeed, beyond the pale of proof. And yet they are more firmly held than opinions, because they are primarily subjective, sweetening our palates and warming our hearts. *De gustibus non est disputandum*: tastes are not to be disputed. So goes the medieval epigram, from the age that refined the arts of logic. You can't argue successfully about tastes, empirical though they be, because they are beyond empirical demonstration. Are peaches better than pears? Whichever you choose, your choice is probably neither logically defensible nor logically vulnerable. The writer's responsibility is to recognize the logical immunity of preferences, and to qualify them politely with "I think," "many believe," "some may prefer," and so forth.

But that preferences are subjective does not eliminate their general interest, nor remove them from discussion. Because they are immune, because they are strong, and because everyone has them, preferences have a certain "validity" that repays investigation. The medieval logicians notwithstanding, tastes are indeed worth disputing, because discussing them may lead to assertions demonstrable enough to be, in some measure, persuasive. You will probably never convince a pear man, but you may make a fairly sound case for peaches. I would guess that the annual consumption of peaches exceeds that of pears three to one. And in a best-selling cookbook, recipes for peaches outnumber those for pears three to one. Of course, popularity is no criterion for quality; but a continued preference by large numbers of people, if you can establish that as fact, shows that what had seemed a private preference actually has a public acceptance worth analyzing. Your private taste for peaches may then translate into a perfectly demonstrable thesis: "Men seem to prefer peaches to pears." You could probably make even a qualitative judgment stand up, with a thesis something like: "Although chilled pears are delicious, Americans seem to consider peaches more satisfying, as the annual sales figures would indicate."

So go ahead, dispute over tastes, and you may find some solid grounds for them. Shakespeare *is* greater than Ben Jonson, his friend and greatest competitor. Subjective tastes have moved all the way up beside fact: the grounds for Shakespeare's margin of greatness have been exhibited, argued, and explored over the centuries, until we accept his superiority, as if empirically verified. Actually, the questions that most commonly concern us are beyond scientific verification. But you can frequently establish your preferences as testable opinions by asserting them reasonably and without unwholesome prejudice, and by using the secondary evidence that other reasonable men agree with you in persuasive strength and number.

Assumptions and Implications

Check your statements, root and branch.

Your statements spring from assumptions below the surface and sprout all kinds of unwritten sprigs. These latter, the implications, you can more readily control. Actually, language is at its best when implying more than it says. Irony, for instance, is a constant shadow-play of implication. When you say, "As a general, he certainly had command of his tailor," you clearly imply that he could command little else. The only danger in implications (beyond risking a black eye) is in your not seeing them yourself. When you thank your hostess by saying "Your salad was good," you may leave her in tears over the rolls, which were actually as splendid as everything else. If you say "The demonstration was unfair to the management," you must face your implication that the management has been fair to the customers and the help. Keep your eyes open for where your words are pointing, and either trim the pointers or follow them out.

Language naturally looks ahead, so we look for our implications almost by second nature. But we do not naturally check our assumptions, because our whole lives rest on acquired assumptions we hardly think to question: love is better than hate; life is better than death; self-preservation is primary; giving your life for others is good; security is good; success is good; and so on and on. Many of our assumptions conflict, as when our approvals of selfless dedication and of self-sufficiency clash. Sacrifice can be truly selfless, or morbidly self-serving; and selfishness can have a certain forthright honesty that works not too badly in the social mix. As when you first shaped your thesis (pp.

27–30), you should continue to check your assumptions to see what your readers, or your opponents, will take for granted, and what they will not grant until proved. If you assume, simply, that football builds character or that socialism ruins it, that some races are inferior or all men equal, you may find your platform shot from under you as the opposition hits the narrowness of your assumptions.

Assumptions and implications can be seen as different ends of the same idea. By assuming that football builds character, you may overlook your implications that other things do not and that "character" means, for you, only a healthy competitive tenacity and a measure of physical courage. Overlooking the full width of the term, you may assume its meaning too narrowly; "character" also means a sense of responsibility and humanity, which, along with tenacity and courage, may come readily from other sources. If you acknowledge this breadth of assumption behind your term, you can very well go ahead with the case, arguing that football does indeed build character in certain ways. Perhaps you need merely change your thesis to something like: "Although no magical guarantee, football contributes certain valuable disciplines toward the development of character." You immediately show that you are neither claiming nor assuming more than the reasonable truth. You have found a solid premise.

Assumptions and implications have to do with your thesis, or with any subordinate assertion you make in demonstrating it. Your proof is what makes your assertions stick. Proof is just enough of evidence and reasoning to persuade your readers that what you are saying is true. Usually, as I have already said, all you need is common sense and enough delicacy not to shout "proved" too loudly. Anything within reason goes; but keep in mind the kinds of proving within reason, and the traps beyond reason.

Proof Beyond Logic

Know your authorities.

An appeal to some authority to prove your point is really an appeal beyond logic, but not necessarily beyond reason. "Einstein said . . ." can silence many an objection, since we believe Einstein knew more about physical fact than anyone. "According to Freud" may win your point on human personality, as may an appeal to Winston

Churchill or Matthew Arnold or H. W. Fowler on English usage. Shakespeare, the Bible, and Samuel Johnson can authenticate your claims about the ways of the world and the spirit.

Since authority has long since proved itself right, appeals to authority are not beyond reason. But they are beyond logic, because the logical proof that first established the authority has long since retired to the bookshelves. What Einstein said, we tend to take on faith, without demanding proof, which may well be beyond us. The greatest men in the field have accepted Einstein's logic and acknowledged his achievement. Who are we to question that? In this apparent infallibility, of course, reside the hazards of relying upon authority.

Appeals to authority risk four common fallacies. The first is in appealing to the authority outside of his field, even if his field is the universe. Although Einstein was a man of powerful intellect, we should not assume he knew all about women too. Even if a chance remark of Einstein's sounds like the quantum theory of womanhood, you will do best to quote it only for its own rational merits, using Einstein's having said it only as a bonus of persuasive interest; otherwise, your appeal to his authority will seem naïve in the extreme. The good doctor, of the wispy hair and frayed sweater, was little known as a man for the ladies.

The second fallacy is in misunderstanding or misrepresenting what the authority really says. Sir Arthur Eddington, if I may appeal to an authority myself, puts the case: "It is a common mistake to suppose that Einstein's theory of relativity asserts that everything is relative. Actually it says, 'There are absolute things in the world but you must look deeply for them. The things that first present themselves to your notice are for the most part relative.' "* If you appeal loosely to Einstein to authenticate an assertion that everything is "relative," you may appeal in vain—since *relative* means relative *to* something else, even to some absolute.

The third fallacy is in assuming that one instance for an authority represents him accurately. Arguments for admitting the split infinitive to equal status with the unsplit, for instance, often present split constructions from prominent writers. But they do not tell us how many splits a writer avoided, or how he himself feels about the construction. A friend once showed me a split infinitive in Walter Lippmann's

* *The Nature of the Physical World* (Ann Arbor: University of Michigan Press, 1958), p. 23.

column after I had boldly asserted that careful writers like Lippmann never split their infinitives. Out of curiosity, I wrote Mr. Lippmann; after all, he might have changed his tune. He wrote back that the split had been simply a slip, that he disliked the thing and tried to revise it out whenever it crept in.

The fourth fallacy is deepest: the authority may have faded. New facts have generated new ideas. Einstein has limited Newton's authority. Geology and radioactive carbon have challenged the literal authority of Genesis. Jung has challenged Freud, and Keynes, Marx.

The more eminent the authority, the easier the fallacy. Ask these four questions:

(1) Am I citing him outside his field?
(2) Am I presenting him accurately?
(3) Is this instance really representative?
(4) Is he still fully authoritative?

Do not claim too much for your authority, and add other kinds of proof, or other authorities. In short, don't put all your eggs in one basket; write as if you knew the market and the risks. Every appeal to authority is open to logical challenge.

Handle persistences as you would authorities.

Persistence, a kind of unwritten or cumulative authority, is also open to logical challenge. Because a belief has persisted, the appeal goes, it must be true. Since earliest times, for example, man has believed in some kind of supernatural beings or Being. Something must be there, the persistence seems to suggest. But the appeal is not logical; the belief could have persisted from causes other than the actuality of divine existence, perhaps only from man's psychological need. As with authority, new facts may vanquish persistent beliefs. The belief that the world was a pancake, persistent though it had been, simply had to give way to Columbus and Magellan. For all this, however, persistence does have considerable validating strength. Shakespeare's supremacy, upheld now for three centuries, and by men of many nations, has considerable force in upholding the assertion that he is, so far, supreme. As with appeals to authority, appeals to persistence are most effective when acknowledged as *indications* of validity rather than as logical proofs and validities themselves.

Don't let documentary evidence fool you.

Documents are both authoritative and persistent. They provide the only evidence, aside from oral testimony, for all that we know beyond the immediate presence of our physical universe, with its physical remains of the past. Documents point to what has happened, as long ago as Nineveh and Egypt and as recently as the tracings on last hour's blackboard. But documents are only records or traces, not events themselves, and you must be wary of taking them at face value. Documents vary in reliability. The inscription on tombstone and monument would seem a firmer testimonial than the name in a legend; the diplomat's diary firmer than the public announcement; the eyewitness's description firmer than the historian's summary. You must consider a document's historical context, since factuality may have been of little concern, as with stories of heroes and saints. You must allow, as with newspapers, for the effects of haste and limited facts. You should consider a document's author, his background, his range of knowledge and belief, his assumptions, his prejudices, his probable motives, his possible tendencies to suppress or distort the facts.

Finally, you should consider the document's data. Are the facts of a kind easily verifiable or easily collected? Indeed, can you find verification elsewhere? For example, numerical reports of population can be no more than approximations, and they are hazier the farther back you go in history, as statistical methods slacken. Since the data must be selected from almost infinite possibilities, does the selection seem reasonably representative? Are the conclusions right for the data? Might not the data produce other conclusions? Your own data and conclusions, of course, must also face questioning.

Statistics are particularly persuasive data, and, because of their psychological appeal, they can be devilishly misleading. To reduce things to numbers seems scientific, incontrovertible, final. But each "1" represents a slightly different quantity, as one glance around a class of 20 students will make clear. Each student is the same, yet entirely different. The "20" is a broad generalization convenient for certain kinds of information: how many seats we will need, how many people are absent, how much the instruction costs per head, and so forth. But clearly the "20" will tell us nothing about the varying characteristics of the students or the education.

Averages and percentages are even more misleading, carrying the numerical generalization one step further from the physical facts. The truth behind a statement that the average student earns $10 a week could be that nine students earn nothing and one earns $100. A statement in an eminent professional journal that 73 percent of the "cultivated informants" in the North Central States say "ain't I" is actually reporting on a group of only 31 cultivated informants, a mere 11 of whom answered the question about "ain't I"—and only 8 of these used "ain't I." Dividing 8 by 11 does give .73. But put "73 percent" in print, and you seem to have scientific proof that 73 of every 100 cultivated persons say "ain't I." Even a figure of 26 percent (dividing 8 by 31) would badly overstate the evidence, implying a statistical base of some breadth, whereas the figure represents merely 31 people in a population of some 35 million. How many of 35 million persons are cultivated, and exactly how we test for cultivation, are questions not easily answered. The survey ignored how often the "ain't I" people said "ain't" as against other possibilities, or how they felt about it—whether they used it humorously, or accidentally, or only with intimate friends, and so forth. Be wary of statistics, especially when each number, so firm and final, can conceal variations beyond the reach of calipers and scales.

Logical Proof: Induction

In Chapter 4, we considered induction and deduction as ways of leading your reader: *in*duction leads him through the evidence to the main point (*in* + *ducere*, "to lead"); *de*duction leads away from your thesis into the evidence that supports it. In logic, you simply follow one or the other of these directions, either toward or away from the Big Idea.

Induction is the way of science: one collects the facts and sees what they come to. Sir Francis Bacon laid down in 1620 the inductive program in his famous *Novum Organum, sive indicia vera de interpretatione naturae* ("The New Instrument, or true evidence concerning the interpretation of nature"). Bacon was at war with the syllogism; its abstract deductions seemed too feeble to measure nature's subtlety. His new instrument changed the entire course of thought. Before Bacon, the world had deduced the consequences of its general ideas; after Bacon, the world looked around and induced new generalizations from what it saw. Observed facts called the old ideas into question, and theories replaced "truths." As you probably know, Bacon died from a cold caught while stuffing a chicken's carcass with snow for an inductive test of refrigeration.

Induction has great strength, but it also has a basic fallacy. The strength is in taking nothing on faith, in having no ideas at all until the facts have suggested them. The fallacy is in assuming that the mind can start blank, with no prior ideas. Theoretically, Bacon had no previous ideas about refrigeration. Theoretically, he would experiment aimlessly until he noticed consistencies that would lead to the icebox. Actually, from experience, one would already have a hunch, a half-formed theory, that would suggest the experimental tests. Induction, in other words, is always well mixed with deduction. The major difference is in the tentative frame of mind: in making a hypothesis instead of merely borrowing an honored assumption; and in keeping the hypothesis hypothetical, even after the facts seem to have supported it.

Use analogies to clarify, not to prove.

The simplest kind of induction is analogy: because this tree is much like that oak, it too must be some kind of oak. You identify the unknown by its analogy to the known. You inductively look over the similarities until you conclude that the trees are very similar, and therefore the same kind. Analogies are tremendously useful indications of likeness; analogy is virtually our only means of classification, our means of putting things into groups and handling them by naming them. Analogy also illustrates the logical weakness of induction: assuming that *all* characteristics are analogous after finding one or two analogous. We check a few symptoms against what we know of colds and flu, and conclude that we have a cold and flu; but the doctor will add to these a few more symptoms and conclude that we have a virulent pneumonia.

Similarity does not mean total identity, and analogies must always make that shaky assumption, or clearly demonstrate that the mismatching details are unimportant. In your writing, you may use analogy with tremendous effect, since it is almost the very basis of knowledge. But watch out for the logical gap between *some* and *all*. Make sure that:

1. A reasonably large number of details agree.
2. These details are salient and typical.
3. The misfitting details are insignificant and not typical.

If the brain seems in some ways like a computer, be careful not to assume it is in all ways like a computer. Keep the analogy figurative: it can serve you well, as any metaphor serves, to illustrate the unknown with the known.

Look before you leap.

The hypothetical frame of mind is the essence of the inductive method, because it acknowledges the logical flaw of induction, namely, the *inductive leap*. No matter how many the facts, or how carefully weighed, a time comes when thought must abandon the details and leap to the conclusion. We leap from the knowledge that *some* apples are good to the conclusion: "[All] apples are good." This leap, say the logicians, crosses an abyss no logic can bridge, because *some* can never guarantee *all*—except as a general *probability*. The major lesson of induction is that *nothing* can be proved, except as a probability. The best we can manage is a *hypothesis*, while maintaining a perpetual hospitality to new facts that might change our theory. This is the scientific frame of mind; it gets as close to substantive truth as we can come, and it keeps us healthily humble before the facts.

Probability is the great limit and guarantee of the generalizations to which we must eventually leap. You know that bad apples are neither so numerous nor so strongly typical that you must conclude: "Apples are unfit for human consumption." You also know what causes the bad ones. Therefore, to justify your leap and certify your generalization, you base your induction on the following three conditions:

1. Your samples are reasonably numerous.
2. Your samples are truly typical.
3. Your exceptions are explainable, and demonstrably not typical.

The inductive leap is always risky because all the data may not be known. The leap might also be in the wrong direction: more than one conclusion may be drawn from the same evidence. Here, then, is where the inductive frame of mind can help you. It can teach you always to check your conclusions by asking if another answer might not do just as well. Some linguists have concluded that speech is superior to writing because speech has many more "signals" than writing. But from the same facts one might declare speech inferior: writing conveys the same message with fewer signals.

The shortcomings of induction are many. The very data of sensory observation may be indistinct. Ask any three people to tell how an accident happened, and the feebleness of human observation becomes painfully apparent. If the facts are slippery, the final leap is uncertain. Furthermore, your hypothesis, which must come early to give your investigation some purpose, immediately becomes a *deductive* proposition that not only will guide your selection of facts, but may well distort slightly the facts you select. Finally, as we have seen with statistics and averages, scientific induction relies heavily on mathematics, which requires that qualities be translated into quantities. Neither numbers nor words, those two essential generalizers of our experience, can adequately grasp all our diversities. The lesson of induction, therefore, is the lesson of caution. Logically, induction is shot full of holes. But it makes as firm a statement as we can expect about the physical universe and our experience in it. It keeps our feet on the ground, while it makes remarkable sense of our facts. The ultimate beauty of science is perhaps not that it is efficient (and it is), but that it is hypothetical. It keeps our minds open for new hypotheses. The danger lies in thinking it absolute.

Logical Proof: Deduction

Establish your premise.

De-duction, as I have said, leads *away from* your premise, your basic assumption. A premise is a kind of weathered hypothesis, a general idea so well fitted and durable as to seem part of the natural order of things and beyond question: *life is essentially good,* for instance. Deductive reason characteristically operates in those areas of *values* and *qualities* where factual induction finds little to grasp. Induction starts with the particulars and sees what general proposition they make. Deduction, the only other possible way to reason, starts with the general proposition and sees what it implies for the particulars: granted that such and such is true, then these things also must be true. Both methods can fall down when the numbers or words they employ generalize too far from the skin of physical and mental actuality—which we can scarcely reach without them. Like induction, deduction can make some notorious mistakes. The greatest mistake may be in the premise itself. Since deductive reasoning depends on your premise—literally "hangs from" it—you must bolt your premise to solid assumptions, or your whole chain of logic will fall in a heap. First check your assumptions with an eye for termites; then attend to the logical linkage.

Deductive reasoning has produced the syllogism, the deducer's standard computer. We are sometimes put off by syllogisms, since they seem a ponderous device for producing what we already know. And when the input is faulty, they tell us that all men are Harry Truman or that Republicans wear blue neckties. But if you take the syllogism as a machine to test your logical alignment, or to attack the illogic of your adversaries, you will certainly improve the quality of the thoughts you commit to paper.

The *standard categorical syllogism* tests the validity of your classifications—your "categories." When you prove that all men are Harry Truman, something has gone wrong with your sorting: you should have "Truman" in some larger class, like "men," and not the other way around. A syllogism does its classifying in three steps, as with this famous example (the size of the print denotes the size of the class):

All MEN are MORTAL CREATURES.	**(major premise)**
***Socrates* is a MAN.**	**(minor premise)**
Therefore, *Socrates* is a MORTAL CREATURE.	**(conclusion)**

Socrates (the *minor term*) fits in the larger class of MEN (*middle* [*middle-sized*] *term*), which fits in the still larger class of MORTAL CREATURES (*major term*), as shown in the diagram on page 227.

The first step in classifying by syllogism is to construct a "categorical proposition"—an assertion containing a subject (which we may call S), a linking *is* (*are, were*), and a predicate nominative (a noun or noun clause that completes the linking *is*; such a noun or noun clause we may conveniently think of as the "predicate term" or P). Your verb, I repeat, must be *is* (*are, were*) and no other; and it must be completed by a noun or noun clause (the predicate term, or P). Both your subject (S) and your predicate term (P) must be the same kind of grammatical entities—nouns or noun clauses. You must change "Socrates is mortal" (*noun*-is-*adjective*) to "Socrates is a mortal creature" (*noun*-is-*noun*); otherwise you cannot manipulate your predicate term in logical equivalence with your subject. Similarly, to put into a syllogism the assertion that "you can't teach an old dog new tricks," you must manufacture the categorical proposition: "All new tricks are things that you can't teach old dogs." Such prose is atrocious, of course, but syllogisms often must untune the language to get at the logic. If you need to state a syllogism directly in your writing, there it must stand, clumsy or not. But more often you use the syllogism to check a question of logic on the side, and what appears in your paper will be a recasting of the same idea in your best-tuned language.

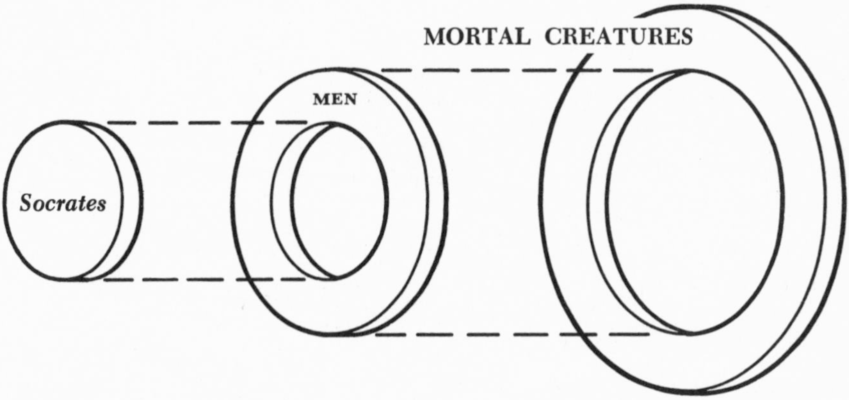

Or in syllogistic form:

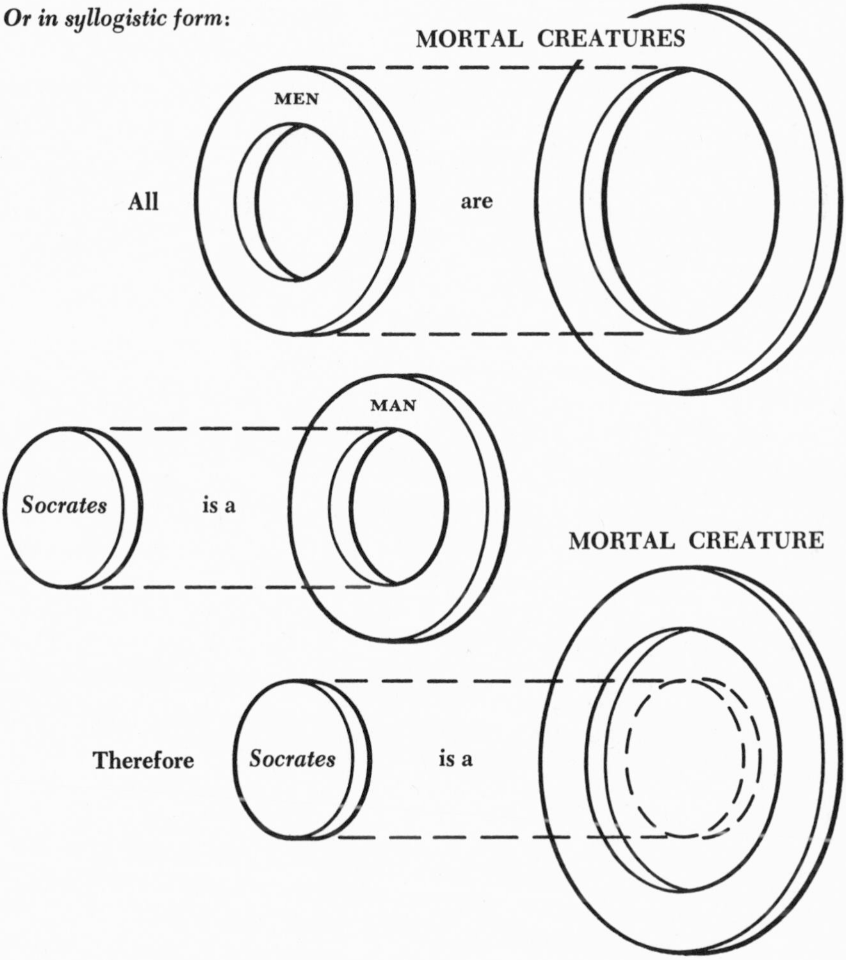

Now, there are only four kinds of categorical propositions:

I. All students are pragmatists.
II. No students are pragmatists.
III. Some students are pragmatists.
IV. Some students are not pragmatists.

As you have seen with Socrates, a syllogism has three propositions: (1) a major premise, (2) a minor premise, and (3) a conclusion. Our categorical Socrates-syllogism takes its three propositions from category I ("Socrates" is naturally "all Socrates"). Furthermore, a syllogism always uses three and only three terms: a MAJOR term, a *minor* term, and a MIDDLE term. The syllogism must always begin with the major premise (1), which contains the MAJOR term and the MIDDLE term. It must then assert the minor premise (2), which must contain the *minor* term and, again, the MIDDLE term. Thus the MIDDLE term appears in both major and minor premises to help show the relationship of the *minor* term to the MAJOR term. That relationship is finally expressed in the conclusion(3), which must always state the *minor* term as its subject (S) and the MAJOR term as its predicate term (P), and which must not mention the MIDDLE term at all.

Unfortunately, classification by size does not work out so neatly in syllogisms using propositions of categories II, III, and IV. In these, size of class may be irrelevant. Your minor class could well be larger than your major, as in the conclusion "No men [minor] are workhorses [major]," or "Some girls [minor] are sophomores [major]"; the world obviously contains more men than workhorses, and more girls than sophomores. Nevertheless, except for our negative statements, we tend to think uphill, putting smaller into larger ("Some sophomores are girls"), as the traditional terms themselves suggest: *minor* ————→ MAJOR.

As we have said, the syllogism aims to draw a valid conclusion that states the minor term as its subject (S) and the major term as its predicate term (P). It is extremely useful, then, *to think of the minor and major terms as* S *and P,* their eventual functions in the conclusion, *and to think of the middle term as M.* In other words, the syllogism first fits the P(redicate) to the M(iddle term), then the S(ubject) to the M(iddle term), and finally the S(ubject) to the P(redicate). The M is merely a means of getting the S correctly related to the P. By way of review, we may now use these symbols in setting down the basic constituents of the syllogism:

Major premise:	P, M	(major term, middle term)
Minor premise:	S, M	(minor term, middle term)
Conclusion:	S, P	(minor term [subject], major term [predicate term])

Notice that the middle term (M) *always* appears in both major and minor premises. Notice, too, that the conclusion *always* states that "subject is predicate term," something-is-something: S ⟶ P.

Our schematic presentation above indicates the necessary sequence of S and P in the conclusion; but it does not show all the sequences S, P, and M may follow in the major and minor premises. Actually, S, P, and M may appear in the premises as in any one of these four figures:

FIRST FIGURE

M ⟶ P	(Middle term *is* predicate term.)
S ⟶ M	(Subject *is* middle term.)
Therefore, S ⟶ P	(Therefore, subject *is* predicate term.)

SECOND FIGURE

P ⟶ M	(Predicate term *is* middle term.)
S ⟶ M	(Subject *is* middle term.)
Therefore, S ⟶ P	(Therefore, subject *is* predicate term.)

THIRD FIGURE

M ⟶ P	(Middle term *is* predicate term.)
M ⟶ S	(Middle term *is* subject.)
Therefore, S ⟶ P	(Therefore, subject *is* predicate term.)

FOURTH FIGURE

P ⟶ M	(Predicate term *is* middle term.)
M ⟶ S	(Middle term *is* subject.)
Therefore, S ⟶ P	(Therefore, subject *is* predicate term.)

Since these four figures describe the *only* forms a categorical syllogism may take, they help tremendously in checking to see if the terms of a syllogism are in proper order. You first label the S and P in the conclusion, and then you trace back and label each appearance of S and P in the two premises. The terms left over you then label M (twice). Comparing the labeled syllogism with the four figures, you may find that any one of the three propositions is running backwards, or that the minor premise precedes the major. Putting the terms in proper order will not guarantee a valid conclusion, but it is a necessary first step.

Now, let's try a syllogism in the First Figure:

Some Republicans (M) are John Birchers (P).
Smith (S) is a Republican (M).
Therefore, Smith (S) is a John Bircher (P).

How was that again? The syllogism follows the First Figure, but something has gone wrong. We have violated another principle of classification, a most important one, concerning the "distribution" of our classes.

Learn how to distribute your terms.

The question of *all* and *some* is at the center of classifying ideas in syllogisms. The rules for distributing and not distributing your terms—that is, for making them assert information about every member, or only some members, of a class—are a little tricky. Let us look again at our Socrates syllogism, which we find, incidentally, is a syllogism in the pattern of the First Figure:

All MEN (M) are MORTAL CREATURES (P).
***Socrates* (S) is a MAN (M).**
Therefore, *Socrates* (S) is a MORTAL CREATURE (P).

In the major premise, "All MEN" is a *distributed* term; that is, it asserts information about the entire class MEN. Had we said "Some MEN," that would be an undistributed term, since it asserts something about only part of the class MEN; on the other hand, MORTAL CREATURES, in the major premise, is *undistributed,* because the statement does not assert something about the entire class of mortal creatures: it concerns only those mortal creatures known as men. In the minor premise, "Socrates" is *distributed,* because he is "all Socrates"; but "MAN" is *undistributed,* because the statement asserts nothing about the entire class of man. In this sound syllogism, then, we find that the middle term (MAN), which appears twice, is distributed once ("All MEN"), in the major premise. We find also that major term P (MORTAL CREATURES) is undistributed in both its premise (the major premise) and the conclusion, and that minor term S (*Socrates*) is distributed in both its premise (the minor premise) and the conclusion. Our findings have now brought us to the two rules that insure against the most common of syllogistic fallacies:

1. Your middle term (M) *must* be distributed at least once.
2. Neither major term (P) nor minor term (S) may be distributed ("All") in the conclusion if undistributed ("Some") in its premise.

In our Republican syllogism, we have not kept our eyes on the *all* and *some.* Our middle term, Republicans (M), is not distributed in either premise: "Some Republicans are John Birchers" asserts nothing about *all* Republicans; and "Smith is a Republican" similarly asserts nothing about *all* Republicans. In short, we have fallen into that common fallacy known as "the undistributed middle."

Here is a table to check your distributed and undistributed terms in the four kinds of categorical propositions (p. 228):

	DISTRIBUTED	UNDISTRIBUTED	DISTRIBUTED
I.	**All [*term*]**	**. . . is [*term*].**	
II.	**No [*term*] is [*term*].**		
III.		**Some [*term*] is [*term*].**	
IV.		**Some [*term*]**	**. . . is not [*term*].**

If your syllogism looks queer—or downright crazy—you simply take your major premise (or minor premise, or conclusion), and then check against this table to determine: (1) which kind of proposition it is, (2) which of its terms are distributed and which not, and (3) what changes in terms will give you the right distribution and a valid syllogism.

Take our statement "Some Republicans are John Birchers," which turned out a bit weird when we brought in "Smith." The table shows that we are in category III, and that both terms are undistributed. Since our rule for distribution requires that middle term (M) *must* be distributed at least once, you must devise a minor premise in which *Republicans* (M) is distributed (stated in some way as "all"), since this is your last chance at M. Or you could cast *John Birchers* in the role of M, and distribute *John Birchers.* Either way you produce a valid syllogism. First, by distributing *Republicans*:

Some Republicans (M) are John Birchers (P).
All Republicans (M) are supporters of the Constitution (S).
Therefore, some supporters of the Constitution (S) are John Birchers (P).

Or by distributing *John Birchers*:

> **Some Republicans (P) are John Birchers (M).**
> **All John Birchers (M) are critics of the Supreme Court (S).**
> **Therefore, some critics of the Supreme Court (S) are Republicans (P).**

To build a valid syllogism, then, take the steps summarized below.

Check your procedure.

A. Assure that your only verb is *is* (*are, were*) by recasting all three of your syllogism's statements as standard categorical propositions, changing "Girls wear skirts" to "All girls are skirt-wearing creatures."
B. See that each of your two premises, major and minor, makes a truthful, sensible statement.
C. Label the terms in your syllogism: two M's, a P, and an S in your two premises; an S and a P in your conclusion.
D. Make sure that you have one of the four "Figures" (p. 229), with the conclusion running S ⟶ P.
E. Make sure that your syllogism observes the six standard rules for a valid syllogism.

Check the Six Standard Rules.

Rule 1. The syllogism must contain exactly three terms, with no change in sense—no "All girls are *bright creatures;* stars are *bright creatures.*" Such a shift in meaning is called the Fallacy of Four Terms because the shift adds an illegitimate fourth to the required three terms.

Rule 2. The middle term (M) must be distributed at least once. This is the rule most commonly violated, to produce the frequent Fallacy of the Undistributed Middle.

Rule 3. Neither major term (P) nor minor term (S) may be distributed ("All") in the conclusion *if it is undistributed* ("Some") *in its premise.* This kind of illegitimate distribution is called the Fallacy of Illicit Process.

Rule 4. The syllogism may have only one negative premise.

Rule 5. If either premise is negative, the conclusion must be negative.

Rule 6. If the conclusion is "particular" ("Some"), the syllogism may have only one "universal" ("All" or "No") premise.

Learn the practical tricks of the trade.

A little practice with syllogisms will reveal these five convenient points:

1. In positive premises ("Men are mortal creatures"), any and every term before "is"—every subject of a positive "is" sentence—is *distributed,* unless *specifically preceded by "Some."* In other words, "Men" equals "All men" at the start of a premise.

2. In negative premises ("No men are angels"; "Some men are not angels") *every* term following the negation ("No" or "not") is *distributed,* since you are asserting something about the whole class. In other words, when you start with "No," you distribute *both* terms: that is, "No men are angels" asserts something about all men and all angels, as does its equivalent, "No angels are men." In "Some men are not angels" the negation distributes only the "angels."

3. Starting with an "All" major premise, any one of the four types of categorical propositions will work as a minor premise, providing that M is distributed in the major ("All M"), or in the minor ("All M," "No ______," or "not M"), or in both premises.

4. Starting with a "Some" major premise, you cannot begin your minor premise with "Some."
   (a) "Some ______ are ______" produces an *undistributed middle.*
   (b) "Some ______ are not ______" produces either an *undistributed middle* or an *illicit process.*

Therefore, starting with a "Some" major premise, you must look for an "All M" or "No ______" minor premise—and your S-term must be something *more general* than your M, or you will still produce an *undistributed middle* (this is what happened when we tried "Smith" as our S, following our major premise, "Some Republicans are John Birchers").

5. Starting with a negative major premise (either II "No ______ are ______," or IV "Some ______ are not ______"), you must look for a positive minor premise (either I "All ______ is ______," or III "Some ______ is ______").

The syllogism, in short, reveals ideas misclassified by confusing *all*'s and *some*'s. Syllogisms also help detect slips in the opposition's argument, and they hand you an invincible weapon to knock an opponent's shaky reasoning off its props. Suppose your opponent has asserted: "Some members of the faculty are Communists because they respect Karl Marx." Actually, they respect Marx's tremendous historical importance, a fact you would point out; then you could utterly demolish the opponent's argument by first putting it in a syllogism:

All Communists (P) are respecters of Marx (M).
Some faculty members (S) are respecters of Marx (M).
Therefore, some faculty members (S) are Communists (P).

Now, you know this is invalid. It flunks Rule 2: it has an undistributed middle ("respecters of Marx"). To display its bad logic, you devise a second and obviously absurd syllogism in exactly the same form, writing:

This argument is obviously absurd. It is exactly like saying:
All fish are good swimmers.
Some birds are good swimmers.
Therefore, some birds are fish.

The standard categorical syllogism, then—the kind we have been discussing—can help you firmly to establish, or to crush, all arguments containing three terms susceptible of being phrased as categorical propositions. Two other kinds of syllogisms—the *disjunctive,* or alternative, and the *hypothetical,* or conditional—are equally good as fault finders.

Beware of the horns.

The disjunctive syllogism is built on *either-or.*

Either the world began, or it did not.	**(major premise)**
Not-beginning is inconceivable.	**(minor premise)**
Therefore, the world began.	**(conclusion)**

The *either-or* syllogism has three basic pitfalls. The first is that the minor premise may make some assumption beyond the major: the inconceivability of "not-beginning" assumes that what we cannot conceive cannot exist. Aware of our limited powers, we know such an assumption is shaky. It may be true, but we cannot know for certain that it is. Its proof is literally beyond us. So when we cancel one half of the *either-or,* we may do so on extralogical grounds. You should see that your cancellations are reasonable and probable, even if beyond logical certainty.

The second pitfall in disjunctive reasoning is that your choices are often more than two; the choice may not really be *either-or.*

This organism is either animal or vegetable.	**(major premise)**
This organism is not vegetable.	**(minor premise)**
Therefore, this organism is an animal.	**(conclusion)**

This seems incontrovertible enough, yet the assumptions behind the major premise and the knowledge behind the minor may actually be faulty. We *assume* that animals and vegetables divide the living world, and we *know* of no exceptions. But biochemists have discovered organisms that seem to belong to both classes and to neither. In everyday thinking, we are forever assuming—when we rise from our desks and can't find our keys—that we *either* dropped our keys on the way to the office *or* left them in the car, only to discover them sticking in the office door. Our detectives are constantly discovering that it was *neither* the son *nor* the nephew, but the distraught widow after all.

The third pitfall in *either-or* statements is that the two terms may not be exclusive: "*Either* the Democrats win, *or* our foreign policy will fail." But experience has shown *our foreign policy* continuing under the Republicans almost unchanged. The policy's failure is not the exclusive alternative to a Democratic victory.

Know your truths and consequences.

The hypothetical syllogism is built on *if* and *then*: "If you work very hard on an essay, your grade will be better than last time"; or in full syllogistic dress:

If you work very hard on an essay, your grade will be better than last time.	**(major premise)**
You worked very hard on this essay.	**(minor premise)**
Therefore, this grade will be better than last time.	**(conclusion)**

But as you well know, the condition does not always bring the consequence. Other conditions, favorable and unfavorable, also operate. Although you dashed off your previous paper at a run, it came from ideas you had lived with. You earned a B, and, with a little more thought and polish, might have earned an A. Now you spend a week of hard reading and writing about an unfamiliar subject. Again your grade is B, or perhaps even C. Obviously, hard work is only one of several conditions for success.

Conditions are of two kinds: sufficient and necessary. A sufficient *if* will always bring a result, but it is not necessary to the result. If you light a match under dry paper, in quiet air, the paper will always burn. The lighted match is a sufficient condition, but it is not a necessary condition for burning paper: a cigarette lighter, hot coal, or tinder box will also do. Lacking a necessary condition, however, the fire *never* occurs. And this is what led me to give my sentence some air (which I had first left out), and then to keep it quiet. Air is necessary to combustion, but too much will blow out the flame. As with *either/or*, you should check your *if-then*'s for hidden alternatives.

Watch out for fallacies.

The syllogism helps to display our fallacies, but most of them you can detect by simply knowing they are lurking. Here are the most common:

(1) *Equivocation.* A word may illogically shift meanings in the same argument, as when someone attempts to argue that a *liberal* education makes people *liberal* with their money or in their politics. Within the syllogism, as we have seen, this slippage of meaning is the Fallacy of Four Terms.

(2) *Oversimplification.* The *either-or* proposition is usually an oversimplification. That every question has two sides—an *either* and an *or*—is not true; it will usually have more than two. Similarly, analogies always risk oversimplification: comparing the brain to a computer may seem to reduce it to nothing but wires and transistors. Sweeping generalizations may so simplify as to omit pertinent considerations, as with "Africans are not ready for self-government." Certainly some Africans are, if some are not; certainly there are many degrees of readiness and many kinds of self-government.

(3) *Begging the question.* As we have already seen (page 29), this somewhat unhandy but established term means assuming as proved something that really needs to be proved. "When are you going to stop beating your wife?" is the classic example of hooking the opponent

with a begged question. No matter what his answer, he seems to grant that which should still be up for proof: that he beats his wife. Similarly, "All the Communists must be rooted out of our colleges" begs the questions of how many Communists, if any, there are in our colleges, of whether anything harmful or illegal is going on, and of whether toleration of Communists is more dangerous than a policy of firing academicians and suspending students for their political beliefs.

(4) *Posing the complex question.* A close relative of *begging the question,* this fallacy lies in answering or giving a simple answer when a question really contains, undetected, several questions. For instance, I might have posed our old question-begging thesis (p. 28) as a fallacious complex question: "Are old age pensions the principle cause of our eroding responsibility?" A simple answer of "Yes" or "No" would mask the three questions entailed: (1) "Is responsibility eroding?"; (2) "If so, are old age pensions the chief cause?"; and (3) "Are old age pensions any part of the cause at all?" Obviously, we must look for the real questions behind any question, and not ignore them with a simple answer.

(5) *Ignoring the question.* This fallacy is so common that one wonders if we prejudiced and touchy creatures can ever face the question, the whole question, and nothing but the question. The issue of whether it is right for a neighborhood to organize against a newcomer is immediately diverted to questions of unkempt yards, reduced land values, and miscegenation. All arguments *ad hominem*—directed "to the man," that is, either against an opponent's character, or to an audience's prejudices, rather than to the issue—are logically fallacious in just this way. Similarly, we often argue only part of the question, ignoring the rest. A discussion of whether to vote an increase in taxes for a new school shifts to questions of who pays the taxes and how much they can pay, ignoring altogether the question of how badly a new school is needed.

(6) *Non sequitur* ("it does not follow"). The asserted conclusion does not logically follow from the stated conditions, as with "He's certainly sincere; he must be right," or "He's the most popular boy in class; he ought to be president." Our man may indeed be right and our boy deserving, but sincerity and popularity are not the logical reasons.

(7) *Post hoc, ergo propter hoc* ("after this, therefore because of this"). Since effects must by nature follow causes, we fallaciously

argue that the mere fact of following *proves* the cause. A new administration comes in; prosperity increases; the country hails the administration's economic genius. But if the new administration has kept all the old machinery, the causes may well lie elsewhere. What follows a thing is not necessarily caused by it—but then again what follows *may* be directly caused by it. To avoid the fallacy, find the real causes, and never base your proof simply on posteriority.

Exercises

1. Write an essay on the subject "The Mind Is a Wonder," illustrating it with mental curiosities of your own—the difficulty of finding words for things and feelings; the words that find you; the pictorial and the verbal; the obsessive inner argument that, even as it runs, you know to be wrong; the clarifications on paper; the hunches traced to their sources. Perhaps your own experience contains something similar to that of the late Benjamin P. Kurtz. Professor Kurtz maintained that, when working on a problem—the significance of Shelley's *Epipsychidion,* for instance—or when trying to remember where he had read something, he would instruct his mind, "All right, get to work on it now; I want some kind of answer on Wednesday morning"; he would then turn completely to other things. Wednesday morning's reports were not always impressive, but they were invariably better than zero; and he had saved two days of conscious stewing.

2. Collect from your dictionary five or six words having several meanings. Write a sentence for each meaning, the context making each perfectly distinct.

3. Write five sentences illustrating the inadvertent pun, as in "The muffins were *hardly* baked."

4. Write out an opinion you have about something, and beneath it draw up two lists: (1) four or five ways it might be documented; (2) four or five ways it might be discredited.

5. In a brief essay, explain and illustrate the differences among fact, belief, opinion, and preference, using as your thesis an assertion that the terms are frequently confused.

6. Write five sentences with ironic implications: "Professor Blank's lectures follow the text faithfully, word for word."

7. Write five assertions based on imperfect assumptions ("Football builds character"), explaining the imperfections briefly under each sentence.

8. Write two sentences illustrating each of the four faulty appeals to authority (pp. 219–220).

9. Write an essay on "Persistences I Have Known," showing how unfounded ideas persist, and how they are commonly cited as authoritative. You may range from superstitions concerning ladders and black cats, to rumors about teachers and other notorious citizens, and on to extrasensory perception.

10. Make up an anecdote entitled "The Clue on the Blackboard," in which something left on the board combines with other documentary and circumstantial evidence to suggest, inductively, a logical but completely false conclusion about the facts.

11. Selecting the author of any factual, expository book, write a case history of him in which you consider his probable dependability, biases, prejudices, and blind spots. This will require a little detective work. Find out his social, cultural, religious, and educational background, and from these details make some reasonable report to Sherlock Holmes about how well your author can be expected to treat the subject matter of his book, including the regions, if any, where one should at least be wary.

12. Look through the newspaper for some statistics—about how many people are killed by automobiles, cigarettes, slippery bathmats, or whatnot. Write a paragraph or two suggesting all the possibilities and details the figures do *not* represent.

13. Write an essay on "The Errors of Induction," taking some conveniently generalized concept like *boys, girls, freshmen, lectures, professors,* and showing the errors in the inductive evidence behind it ("All lectures are dull"), making sure to consider the three conditions for sound induction: (1) number of samples, (2) typicality, (3) explainability of exceptions.

14. Write an essay on the thesis "The exception proves the rule." (Consult your dictionary for the precise meaning of *proves* in this context.)

15. Write five nonsensical syllogisms in which the major and minor premises are perfectly true, but in which the conclusion is unproved because:

(a) The middle term (M) is undistributed (see "Republicans," pp. 230–232).

(b) The major term (P) is distributed in the conclusion but not distributed in the major premise (making M irrelevant).

All Dubliners (M) are city dwellers (P).
Some Dubliners (M) are policemen (S).
Therefore, some policemen (S) are not city dwellers (P).

(c) The minor term (S) is distributed in the conclusion but not distributed in its premise.

No Irishmen (M) are Englishmen (P).
Some Irishmen (M) are policemen (S).
Therefore, no policemen (S) are Englishmen (P).

(d) The syllogism contains two negative premises (M irrelevant).

No astronauts (M) are grandfathers (P).
No girls (S) are astronauts (M).
Therefore, no girls (S) are grandfathers (P).

(e) The syllogism contains one negative premise but an affirmative conclusion (undistributed M).

No astronauts (P) are grandfathers (M).
Some grandfathers (M) are skeptics (S).
Therefore, some skeptics (S) are astronauts (P).

16. Write four syllogisms, each beginning with a different one of the four possible categorical propositions (p. 228) as its major premise.

17. Turn the following statements into categorical propositions ("Women are creatures who live longer than men"); then make a syllogism of each, explaining in a note the logical invalidities, if any (the mistakes in classification and distribution), and any further errors in the implications even when the statement is made logical:

a. Women live longer than men.
b. Buicks are more expensive than Fords.
c. No bet is sure.
d. Cheaters never prosper.
e. Some people never learn.
f. Some apples are bad.
g. You can't teach an old dog new tricks.
h. Teen-agers are irresponsible.

Example: "Southerners suppress the Negro."

Some Southerners (M) are in the class of "those who suppress the Negro" (P) (major premise)
This man (S) is a Southerner (M). (minor premise)
Therefore, this man (S) is in the class of "those who suppress the Negro" (P). (conclusion)

(1) The major premise must be adjusted to what we know, and what common sense tells us: namely, that the "Southerners" of the original statement can rightly mean only "Some Southerners" and not "All Southerners." The original statement unjustifiably extends the middle term.

(2) With the premise adjusted, we see that the syllogism fails logically because the middle term is not distributed at least once (Rule 2); that is, "Some Southerners" is obviously not distributed, and neither is "Southerner" distributed, since "This man" occupies only a small part of the whole.

(3) The premise "Some Southerners are in the class of those who suppress the Negro," though technically sound, still carries the unsound implication that no one else outside the class of "Southerners" is culpable —no Northerners, no Westerners. The premise also implies that Negroes are not Southerners, and that some Negroes do not suppress others.

18. Make up one faulty and one valid disjunctive syllogism (*either-or*), explaining the machinery in both.

19. Do the same for the hypothetical syllogism (*if-then*).

20. Write a sentence or two illustrating each of the seven fallacies outlined on pages 236–238, adding a note explaining the fallacy in each. In other words, make up some bad examples, and explain them.

The Research Paper 14

Now to consolidate and advance. Instead of one thousand words you will write three thousand. Instead of a self-propelled debate you will write a scholarly argument. You will also learn to use the library, and to take notes and give footnotes. You will learn the manners of scholarship. You will learn to acknowledge your predecessors as you distinguish yourself, to make not only a bibliography, but a contribution.

The research paper is very likely not what you think it is. *Re-search* is searching again. You are looking, usually, where others have looked before; but you hope to see something they have not. Research is not combining a paragraph from the *Encyclopaedia Britannica* and a paragraph from *The Book of Knowledge* with a slick pinch from *Life.* That's robbery. Nor is it research if you carefully change each phrase and acknowledge the source. That's drudgery. Even in some high circles, I am afraid, such scavenging is called research. It is not. It is simply a cloudier condensation of what you have done in school as a "report"—sanctioned plagiarism to teach something about ants or Ankara, a tedious compiling of what is already known. That such material is new to you is not the issue: it is already in the public stock.

Choosing Your Subject

Find a thesis.

What, then, can you do, with things so well stocked? You move from facts to ideas. Here the range is infinite. Every old idea needs new assertion. Every new assertion needs judgment. Here you are in the area of values, where everyone is in favor of virtue but in doubt about what is virtuous. Your research problem is to make a judgment of right or wrong on some controversial issue.

I have put it bluntly to save you from drowning in slips of paper. Remember that an opinion is not a private fancy; it is an opinion *about* what the right is, what the truth is, what the facts mean. It is a judgment of what *is*—out there somewhere, not merely in somebody's head. An opinion, when careful and informed, is usually as close as you will get to truth: a statement of what the truth of the matter seems to be. Your opinion may be just as accurate as anybody's, and the major task of the research paper is to sift opinions.

Your sifter, as always, is your thesis, right there at the neck of your beginning paragraph. Your thesis, as always, is your essay in miniature. Make your thesis first, *before you begin research.* Call it a hypothesis (a "subthesis") if that will make you comfortable. It does seem unscientific. But it is nearer the scientific method than it looks. The scientist, too, plays his hunches. James Watt saw the steam condenser in the lid of his aunt's teakettle; Donald Glaser saw the tracks of atomic particles in the bubbles of his beer. As with scientific experiment and the simple essay, if the hypothesis proves wrong, the testing will have furnished means to make it more nearly right. With the research paper, if you do not have a thesis to lead you through the twists and turns of print, you will never come out the other end. Unless you have a working hypothesis to keep your purpose alive as you collect, you may collect forever, forever hoping for a purpose. If you have a thesis, you will learn—and then overcome—the temptations of collecting only the supporting evidence and ignoring the obverse facts and whispers of conscience. If further facts and good arguments persuade you to the other side, so much the better. You will be the stronger for it.

Persuade your reader you are right.

You do not search primarily for facts. You do not aim to summarize everything ever said on the subject. You aim to persuade your reader that the thesis you believe in is right. You persuade him by: (1) letting him see that you have been thoroughly around the subject and that you know what is known of it and thought of it, (2) showing him where the wrongs are wrong, and (3) citing the rights as right. *Your* opinion, *your* thesis, is what you are showing; all your quotations from all the authorities in the world are subservient to *your* demonstration. You are the reigning authority. You have, for the moment, the longest perspective and the last word.

Pick an argument.

The tactics of the research paper, then, are exactly those of any argumentative essay. Of course, you can give even straight exposition an argumentative edge; you can take as a subject not just "House Cats" but "House cats are more intelligent than most people realize." You can find something to prove even in straight description: "See," you say, "this has been overlooked; this has not been appreciated; this has been misunderstood." But you will be stronger yet in dealing with a controversial topic. Therefore: (1) pick a subject in which much is to be said on both sides; (2) take the side where your heart is; (3) write a thesis-sentence with a *because* in it; (4) gather your material around and about the *pro* and *con;* (5) write an essay with beginning, middle, and end, and with a *pro*-and-*con* structure like one of those described on pages 55–57.

Pick something that interests you.

You need not shake the world. Such subjects as "Subsidized College Football," "Small College Versus Big University," or the worth of "A Best-Selling Novel" well suit the research paper—a three-fold elaboration of the simple essay involving: (1) the handling of your argument, (2) the citation of others' facts and arguments *as part of your own,* and (3) the managing of footnotes and bibliography. Bigger subjects, of course, will try your mettle: subjects like "The Rights of Slaveholders in the Old South," "Euthanasia," "Legal Abortion." The whole question of governmental versus private endeavors affords many lively issues for research and decision—the ills and virtues of commercial television, for instance.

The Uses of the Library

Find the library, and walk in.

Sweet are the uses of diversity—books in the open stacks, sermons in tomes, and good in everything. But, in this plenteous Forest of Arden, you need some guidance if all is to be as you like it. First, find the card catalog. It catalogs all the library's holdings—books, magazines, newspapers, atlases, books on books, guides to guides. It also will catalog all holdings in any of its satellites around the campus—the law library, the medical library, the forestry library, the transportation library, and whatever else has spun off recently, including storage libraries, which the growing pressures of our collections have forced into remote orbit.

The catalog's 3 x 5 cards, filed in drawers, alphabetize every entry of every kind, from *A* to *Z*. Whether you are looking for an author's name, a book's title, or a general subject, whether the item is ten feet away or across the river in storage, you will find it in proper alphabetical order. John Adams and *The Anatomy of Melancholy* and Atomic Energy will all be found, in that order, in the *A* drawers. You do not need to shift catalogs as your need shifts from authors to titles to subjects. The one big catalog covers them all. (This convenience may not extend to some computer-generated catalogs, however.)

The Library of Congress and a few commercial firms prepare and sell author cards as a service for all libraries; from these, the libraries make their title and subject cards, and select their call numbers. On the cards in the illustration, notice the call number, the same on all cards for that book, typed by the library according to its classification system. This number locates the book on the shelves, leads you to it (in open stacks), and identifies it on your call slip, if you wish to "call" for it. Notice that the title card is made simply by adding the

Author Card: the "Main Entry"

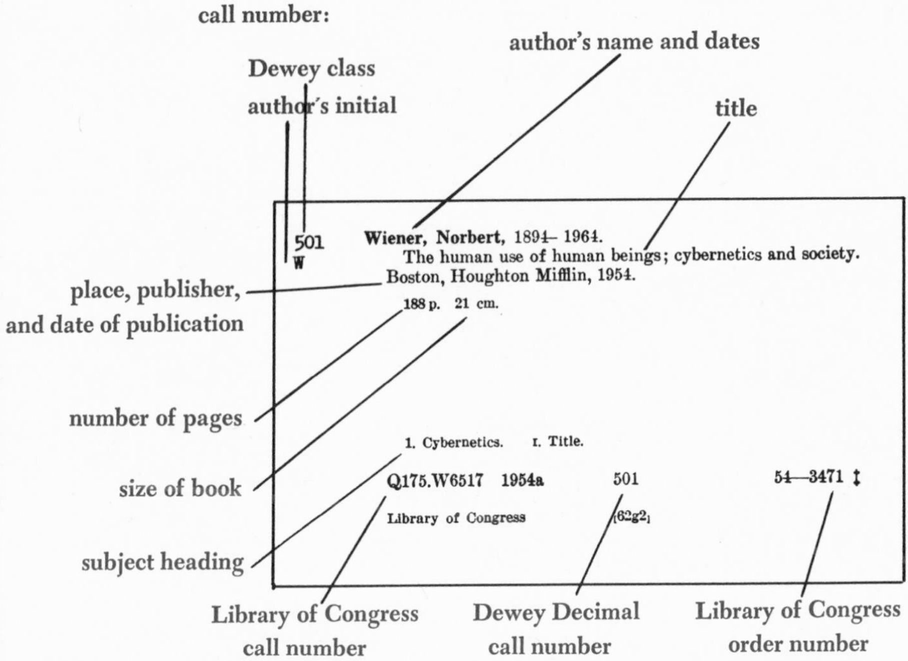
call number:
Dewey class
author's initial
author's name and dates
title
501
W
Wiener, Norbert, 1894– 1964.
The human use of human beings; cybernetics and society.
Boston, Houghton Mifflin, 1954.
188 p. 21 cm.
1. Cybernetics. I. Title.
Q175.W6517 1954a 501 54—3471 ‡
Library of Congress [62g2]
place, publisher, and date of publication
number of pages
size of book
subject heading
Library of Congress call number
Dewey Decimal call number
Library of Congress order number

Subject Card

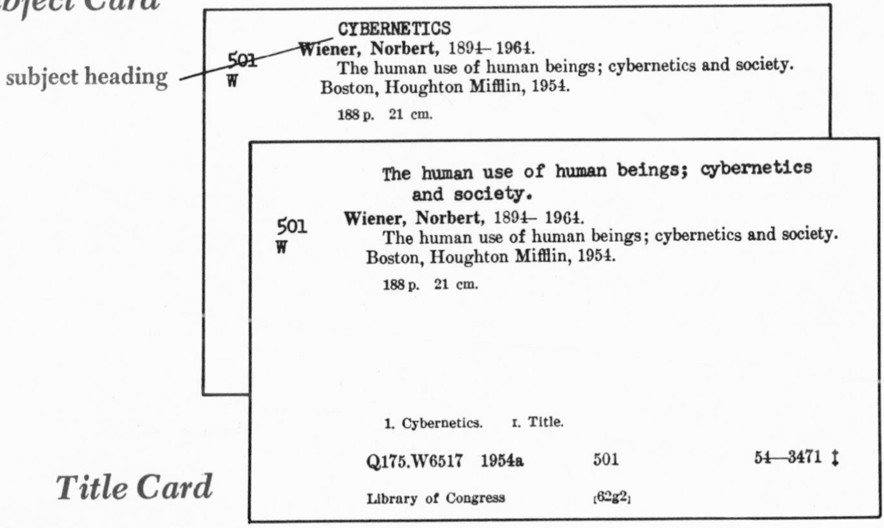
subject heading
CYBERNETICS
501
W
Wiener, Norbert, 1894– 1964.
The human use of human beings; cybernetics and society.
Boston, Houghton Mifflin, 1954.
188 p. 21 cm.
The human use of human beings; cybernetics and society.
501
W
Wiener, Norbert, 1894– 1964.
The human use of human beings; cybernetics and society.
Boston, Houghton Mifflin, 1954.
188 p. 21 cm.
1. Cybernetics. I. Title.
Q175.W6517 1954a 501 54—3471 ‡
Library of Congress [62g2]

Title Card

title at the top of an extra author card. Subject cards are made in the same way. The librarian usually follows the Library of Congress's recommendations for identifying the subject. The author card is filed under W (for Wiener), the title card under H (Human), and the subject card under C (cybernetics).

You will notice the two systems of call numbers printed at the bottom of the card: the Library of Congress and the Dewey Decimal. The Library of Congress's method has by no means supplanted the older system devised by Melvil Dewey in 1876. The Dewey system, with its ten divisions of knowledge, easily subdivided by decimals, brought order out of confusion. It became virtually standard throughout the United States, and made considerable headway in England. As our illustrative cards suggest, Dewey Decimal is still widely used. But Library of Congress is gaining ground. Big libraries need more and more subdivisions, to place a book among hundreds of a class. The Library of Congress, using letters for its general headings, offers twenty categories for Dewey's ten, and additional possibilities by combining letters with numbers.

The Dewey Decimal System

000 General Works
100 Philosophy
200 Religion
300 Social Sciences, Government, Customs
400 Philology
500 Natural Sciences
600 Useful Arts
700 Fine Arts
800 Literature
900 History, Travel, Biography

The Library of Congress System

A General Works
B Philosophy, Religion
C History
D Foreign History
E,F American History
G Geography, Anthropology
H Social Sciences
J Political Science
K Law
L Education
M Music
N Fine Arts
P Language and Literature
Q Science
R Medicine
S Agriculture
T Technology
U Military Science
V Naval Science
Z Library Science, Bibliography

Letters present some difficulties, of course. *I* and *O* have been skipped to avoid their confusion with numerals, and only three letters stand as initials for their categories. But in the older and the newer systems, you can see some interesting changes in the shape of human knowledge. "Religion" has lost some distinction, now sharing a category with "Philosophy"; "Philology" has become "Language" and has moved in with "Literature"; "History" has proliferated; "Politics" has become a science, with a category of its own. The newer system is far from perfect: "American History" has two letters, for instance, but "Anthropology" shares one with "Geography," which no longer seems its nearest relative. Knowledge, and the categories of knowledge, will change; the stock of books, and microfilms, will fluctuate in proportion; and our librarians will adjust their systems, endlessly keeping their cards up to date.

Learn the catalog's inner arrangements.

If you have ever tried to find your library's file of the *New Yorker,* or the New York *Times,* your heart probably sank before the drawers and drawers in the N-section labeled "New York." The alphabet seems to have collapsed under the dominance of our city of cities. You discover that you need to know a little more than the alphabet to find your way. Here are some finer details of arrangement in the card catalog:

1. Not only men, but organizations and institutions, can be "authors" if they publish books or magazines, as do the following:

Parke, Davis & Company, Detroit
The University of Michigan
U.S. Department of State

2. Initial *A, An, The,* and their foreign equivalents (*Ein, El, Der, Une,* and so forth) are ignored in alphabetizing a title. *A Long Day in a Short Life* is alphabetized under *L.* But French surnames are treated as if they were one word: De la Mare as if *Delamare,* La Rochefoucauld as if *Larochefoucauld.*

3. Cards are usually alphabetized *word by word*: *Stock Market* comes before *Stockard* and *Stockbroker.* "Short before long" is another way of putting it, meaning that *Stock* and all its combinations with other separate words precede the longer words beginning with *Stock-.*

Whether a compound word is one or two makes the apparent disorder. Hyphenations are treated as two words. The sequence would run thus:

Stock
Stock-Exchange Rulings
Stock Market
Stockard

4. Cards on one subject are arranged alphabetically by author. Under *Anatomy*, for instance, you will run from "Abernathy, John" to "Yutzy, Simon Menno," and then suddenly run into a title—*An Anatomy of Conformity*—which happens to be the next large alphabetical item after the subject *Anatomy*.

5. Identical names are arranged in the order (a) person, (b) titles and places, as they fall alphabetically.

Washington, Booker T.
Washington, George
Washington (State)
Washington, University of
Washington, D.C.
***Washington Square* [by Henry James]**

"Washington," the state, precedes the other "Washingtons" because "State" (which appears on the card only in parentheses) is not treated as part of its name. The University of Washington precedes "Washington, D.C." because no words or letters actually follow the "Washington of its title.

6. Since *Mc, M'*, and *Mac* are all filed as if they were *Mac*, go by the letter following them: *M'Coy, McDermott, Machinery, MacKenzie.*

7. Other abbreviations are also filed as if spelled out: *Dr. Zhivago* would be filed as if beginning with *Doctor; St.* as if *Saint; Mrs. Miniver* as if *Mistress*—except that many libraries now alphabetize *Mr.* and *Mrs.* as spelled.

8. Saints, popes, kings, and people are filed, in that order, by name and not by appellation (do not look under *Saint* for St. Paul, nor under *King* for King Henry VIII). The order would be:

Paul, Saint
Paul VI, Pope
Paul I, Emperor of Russia
Paul, Jean

9. An author's books are filed first by collected works, then by individual titles. Different editions of the collected works and different editions of the same title are arranged chronologically. Books *about* an author follow books *by* him.

Fielding, Henry 1707–1754	
***The Works of Henry Fielding, esq. . . .* London . . . .**	**1784**
***The Works of Henry Fielding, esq. . . .* London . . . .**	**1806**
The Complete Works of Henry Fielding	**1840**
Selections	**1923**
Amelia	**1752**
The History of Amelia	**1857**
The History of the Adventures of Joseph Andrews	**1893**
The History of Tom Jones, a foundling	**1749**
The History of Tom Jones, a foundling	**1836**
[works about]	
Allen, Walter, *Six Great Novelists*	

Notice that this library owns only a later edition of *Joseph Andrews*, printed long after the author's death in 1754.

Locate the books you need.

The card catalog may tell you: "Undergrad Library," "Graduate Reading Room," "Rare Book Room," "Engineering Library," "Storage." You will learn your own library's system, of course, from the staff and from your fellow students: which stacks are open, which closed, where the several rooms and libraries are, how to make out call slips, how to get at the books and get them out. But the card catalog tells you the primary fact of whether the library has the book at all. No card, no book. All the library's holdings are indexed: newspapers, magazines, encyclopedias, dictionaries, indexes, atlases, microfilms. Your library can also help you to locate the book in another library, or to get information about it. For graduate research, if the book is not too rare, the library can arrange to borrow it for you from another library, or to supply you with microfilms or photostats of the parts you want.

Several other guides can help you find where in the world a book may be:

1. *A Union Card Catalog.* A few large libraries keep one of these: a catalog of cards in other libraries. Find out if your library has one, and browse it. It may prove useful someday.

2. The *Library of Congress Catalog of Printed Cards* and the *Library of Congress National Union Catalog.* These are big alphabetized volumes in which the cards, or their contents, are reproduced, eight or ten to the page. Cards for new acquisitions are reproduced in supplements issued quarterly.

3. The British Museum's *General Catalogue of Printed Books.* Similar to the Library of Congress's catalog, it lists the holdings in England.

4. The *United States Catalog* and its supplements, the *Cumulative Book Index,* are volumes listing books printed in English. These identify publisher and date of publication but not location in a library.

Know the encyclopedias.

The encyclopedias will probably be in the reference room. The card catalog will, of course, tell you where each one is, but the reference room will probably have them all together on open shelves, with perhaps a separate catalog of the room's holdings nearby for your convenience. The best general encyclopedias, with authoritative articles on subjects and people arranged alphabetically, are these:

Encyclopaedia Britannica
Encyclopedia Americana
Collier's Encyclopedia
Columbia Encyclopedia

Here are some encyclopedias on special subjects:

Agriculture.

Agricultural Index. 1916–. [Monthly]
Yearbook of Agriculture. 1894–. [U.S. Department of Agriculture]

The Arts.

Encyclopedia of World Art. 1959–1968.
Grove, Sir George. *Dictionary of Music and Musicians.* 9 vols. 1954.
Harper's Encyclopedia of Art. 1937.
Thompson, O. *International Encyclopedia of Music and Musicians.* 8th ed., 1958.

Education.

Harris, Chester W., ed. *Encyclopedia of Educational Research.* 1960.
Monroe, Paul, ed. *Cyclopedia of Education.* 5 vols. 1911–1913, repr. 1926–1928.

History.

Adams, J. T., ed. *Dictionary of American History.* 6 vols. 1940–1963.

Encyclopedia of World History. 1968.

Worldmark Encyclopedia of the Nations. 1971.

Religion.

Catholic Encyclopedia. 17 vols. 1907–1922. Revised 1936–, with loose-leaf supplements.

Hastings, James, ed. *Dictionary of the Bible.* 5 vols. 1898–1904.

———. *Encyclopedia of Religion and Ethics.* 13 vols. 1911–1912.

The Interpreter's Dictionary of the Bible. 4 vols. 1962.

Jewish Encyclopedia. 12 vols. 1925.

New Schaff-Herzog Encyclopedia of Religious Knowledge. 13 vols. 1949–1950.

Twentieth-Century Encyclopedia of Religious Knowledge. 2 vols. 1955.

Universal Jewish Encyclopedia. 10 vols. 1939–1943.

Science.

McGraw-Hill Encyclopedia of Science and Technology. 15 vols. 1966.

Van Nostrand's Scientific Encyclopedia. 1968.

Social Science.

Baldwin, J. M., ed. *Dictionary of Philosophy and Psychology.* 1940–1949.

Encyclopedia of the Social Sciences. 15 vols. 1930–1935.

Munn, Glenn G. *Encyclopedia of Banking and Finance.* 6th ed., 1962.

Biographical Encyclopedias.

Current Biography. 1940–.

Dictionary of American Biography. 20 vols., index. 1928–1943, plus current supplements. [Abbreviated as "DAB" in footnotes.]

Dictionary of National Biography [British]. 22 vols. 1908–1909, indexes, plus current supplements. [Abbreviated as "DNB."]

International Who's Who. 1935–.

Kunitz, S. J., and Howard Haycraft. *American Authors, 1600–1900.* 1938.

———. *British Authors of the Nineteenth Century.* 1936.

———. *Twentieth Century Authors.* 1942. Supplement, 1955.

———. *British Authors Before 1800.* 1952.

Webster's Biographical Dictionary. 1964.

Who's Who [British]. 1848–. [Issued annually.]

Who's Who in America. 1899–. [Issued biennially.]

Investigate the almanacs.

Benjamin Franklin compiled a collection of pithy sayings to see us through the year—*Poor Richard's Almanac.* But more useful to your research will be the modern almanacs of facts, statistics, and events, year by year. If you want to know what the population of Nevada was in 1940, what the wheat crop was in 1950, what the rainfall was in 1960, or who your senator was in 1970—these are the books for you. Suppose you are writing about Eugene O'Neill's *Mourning Becomes Electra*. You could say many different kinds of things about that play: what each character represents in the play's diagram of forces, how the play relates to O'Neill's other plays, or to the Greek drama, which its title invokes. But if you want a glimpse of the play's career on Broadway, go to an almanac. Here you will find what other plays were running, how long O'Neill's play ran, who played the leading roles, when and where the actors were born, whether O'Neill won a Pulitzer Prize (he did) and for which play (not this one). This is not all on one page, of course; but the index will lead you. For almost any subject, you can find interesting facts and figures in the almanacs. Here are the most useful ones:

American Year Book. 1910–.
Americana Annual. 1923–.
Annual Register of World Events [British]. 1758–.
Britannica Book of the Year. 1938–.
Economic Almanac. 1940–.
Information Please Almanac, Atlas, and Yearbook, 1947–.
New York Times Encyclopedic Almanac. 1970–.
Statesman's Year-Book. 1864–.
Statistical Abstract of the United States. 1878–.
The World Almanac and Book of Facts. 1868–.

Find the indexes to periodicals and newspapers.

Indexes to periodicals do for articles what the card catalog does for books. Some index by subjects only, others by subjects and authors. They, too, will probably be in your reference room. The card catalog or list of magazine holdings will tell you whether your library has a particular magazine, and where the bound volumes of it are shelved. Issues for the current year will be available, unbound, in some kind of periodical section, or room. But to find what is in the popular magazines, bound or unbound, you start with the *Readers' Guide to Periodical Literature*.

This is a long file of fat volumes, beginning in 1900, and kept current with supplements, now issued twice monthly, running only a few weeks behind the flood of articles in the magazines they index. They list these magazines inside the front cover; check this list first if, for instance, you are trying to find an article you once read at the barbershop in some magazine called *Thrill.* You will discover that *Thrill* is not indexed, which is probably just as well, and you can shift your search to another sector. Also inside the front cover is a list of the abbrevations used in describing the articles. Studying them will enable you to read an entry such as this:

GAMBLING
It's bye! bye! blackjack. D. E. Scherman.
il Sports Illus 20:18-20+ Ja 13 '64

—and translate it into this:

Scherman, D. E., "It's Bye! Bye! Blackjack," ***Sports Illustrated,*** **January 13, 1964, pp. 18-20. . . .**

You learn that the article is illustrated ("il") and in volume 20, which you may need for finding it. You also learn that the article continues on back pages: "18–20+—which you would complete after you had found the article and read it through, as: "pp. 18–20, 43, 46–47." You will do well to write out as full a translation as you can on your own bibliographical card, or you may not understand the abbreviations when going to find the magazine or writing your bibliography. Other important general indexes are:

Book Review Digest. 1905–.

New York Times Index. 1913–. [A wonderful guide to the news. Get the date, and you can read about the incident in most other newspapers for the same day, if your library lacks the *Times.*]

Nineteenth Century Readers' Guide . . . . 1890–1899, with supplementary indexing, 1900–1922.

Poole's Index to Periodical Literature. 1802–1906. [By subject only, but admirably supplemented by Marion V. Bell and Jean C. Bacon, *Poole's Index, Date and Volume Key* (Chicago, 1957). If you want to know what the reviewers thought of Webster's first *Dictionary,* or Hawthorne's *Scarlet Letter,* dip into *Poole's.*]

Social Sciences and Humanities Index. 1965–. [Formerly *International Index to Periodicals,* 1913–1964, this does for scholarly journals what the *Readers' Guide* does for popular ones.]

The Subject Index to Periodicals. 1915–1951. [Covers more than 450 periodicals in all fields, American and British. In 1961, it split into two, limited to Britain: *British Humanities Index* and *British Technology Index.*]

Here are some special indexes:

Annual Magazine Subject-Index. 1908–1949. [Particularly for history.]
Art Index. 1929–.
Bibliographic Index. 1937–.
Biography Index. 1946–.
Biological and Agricultural Index [formerly *Agricultural Index,* 1916–].
Catholic Periodical Index. 1930–.
Dramatic Index. 1909–1950.
Education Index. 1929–.
Engineering Index. 1884–.
Essay and General Literature Index. 1900–. [Very useful for locating particular subjects within books of essays.]
Index Medicus. 1879–1926; *Quarterly Cumulative Index Medicus.* 1927–.
Industrial Arts Index. 1913–1957. Succeeded by *Applied Science and Technology Index.* 1958–; and by *Business Periodicals Index.* 1958–.
International Catalogue of Scientific Literature. 1902–1921.
Music Index. 1949–.
Psychological Index. 1894–1936.
Public Affairs Information Service. Oct. 15, 1914–.
Technical Book Review Index. 1917–1929; 1935–.
Thompson, Stith. *Motif-Index of Folk-Literature.* 6 vols. 1932–1936.

And check your particular field for "abstracts"—indexes that publish brief summaries of articles—such as, *Biological Abstracts,* 1926–; *Chemical Abstracts,* 1907–; *Geological Abstracts,* 1953–; *Psychological Abstracts,* 1927–. These lists should prove more than adequate for your beginnings in any subject. You may expand your knowledge of such aids to research by examining Constance M. Winchell's *Guide to Reference Books* (eighth edition, with current supplements).

Browse the literary bibliographies.

In no field are books and articles so thoroughly and variously listed as in literary studies—by period, by field, by literary genre, by author, and so on. *Selective Bibliography for the Study of English and American Literature* (New York, 1960), by Richard D. Altick and Andrew Wright, admirably outlines the field. Begin here. It is the best, for amateur and professional alike, an indispensable guide to the guides. It will lead you to what others have said about the novels and stories and poems and authors you are studying. Here are some important landmarks:

I. *English Literature: General.*

The Cambridge Bibliography of English Literature, 4 vols. Cambridge, 1941. Supplement (Vol. V), Cambridge, 1957.

The Concise Cambridge Bibliography of English Literature. Cambridge, 1958. [Handy and inexpensive.]

II. *American Literature: General.*

Robert E. Spiller, et al., *Literary History of the United States.* Bibliography. *Supplement,* 1962, 1963.

Lewis Leary, *Articles on American Literature, 1900–1950.* Durham, 1954.

Jacob Blanck, *Bibliography of American Literature.* New Haven, 1955–. [Appearing in volumes, author by author, this promises to be the definitive bibliography for some time to come.]

Clarence L. F. Gohdes, *Bibliographical Guide to the Study of the Literature of the U.S.A.* Durham, 1959.

III. *Current Literary Bibliography: General.*

"Annual Bibliography," *PMLA* (Publications of the Modern Language Association of America). 1922–. [Each April issue of this quarterly magazine. Since 1957, its international coverage has made it the supreme bibliography.]

Modern Humanities Research Association, *Bibliography of English Language and Literature.* 1920–. [Annual.]

English Association, *The Year's Work in English Studies.* 1921–. [Annual.]

IV. *English Literature: Current.*

"Bibliography of American Periodical Literature," *Speculum.* 1926–. [Quarterly. Scholarly essays on medieval subjects in American journals.]

"Literature of the Renaissance," *Studies in Philology.* 1917–. [Annual, April issue.]

"Shakespeare: An Annotated Bibliography," *Shakespeare Quarterly.* 1950–. [Annual, Spring issue.]

"English Literature, 1660–1800," *Philological Quarterly.* 1926–. [Annual, April issue, 1926–1948; July issue, 1949–.]

"The Romantic Movement: A Selective and Critical Bibliography," *English Literary History.* 1937–1949. Transferred to *Philological Quarterly.* 1950–. [Annual, April issue.]

"Current Bibliography," *Keats-Shelley Journal.* 1952–. [Annual, Winter issue.]

"Victorian Bibliography," *Modern Philology.* 1933–1957. [Annual,

May issue.] Transferred to *Victorian Studies.* 1957–. [Annual, May issue.]

"Current Bibliography," *Twentieth-Century Literature.* 1955–. [Quarterly.]

V. *American Literature: Current.*

"Articles on American Literature Appearing in Current Periodicals," *American Literature.* 1929–. [Quarterly.]

"Articles in American Studies," *American Quarterly.* 1955–. [Annual, Summer issue.]

The Job of Research

Now that you have looked over the library and its possibilities, you are ready to dig in. You have already decided on your subject and your tentative thesis. Getting these in hand before you even learn where the library is will emphasize the point made at the start of this chapter: *make your thesis, or hypothesis, first,* before you begin looking at the work of others. Let us suppose that you have grown weary of the interrupting commercials on television, that you have heard something of England's BBC, with its freedom from interruptive advertisements, but that you also have heard that a commercial television system, complete with sponsors and advertising spots, has sprung up in England beside the government's noncommercial one. You would like to look into the matter. Testing your own feelings, and suspecting that the better argument is that which challenges the status quo, you decide tentatively to argue "the case for socialized television" (and, indeed, the very phrase strikes you as a properly saucy title for your paper).

Get the equipment, and gather the material

You will need some 3 x 5 cards for your bibliography, some 3 x 5 slips of paper for notes, and some kind of envelope to hold them. Since you will work up your bibliography first, you may find that your cards still have enough room on face and back for whatever notes you need. Since notes should be brief and few, the limit of your one bibliographical card per source may keep you trim. If you take several notes from each source, however, use your slips of paper and put only one note, even if only a phrase, on each slip. This will facilitate your shuffling and organizing. You will fill out your bibliographical cards as you find what you want in card catalogs and indexes.

Your instructor may ask you to keep your bibliographical cards free of notes, to facilitate his giving you exercises in bibliographical form. And it is extremely important to get the form exactly right on your cards; otherwise, you may have to look everything up again in the library when you come to type your bibliography. Make sure to catch the following details in full, exactly as they appear on the book or article itself:

1. *Author's full name* (last name first).
2. *Title of the work.* Italicize (that is, underline) titles of books and magazines; put titles of chapters and articles found *within* books and magazines in quotation marks.
3. *Facts of publication.* For a book, give the place, the publisher, and year of publication, all within parentheses; the year should be the copyright year, usually given on the back of the title page. For an article, give the magazine's full title, underlined, its volume number if any, its date (in parentheses), and the pages through which the article runs.

I find a great advantage in using my bibliographical cards for notes —indeed, in limiting my notes as far as possible to what the bibliographical card can hold, front and back. (Using the back is heretical, but handy.) Your cards will look something like those on pages 260 and 261.

Plan on some ten or fifteen sources for your 3,000 words of text. Make all entries, take all notes, in *ink.* After the thumbing, you will be thankful. Check spellings, volume numbers, places, dates, and pages when you finally get your magazine or book in hand, putting a light checkmark (√) in pencil to assure yourself that your card is authoritative, safe to use in checking your finished paper. Get the author's name as he signed it, adding detail in brackets if helpful: D[elmar] P[rince] Smith. Get all the information; the sample footnotes on pages 267–272 will show you what you may need, especially in complicated references.

Start with encyclopedias.

Now that you have located the card catalog, find the *Encyclopaedia Britannica* and the *Readers' Guide to Periodical Literature,* and your problems are nearly solved. Begin with the *Britannica.* This will survey your subject (for latest news, see latest editions, and the annual supplementary "year books"). Each article will refer you, at

Book

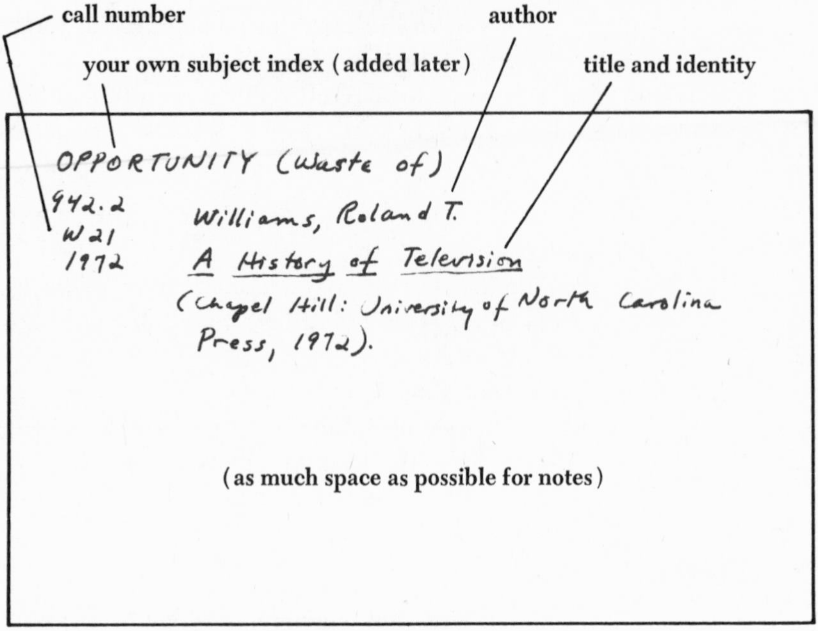
call number
author
your own subject index (added later)
title and identity
OPPORTUNITY (Waste of)
942.2
W21
1972
Williams, Roland T.
A History of Television
(Chapel Hill: University of North Carolina
Press, 1972).
(as much space as possible for notes)

Article

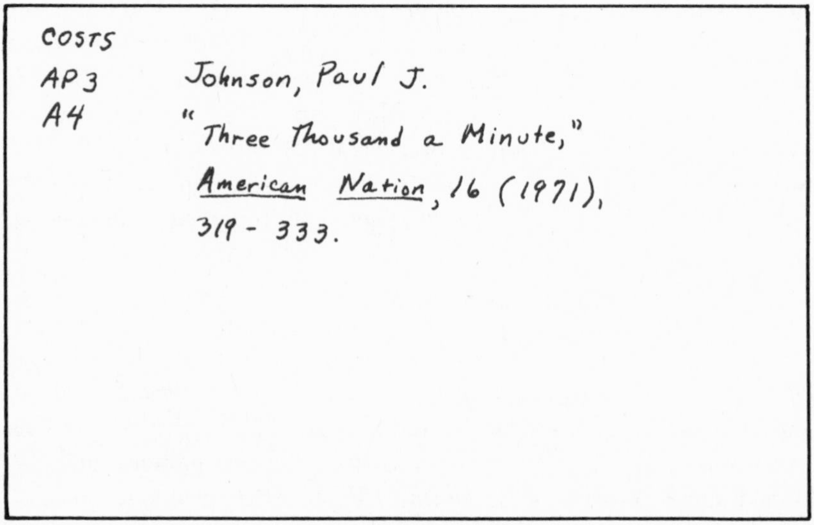
COSTS
AP3
A4
Johnson, Paul J.
"Three Thousand a Minute,"
American Nation, 16 (1971),
319 - 333.

News Story

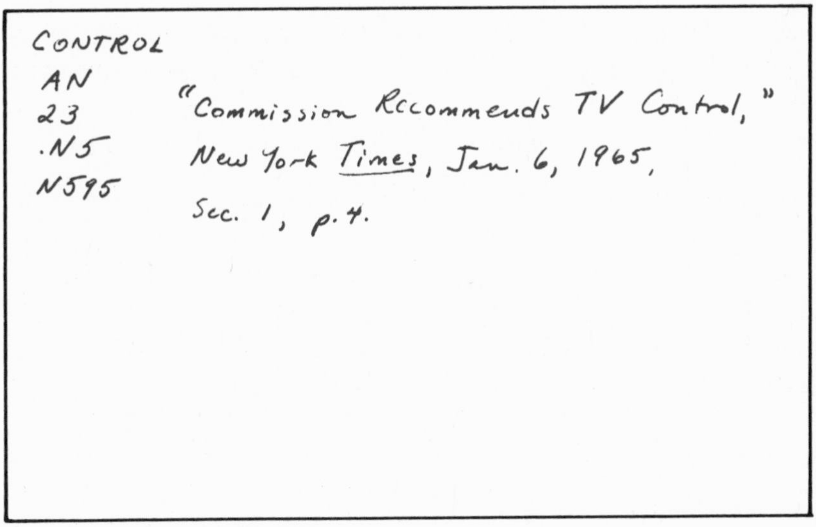
CONTROL
AN
23
.N5
N595

"Commission Recommends TV Control," *New York Times*, Jan. 6, 1965, Sec. 1, p. 4.

the end, to several authorities. If someone's initials appear at the end, look them up in the Contributors' List, or in the Index (the last volume of the set). The author is an authority himself; you should mention him in your paper. Furthermore, the Contributors' List will name several of his works, which will swell your bibliography and aid your research. The index will also refer you to data scattered through all the volumes. Under "Medicine," for instance, it directs you to such topics as "Academies," "Hypnotism," "Licensing," "Mythology," and so on. Since the *Britannica* now revises progressively, subject by subject, note the date on the copyright page to see how much you may need to bring your subject up to date. The *Encyclopedia Americana* and *Collier's Encyclopedia*, though less celebrated, will here and there challenge the *Britannica's* reign. Others from the list on pages 252–253 will also help.

Comb the indexes.

With your encyclopedic background sketched, go next to the card catalog, then to the magazine indexes. The card catalog directs you around within itself rather well. So, for your research paper, simply take your subject and see what books your library lists under it. Two or three of the most recent books will probably give you all you want, because each of these, in turn, will refer you, by footnote and bibliography, to important previous works. Make your bibliographical cards as you go.

Now for the *Readers' Guide*. Again, take the most recent issue, look up your subject, and make out your cards—spelling out the abbreviations of titles and dates. You can drop back a few issues and years to collect more articles; and if your subject belongs to the recent past (after 1907), you can drop back to the right year and track your subject forward.

You can do the same with the *New York Times Index*, beginning with 1913, and with the *Social Sciences and Humanities Index*. Add to these the *Book Review Digest* and the *Biography Index* (which nicely collects scattered references), and you will probably need no more, unless working in a subject having special indexes or bibliographies, such as the *Art Index*, the *Psychological Index*, or the annual literary bibliographies in *PMLA* and others (see pp. 255–258).

Then take a dip in the *World Almanac* or *Statistical Abstract of the United States* to see what interesting statistic or odd fact you can turn up for your subject. And finally—but here I urge great restraint, to avoid seeming puffed up—look into *Bartlett's Familiar Quotations*, *Oxford Dictionary of Quotations*, or some such, to see what ringing and authoritative words may support your crucial point.

Take few notes.

Now, first the books, then the magazines. With cards in hand, begin with a likely-looking book. Read quickly, with an eye for the general idea, and the telling point. Having a clear thesis will guide your note-taking. You can be sparing and spare. Some of your sources will need notes no fuller than "Violently opposed; recommends complete abolition." This violent and undistinguished author will appear in your paper only among several others in a single footnote to one sentence: "Opposition, of course, has been long and emphatic.[2]" Now is the time, too, to put a *pro* or a *con* in the upper right corner of your card so that you may sort your cards when you begin to organize.

You have been evaluating your authors, of course, noting the biased and the judicious, checking their credentials to decide how authoritatively they may speak on the subject, and from what cultural and religious background. You can quickly take something of an author's measure by his cards in the catalog; and magazines frequently give a note about their authors. Be cautious—and generous. Tempers and antagonisms change, and one slip doesn't always make a slide. But from a man's tone and background you may occasionally put down a helpful note to yourself, something like: "[violently anti-British]."

Your next source, however, turns out to have something substantial to say, though still in opposition. This man writes well enough to be quoted. A *con* will put him in his place; a summary phrase will cover him: "Bases argument entirely on practical grounds, sets moral issue aside as irrelevant and 'Utopian.'" Now, within exaggerated quotation marks, put down the sentence or two you want. Your card would look like the example on this page.

Take care with page numbers. Notice how I have put "214" where the quotation turns the page—I might want to use only part of the excerpt and then be uncertain as to which of the two pages held it. Notice also how I have put brackets around my own words, just to make sure that I don't later confuse them with quoted material. Check your quotation against the original, word by word, and give it a penciled check when you know it is accurate.

TAXATION - Private Property
420.6 Adamson, Charles C.
AM 40 "How Much Can the Traffic Bear?"
American Investigator, 16 (1960), 210-219.
Bases argument entirely on practical grounds.
Moral issues "Utopian." (210)
"Morals in the T.V. trade are always tied to purse strings. Where the haves /214 and have-nots haggle, only practical questions can yield practical answers." (213-214) [But couldn't the moral issues be there anyway? Truth?]

Use your slips of paper only if you feel you need more notes than these. Put a "2" in the upper right corner of your first slip; copy and summarize away, using brackets and big quotation marks and putting page numbers in parentheses right where they belong. At the bottom of the slip, note the author and page numbers—you will need catchwords to designate different works by the same author: **Adamson, "TV Nets," 215; Adamson, *Money*, 109–112**—and start slip 3, if you must. When all your notes are taken, you are ready to write.

The First Draft

Start to plan your paper by writing a beginning paragraph.

Formal outlines, especially those made too early in the game, can sometimes take more time than they are worth, but a long paper with notes demands some planning. First, draft a beginning paragraph, incorporating your thesis:

The Case for Socialized Television

Freedom for all is the essential idea in a democracy; and free enterprise, many believe, has made America strong. From the first, we have resisted governmental controls, throwing tea into Boston harbor and overthrowing British rule. To this day, "Big Government" usually spells "bad government" to most people, suggesting dictators, inhuman regimentation and terror, and societies of robots. Freedom for the individual is our belief and our goal. But the idea also involves freedom of opportunity, and here, I think, "Big Government" can function, as it has functioned in the past, to prevent one man's enterprise from seizing another man's opportunity. Some such seizure has taken place in the television enterprises of the United States. A brief comparison with the British system, and a little thought, will show that the United States Government could control television with no real damage to free enterprise and with a great widening of opportunity for all. American television is not living up to its opportunities.

Canvass your notes and plot your course.

Next, read through your notes, sorting them into three piles: *pro*'s, *con*'s, and *in-between*'s (often simply facts). Now you are ready to make your formal outline, if the assignment requires it, using one of the schemes on pages 65–70, refining it as you work further into your notes and your paper.

Or you may use a working outline, intended for no eyes but your own, a private guide for the job ahead. Make three or four general headings on a sheet of paper, with ample space between. Let us assume a complex *pro*-and-*con* structure. Under each of your headings, make a list of the *con*'s against a list of your *pro*'s, as they seem to mount and to balance each other. Start with a list of insignificant *con*'s, to be finished in a sentence, and move to the more significant. Your sketch will look something like this:

I. Commercial argument—Gov't would still leave room for advertising.

PRO	CON
	Allenberg
	Hawkins, Weiss
	Smith
	Dillon
	Jones (p. 20)
But—Jones (p. 23)	
Lecky's facts	
N.Y. Times	
Cummings	

II. Educational argument

PRO	CON
	Perkins
But—Brown (hrs./day that children watch)	
Facts { Johnson, Flemming, Steinberg, Lane	

III. Freedom to choose—Collins, Williams, Thos. Jefferson's "aristocracy of talent"

IV. Opportunity to learn and to be amused—Wilkins

Notice, first, that your references are thick at first and thin toward the end. As I have said, you will handle each of the first four or five *con*'s in a sentence or two; the rest will get more space. But with Perkins's protests you will leave the *con* side altogether, well before you are halfway through. You will still be citing and quoting under heading III, but these men will all be on your side; and in section IV you will be entirely on your own, except for one stirring quotation from Wilkins.

Put in your references as you go.

Your first draft should have all your footnotes, abbreviated, right in the text. Otherwise you will lose your place, and go mad with numbers. Put the notes at the *end* of the last pertinent sentence, with as many of your references as possible grouped in one note. Write out your quotations in full, so you can have them directly before you, and see how much space they take, as you type your smooth copy; and include the author's surname and the page number with each citation. You will change these in your final draft, of course, filling in the names or leaving them out of the note altogether if they appear in the text. But it will help you in checking against your cards to have an author's name and a page number for each citation. *Don't number your footnotes yet.* When your draft is finished, add the numbers in pencil, so you can change them; circled in red, so you can see them (a red pencil is really worth its price). As you type along, mark your notes with triple parentheses: (((. . .)))—the easiest distinction you can make. Check the rules about quotation marks on pages 160–162. You should single-space, and indent (as shown in the following example), all quotations of more than fifty words, unless you want to emphasize shorter quotations by thus setting them apart, as you would do with poetry. (If the quoted matter itself begins as a paragraph, indent the first quoted line further.) Now, settle down to the keyboard and begin your second paragraph.

> **Free enterprise and freedom of opportunity, of course, are the first appeals of those who defend American television as it now is. Any mention of governmental control, or even of change in the present system, is likely to be met with cries of "socialism" and lectures on the American heritage. (((Allenberg, p. 10; Hawkins, p. 16; Weiss, p. 5; Smith, "This is creeping socialism. This is not the American way," p. 77))) Miles W. Dillon argues that the television networks must awake to their national responsibility in helping keep America free by "cleaning their own house," thus forestalling the governmental intrusion that will be a first step toward absolute governmental control, propaganda, and dictatorship. (((Dillon, pp. 23–25))) Bingham Jones, a proponent of mild governmental regulation, acknowledges these same dangers and concedes that the best solution would be a general renovation by the networks themselves. (((Jones, p. 20)))**
>
> **But, Jones continues, the networks will never do it; the sponsors are too firmly entrenched:**
>
> > **If the general housecleaning, so frequently recommended, so frequently attempted, could work, the entire problem would disappear. Our television systems would have arrested their slow deterioration. The lost adult audiences would have been regained . . . . We could again see great works of literature drama-**

tized frequently; we could again explore the world with the informed camera and explore ideas with the best minds of the country. But so long as advertising agents select programs with sales their sole consideration, no house will be cleaned. Indeed, up to the present, every effort at housecleaning has failed after a few preliminary sweeps. Commerce dictates as strongly as ever. (p. 23)

Hans J. Lecky's survey in *T.V. News* indicates that Jones is correct. More than 30 percent of all television time, Lecky calculates, is given to advertisement. Of the 1,000 hours in Lecky's sample, only 50 were "live." (((Lecky, pp. 93–94))) Moreover, the decline in "live" hours of commercial television may be directly proportional to the decline in quality. (((*Times*, p. 8)))

And so on, until your carded sources run out and your own resources take over completely.

Your Final Draft: Documenting Your Sources

Allow space for notes at the foot of the page.

You can see from your preliminary drafts about how many footnotes will fall on your page, and about how much space to allow at the bottom. Allow plenty. You will begin your notes three spaces below your text. You have been double-spacing your text; now use a triple-space. Do *not* type a line between text and notes: this indicates a footnote continued from the preceding page. Single-space each note, but double-space between notes. Indent as for a paragraph. To type the number, use the variable line spacer and roll down about half the height of a capital letter. After you have typed the number, return to your normal typing line and begin typing your note without hitting the space bar: "[1] Albert Kurtz, p. 5." After the first line, notes run out to the left margin again, as in paragraphs. The notes to our sample would come out like this:

[1] Donald Allenberg, *The Future of Television* (New York, 1973), p. 10; A. H. Hawkins, "Our Greatest Salesman," *American Thought,* 4 (1968), 16; J. Weiss, "Government Control, a Growing Concern," *Saturday Night Journal,* September 20, 1971, p. 5; see especially W. W. Smith, "Television and the Modern World," *American Politician,* 19 (1968), 77: "This is creeping socialism. This is not the American way."

[2] "American Television and Responsibility," ***Space,*** **August 16, 1970, pp. 23–25.**

[3] "Television and Vision: The Case for Governmental Control," ***Independent Review,*** **8 (1972), 20.**

[4] "A Survey of Programming," May 10, 1967, pp. 93–94.

[5] "The Trouble with Television" (editorial), New York ***Times,*** **April 10, 1972, Sec. 4, p. 8.**

[Notice the comma here: omitted after "Television" and inserted after the parenthesis. Do the same with any parenthetical explanation of a title.]

Footnotes carry only information that does not appear in the text. In note 4, for example, only the title of the article, the date, and the pages appear, since the text gives the author and publication. Put as much in the text as possible, without cluttering it. You may have noticed that our long quotation from Jones carried "(p. 23)" at the end, without dropping down to a footnote, and that we needed no title, publication, nor date because we had already given them in footnote 3. Use parentheses like this, even in your own sentences, once you have cited a source (notice where the periods and the quotation marks go):

Jones further states that advertisers control hiring and firing (p. 24).

Jones further states that "advertisers actually control hiring and firing, one way or another" (p. 24).

Punctuate your footnotes meticulously.

The first three entries under our footnote 1 illustrate the three principal kinds of references:

BOOK

Donald Allenberg, ***The Future of Television*** **(New York, 1973), p. 10.**

QUARTERLY MAGAZINE

A. H. Hawkins, "Our Greatest Salesman," ***American Thought,*** **4 (1968), 16. ["4" is volume number.]**

POPULAR MAGAZINE

J. Weiss, "Government Control, a Growing Concern," ***Saturday Night Journal,*** **September 20, 1971, p. 5. [Ignore volume number, if any.]**

As in this last example, give the full date for a popular magazine, instead of volume number and year, and *use no parentheses.* Newspaper articles (see our footnote 5, above) follow the same pattern. With a book, a popular magazine, or a newspaper you use "p." before the page number; with a magazine having a volume number, do not use "p."; just give volume number, date (in parentheses), and page numbers, in that order: "29 (1919), 23–26." (But give the month if a month's issue within a volume has separate pagination.) Convert all roman volume numbers into arabic: "XXIX" becomes "29." Give the second page number in full: "23–26," not "23–6." The point of footnoting, of course, is to identify author, title, name of publication, and page, to exhibit your sources fully to the reader, who might want to use them himself. Here are some complications:

[1] Abraham B. Caldwell, "The Case for Subsidized Television," *American Questioner*, June 20, 1971, p. 37, quoted in Albert N. Mendenhall, *The Time Is Now* (Princeton, 1973), p. 308.

[You have found the quotation in Mendenhall's book.]

[1] D. C. Hill, "Who Is Communicating What?" in *Essays for Study*, ed. James L. McDonald and Leonard P. Doan (New York, 1973), p. 214, reprinted from *Era*, 12 (1972), 9–18.

[McDonald and Doan have edited the collection. You could have cited *Era* first, and given the page for both. A title ending in a question mark should not take a comma.]

[1] David R. Small, "The Telephone and Urbanization," in *Annals of American Communication*, ed. Walter Beinholt (Boston, 1969), III, 401.

[The *Annals of American Communication* are a series of bound books, not a magazine: the volume-number is in Roman numerals, and it *follows* the parenthesis. Had this been a magazine, the entry would have omitted the "in," the editor, and the place of publication, and would have read ". . . *Annals of American Communication*, 3 (1969), 401."]

[1] Arnold Peters, "Medicine," *Encyc. Brit.* (Chicago, 1967).

[Abbreviate familiar titles, so long as they remain clear. You need neither volume nor page numbers in alphabetized encyclopedias. Here the article was initialed "A.P.," and you have looked up the author's name in the Contributors' List.]

[1] "Prunes," *Encyc. Brit.* (Chicago, 1967).

[Here the article was not initialed.]

[1] George L. Gillies, "Robert Herrick's 'Corinna,'" *Speculation*, 2 (1881), 490.

[This shows where to put the comma when the title of a magazine article ends in a quotation, and you have to use both single and double quotation marks. Gillies's original title would have looked like this: Robert Herrick's "Corinna."]

[1] *The Merchant of Venice* I.ii.102, in *The Complete Works of Shakespeare*, ed. George Lyman Kittredge (Boston, 1936).

[Note the absence of the comma after the title, and the periods and close spacing between Act.scene.line. Subsequent references would go directly in your text within parentheses: (*Merch.* IV.iii.11–12). See further instructions below.]

[1] P[aul] F[riedrich] Schwartz, *A Quartet of Thoughts* (New York, 1943), p. 7.

[1] [Lewes, George H.] "Percy Bysshe Shelley," *Westminster Review*, 35 (April 1841), 303–344.

[These two footnotes show how to use brackets to add details not actually appearing in the published work. Of course, famous initials are kept as initials, as with T. S. Eliot, H. G. Wells, or D. H. Lawrence.]

[1] *The Reading Problem*, mimeographed pamphlet, Concerned Parents Committee, Center City, Arkansas, December 25, 1973, p. 8.

[1] U. S. Congress, House Committee on Health, Education, and Welfare, *Racial Integration*, 101st Cong., 2nd sess., 1969, H. Rep. 391 to accompany H. R. 6128.

[These represent the infinite variety of pamphlets, and other oddities, that may contain just the information you want. These you must play by instinct, including all the details that would help someone else hunt them down, as briefly as possible.]

These should cover most footnoting problems, or suggest how to meet them.

Abbreviate your references after the first full citation.

Two old favorite abbreviations are now mercifully out of style. Do NOT use:

ibid.—***ibidem*** ("in the same place"), meaning the title cited in the note directly before. Instead, USE THE AUTHOR'S LAST NAME, AND GIVE THE PAGE.

op. cit.—***opere citato*** ("in the work cited"), meaning title referred to again after other notes have intervened. Again, USE THE AUTHOR'S LAST NAME INSTEAD, AND GIVE THE PAGE.

Four are still used and especially useful (do *not* italicize them):

cf.—confer (means "compare"); do not use it for "see."

et al.—***et alii*** ("and others"); does not mean "and all"; use it after the first author in multiple authorships, "Ronald Elkins, et al."

loc. cit.—***loco citato*** ("in the place cited"); use without page number, when you cite a page previously noted. Best in parentheses *in the text:* "Allenberg (loc. cit.) also considers this important."

passim—(not an abbreviation; a Latin word meaning "throughout the work; here and there"). Use when a writer makes the same point in many places within a single work; use also for statistics you have compiled from observations and tables scattered throughout his work.

Other useful abbreviations for footnotes are:

c. or *ca.*	*circa,* "about" (*c.* 1709)
ch., chs.	chapter, chapters
ed.	edited by, edition, editor
f., ff.	and the following page, pages
l., ll.	line, lines
MS., MSS.	manuscript, manuscripts
n.d.	no date given
n.p.	no place of publication given
p., pp.	page, pages
rev.	revised
tr., trans.	translated by
vol., vols.	volume, volumes

Our footnotes to the television paper might continue like this, with abbreviations for works already fully cited:

[6] Allenberg, p. 12.
[7] Allenberg, p. 13.
[Formerly would have been "Ibid., p. 13," but the name is clearer.]

[8] Jones, passim.
[9] Allenberg, p. 4.
[Formerly would have been "Allenberg, op. cit., p. 4."]

[10] Cf. Dillon, et al., p. 191—exactly the opposite position.

[11] See Jones, p. 24, for a reasonable and full denial of this claim.

[12] See Weiss, p. 6, and Smith, p. 71.

[13] Jones, loc. cit.; cf. Weiss, p. 3.

["Loc. cit., means the last Jones citation—p. 24—to which we are asking our readers to compare Weiss's position, indicating simply that Weiss is a little extreme.]

If we had two Joneses, our short references would simply have repeated their first initials; if Jones had written two articles or books, we would have devised two convenient but clear short titles for subsequent references. In addition to Jones's article "Television and Vision: The Case for Governmental Control," suppose we have also cited his book *The Kinescopic Arts and Sciences* (Princeton, 1970). Our further references to him would look like this:

[4] Jones, "Vision," p. 27.

[5] Jones, *Kinescopic Arts*, p. 291.

Abbreviate books of the Bible, even the first time.

The Bible and its books, though capitalized as ordinary titles, are never italicized. Biblical references go directly into your text, within parentheses—no footnote, no commas, *small* roman numerals for chapter, arabic for verse: Mark xvi.6; Jer. vi.24; II Sam. xviii.33. No comma—only a space—separates name from numbers; periods separate the numbers, *with no spacing*. The dictionary gives the accepted abbreviations: Gen., Exod., Lev., Deut. Make biblical references like this:

There is still nothing new under the sun (Eccl. i.9); man still does not live by bread alone (Matt. iv.4).

As Ecclesiastes tells us, "there is no new thing under the sun" (i.9).

Abbreviate plays and long poems after the first time.

Handle plays and long poems like biblical citations, after an initial footnote identifying the edition (see page 270). Italicize the title: *Romeo* II.iv.72–75 [this is *Romeo and Juliet*, Act II, Scene iv, lines 72–75]; *Caesar* V.iii.6; *Ham.* I.i.23; *Iliad* IX.93; *P.L.* IV.918 [*Paradise Lost*, Book IV, line 918]. Use the numbers alone if you have already mentioned the title, or have clearly implied it, as in repeated quotations from the same work.

Match your bibliography to your footnotes.

When your paper is finally typed, arrange the cards of the works cited in your footnotes in alphabetical order (by authors' last names or, with anonymous works, by first words of titles—ignoring initial *The, A,* or *An*). You will not have used all your notes, nor all the articles you have carded. In typing your bibliography, pass over them in decent silence. *Include no work not specifically cited.* Your bibliographical entries will be just like your footnotes except that: (1) you will put the author's last name first; (2) you will give the total span of pages for magazine articles—none at all for books; (3) you will reverse indentation so that the author's name will stand out; (4) you will punctuate differently—putting one period after the alphabetized name or title, and another (no parentheses) after a *book's* place and date of publication; (5) you will include the publisher's name—New York: Thomas Y. Crowell Co., 1972—between the place and date; and (6) you will double-space, triple-spacing between entries. Your single-spacing has been the typewriter's approximation of passages set in small print. If you had been actually writing for print, you would have double-spaced everything and would not have put your footnotes at the bottoms of pages: you would have collected them serially at the end of the paper in a section headed "Footnotes." In many publications you would not have a bibliography; in many others, you would. Your research paper requires one, something like this:

BIBLIOGRAPHY

Allenberg, Donald. *The Future of Television.* New York: Nosuch Co., 1973.

Brown, J. P. "Some Facts About Television and Education," *New Mercury,* July 10, 1971, pp. 20–31.

Cummings, John L. "How Good Are Our Programs?" *Time and Tide,* 46 (1969), 163–176.

***Encyclopaedia Britannica.* 24 vols. Chicago, 1967.**

Hill, D. C. "Who Is Communicating What?" in *Essays for Study,* ed. James L. McDonald and Leonard P. Doan. New York: Appleton Hall, Inc., 1973. Pp. 211–219. Reprinted from *Era,* 12 (1972), 9–18.

[Notice the capitalized "Pp. 211–219." Since this article is in a book, the publishing data have required a period after "1973."]

Jones, Bingham. *The Kinescopic Arts and Sciences.* Princeton: The Little House, Inc., 1970.

———. "Television and Vision: The Case for Governmental Control," *Independent Review,* 8 (1972), 18–31.

Small, David R. "The Telephone and Urbanization," in *Annals of American Communication,* ed. Walter Beinholt. Boston: Large, Green, and Co., Inc., 1969. III, 398–407.

"The Trouble with Television." Editorial, New York *Times,* April 10, 1972, Sec. 4, p. 8.

[Each new section of this newspaper begins its numbering anew; hence, "Sec. 4." Notice that the city, which practically forms a part of the title, is nevertheless NOT italicized with newspapers: New York *Herald Tribune,* Detroit *Free Press.*]

I have based these instructions on *The MLA Style Sheet* (compiled by the Modern Language Association of America), which you may consult for further detail. It is standard for work in literature and the humanities. The sciences use slightly different conventions. Bingham Jones's article would look like this in a botanical bibliography (no italics, no quotation marks, no year, no parentheses): Television and Vision: The Case for Governmental Control. Independent Review. 8:18–31. For some advanced courses you may want to consult:

McCrum, Blanche, and Helen Jones. *Bibliographical Procedures & Style: A Manual for Bibliographers in the Library of Congress.* Washington, D.C.: Superintendent of Documents, 1954.

Publication Manual of the American Psychological Association. Washington, D.C., 1957.

Style Manual. U.S. Government Printing Office. Rev. ed. Washington, D.C.: 1967.

Style Manual for Biological Journals. Washington, D.C., 1960.

Turabian, Kate L. *A Manual for Writers of Term Papers, Theses, and Dissertations.* Rev. ed. Chicago: University of Chicago Press, 1955.

———. *Student's Guide for Writing College Papers.* Chicago: University of Chicago Press, 1963.

Wood, George McLane. *Suggestions to Authors . . . , United States Geological Survey.* 4th ed. rev. by Bernard H. Lane. Washington, D.C., 1935.

But for the present, let us suppose that you have finally turned your paper in. After all that researching, carding, plotting, revising, and typing, you are now dismayed as your instructor hands back your paper thoroughly penciled (with marks much like those inside the back cover of this book). Pages 276 and 277 give a sample of your trouble and of your final corrections. They should also demonstrate the value of a good antagonistic friend in helping you check our common tendency to become hypnotized by our own writing, and to stand convinced that our words say what we intended, when in fact they may say other things to our readers. If you have the foresight to plan and revise your writing against the Checklist inside the front cover before submitting your paper in final form, you can save such a friend some trouble. And you may even win his praise.

Research and the Final Product

Follow the conventional format.

In your hypothetical paper on television, you have seen, in skeleton, the job of research and writing. Since the full-dress research paper usually has four parts, each with certain formal requirements, here are the points to watch, outlined for your convenience:

I. Title Page (not numbered)
   A. In the upper half, type your title in capitals, and beneath it, your name.
   B. In the lower third, designate on separate lines the course and section, your instructor's name, and the date.

II. Outline (page not numbered unless it runs to more than one; if so, use small roman numerals: i, ii, iii, iv)
   A. Head the page with your title.
   B. State your thesis in a sentence.
   C. Present your outline—topic or sentence as your instructor specifies. It will serve as your paper's table of contents.

III. Text with Footnotes (pages numbered in arabic numerals from first to last)
   A. After heading the first page with your title, type your text double-spaced—except for long quotations, which you indent and single-space, without quotation marks, to simulate smaller print.
   B. Type your footnotes at the bottom of your text pages, each single-spaced, but with a space between notes, and in proper form (see pp. 267–272). (Or your instructor may ask you to group all your footnotes together following the text, beginning on a new page headed "Footnotes," and continuing the page numbering of the text. You would prepare an article for publication in this way, so that the printer may conveniently set the notes in smaller type all at the same time.)

Your Last Page as the Instructor Marked It

13

old hat[4].) Government television control should be exercised by a committee of prominent citizens and people interested in entertainment-type programs appointed by the President. The people are interested in T. V., and the people should be given a voice. By the use of a committee T. V. could be fairly and effectively controlled. This would be Modern. Returning to finances, the companies could still place their advertisements between shows but they would not control the shows. Advertising and showmanship would be kept seperate. It would still sell soap and gasoline and everything the public demands and maybe make a contribution toward making this a better world in which to live, for not only the people but for the advertisers too.

Sensible control would be both democratic and help improve the intellectual level.

C– Idea good, plan good, research good – and your argument is persuasive. You still can catch an apt phrase now and then, BUT (!) you've fallen into all your old habits in the rush. Avoid clusters of nouns like government television control – 3 in a row! Avoid the passive voice and all the excess wordage. The end seems lame. And please learn to punctuate. This deserves rewriting. Spend some time on it, sentence by sentence. I'll be happy to reconsider the grade.

(Margin marks: awk; wordy; DM; transition; ref; S; – trite; // st; // st)

Your Last Page Rewritten

13

old hat." The government should control television only through a committee of prominent citizens appointed by the President. For balance, the committee should include a few champions of light entertainment. Since, in a sense, television is really public property, the public should have some voice in television's affairs. After all, representative government is the modern way.

Nor would business go unrepresented. Business would still manage its own house, and it would have seats on the governmental committee. Companies could still bid for advertising space between the best programs, but they could no longer influence the programs themselves. Advertising would exercise its showmanship only in advertising. It would still sell its soap and gasoline, but the programs themselves would be freed for variety and creativity. New audiences might even benefit the advertisers, and sensible control of the commercial motive would certainly increase everyone's opportunity to see for himself.

A- Nice work! I like "champions of light entertainment" and "see for himself." This is the style you've been working for: not too big, not too little, sensible, clear, on its toes. You are touching the concrete beautifully: house, seats, soap, and gasoline.

Since this is a second chance, I can't give highest honors. But it's a fine job. Congratulations. You're really writing in Style ——!

IV. Bibliography (pages numbered in continuation of text paging)
   A. Head the first page "Bibliography" or "Works Cited."
   B. Arrange the works in one of two ways: (1) alphabetized, by author's last name (Eliot, T. S.), and by title when the author is unknown ("Medicine," *Encyclopaedia Britannica*); or (2) grouped by kind of source, the entries within each group arranged alphabetically: "Primary Sources" (works of literature, historical documents, letters, and the like) and "Secondary Sources" (works *about* your subject)—and you may further divide these groups, if your bibliography is long enough to justify it, into "Books" and "Articles."

Sample Papers

Here (pp. 279–314) are two papers by students in one of my classes in American literature. They have revised and polished their work a bit for public display, but they are essentially the same papers I read with delight one evening among those of a very good set. Miss Ferris, a history major, suspecting that Hawthorne's picture of the Puritans was not accurate, looked into the historical background with this thesis in view. Her paper is an unusually fine application of historical research to literary understanding. I have included some of her note cards, and a page of her first draft, to illustrate part of the process. She omits the call number of *The Portable Hawthorne* because this was our textbook, and she did not need to look it up in the library.

Mr. Blaske's paper emerged from a vigorous classroom discussion as to whether Hemingway was a symbolist or not. We had turned to Hemingway from the distinct symbolism of Hawthorne, and the difference was vividly apparent. Mr. Blaske wrote a short paper on Hemingway's "The End of Something," setting forth his very interesting theory of "traces," and quoting Freud briefly for support. I suggested a full-scale researching of the question for a term paper. He discovered, of course, that a number of scholars had already touched upon his idea in one way or another, but he also discovered that he still had something left to say. His adjusting of his original thesis to the work of previous critics provides an excellent example of the way to handle literary research.

HAWTHORNE'S PURITANS

by

Marilyn Ferris

English 269
Mr. Baker
April 16, 1970

NOTE ON THE TEXT

To give a sense of this paper's evolution, we have reproduced in color, on the backs of the next three leaves, some of Miss Ferris's note cards and a page of her first draft. The cards correspond to her first four footnotes. She has recorded the library's call number, the author's name, the title, and all the other details necessary for her footnotes and bibliography. She has made brief summaries of her own, has quoted only briefly, has checked over her quotations for accuracy while still having the book in hand, and has recorded the page. Everything she needs, and more than she used, is there.

The first-draft page matches the text it faces at the line (mid-page) beginning "about the difficulty of writing . . . ." Miss Ferris has indicated her footnotes directly on her draft, between triple parentheses ((( ))). Notice how the author's name eventually goes into her text and his title into her note, how some page numbers appear in the text itself, once the source is established by a footnote, and especially how "(((Schwartz, loc. cit.)))" expands at footnote 6. She has polished her style directly on the draft, and then has modified it further, here and there, while typing her final copy.

HAWTHORNE'S PURITANS

Thesis: Despite its moral power and claims to authenticity, The Scarlet Letter is historically untrue.

I. Hawthorne's claims of historical accuracy
   A. The "Custom House" introduction
   B. Phrases in the text implying historical accuracy
   C. Hawthorne's prior references to a scarlet "A"

II. The critical estimate
   A. Baughman's assertion "sure of historical grounds"
   B. Green's attack
   C. Trollope's view as "romance"
   D. Hawthorne's own belief (Schwartz, Waggoner)
   E. Hawthorne's "Puritan myth"

III. Hawthorne's actual use of history
   A. Union of religion and law
   B. The Puritan's idea of community
   C. Isolation by sin
   D. Reunion by confession and repentance

IV. Hawthorne's unique characters
   A. Hester
   B. Dimmesdale
   C. Chillingworth

V. Hawthorne's projecting unique cases from general Puritan practices, and making them universal

F Baughman, Ernest W.
1 "Public Confession and *The Scarlet Letter*,"
N4 *The New England Quarterly*, 40 (1967), 532-550.

Public confession, an English custom-required by church and state in Mass. Bay Colony from its founding on, in Plymouth from 1624, in Va. at least 30 years before *SL* takes place. (533)

H. familiar with John Winthrop's *Journals*,

front

1630-1650. W. records 16 pub. confessions, 4 for adultery. (539)

Hester not reunited w. community because she refuses to repent and name her partner. (544)

Hawthorne "was on sure historical grounds at all times."✓ (548) He uses custom of confession of sins that isolate "from the fellowship of the church."✓ (544) Characterization consistent w. Puritan thought "though, until the end, much of their conduct is at odds w. the tradition."✓ (549)

back

813 Levin, David
S 816 "Nathaniel Hawthorne, *The Scarlet Letter*," in *The American Novel from James Fenimore Cooper to Wm Faulkner*, ed. Wallace Stegner (New York: Basic Books, Inc., 1965), pp. 13-24.

"... he studied Puritan history w. a persistence that some scholars (along with H. himself) have considered obsessive."✓ (13)

single entry

HAWTHORNE'S PURITANS

In The Scarlet Letter, Hawthorne presents the system of ethics, law, and punishment in a Puritan New England town. He introduces his story of adultery and expiation with an elaborate account of finding a faded red-cloth "A" twisted around a roll of papers, among other documents in the Salem Custom House, which he intends to give to the Essex Historical Society. The roll of papers contains, in "Surveyor Pue's" handwriting, the story of Hester Prynne. In the narrative itself, Hawthorne makes numerous other assertions of historical fact. But all of this is fiction. Actually, The Scarlet Letter, though generally acknowledged as a great moral novel, is historically untrue.

Ernest W. Baughman, however, claims that Hawthorne "was on sure historical grounds at all times," because he employs the Puritan idea that public confession reunites the sinner with the community.[1] Baughman concedes that "until the end, much of [the] conduct is at odds with the tradition," but he insists that the essential characterization and the underlying idea are historically faithful (loc. cit.). Baughman states that Hawthorne was familiar with John Winthrop's journals and other Puritan documents (p. 539). According to David Levin, Hawthorne "studied

[1]"Public Confession and The Scarlet Letter," The New England Quarterly, 40 (1967), 548-549.

Cowley, Malcolm

The Portable Hawthorne, ed., with Introduction and Notes, by Malcolm Cowley (New York: The Viking Press, 1948).

Character wearing "the letter A on the breast of her gown" appears in 1 sentence, "Endicott and the Red Cross," pub. 1837 – first hint of SL. (269)

Seven yrs. later, in one of H.'s note books is

front

back

"plot of a new story he planned to write: 'The life of a woman who, by the old colony law, was condemned always to wear the letter A, sewed on her garment, in token of her having committed adultery.'" (269)

820.6 E58e Green, Martin

"The Hawthorne Myth: A Protest," Essays and Studies by Members of the English Association, 16 (1963), 16-36.

"T.S. Eliot has said that H.'s is a true criticism of the Puritan morality, true because it has the fidelity of the artist + not a mere conviction of the man, but there is very little that is Puritan in The SL. The thoughts and emotions expressed all belong to /30 the nineteenth century." (29-30) Claims "to be historical are so insistent and so unacceptable..." (29)

all on one side

Puritan history with a persistence that some scholars (along with Hawthorne himself) have considered obsessive."[2]

But the evidence undermines Hawthorne's claims of factuality. First, a character wearing a "letter A on [her] breast" appears briefly in an early Hawthorne story ("Endicott and the Red Cross," 1837); then seven years later and six years before he started The Scarlet Letter, Hawthorne records in his notebook plans to write: "The life of a woman, who, by the old colony law, was condemned always to wear the letter A, sewed on her garment, in token of her having committed adultery."[3] Hawthorne mentions discovering no manuscript and faded letter, and such a discovery would certainly have been exciting news, to be recorded in his notebook and in letters to his friends. He records no such discovery. Clearly, his "document," and his claims of finding it, are fictitious, if not fraudulent.

Martin Green is the severest of Hawthorne's critics. He sets aside T. S. Eliot's claim that Hawthorne's picture of Puritan morality is true "because it has the fidelity of the artist." The book's claims to historicity, says Green, are "so insistent and so unacceptable": ". . . there is very little that is Puritan in The Scarlet Letter. The thoughts and emotions all belong to

[2]"Nathaniel Hawthorne, The Scarlet Letter," in The American Novel from James Fenimore Cooper to William Faulkner, ed. Wallace Stegner (New York, 1965), p. 13.

[3]Malcolm Cowley, The Portable Hawthorne (New York, 1948), p. 269.

of writing ~~entertaining and~~ lively children's stories ~~for children using~~ with "such unmaleable material as the somber, stern, and rigid Puritans," ((("Three Aspects of Hawthorne's Puritanism," *The New England Quarterly*, 36 (1936), 202.))) ~~He also~~ not~~es~~ing ~~that~~ Hawthorne consistently viewed ~~looked upon~~ his Puritan ancestors as "gloomy, joyless, and rigid." (((Schwartz, loc. cit.))) Apparently Hawthorne's view of the Puritans distorted his picture of the past. ~~was distorted.~~ As Hyatt H. Waggoner puts it: "Despite his long absorption in Puritan writings, it is pretty clear that Hawthorne had a typical nineteenth-century view of his ancestors. He exaggerated their gloominess and their intolerance and probably attributed their persecution of sexual offenses to ideas other than those they actually held." (((*Hawthorne, A Critical Study* (Cambridge, 1963), p. 14))) As A. N. Kaul says, "This archaism appears to have been a necessary condition for the richest engagement of his imagination, and also, paradoxically, for his deepest intuitions of the modern spirit." ((("Introduction," *Hawthorne: A Collection of Critical Essays* (Englewood Cliffs, 1966), p. 2.)))

But we must concede that ~~Of course~~, Hawthorne ~~does~~ follow, ~~history~~ historical facts at least part of the ~~time~~ way. As he states in Chapter 2, the Puritans were in fact "a people amongst whom and religion and law were almost identical." Page Smith~~, in his book *As a City Upon a Hill*, tells about how~~ reports that the early Puritans were forced to confess their sins before the entire congregation, which consisted of almost the entire population of the town. The penitent sinner ~~who was penitent~~ was then accepted ~~taken~~ back into the congregation, but the impenitent sinner ~~who was not~~ was excommunicated, regardless of the relative mildness of ~~how mild~~ his sin. ~~was.~~

the nineteenth century."[4] Of course, Hawthorne called his book "A Romance" on the title page. Anthony Trollope, writing in 1879, is probably typical of Hawthorne's readers in accepting the historical pretense as a usual part of fiction: "His is a mixture of romance and austerity, quite as far removed from the realities of Puritanism as it is from the sentimentalism of poetry."[5]

Nevertheless, in spite of the fictional deceit of the Custom House introduction, Hawthorne himself probably thought he was more historically accurate than Trollope allows. His statement in his notebook about "the old colony law" shows his belief in its authenticity. Joseph Schwartz quotes Hawthorne's complaint about the difficulty of writing lively children's stories with "such unmalleable material as the somber, stern, and rigid Puritans," noting that Hawthorne consistently viewed his Puritan ancestors as "gloomy, joyless, and rigid."[6] Apparently, Hawthorne's view of the Puritans distorted his picture of the past. As Hyatt H. Waggoner puts it:

> Despite his long absorption in Puritan writings, it is pretty clear that Hawthorne had a typical nineteenth-century view of his ancestors. He exaggerated their gloominess and their intolerance and probably attributed their persecution of sexual offenses to ideas other than those they actually held.[7]

[4]"The Hawthorne Myth: A Protest," Essays and Studies by Members of the English Association, 16 (1963), 29-30

[5]"The Genius of Nathaniel Hawthorne," The North American Review, 129, No. 274 (September 1879), 206.

[6]"Three Aspects of Hawthorne's Puritanism," The New England Quarterly, 36 (1963), 202.

[7]Hawthorne, A Critical Study (Cambridge, 1963), p. 14.

As A. N. Kaul says, "This archaism appears to have been a necessary condition for the richest engagement of his imagination, and also, paradoxically, for his deepest intuitions of the modern spirit."[8]

But we must concede that Hawthorne follows historical facts at least part of the way. As he states in Chapter 2, the Puritans were "a people amongst whom religion and law were almost identical." Page Smith reports that the early Puritans were forced to confess their sins to the congregation, which consisted of almost the entire population of the town. The penitent sinner was then accepted back into the congregation, but the impenitent sinner was excommunicated, regardless of the relative mildness of his sin.[9] Hester, as Baughman points out, refuses to repent, and to name her partner, and is thus isolated from the community (p. 544).

This tradition of public confession was continued later in larger Puritan towns. Cases involving morals and religious beliefs were tried in civil courts and also punished by the church.[10] The Scarlet Letter takes place in Boston, and apparently at such a later date, with civil and religious authority collaborating, and yet Hawthorne clearly dates his events in very early Puritan times. The action occurs, he says, "not less than two centuries ago" (Ch.2), that is, at some time before 1650, since The Scarlet

[8]Introduction, Hawthorne: A Collection of Critical Essays (Englewood Cliffs, 1966), p. 2.

[9]As a City upon a Hill (New York, 1966), pp. 60-61.

[10]Smith, pp. 129-130.

Letter was published in 1850. Hawthorne mentions that Hester has been sentenced by the magistrates. But when she is forced to stand on the scaffold, a civil punishment, the church, in the persons of the clergymen Wilson and Dimmesdale, urges her to reveal the name of her partner in sin. Years later, when Hester and Pearl visit the governor, he discusses the case with the Reverend Mr. Dimmesdale.

Not only civil and religious authorities were involved in the punishment of sin, but the people themselves. The townspeople are present at Hester's punishment. They avoid her when they meet her in public, and they tell their children stories about her. The punishments of standing on the scaffold and wearing the scarlet letter are effective only because they make Hester aware of the way the townspeople feel about her. Facing the stares of the people, on the scaffold and for years afterward, is her real punishment.

Beyond this union of church authority, state authority, and public opinion in the punishment of sin, Hester's treatment is not characteristic of Puritan justice and mercy. The scaffold itself, and Hester's being forced to stand on it for public scorn, are probably not historically accurate. In the early Puritan community, the sinner was usually punished only mildly, if at all, and was forgiven and reunited with the community after a public confession. Later, sinners were punished more severely, but the punishment was usually brief, such as an afternoon in the stocks or a whipping. Long-term punishments, such as jail sentences, were almost nonexistent.[11] Some cases are recorded of women being branded or forced to wear the letter "A," but such cases were rare, and, according to Curtis P. Nettels, concerned only habitual offenses:

> In seventeenth-century New England, women guilty of repeated moral lapses were whipped or occasionally forced to wear the scarlet letter; after 1720, whipping was resorted to only for serious offenders.[12]

Hester's offense is clearly not habitual: Hawthorne presents her only arrest, and she has offended with one man only. Hawthorne's townswomen who call for branding, and even death, are evidently not authentic, as Hawthorne claims them to be: ". . . there was a coarser fiber in those wives and maidens of old English birth and breeding, than in their fair descendants . . . ." (Ch. 2).

Puritan religious and civil law covered such a wide range of sins that everyone must have committed some sin at one time or another, and, in fact, in some towns, nearly every citizen was brought before the court during the course of a few years. Court records are full of cases in which a man and a woman were forbidden to see each other or a woman was awarded payment from the father of an illegitimate child.[13] Since these cases were public knowledge, the sinner knew that he was not alone.

[11]Henry W. Lawrence, The Not-Quite Puritans (Boston, 1928), p. 171.

[12]The Roots of American Civilization: A History of American Colonial Life. Second Ed. (New York, 1963), p. 463.

[13]Edmund S. Morgan, "The Puritans and Sex," in Pivotal Interpretations of American History, ed. Carl N. Degler (New York, 1966), I, 11, 14.

The members of the early Puritan community were bound to forgive the penitent sinner and restore him to their community. Even when a member was excommunicated, he automatically became a member again if he confessed his guilt.[14] Baughman points out that the English Puritan societies practiced public confession, and naturally imported it to America when they came. Public confessions were required by the church and state in the Massachusetts Bay Colony from its beginning, and in Plymouth from 1624. John Winthrop's journal, with which Hawthorne was familiar, describes sixteen cases of public confession between 1630 and 1650, four of them for adultery.[15] In Groton, Massachusetts, sixty-six of the two hundred persons who were members of the town by baptismal covenant between 1761 and 1775 confessed to fornication before marriage. Nine of the sixteen couples admitted to full communion between 1789 and 1791 had confessed to fornication.[16]

The Puritans felt that the entire community was united in a covenant with God. The sins of one person could bring God's judgment on all. Therefore, for the common good, the community tried to redeem all sinners as quickly as possible and reunite them with the community.[17] Confession and punishment were forms of cleansing after which the sinner could rejoin the community,

[14]Smith, pp. 60-61.

[15]Baughman, pp. 533, 539.

[16]Smith, p. 62.

[17]Smith, pp. 7-8.

both religiously and socially, on an equal level with everyone else and with no stigma. When one member of the community was purged of sin and forgiven, the community was reunited, as a child is reunited with his parents after being spanked.

Hester's permanent alienation from the community, though partially self-imposed, is not characteristic of the Puritans. Her punishment must be seen not as an example of the way the Puritans dealt with sinners, but as an example of an individual's failure to accept the moral and legal system designed to reunite him with the community, and of the community's failure to forgive a sinner and restore him to full fellowship, under God's covenant. Hawthorne has freely interpreted Puritan beliefs about the community, and about sin as isolating the individual and harming the community.

Hester's public admission of her act, whether or not she considered it sinful, and her punishment cleanse her of guilt, just as they would have in historical times, but only if she had fully confessed and repented. But Hester does not name her partner, and she remains impenitent and even, at first, defiant. She refuses to accept the moral and legal system for reuniting the sinner with the community; then she works out her own way, through her needlecraft and care of the sick, to rejoin the community while still remaining isolated and independent.

Hawthorne does not present Hester as a case of Puritan injustice, as the beginning of his story suggests. Hester's story presents not the injustice of the Puritan code, but a specific instance wherein the code fails to preserve justice. Hawthorne imagines a unique personality and a unique experience within the general context of Puritan beliefs. He creates not Puritan history, but what Kaul refers to as "the interpretative Puritan myth" (p. 9).

Dimmesdale and Chillingworth are similarly interpretative projections of Puritan beliefs, rather than authentic types. When one person broke the community's covenant with God by sinning, and was cast out for not repenting, the community was not whole. The sin spread throughout the community, as its members were tempted to hate or ignore the outcast, to gossip and act hypocritically. Smith gives the historical context:

> The congregations were doubtless on occasion cruel, and the system itself put fearful strains on the delinquent saints as well as their judges. But the records are impressive evidence of the fidelity with which most congregations observed scriptural injunctions to charity. Within a harsh system, they frequently showed great patience and forbearance with the sinners who appeared before them. If their church was a community of justice, it was also a community of mercy, surrogate for a Christ who had spoken of God's forgiveness as inexhaustible. (p. 63)

Smith further reports that the Puritans had "a country realism about sex that is in sharp contrast to late nineteenth-century sexual attitudes," which have pictured the Puritans inaccurately "as full of inhibitions, prudery, and repressions" (loc. cit.). The small Puritan town contained a great deal of illicit sex, most of it eventually confessed in public, repented, and accepted by the community as the usual human weakness. The Puritan community aimed chiefly to bring the lost soul back into fellowship with the community and with God, and to repair the break in their communal covenant.

Chillingworth is, of course, not a Puritan. But Hawthorne presents him as a kind of obsessive Puritan, in nineteenth-century terms, ruined by his inability to forgive sin, as an actual Puritan would have done. His psychological torture of Hester and Dimmesdale leads not to their reunion with society but to their further alienation. Dimmesdale lives a tortured life, unable to experience the purging from sin by confession and punishment that would reunite him psychologically with the community. His inhibitions and conscience, which shut him off from the Puritan system, probably belong, as Green would claim, to the nineteenth century rather than the seventeenth.

Hawthorne, in fact, has not created a historically accurate story. From the general Puritan beliefs about the wholeness of the community and the isolation of sin, he has projected three unique and atypical individuals. Through them, he works out his universal themes of alienation and social community, of sin, guilt, confession, punishment, and redemption. He has combined aspects of Puritan America with aspects of nineteenth-century America to create a story that is universal and symbolic, rather than historical. The story's only flaw lies in Hawthorne's misleading his readers to believe that his Puritans are historically authentic, as perhaps he himself mistakenly believed them to be.

BIBLIOGRAPHY

Baughman, Ernest W. "Public Confession and The Scarlet Letter," The New England Quarterly, 40 (1967), 532-550.

Cowley, Malcolm. The Portable Hawthorne, ed., with Introduction and Notes. New York: The Viking Press, 1948.

Green, Martin. "The Hawthorne Myth: A Protest," Essays and Studies by Members of the English Association, 16 (1963), 16-36.

Kaul, A. N. Introduction, Hawthorne: A Collection of Critical Essays. Englewood Cliffs: Prentice-Hall, Inc., 1966.

Lawrence, Henry W. The Not-Quite Puritans. Boston: Little, Brown, and Co., 1928.

Levin, David. "Nathaniel Hawthorne, The Scarlet Letter," in The American Novel from James Fenimore Cooper to William Faulkner, ed. Wallace Stegner. New York: Basic Books, Inc., 1965. Pp. 13-24.

Morgan, Edmund S. "The Puritans and Sex," in Pivotal Interpretations of American History, ed. Carl N. Degler. New York: Harper and Row, 1966. I, 4-16.

Nettels, Curtis P. The Roots of American Civilization: A History of American Colonial Life. Second Ed. New York: Appleton-Century-Crofts, 1963.

Smith, Page. As a City upon a Hill. New York: Alfred A. Knopf, 1966.

Schwartz, Joseph. "Three Aspects of Hawthorne's Puritanism," The New England Quarterly, 36 (1963), 192-208.

Trollope, Anthony. "The Genius of Nathaniel Hawthorne," The North American Review, 129, No. 274 (September 1879), 203-223.

Waggoner, Hyatt H. Hawthorne: A Critical Study. Cambridge: Harvard University Press, 1963.

HEMINGWAY'S SYMBOLIC TRACES

by

Tom Blaske

English 269
Mr. Baker
April 16, 1970

HEMINGWAY'S SYMBOLIC TRACES

Thesis: Hemingway's writing does not generally contain conscious literary symbols, but rather "traces" of subconscious symbols.

I. Hemingway's spare style
   A. His apparent lack of symbolism
   B. The "something there" of psychic traces

II. Critical views of Hemingway's symbolism
   A. The proponents of shallowness
   B. Hemingway's own estimate
   C. The proponents of symbolism

III. Hemingway's borderline symbolism, or "traces"
   A. Heart versus head
   B. Subconscious versus conscious

IV. "The End of Something" as illustration
   A. Alienation theme
      1. The castle
      2. Conscious symbolism
   B. Death-and-birth theme
      1. Freud's dream symbols
      2. Hemingway's preoccupation with death-and-birth
      3. Death-and-birth traces in "The End of Something"
         a. The lake
         b. The moon
         c. Psychological corroboration
            i. Freud's dream-symbols as universals
            ii. Jung's collective unconscious
         d. "Not touching"
   C. The woman theme
      1. Hemingway's challenged manhood
         a. His mother
         b. His father
      2. Nick's rejection of Marjorie
         a. Baiting the perch
         b. "You know everything"
         c. Marjorie's self-sufficiency
         d. Nick's alliance with Bill

V. Subconscious communication through traces
   A. Summary of psychic categories
   B. Hemingway's primitive eloquence

HEMINGWAY'S SYMBOLIC TRACES

Hemingway's sparse and "reportive" style seems at first glance to contain none of the symbolism characteristic of great literature. In fact, critics have differed widely in trying to describe just where Hemingway's greatness lies. When his _The Old Man and the Sea_ appeared in 1952, Scribner's dust jacket pessimistically crystallized the problem: "One cannot hope to explain why the reading of this book is so profound an experience." That story, like all of Hemingway's best, leaves the reader with a pause, a feeling that something was there--something nonintellectual and nonallusive, playing on the emotions not on the mind, something suffused and inexpressible, but something, nonetheless. Hemingway's something, his "symbolism," I believe, comes from an unconscious and highly personal facing of his inner self, as an almost accidental trace of more universal human feelings.

Some critics have dismissed Hemingway as shallow, a view Robert P. Weeks summarizes:

> Hemingway is too limited, they say. His characters are mute, insensitive, uncomplicated men; his "action" circles narrowly about the ordeals, triumphs, and defeats of the bull ring, the battlefield, the trout stream, and similar male proving grounds; his style (some deny Hemingway's writing the benefit of this term) has stripped so much away that little is left but "a group of clevernesses"; and his "code" is at best a crudely simple outlook, in no sense comparable to the richer, more profound Stoicism which it is sometimes thought to resemble.[1]

Hemingway himself presents the first line of defense against this critical onslaught: ". . . a writer . . . may omit things

[1]Introduction, _Hemingway: A Collection of Critical Essays_, ed. Robert P. Weeks (Englewood Cliffs, 1962), pp. 1-2.

that he knows, and the reader, if the writer is writing truly enough, will have a feeling of those things as strongly as though the writer had stated them. The dignity of movement of an ice-berg is due to only one-eighth of it being above water."[2] His word "feeling" clearly suggests the nonintellectual impact of things presented without statement, that is, things symbolized. But no critic before Malcolm Cowley, in 1944, had suggested that Hemingway might contain symbolism. Today a full complement of critics has found rich, sophisticated textures, at once deep and powerful and elemental in their simplicity, layered into Hemingway's apparently shallow work. Less becomes more, as Weeks has pointed out (loc. cit.), applying Mies van der Rohe's architectural formula; and many critics find ironic method, symbolic effects, and a simple style that touches the reader too deeply to be insignificant.

Many have verged upon the point I hope to amplify--that Hemingway is almost accidentally and unconsciously symbolic, rather than overtly and conventionally so. Harry Levin answers the common criticism that Hemingway is barren: "The powers of connotation, the possibilities of oblique suggestion and semantic association, are actually grasped by Hemingway as well as any writer of our time."[3] Philip Young finds "shadows" of meaning that place Hemingway among such deliberate symbolists as Haw-

[2]Death in the Afternoon (New York, 1932), p. 192.

[3]"Observations on the Style of Ernest Hemingway," in Weeks, p. 75.

thorne, Melville, and Poe.[4] Carlos Baker sees Hemingway as less overtly and intellectually symbolic, a writer "deeply interested in the communication of an effect, or several effects together, . . . to evoke the deep response of shared human experience," by using naturally emotive images.[5] Yet he, like Young, assumes in Hemingway a rational symbolic intention.

E. M. Halliday devastates Carlos Baker's excesses, concluding that Hemingway selects details not so much to "produce" an emotion as to "epitomize it."[6] Joseph DeFalco similarly sees Hemingway examining "the effect upon the inner being of the traumata" of modern man, getting beneath the surface to the "more basic, primal contexts," and applying "certain distinct, psychologically symbolic techniques."[7] Sheridan Baker, analyzing the symbolism of "The Big Two-Hearted River," makes a similar point:

> Every sentence seems to sound a harmonic of larger and parallel meaning. . . . And the power . . . lies in its intensely suggested meaning--which depends on never being stated, always being poised, like a trout, under the noncommittal surface. His bell-like prose makes resonant the slightest poetic suggestion: former happiness on the shore of the Black River, fishing the Big Two-Hearted River toward the final swamp.[8]

Yet all of these critics assume some conscious intention and stop short of the elemental psychic roots in the human mind.

[4]Ernest Hemingway, University of Minnesota Pamphlets on American Writers, No. 1 (Minneapolis, 1964), p. 18.

[5]Hemingway: The Writer as Artist (Princeton, 1952), p. 131.

[6]"Hemingway's Ambiguity: Symbolism and Irony," in Weeks, p. 57.

[7]The Hero in Hemingway's Short Stories (Pittsburgh, 1963), p. 14.

[8]Ernest Hemingway: An Introduction and Interpretation (New York, 1967), pp. 32-37.

Malcolm Cowley comes closer, seeing in Hemingway "nightmares at noonday, accurately described, pictured without blur, but having the nature of obsessions or hypnagogic visions between sleeping and waking."[9] This describes Hemingway's mysterious "something," which moves the reader with subliminal powers at the center of what it means to be human. No analysis "can speak for long of the style without speaking of the man," writes Harry Levin:

> It has cast him in the special role of our agent, our plenipotentiary, our roving correspondent on whom we depend for news from the fighting fronts of modern consciousness. Here he is, the man who was there. His writing seems so intent upon the actual, so impersonal in its surfaces, that it momentarily prompts us to overlook the personality behind them. That would be a serious mistake; for the point of view, though brilliantly intense, is narrowly focused and obliquely angled. We must ask: who is this guide to whom we have entrusted ourselves on intimate terms in dangerous places? Where are his limitations? What are his values?[10]

Whose nightmares? Hemingway's own.

Each of these critics describes Hemingway's "something," but none, I think, accurately places Hemingway between the borders of conventional symbolism and unconscious accident. I believe that Hemingway is indeed a symbolist, but that his work speaks to readers primarily on a primitive, subconscious, psychological, elemental level. He writes from the heart, from the depths of his own psyche, almost unaware of what he is doing. He does not write from the head, from the intellect. This profound kind of

[9]"Nightmare and Ritual in Hemingway," in Weeks, p. 41.

[10]Levin, p. 83.

psychological symbol, which I prefer to call a "trace," is imbedded deep in Hemingway--both the man and his work.

By way of illustration, let us examine his early story "The End of Something." Early in the story, Nick and Marjorie are trolling for trout. They pass by the crumbling white limestone ruins of a sawmill. Marjorie muses that "it seems more like a castle." Like a castle, once the center of medieval life, this mill, now eroding away with the wind and water, had once been the center of life in this little lumbering community. The decrepit mill symbolizes "the end of something," a dead town, a sense of lost contact with the past, of isolation in their own time, of alienation.

But this consciously perpetrated symbol seems somehow strangely inconsistent with the flow of Hemingway's prose. Marjorie's observation caps the entire nostalgic scene of Horton's Bay as it once was; and her comment seems a sudden, abrupt finale to the story's introduction. Its impact seems disproportionate to its intrinsic weight. It sticks out, a planned device to convey a certain meaning. Yet we may have a kind of mixture here, for this symbol also has an element vital to "traces." Hemingway was himself alienated from his past, and consumed with the feeling that something had gone wrong with the old and the traditional. This symbol may seem to spring, in part, from Hemingway's own sense of himself--as his "traces" surely do. Nevertheless, the sawmill as castle is largely a conventional and intentional symbol.

But "traces" are intuitional. Perhaps their broadest category in this story is the Freudian notion of death-and-birth. Death seems somehow always at the center of life for Hemingway. As Richard P. Hovey says, "It is impossible any longer to question Hemingway's obsession with death and suicide."[11] His preoccupation with suicide was widely manifest: his father committed suicide; Hemingway himself committed suicide; his first story, written while he was yet in high school, ends in suicide;[12] the first story of In Our Time, his first major work, ends in suicide. Further, as Philip Young suggests, the central traumatic experience in his life was when he lay near death after being wounded by a mortar shell while carrying candy bars to the soldiers on the front lines at Fossalta di Piave, Italy, 1918.[13] Much of Hemingway's biography, most of his preoccupations, and many of his writings may be explained by post-Freudian analysis of the Hemingway psyche as it was shaped by this experience, as Young has already suggested.[14] Hemingway's "traumatic neurosis," his "shell shock," became an omnipresent influence. One critic has even said, "A clumsy but accurate title for his collected works might be 'How to Die Correctly in Ten Not Very Easy Lessons.'"[15] This basic psychological fact of Hemingway's existence is revealed beautifully through symbolic "traces."

[11]Hemingway: The Inward Terrain (Seattle, 1968), p. 215

[12]Sheridan Baker, p. 7.

[13]Ernest Hemingway: A Reconsideration (University Park, Pennsylvania, 1966), pp. 120, 164.

[14]Reconsideration, p. 165 ff.

[15]Bern Oldsey, "The Snows of Ernest Hemingway," Wisconsin Studies in Contemporary Literature, 4 (1963), 193.

After Nick and Marjorie set their night lines from the point, they build a driftwood fire for a picnic. Hemingway is careful to say that the light reaches out only to the water, and not beyond, thus creating an air of mystery about the lake itself. The world, for the two by the fire, extends no farther than the circle of flickering light. Freud has said that "the womb is represented countless times by recurring images of water, especially darkened water."[16] He equated that water with the amniotic fluid of the mother's womb. Amazingly, Hemingway has produced just such a Freudian image in his darkened lake, with his characters distinctly removed from the maternal warmth, dark security, and comfort. When Marjorie leaves, Hemingway writes another Freudian trace: "She was afloat in the boat in the water with the moonlight on it." Freud describes one patient who dreamed about diving into the dark waters of a lake just where the pale moon was mirrored in it. Freud interprets this as a dream of death, a return to the mother's womb: "The water theme recurs here and implies, of course, the womb. We can discover the locality from which a child is born by calling to mind the slang use of the word '_lune_' in French (viz., 'bottom'). The pale moon was thus the white bottom which children are quick to guess they came out of."[17]

What to make of all this? Certainly, Hemingway leaves suggestive traces that correlate remarkably with Freud's interpreta-

[16]_The Interpretation of Dreams_ (New York, 1953), p. 403n.

[17]Freud, p. 400.

tion of dream-symbols. That Hemingway actually knew his characters in such depth as to include these symbols deliberately does not seem probable. He could not have known his Freud that well, nor, even less, could he have expected his readers to know Freud well enough to derive any intellectual meaning from these descriptions. Furthermore, these same features correlate well with what critics have deduced about Hemingway's own psychic preoccupation with death. The coincidence is virtually conclusive by itself. Thus we can hypothesize two ways in which such psychological traces could reach so deeply into Hemingway's stories: one, a long, devious, intellectual route, presuming deliberate manipulation of subconscious symbols; the other, a short, direct, subconscious one. Using Occam's razor and following the path of least resistance, which is also the path of greatest psychological coincidence, we must assume, I think, that Hemingway traveled the subconscious path.

Psychological case studies corroborate such subconscious trace-making. That "dreams contain the essentials of a person's central conflicts"[18] is axiomatic in modern psychoanalysis. Freud believed that "some [dream] symbols . . . bear a single meaning almost universally,"[19] and other clinical studies have borne him out, especially those of Morton Prince.[20] That these

[18]Leopold Caligor and Rollo May, Dreams and Symbols (New York, 1968), p. v.

[19]On Dreams (New York, 1952), p. 108.

[20]Clinical and Experimental Studies in Personality (Cambridge, Massachusetts, 1939), passim.

universal psychic symbols may extend beyond the sleeping world and may be present in all consciousness is the essence of C. G. Jung's "transcendent function."[21] Numerous case studies have shown the subconscious mind overruling the conscious in writing. We can safely assume that Hemingway's subconscious was also leaving its traces in the very fabric of his art. "Dream symbolism extends far beyond dreams," Freud writes: "it is not peculiar to dreams, but exercises a similar dominating influence on representation in fairy tales, myths, and legends, in jokes, and in folklore."[22] Finally, Jung's theory of the "collective unconscious" suggests a symbolic communication among human subconscious psyches, since he believes that the transpersonal matrix of such communication is omnipresent, and that communication will occur as the appropriate symbols of primordial urges and drives are touched.[23]

From a psychoanalytical point of view, then, Hemingway's symbolic traces are not only possible, but indeed likely and perhaps inevitable. And Hemingway's insistent clarity of style, his manifest desire--particularly in the early stories--to avoid intellectual devices and the usual contrivances of symbolism and imagery, makes these traces much more easily decipherable and undeniably powerful than in any other great writer.

We can see the death-and-birth theme again in Hemingway's

[21] C. G. Jung, Psyche and Symbol (Garden City, 1958), passim.

[22] On Dreams, p. 111.

[23] Jung, p. xxx.

cursory, almost awkward insistence that neither Marjorie nor Bill touched Nick. Marjorie and Nick sit on the blanket "without touching each other," and later, "Bill didn't touch him, either." No one would expect Bill to touch him, nor to find any significance in Bill's not touching him. Again we sense some unspecified psychological emphasis. Behavioral psychologists stress the vital importance to normal development of parental fondling in infancy, particularly by the mother. Nick is explicitly denied such physical contact. More and more clearly, one senses in this story some deep, psychological subconscious identification between Nick and Hemingway himself.

Many scholars have pointed to the considerable autobiographical content in Hemingway's early stories: "The connection between Hemingway and his hero has always been intimate."[24] And several have noted that Hemingway himself "acted out themes and motifs frequent in his fiction."[25] Nevertheless, the point is not that Hemingway is autobiographical, but rather that, as Malcolm Cowley says, "He is one of the novelists who write not as they should or would, but as they must."[26]

Nick, too, seems to act as he must. After his separation from Marjorie, Nick lies face down on the blanket. He refuses, therefore, to look at the moon and the lake, those traces of maternal warmth and security. He even wants Bill to leave him

[24]Young, Ernest Hemingway (Minneapolis, 1964), p. 13.

[25]Hovey, p. 220.

[26]Cowley, p. 51.

alone. He wants no contact with the world or with other people, or, symbolically, with the traces of subconscious relief. He has, in a sense, died. Something has truly ended.

Nick has rejected not only Marjorie, but the female element itself, and he lies in psychic pain, face down on the blanket, his only comforter. Richard P. Hovey documents in superb detail how Hemingway's dominant mother impaired his acceptance of the feminine and shook his faith in his father and in his own masculinity (pp. 212-213). As Leslie Fiedler says: "Hemingway is only really comfortable in dealing with 'men without women.'"[27] We have, then, a man profoundly negative in outlook toward women, with a constant corollary need to reassert his masculinity and to prove his superiority to them.

Numerous traces in "The End of Something" suggest this subconscious fact of Hemingway's life. First, as Nick and Marjorie prepare bait, Nick grabs three small perch from the bucket, "while Marjorie chased with her hands in the bucket" and "finally caught a perch." Nick has dominated, but he remains unsatisfied. Psychologically and dramatically, Hemingway now needs some sort of tiff for Nick finally to get up the nerve to tell Marjorie, "It isn't fun any more." From Hemingway's subconscious resentment of women, we could almost predict the irritant. Nick remarks that "There's going to be a moon tonight." "I know it," Marjorie says happily. "You know everything," retorts Nick, turning upon her as a know-it-all, though he in fact has given

[27]"Men Without Women," in Weeks, p. 86.

all the directions and has taught her all she knows.

As Marjorie leaves, Nick somewhat contritely offers the normal gentlemanly courtesy of pushing off the boat for her. She shrugs away his offer and does it easily by herself, almost as if to imply--a bitter pill to Hemingway's subconscious and yet something he could not escape--that women perhaps really do not need men, that they can manage very nicely alone. Then Bill appears, by prearrangement, and we see that the two had planned the whole episode, that Marjorie could not have changed the outcome, that Nick's relationship with Bill is stronger than that with Marjorie.

Except possibly for the last example, these details seem truly to be "traces." They are really little things, descriptions, contrivances of plot, and the like, all normal devices that any author must construct; yet they are distinctly Hemingway. They correlate precisely with what critics have surmised and biographers have affirmed about the personal inner workings of Hemingway's mind. These traces help to confirm our general notion of Hemingway's subconscious symbolism.

Actually, these traces in "The End of Something" fall into three major thematic categories: alienation, death-and-birth, and women. The death-and-birth theme especially is remarkable in its correlation with Freudian dream symbolism. Moreover, the themes that leave these traces are also basic themes in Hemingway's life. From the first, he is alienated from society and tradition. Death seems always at the focal point of his life: he never forgot the traumatic experience of 1918, nor, later, his father's suicide. His mistrust of women sprang from his dominating mother. That traces of these psychic preoccupations should be so varied and plentiful in one very short story is truly remarkable, and yet we could undoubtedly find abundant examples in all of Hemingway, especially in the early stories.

Hemingway once jestingly commented that the typewriter was his psychiatrist[28]--more than he knew, his fiction was his psychoanalytical couch. His readers were the psychological observers, sometimes unaware that they were watching, or rather, feeling, a man working out his own inner torments, but always aware that mysteriously they too were profoundly moved by what he told. He wrote "commencing with the simplest things,"[29] viewing the world behavioristically, not consciously regarding what he wrote as symbolic, not deliberately employing symbolism, only knowing that his stories had that special something, that suffused and inexpressible pause of feeling: "It is hard enough to write books and stories without being asked to explain them as well."[30]

"Read anything I write for the pleasure of reading it. Whatever else you find will be a measure of what you brought to the reading" (loc. cit.). What you brought to the reading--what readers have probably responded to most deeply from the first--is a natural empathy for those deep psychic symbols of which Hemingway's spare prose bears the traces. Symbolism that is not

[28]Young, <u>Reconsideration</u>, p. 165.

[29]Hemingway, quoted by Cowley, p. 46

[30]"An Interview with Ernest Hemingway," with George Plimpton, <u>The Paris Review</u>, 18 (1958), 76, quoted by Oldsey, p. 195.

symbolism in the usual literary sense, but rather traces that speak directly to the reader's subconscious mind, powerful because they spring unaltered from the author's own subconscious--perhaps this kind of primitive, deep eloquence that we find in Hemingway's traces gives a clue to his real power and greatness.

BIBLIOGRAPHY

Baker, Carlos. Ernest Hemingway, A Life Story. New York: Charles Scribner's Sons, 1969.

_________. Hemingway, The Writer as Artist. Princeton: Princeton University Press, 1952.

Baker, Sheridan. Ernest Hemingway: An Introduction and Interpretation. American Authors and Critics Series. New York: Holt, Rinehart, and Winston, Inc., 1967.

Caligor, Leopold, and Rollo May. Dreams and Symbols. New York: Basic Books, Inc., 1968.

DeFalco, Joseph. The Hero in Hemingway's Short Stories. Pittsburgh: University of Pittsburgh Press, 1963.

Freud, Sigmund. The Interpretation of Dreams. New York: Basic Books, Inc., 1953.

_________. On Dreams. New York: W. W. Norton and Co., Inc., 1952.

Hemingway, Ernest. Death in the Afternoon. New York: Charles Scribner's Sons, 1932.

_________. "The End of Something," in In Our Time, pp. 35-41. New York: Charles Scribner's Sons, 1955.

Hovey, Richard P. Hemingway: The Inward Terrain. Seattle: University of Washington Press, 1968.

Jung, C. G. Psyche and Symbol. Garden City: Doubleday and Co., Inc., 1958.

Oldsey, Bern. "The Snows of Ernest Hemingway," Wisconsin Studies in Contemporary Literature, 4 (1963), 172-198.

Prince, Morton. Clinical and Experimental Studies in Personality. Cambridge, Massachusetts: Sci-Art Publishers, 1939.

Weeks, Robert P., ed. Hemingway: A Collection of Critical Essays. Englewood Cliffs: Prentice-Hall, Inc., 1962.

Young, Philip. Ernest Hemingway. University of Minnesota Pamphlets on American Writers, No. 1. Minneapolis: University of Minnesota Press, 1964.

__________. Ernest Hemingway: A Reconsideration. University Park: The Pennsylvania State University Press, 1966.

Exercises

1. Go to the card catalog and pick a card, any card. Write down everything you can learn from it about the author and the book. Is it classified according to Dewey Decimal or the Library of Congress? What general category is it in—Philosophy, Agriculture? What can you surmise from the other numbers and letters of the call number? What other cards have probably been made for it? Record everything you can learn or guess from the single card. Now, find the book itself, and report everything else you learn about it from the title page and the back of the title page.

2. Select some well-known literary work: *Walden, David Copperfield, Huckleberry Finn, Alice in Wonderland, The Wind in the Willows, A Farewell to Arms.* Describe how thoroughly it is cataloged by your library. Check cards for author, title, and subject. How many editions does the library have? Is the work contained within any *Works?* How many cards treat it as a subject? Does your library own a first edition? This last may require that you find the date of the first edition by looking up your author in an encyclopedia, checking available books about him, and perhaps checking in the British Museum's *General Catalogue of Printed Books,* or, for a twentieth-century book, *United States Catalog of Printed Books* or *Cumulative Book Index* to discover the earliest cataloging.

3. Read an article in one of the specialized encyclopedias, such as the *Catholic Encyclopedia,* the *Encyclopedia of World Art,* or the *Cyclopedia of American Government.* Then read articles on the same topic in two of the general encyclopedias, such as the *Britannica* and *Collier's.* Write an analysis that compares and evaluates the differing treatments.

4. Consult the current *World Almanac* or the *New York Times Encyclopedic Almanac* for the date of some memorable event: the sinking of the *Titanic* or the *Lusitania,* Lindbergh's flight over the Atlantic, the United States' entry into war, the founding of the United Nations, the great stock-market crash, or the like. Now go to one of the other almanacs for the year of your event, and write an essay entitled, let us say, "1918"—a synopsis of the monumental and the curious for that year, as lively and interesting as you can make it.

5. Choose a subject—"Dog Racing," "Vietnam," "Bowling," "Mushrooms," or what not—and write a short statistical report on the listings

under this subject in the *Reader's Guide to Periodical Literature* over the past ten years. Does your subject have unusually fat or lean years? What kinds of magazines treat the subject? Can you infer anything from your data about fashions in magazines, or happenings in the world? Go to one article in the most prolific year to discover the reason for your subject's popularity.

6. Look up some event of the recent past (after 1913) in the *New York Times Index*. Write a paper on how the event is reported in the *Times* and in the other newspapers available in your library.

7. Write a brief description of four specialized indexes—for example, the *Art Index*, the *Dramatic Index*, the *Essay and General Literature Index*, the *Music Index*—telling what kinds of things you can learn from each, what kinds of things you would like to learn but cannot, and how convenient and informative each seems to be.

8. Selecting any well-known author, English or American (but to keep your task manageable, avoid such giants as Shakespeare and Milton), go to the "Annual Bibliography" in *PMLA* for any year, and copy out the year's crop of articles on your man. Now go to an appropriate specialized bibliography for the same year—the one in the *Philological Quarterly*, for instance, or in *Modern Philology* or in *American Literature*—and write a report comparing the differing treatments of the two.

Suggested Subjects for Research Papers

Who Killed Malcolm X?
Socialized Medicine
Euthanasia
Capital Punishment
Early Reviews of *For Whom the Bell Tolls*
The Tonkin Gulf Incident
Lyndon B. Johnson's Foreign Policy
The Meaning of a Story by Faulkner
The Generation Gap
Assassination in Dallas
Light and Dark in Three Poems by Robert Frost
Interracial Marriage
Censorship
States' Rights
Federal Aid to Education

The Meaning of a Poem by E. E. Cummings
The Theater of the Absurd
The Future of Boxing
The Plight of Our Cities
Death on the Highways
Chemotherapy for Psychosis
Managing the Environment
Our Disappearing Whales (Horses, Eagles, etc.)
Legislation to Control Guns

APPENDICES

A. A Writer's Grammar

B. A Glossary of Usage

C. Rhetorical Devices

A Writer's Grammar
Appendix A

Grammar as Therapy

You have already seen many of the ills of writing—the ailing thesis that weakens the whole system, the *of*-and-*which* disease, the recurring rash of wordiness. But many a sentence suffers from ailments more deeply genetic. You can probably tell when a sentence feels bad, especially after your instructor has marked it up. You can, in other words, detect the symptoms, but to work an efficient cure you need also to find the causes and to treat them directly. You need some skill in the old household remedies of grammar.

Learn to trace symptoms back to causes.

Here are fifteen ailing sentences, each with a different kink, or quinsy, which a knowledge of grammar can help you cure. You will see the specific treatments in a moment, but for a first lesson in home therapy, look over these fifteen different symptoms (italicized and underlined), noting the affected parts (italicized):

The *professor*, as well as the students, *were* glad the course was over. [*Were* does not agree with *professor*.]
***They* study hard here, but *you* do not have to work all the time. [*You* does not agree with *They*.]**

Holden *goes* to New York and *learned* about life. [*Learned* does not agree in tense with *goes.*]

As *he looked up,* a *light could be seen* in the window. [The subject has shifted awkwardly from *he* to *light,* and the verbal construction from active to passive.]

A *citizen* should support the government, but *they* should also be free to criticize it. [*They* does not agree with *citizen.*]

Now we knew: *it* was *him.* [*Him* does not agree in case with the subject, *it.*]

Let's keep this *between* you and *I.* [*I* cannot be the object of *between.*]

The students always elect *whomever is* popular. [*Whomever* cannot be the subject of the verb *is.*]

She hated *me leaving* so early. [She hated not *me* but the *leaving.*]

***Bill* told *Fred* that *he* failed the exam. [*He* can mean either *Bill* or *Fred.*]**

***Father* felt *badly.* [*Badly* describes *Father's* competence, not his condition.]**

They *walked leisurely.* [The adjective *leisurely* makes a poor adverb.]

She said *on Tuesday* she *would call.* [The position of *on Tuesday* confuses the times of *saying* and *calling.*]

***Walking* to class, her *book* slipped from her grasp. [*Walking* refers illogically to *book.*]**

While *playing* the piano, the *dog* sat by me and howled. [Dogs don't play pianos.]

With each of these, you sense that something is wrong. And by applying a little common logic you can usually find the dislocated parts. But that each requires a different diagnosis and a different kind of grammatical cure may not be so readily apparent. We first need to understand something of the basic physiology of grammar.

Know the basic parts of speech.

The parts of speech are the elements of the sentence. A grasp of the basic eight—nouns, pronouns, verbs, adjectives, adverbs, prepositions, conjunctions, and interjections—will give you a sense of the whole.

Nouns. These name something. *A proper noun* names a particular person, place, or thing. A *common noun* names a general class of things; a common noun naming a group as a single unit is a *collective noun.* A phrase or clause functioning as a noun is a *noun phrase* or a *noun clause.* Here are some examples:

Common: stone, tree, house, girl, artist, nation, democracy
Proper: George, Cincinnati, Texas, Europe, Declaration of Independence
Collective: committee, family, quartet, herd, navy, clergy, kind
Noun phrase: *Riding the surf* takes stamina.
Noun clause: *What you say* may depend on *how you say it.*

Pronouns. As their name indicates, pronouns stand "for nouns." The noun a pronoun represents is called its *antecedent.* Pronouns may be classified as follows:

Personal (standing for persons): I, you, he, she, we, they; me, him, her, us, them; my, his, our, and so on
Reflexive (turning the action back on the doer): I hurt *myself.* They enjoy *themselves.*
Intensive (emphasizing the doer): He *himself* said so.
Relative (linking subordinate clauses): who, which, that, whose, whomever, whichever, and so on
Interrogative (beginning a question): who, which, what
Demonstrative (pointing to things): this, that, these, those, such
Indefinite (standing for indefinite numbers of persons or things): one, any, each, few, some, anyone, everyone, somebody, and so on
Reciprocal (plural reflexives): each other, one another

Verbs. These express actions or states of being. A verb may be *transitive,* requiring an object to complete the thought, or *intransitive,* requiring no object for completeness. Some verbs can function either transitively or intransitively. *Linking verbs* link the subject to a state of being.

Transitive: He *put* his feet on the chair. She *hit* the ceiling. They *sang* a sad old song.
Intransitive: He *smiled.* She *cried.* They *sang* like birds.
Linking: He *is* happy. She *feels* angry. This *looks* bad.

Adjectives. These describe nouns or pronouns. An *adjectival phrase* or *adjectival clause* functions in a sentence as a single adjective would.

Adjectives: The *red* house faces west. He was a *handsome* devil. The *old haunted* house was *empty.*
Adjectival phrase: He had reached the end *of the book.*
Adjectival clause: Here is the key *that unlocks the barn.*

Adverbs. These describe verbs, adjectives, or other adverbs. An *adverbial phrase* or *adverbial clause* functions as a single adverb would.

Adverbs: **Though *slightly* fat, he runs *quickly* and plays *extremely well.***

Adverbial phrase: **He left *after the others.***

Adverbial clause: **She lost the gloves *after she left the store.***

Prepositions. A preposition links a noun or pronoun to another word in the sentence. A preposition and its object form a *prepositional phrase.*

By **late afternoon, Williams was exhausted.**
He walked *to* his car and drove *from* the field.

Conjunctions. These join words, phrases, and clauses. Coordinating conjunctions—*and, but, or, yet, for*—join equals:

Mary *and* I won easily.
Near the shore *but* far from home, the bottle floated.
He was talented, *yet* he failed.

Subordinating conjunctions join minor thoughts to main ones:

Since **it was late, they left.**
He worked hard *because* he needed an A.
They stopped *after* they reached the spring.

Interjections. These interrupt the usual flow of the sentence to emphasize feelings:

But, *oh,* the difference to me.
Mr. Dowd, *alas,* has ignored the evidence.
The consumer will suddenly discover that, *ouch,* his dollar is cut in half.

Sentences

Learn to identify the simple subject and its verb. Grammar conveniently classifies the words in your sentences into parts of speech. With the natural and logical joining of parts, thought begins. And the very beginning is the subject and its verb. A noun expresses a meaning, which, when expressed, gathers other meanings to it. The mere idea of *tree* moves on to include some idea of a verb: *tree is.* And other subject-verb thoughts are probably not far behind: *tree sways; it drops its leaves.* With *The poplar tree sways in the wind, dropping yellow leaves on the lawn,* you have a full-grown sentence. At its heart are *tree*—the simple subject (the subject shorn of all modifiers)—and *sways,* the verb. All the rest is a complicating of the simple subject and its verb. You should accustom yourself to locating these two parts in an ailing sentence. They will help you see how its other parts are behaving—or ought to be behaving. First, find the verb, since that names the action: *sways.* Then ask *who* or *what.* The answer gives you your subject, which, with modifiers cut away, is the simple subject. Having found the heart—*simple subject* plus *verb* —you are well on the way to understanding the rest of your sentence's anatomy.

Know the structure—and complications—of the simple sentence.

The simple English sentence can take one of three essential forms:

I. Subject-Verb
II. Subject-Verb-Object
III. Subject-Is-Something

These three incorporate the three major kinds of verbs, which I indicate in brackets:

I. Subject-Verb[*intransitive*]

> **She *smiles.***
> **He *laughs* like a perfect idiot.**
> **The tree *sways* in the wind.**

II. Subject-Verb[*transitive*]-Object

> **Boy *meets* girl.**
> **He *liked* her convertible.**
> **They *cashed* the check.**

III. Subject-Is[*linking*]-Something

> **The temperature *is* up.**
> **They *are* here.**
> **This *tastes* salty.**
> **The pie *smells* good.**

Is is the most common link in the last form's equation; but, as you see, a number of other verbs may serve: *taste, smell, feel, look, seem, appear, act, get, grow, turn, become.*

Although the structure is simple, the simple sentence may exhibit considerable variation. It may contain compounds in subject or predicate:

The *boy and* the *girl,* the *aunt, and* the whole hypocritical *family* smile. [compound subject]

He *hit* the right note with her *and struck* a full sympathetic chord with her parents. [compound predicate]

The *president* of the company *and* the *chairman* of the board *stormed and raged.* [compounds in subject and predicate]

Or it may attach modifiers to subject and verb:

Beautiful beyond imagination, glowing with health, *she* won the contest. [*She* is the subject.]

He *swam,* unaware of sharks, indifferent to snipers' bullets, as if he were merely racing again in the varsity pool. [*Swam* is the verb.]

Or put the verb before the subject:

Near the window *stood* a folding *screen.*

Behind it *was* the *murderer.*

There *is* your *problem.* [The expletive *there* can never be a subject.]

It *was* too bad *that he quit.* [*That he quit,* a noun clause, is the subject. Like *There, it* is an expletive introducing the sentence.]

Or use a verbal form for subject:

***To see* it will be enough.**

***Seeing* it will convince you.**

Or omit the subject (*you* implied) in a command or request—an *imperative* sentence:

Get smart.

If it is not too much trouble, please punctuate accurately.

Take, oh take, those lips away.

Two or more simple sentences can combine into a *compound* sentence:

He drove the car, and she did the talking.

He liked the scenery, she liked the maps, and they both enjoyed the motels.

The food was good; the prices were reasonable.

Either the plan was bad, or the instructions failed.

A simple sentence with one or more subordinate clauses added becomes a *complex* sentence:

When the weather cleared, they started their vacation.

Although the weather was fine, although the timing was perfect, although expenses were no problem, the vacation was miserable. They returned home as soon as they could.

Two or more simple sentences combined with one or more subordinate clauses become a *compound-complex* sentence:

When the weather cleared, they started their vacation; but they returned home as soon as they could.

Practice A

Treat these ailing sentences, consulting Chapter 10 as necessary. In your cured versions, underline the simple subject of each clause once, and the subject's verb twice, and bracket the subordinate clauses.

SIMPLE SENTENCES

1. The old and the young, the feeble and the sprightly; joins the dance.
2. John Stevenson liked everything about the old town, her relatives, and she most of all.
3. There is one or two things left to do.
4. Solving several specific problems are good exercise.
5. Ann, as well as her mother, like to sew.

COMPOUND SENTENCES

6. He drives the car and she, a friendly girl, do the talking.
7. Jim drove the car and her friends, thought him crazy.
8. They liked the dinner, however it was expensive.
9. Either the beds were too hard or the prices.
10. The game was over the season had ended.

COMPLEX SENTENCES

11. Whenever he comes over chaos reigns.
12. Them who gets there first gets the best seats.
13. After many years passed Jim forgot.
14. The old and the young, the feeble and the sprightly, comes when the drum begins to beat.
15. All the people, whoever happened to be in the village was welcome.

Subjects

Avoid awkward changes of subject in midsentence.

Unnecessary shifts in structure can confuse a sentence's vision and its sense of direction. A needless change in subject may make a sentence appear unsure whether it is coming or going.

Faulty: **As *I* entered the room, *voices* could be heard.**
Revised: **As *I* entered the room, *I* could hear voices.**

Faulty: **The *audience* was pleased by his performance, and *he* earned a standing ovation.**
Revised: **His performance pleased the audience and earned him a standing ovation.**

Faulty: **The first *problem* is political, but there are *questions* of economics that are almost entirely involved in the second problem.**
Revised: **The first *problem* is political; the second, principally economic.**

Faulty: ***Jim* rolled up his sleeves, the *axe* was raised, and the *sapling* came down with four powerful strokes.**
Revised: ***Jim* rolled up his sleeves, raised the axe, and cut the sapling down with four powerful strokes.**

Avoid illogical shifts in person and number.

Person refers to the form a pronoun and verb take to indicate who is speaking, who is being spoken to, and who is being spoken about:

***I am*—first person**
***You are*—second person**
***He is, they are*—third person**

Number refers to the form a noun, pronoun, or verb takes to indicate one (*singular*) or more than one (*plural*). A sentence that shifts illogically in person and number is almost completely unhinged: it cannot distinguish between persons, and it has forgotten how to count.

Faulty: ***They* have reached an age when *you* should know better.**
Revised: ***They* have reached an age when *they* should know better.**

Faulty: ***Readers* have difficulty in following the argument. *You* get lost in qualifications.**
Revised: ***Readers* have difficulty in following the argument. *They* get lost in qualifications.**

Faulty: **If *someone* asks her a question, *they* get a straight answer.**
Revised: **If *someone* asks her a question, *he* gets a straight answer.**

Faulty: **A motion *picture* can improve upon a book, but *they* usually do not.**

Revised: **A motion *picture* can improve upon a book, but *it* usually does not.**

Practice B

Revise the following sentences, correcting the awkward shifts of subject, person, and number.

1. A stitch was dropped, and Barbara sighed.
2. Whenever a stitch was dropped, Barbara would sigh.
3. First he investigated the practical implications, and then the moral implications that were involved were examined.
4. Sam sat down at the counter, catsup was poured on the hamburger, and there was hunger in his face as he ate it.
5. These statistics are impressive, but error is evident in them.
6. The United Nations is not so firmly established that they can enforce international law.
7. One should never assume that they have no faults.
8. A person is overwhelmed by the gardens. Everywhere you look is beauty.
9. The buffalo is far from extinct. Their numbers are actually increasing.
10. People distrust his glibness. One feels they are being taken in by him.

Verbs

Keep your verb and its subject in agreement.

Match singulars with singulars, plurals with plurals. You will have little trouble except when subject and verb are far apart, or when the number of the subject itself is doubtful. (Is *family* singular or plural? What about *none?*—about *neither he nor she?*)

Sidestep the plural constructions that fall between your singular subject and its verb:

Faulty: **The *attention* of the students *wander* out the window.**
Revised: **The *attention* of the students *wanders* out the window.**

Faulty: ***Revision*** **of their views about markets and averages *are* mandatory.**
Revised: ***Revision*** **of their views about markets and averages *is* mandatory.**

Faulty: **The *plaster,* as well as the floors, *need* repair.**
Revised: **The *plaster,* as well as the floors, *needs* repair.**

Collective nouns (*committee, jury, herd, group, family, kind, quartet*) are single units; give them singular verbs, or plural members:

Faulty: Her _family were_ ready.
Revised: Her _family was_ ready.

Faulty: The _jury have disagreed_ among themselves.
Revised: The _members_ of the jury _have disagreed_ among themselves.

Faulty: _These kind_ of muffins _are_ delicious.
Revised: _This kind_ of muffin _is_ delicious.

Remember that in clauses introduced by expletive *there* (which can never be a subject though it may look like one), the subject follows the verb and governs its number:

There _is_ only one good _choice._
There _are_ several good _choices._

But expletive *it* always takes a singular verb:

It _is_ [_was_] the _child._
It _is_ [_was_] the _children._

Watch out for the indefinite pronouns *each, either, neither, anyone, everyone, no one, none, everybody, nobody.* Each of these is (not *are*) singular in idea, yet each flirts with the crowd from which it singles out its idea: each of *these,* either of *them,* none of *them.* They all take singular verbs.

Faulty: _None_ of these men _are_ failures.
Revised: _None_ of these men _is_ a failure.

Faulty: _None_ of the class, even those best prepared, _want_ the test.
Revised: _None_ of the class, even those best prepared, _wants_ the test.

Faulty: _Everybody_ on the committee _are_ present.
Revised: _Everybody_ on the committee _is_ present.

Faulty: _Neither_ the right nor the left _support_ the issue.
Revised: _Neither_ the right nor the left _supports_ the issue.

Exception: when one side, or both, of the *either-or* contrast is plural, the verb is plural:

Either the players or the coach _are_ bad.
Neither the rights of man nor the needs of the commonwealth _are_ relevant to the question.

None of them are is very common. From Shakespeare's time to ours, it has persisted alongside the more precise *none of them is,* which now seems to have the edge in careful prose.

When a relative pronoun (*who, which, that*) is the subject of a clause, it takes a singular verb if its antecedent is singular, a plural verb if its antecedent is plural:

The *man* who *tries* cannot fail.
The *men* who *try* cannot fail.

Faulty: **Phil is one of the best *swimmers* who *has* ever been on the team.**
Revised: **Phil is one of the best *swimmers* who *have* ever been on the team.**

Faulty: **Phil is the only *one* of our swimmers who *have* won three gold medals.**
Revised: **Phil is the only *one* of our swimmers who *has* won three gold medals.**

Don't let a plural noun in the predicate lure you into a plural verb:

Faulty: **His most faithful rooting *section are* his girl and his family.**
Revised: **His most faithful rooting *section is* his girl and his family.**

Use the tense that best expresses your idea.

Tense means time (from Latin *tempus*). Using verbs of the right tense means placing the action in the right period of time. Usually, you have no trouble choosing the forms to express simple past, present, and future; but you may have trouble expressing "perfected" forms of past, present, and future—especially when they must appear in the same sentence or paragraph with the simpler forms.

Here, with active and passive examples, are the six principal tenses found in English:

TENSE	ACTIVE VOICE	PASSIVE VOICE
Present	I ask	I am asked
Past	I asked	I was asked
Future	I shall ask	I shall be asked
Present Perfect	I have asked	I have been asked
Past Perfect	I had asked	I had been asked
Future Perfect	I shall have asked	I shall have been asked

Each tense has its own virtues for expressing what you want your sentences to say.

Use the *present tense* to express present action:

Now she *knows*. She *is leaving*.

Use the present also for habitual action:

He *sees* her every day.

or for future action:

Classes *begin* next Monday.

or for describing literary events:

Hamlet *finds* the king praying, but he *is* unable to act; he *lets* the opportunity slip.

or for expressing timeless facts:

The Greeks knew the world *is* round.

or for the "historical present":

King Alfred *watches* as the spider *mends* her web. He *determines* to rebuild his kingdom.

But reserve the historical present for such deliberate literary effect. In ordinary narration or exposition, *avoid* this kind of thing:

One day I *am watching* television when the phone *rings;* it *is* the police.

Use the *past tense* for all action before the present:

He just *left*.

One day I *was watching* television when the phone *rang;* it *was* the police.

Use the *future tense* for action expected after the present:

He *will finish* it next year.

When he *finishes* next year, ...

He *is going to finish* it next year. [The "present progressive" *is going* plus an infinitive, like *to finish*, commonly expresses the future.]

Use the *present perfect tense* for action completed ("perfected") but relevant to the present moment:

I *have gone* there before.

He *has sung* forty concerts.

She *has driven* there every day.

Use the *past perfect tense* to express "the past of the past":

When we *arrived* [past], they *had finished* [past perfect].

Notice that the present perfect (*have* plus past participle) becomes the past perfect (*had* plus past participle) when you step from present or future to past. Everything moves back one step:

The flare *signals* that he *has started.*
The flare *signaled* that he *had started.*

Use the *future perfect tense* to express "the past of the future":

When we *arrive* [future], they *will have finished* [future perfect].
You *will have worked* thirty hours by Christmas.

Avoid unnecessary shifts in tense, voice, and mood.

Inconsistencies in verbal forms will bother your reader, and usually muddle your ideas as well. Choose your tense and stay with it, stepping away only when the thought demands some other tense to make a distinction of time.

Faulty: **Then Antony *looked up* from the body and *begins* to speak.**
Revised: **Then Antony *looked up* from the body and *began* to speak.**

Faulty: **King Alfred *thanks* the peasant, and *went* his way. He *gathered* his men. They *are* overjoyed.**
Revised: **King Alfred *thanks* the peasant, and *goes* his way. He *gathers* his men. They *are* overjoyed.**

Faulty: **While the executives *stayed* in the plant, the strikers *picket* outside.**
Revised: **While the executives *stayed* in the plant, the strikers *picketed* outside.**

Faulty: **Although the government *has stated* its policy [present perfect], the people *have* still *been* confused [present perfect].**
Revised: **Although the government *has stated* its policy [present perfect], the people *are* still confused [present].**

Awkward: **We *will have left* [future perfect] by the time they *will have arrived* [future perfect].**
Revised: **We *will have left* [future perfect] by the time they *arrive* [present functioning to express future action].**

English has only two "voices"—the active and the passive (I *see,* I *am seen*)—and if you have read pages 132–135, you know which is the more efficient. Whether using the active or the passive, avoid awkward shifts, especially if they also bring awkward shifts of subject.

Faulty: **This plan *reduces* taxes and *has been proved* workable in three other cities.**
Revised: **This plan *reduces* taxes and *has proved* workable in three other cities.**

Faulty: **He *had paid* for the new tires and the new upholstery; and now even the car *was paid for.***
Revised: **He *had paid* for the new tires and new upholstery; and now he *had* even *paid* for the car.**

Faulty: **After they *laid out* the pattern, electrical shears *were used* to cut around it.**
Revised: **After they *laid out* the pattern, they *cut* around it with electrical shears.**

Mood (also called *mode*: "manner") is the attitude of the speaker toward the action his verb names. English has three moods. The *indicative mood* declares a fact or asks a question:

> **This pie *is* good. Susan *baked* it.**
> **Susan *baked* it? *Is* there any left?**

The *imperative mood* expresses a command or request:

> ***Get* out. Please *be* careful. *Take* two aspirin.**

The *subjunctive mood* expresses an action or condition not asserted as actual fact. Such conditional, provisional, wishful, suppositional ideas are usually subjoined (*subjunctus,* "yoked under") in subordinate clauses. The form of the verb is often plural, even though the subject is singular.

> **He looked as if he *were* confident.**
> **If I *were* you, Miles, I would ask her myself.**
> **If this *be* error, and upon me [*be*] proved . . .**
> ***Had* he *been* sure, he would have said so.**
> **I demand that he *make* restitution.**
> **I move that the nominations *be closed,* and that the secretary *cast* a unanimous ballot.**

Avoid awkward or faulty shifts of mood:

Faulty: **If I *was* you, John, I would speak for myself.**
Revised: **If I *were* you, John, I would speak for myself.**

Faulty: **If he *would have known,* he never would have said that.**
Revised: **If he *had known,* he never would have said that.**
Revised: ***Had* he *known,* he never would have said that.**

Faulty: **He moved that the club buy the picture, and that the secretary *shall bill* the members.**
Revised: **He moved that the club buy the picture, and that the secretary *bill* the members.**

Faulty: **You *should read* carefully and *don't miss* his irony.**
Revised: **You *should read* carefully *to avoid missing* his irony.**
Revised: ***Read* carefully, and *don't miss* his irony.**

Master the tenses of the troublesome verbs.

Six short verbs are among the most troublesome in English: *lie, lay; sit, set; rise, raise.* These are six separate verbs, with six separate meanings. Master their meanings and their "principal parts" (present tense, past tense, and past participle—the form used with *has* or *had* in compound verbs), and your sentences will comport themselves comfortably and healthily. Indeed, three of the six suggest the convalescing patient: *lie, sit, rise.* These three are intransitive: they never take an object. The other three function more aggressively, always transitively, always taking an object: *lay, set, raise.* Now for the meanings, principal parts, and uses of them all.

First, the intransitive verbs. *Lie, lay, lain* (present, past, past participle) means to recline, or to be at rest.

Present: **The patient *lies* quietly asleep.**
The patient *is lying* quietly asleep.
Past: **After the visitors left, the patient *lay* quietly asleep.**
The purse *lay* unnoticed on the chair.
Past participle: **He has *lain,* quiet and asleep, all afternoon.**

Sit, sat, sat means to assume, or remain in, a sitting position.

Present: **I *sit* by the bed.**
A clock *sits* on the table near the bed.
Past: **The patient *sat* in the sun today.**
Past participle: **He had *sat* by the window yesterday.**

Rise, rose, risen means to stand up, or to move upward.

Present: **When supply is short, prices *rise.***
Past: **To my surprise, he *rose* to greet me.**
Past participle: **To my surprise, he had *risen* to greet me.**

Here are the transitive verbs. *Lay, laid, laid* means to place or put something.

> ***Present:*** **He *lays* the suitcase on the bed.**
> **He *is* already *laying* plans for a new life.**
> ***Past:*** **Yesterday he *laid* new tile in the playroom.**
> ***Past participle:*** **By now he has *laid* the cornerstone of the new city hall.**

Set, set, set means to place something in position.

> ***Present:*** **I *set* the chair near the window.**
> **He *sets* the checkerboard on the table.**
> ***Past:*** **He *set* the chair near the window.**
> ***Past participle:*** **He has *set* the checkerboard on the table.**

Don't confuse it with *sit* or *sit down*:

> ***Faulty:*** **He *sat* the chair near the window.**
> ***Revised:*** **He *set* the chair near the window.**

> ***Faulty:*** **He *set* himself *down* by the entrance.**
> ***Revised:*** **He *sat* himself *down* by the entrance.**

Finally, *raise, raised, raised* usually means to make something move up or grow.

> ***Present:*** **When supply is short, businessmen *raise* prices.**
> ***Past:*** **He *raised* his hand in greeting.**
> ***Past participle:*** **She has *raised* three beautiful children.**

Part of the difficulty is that the first five of these six troublemakers are *irregular verbs*—verbs not forming the past and the past participle by adding the usual *-ed*. Here are some more to watch; learn to control their past and past-participial forms:

> ***arise, arose, arisen***
> ***bear, bore, borne*** **[But: "She was *born* in 1950."]**
> ***beat, beat, beaten***
> ***begin, began, begun***
> ***bid*** **("order"),** ***bade*** **[pronounced "bad"],** ***bidden***
> ***burst, burst, burst***
> ***drag, dragged, dragged*** **[Not *drag, drug, drug*]**
> ***get, got, got (gotten)***
> ***hang*** **("suspend"),** ***hung, hung*** **[But: *hang* ("execute"), *hanged, hanged*]**
> ***lead, led, led*** **[Don't let the *lead* in *lead pencil* trick your spelling.]**
> ***lend, lent, lent***

light, lit (*lighted*), *lit* (*lighted*)
ride, rode, ridden
ring, rang, rung
sew, sewed, sewn (*sewed*)
shine ("glow"), *shone, shone* [Distinct from "polish"—*shine, shined, shined*]
show, showed, shown (*showed*)
shrink, shrank, shrunk
sing, sang, sung
sow, sowed, sown (*sowed*)
spring, sprang, sprung
swim, swam, swum
swing, swung, swung

Practice C

PART I: Treat these troubles, mostly verbal:

1. Conservatism, as well as liberalism, are summonses for change in American life as we now know it.
2. These kind of questions are sheer absurdities.
3. The committee were miles apart.
4. None of these proposals are unworkable.
5. Neither the tweed of his jacket nor the silk of his tie impress us.
6. Neither the question nor the answers seems pertinent to the issue.
7. None of us are perfect.
8. John was the second one of the fifty boys who has volunteered.
9. Each who have come this far have shown real determination.
10. His idea of fine foods are hamburgers and French fries.
11. Doug is the only one of the tall boys who always stand straight.
12. Last year we are warned of higher taxes and getting lower taxes. This year we are promised lower taxes and getting higher taxes. What next year is holding, we can only guess. But sooner or later we are being promised and taxed into disbelief.

PART II: Clinch your mastery of *lie, lay, sit, set, rise,* and *raise* by writing for each a set of three active sentences: the first using the present tense, the second using the past tense, the third using the past participle.

PART III: Straighten out the inconsistencies of tense, voice, and mood in this cripple:

> A third principle that industry should recognize was the need for constant appraisal by management of an employee's progress. Man-

agement would determine what a man, when he would of been hired, were expected by it to achieve; and it then judges whether it now had had him poorly assigned. He probably knows his own limitations, and jobs beyond his capacity are poorly handled by him. But it is not enough that a manager sit down periodically with a man and reviews his performance. The important thing is that the manager understands a man well enough and be articulate enough to make sure the man himself has become conscious of his need for further development. If the manager will have been sufficiently observant, he might have helped the man to an accurate evaluation of his own potential.

Pronouns as Subjects and Objects

Match a pronoun's form to its function.

Unlike nouns, pronouns change form when they change from subject to object. *John* remains *John,* whether on the giving or receiving end of the verb: *John* hit Joe; Joe hit *John.* But the pronoun changes from subjective to objective form: *He* hit Joe; Joe hit *him.* We all know the difference between *who* (subject) and *whom* (object), if only because we are so often uncertain about them. We tend to say, "*Who* did you see," because *who,* though really the object of the verb *see,* comes first—in the slot usually reserved for subjects. But "*Whom* did you see" is correct. We are also sometimes skittish about "between you and me," which is solidly correct, *me* being the object of the preposition *between.* Pronouns can cause considerable uncertainty—but they need not if you merely remember which forms are subjective and which objective. Here are the pronouns that give trouble:

SUBJECTIVE	OBJECTIVE
I	**me**
he	**him**
she	**her**
we	**us**
they	**them**
who	**whom**
whoever	**whomever**

Use subjective pronouns for subjective functions.

Compound subjects, like "Bill and I," are a common source of trouble. For an easy way to check whether *I* or *me* (*he* or *him*) is right, drop the "Bill" and see how well the pronoun alone stands as subject of the verb. You would not, for instance, say "Me reported the incident."

Faulty: **Bill and *me* signed the petition.**
Revised: **Bill and *I* signed the petition.**

Faulty: **Sally and *her* rode up front.**
Revised: **Sally and *she* rode up front.**

Faulty: ***Us* and *them* should have cooperated on this.**
Revised: ***We* and *they* should have cooperated on this.**

Faulty: **Pierce, Finch, and *myself* have resigned.**
Revised: **Pierce, Finch, and *I* have resigned. [Keep *myself* where it belongs, as an intensive (I *myself*) or reflexive (I hurt *myself*), and be unashamed of *me* where it properly fits.]**

A *complement* is a word that "complements" or completes the meaning of a verb. *Subjective complements* are words that complete the meaning of a linking verb, like *is,* while referring back to the subject ("Tom is *chairman*"). Pronouns serving as subjective complements must, of course, be subjective in form:

Faulty: **This is *him.***
Revised: **This is *he.***

Faulty: **He discovered that it was *me.***
Revised: **He discovered that it was *I.***

Faulty: **It was *them* who signed the treaty.**
Revised: **It was *they* who signed the treaty.**

A pronoun *in apposition* with the subject (that is, positioned near, and meaning the same thing as, the subject), or in apposition with a subjective complement, must also take the subjective form:

Faulty: ***Us* students would rather talk than sleep.**
Revised: ***We* students would rather talk than sleep.**

Faulty: **Both of us—Mike and *me*—should have gotten the credit.**
Revised: **Both of us—Mike and *I*—should have gotten the credit. [*Mike and I* are in apposition with the subject, *Both,* not with the object of the preposition, *us.*]**

Faulty: **They were both to blame—Lord Hervey and *him.***
Revised: **They were both to blame—Lord Hervey and *he.***

When a pronoun follows *than* or *as,* it must be subjective if the subject of an implied verb:

Faulty: **She is taller than *me* [am].**
Revised: **She is taller than *I* [am].**

Faulty: **You are as bright as *him* [is].**
Revised: **You are as bright as *he* [is].**

Faulty: **She loves you as much as *me* [love you].**
Revised: **She loves you as much as *I* [love you].**

Faulty: **She loves you better than [she loves] *he.***
Revised: **She loves you better than [she loves] *him.* [Here the pronoun is objective, since it is the object of the implied verb.]**

Use objective pronouns for objective functions.

A pronoun functioning as a *direct object, indirect object,* or *object of a preposition* must be objective in form. Compound objects give most of the trouble:

Faulty: **The mayor complimented Bill and *I.***
Revised: **The mayor complimented Bill and *me.***

Faulty: **She typed the letter for Stuart and *he.***
Revised: **She typed the letter for Stuart and *him.***

Faulty: **Will you have dinner with Mary and *I?***
Revised: **Will you have dinner with Mary and *me?***

Faulty: **Between her and *I,* an understanding grew.**
Revised: **Between her and *me,* an understanding grew.**

Faulty: **Everyone but Mildred and *she* contributed.**
Revised: **Everyone but Mildred and *her* contributed. [*But* is used here as a preposition with the meaning "except."]**

Faulty: **The petition was drafted by Nielsen, Wright, and *myself.***
Revised: **The petition was drafted by Nielsen, Wright, and *me.***

Pronouns in apposition with objects must themselves be objective:

Faulty: **The mayor complimented us both—Bill and *I.***
Revised: **The mayor complimented us both—Bill and *me.***

Faulty: **She gave the advice specifically to us—Helen and *I.***
Revised: **She gave the advice specifically to us—Helen and *me.***

Faulty: **Between us—Elaine and *I*—an understanding grew.**
Revised: **Between us—Elaine and *me*—an understanding grew.**

Faulty: **He would not think of letting *we* girls help him.**
Revised: **He would not think of letting *us* girls help him.**

Use a subjective pronoun for the subject of a noun clause.

This is one of the trickiest of pronominal problems. When a pronoun is the subject of a noun clause, it will often follow a verb or preposition, and therefore look like an object. But it is the subject, after all, and it must take a subjective form:

Faulty: **The sergeant asked *whomever* did it to step forward.**
Revised: **The sergeant asked *whoever* did it to step forward. [*Whoever did it* is a noun clause functioning as direct object of the verb *asked.* But *whoever* is the subject of the clause.]**

Faulty: **They promised the medal to *whomever* would go.**
Revised: **They promised the medal to *whoever* would go. [*Whoever would go* is a noun clause functioning as object of the preposition *to.* But *whoever* is subject of the clause.]**

Similarly, parenthetical remarks like *I think, he says,* and *we believe* often make pronouns seem objects when they are actually subjects:

Faulty: **Ellen is the girl *whom* I think will succeed.**
Revised: **Ellen is the girl *who* I think will succeed.**

Faulty: **Jim will vote for *whomever* they say is a winner.**
Revised: **Jim will vote for *whoever* they say is a winner.**

The *who* pronouns also match form to function in relative adjectival clauses:

Faulty: **The man *whom* had lied to her came in.**
Revised: **The man *who* had lied to her came in. [*Who* is subject of the clause *who had lied to her.*]**

Faulty: **The man *who* she hated came in.**
Revised: **The man *whom* she hated came in. [*Whom* is the direct object of the verb in the clause *whom she hated.*]**
Better: **The man she hated came in.**

But the *subject of an infinitive—and its complements*—is objective in form:

Faulty: **They guessed the author to be *I.***
Revised: **They guessed the author to be *me.***

Faulty: **They will pay *whoever* they find the artist to be.**
Revised: **They will pay whomever they find the artist to be.**

Use the possessive pronoun before a gerund.

Gerunds are verbal forms used as nouns (*hunting, skating, reading, sleeping*). *Participles* look exactly the same, but serve as adjectives.

Gerund: ***Hunting*** **is good exercise.**
Participle: ***Hunting*** **the southern hills, he came upon an old cabin.**

A gerund accompanied by a pronoun often runs into trouble:

Faulty: **She disliked *him* hunting.**
Revised: **She disliked *his* hunting.**

The object of her dislike is not *him* but *hunting;* hence the possessive pronoun merely modifies the true object, the gerund. Sometimes, however, the choice is not so clear:

They caught *him* cheating on the first exam.
They caught *his* cheating on the first exam.

Here the difference is not one of correctness, since both examples are correct, but of meaning as expressed through grammatical structure. In the first sentence, the object of *caught* is *him,* which is modified by the participle *cheating.* In the second sentence, the object is the gerund *cheating,* which is modified by *his.*

Faulty: **Her father disapproved of *me* dating her.**
Revised: **Her father disapproved of *my* dating her.**

Faulty: **I am bothered by *him* not asking me out.**
Revised: **I am bothered by *his* not asking me out.**

Faulty: **He consented to *them* making the trip.**
Revised: **He consented to *their* making the trip.**

Practice D

Cure the disabled pronouns:

1. It was him all right.
2. She disliked him whistling the same old tune.
3. They cheered both of us—Andy and I.
4. I admit it was me to whom they first confided.

5. We all three like it—Helen, Ann, and myself.
6. Us sophomores should all sign the petition.
7. Both her and me were elected.
8. He told her and I to leave.
9. They always elect whomever is popular.
10. They choose whoever they like.
11. My mother insists on me buying my own clothes.
12. Everybody thinks us girls should go.
13. Little love is lost between him and I.
14. In the end, it was them who succeeded.
15. The child who he adored finally broke his heart.

Pronouns and Their Antecedents

Keep your antecedents specific, unambiguous, and close at hand.

The antecedent states your pronoun's meaning. If an antecedent is missing, ambiguous, vague, or too far away, the pronoun will suffer from "faulty reference" and throw your sentence into disarray. Here is the malady in its various forms:

Missing: **In Texas *they* produce a lot of oil.**
Revised: ***Texas* produces a lot of oil.**

Missing: **My father is a doctor, and *this* is the work I want to do too.**
Revised: **My father is a doctor, and *medicine* is the profession I want to follow too.**

Ambiguous: **Pete told Sam that *he* had played terribly. [Is *he* Pete or Sam?]**
Revised: **Pete said that *Sam* had played terribly.**
Revised: **To Sam, Pete admitted having played terribly.**

Ambiguous: **Adams told Andrews that *he* could send *him* to London.**
Revised: **Adams threatened Andrews with being sent to London.**

Ambiguous: **Paul smashed into a girl's car *who* was visiting his sister.**
Revised: **Paul smashed into the car of a *girl* visiting his sister.**

Ambiguous: **He aimed at the tiger's eye, but *it* ran away.**
Revised: **He aimed at the eye, but *the tiger* ran away.**

Ambiguous: **Jane Austen saw Emma as a projection of *her* personality.**
Revised: **Jane Austen saw Emma as a projection of *her* (*Jane Austen's*) personality. [Improved, but awkward.]**

Better: Jane Austen saw *her Emma* as a projection of *her own* personality.

Vague: He is an excellent guitarist. *This* is because he began studying *it* as a child.

Revised: He is an excellent guitarist because he began taking lessons when a child.

Vague: Because Ann had never spoken before an audience, she was afraid of *it.*

Revised: Because Ann had never spoken before an audience, she was afraid.

Vague: He shouted outside the window and pounded on the frame, *which* finally broke the glass.

Revised: He shouted outside the window and pounded on the frame till he finally broke the glass.

Remote: The mayor's committee reported on the remaining problems of polluted air, poor traffic control, inadequate schools, and rat-infested slums. The mayor was proud of *it.*

Revised: The mayor's committee reported on the remaining problems of polluted air, poor traffic control, inadequate schools, and rat-infested slums. The mayor was proud of *the report.*

Remote: The castle was built in 1337. The rooms and furnishings are carefully kept up for the eyes of tourists, and at the entrance stands a coin-fed turnstile. *It* still belongs to the Earl.

Revised: The castle, which still belongs to the Earl, was built in 1337. The rooms and furnishings are carefully kept up for the eyes of tourists, and at the entrance stands a coin-fed turnstile.

With an indefinite antecedent, use a singular pronoun.

Prominent among the indefinite antecedents are *anybody, anyone, each, either* (*neither*), *everybody, everyone, no one, nobody.* Also included are generic nouns like *kind, sort, man, woman,* and *person,* and the collective nouns like *family, jury,* and *clergy.* All of these, collecting plural items under one head, retain a certain misleading plural feeling, which may wrongly tempt you to plural pronouns of reference.

> ***Faulty:*** **Modern suburban *woman* is often more interested in *their* social standing than in *their* children.**
> ***Revised:*** **Modern suburban *woman* is often more interested in *her* social standing than in *her* children.**

> ***Faulty:*** ***Everybody* paid for *their* ice cream.**
> ***Revised:*** ***Everybody* paid for *his* ice cream.**

> ***Faulty:*** ***Each* of the students hoped to follow *their* teacher's footsteps.**
> ***Revised:*** **Each of the students hoped to follow *the* teacher's footsteps.**

> ***Faulty:*** **After *everybody* in the crowd had contributed, Stan thanked *him.* [The grammar is correct, but the meaning is wrong.]**
> ***Revised:*** **After *all* the crowd had contributed, Stan thanked *them.***

> ***Faulty:*** **If the *clergy* dares to face the new philosophy, *they* should declare *themselves.***
> ***Revised:*** **If the *clergy* dares to face the new philosophy, the *clergy* should declare *itself.***

Practice E

Strengthen the faulty references:

1. He sent him his high-school pictures.
2. He kicked the child's toy by accident who was visiting.
3. Everyone knows their own best interest.
4. He missed several classes, which in the end defeated him.
5. When industries fail to make plans far enough into the future decades, they often underestimate them.
6. She ended her performance, but it was too late.
7. He opened the bird's cage, and it flew away.
8. My family is always throwing their weight around.
9. Shakespeare has Edgar portray his essential position.
10. These sort of snakes are very deceptive in their coloring.
11. The roofers finished early, after last touches to the trim and shingles, and they had really made it sparkle.
12. She loves swimming especially in the surf, thinking it the best exercise in the world.
13. His article was accepted by *Sport* magazine, for which he acknowledged his gratitude.
14. People should insure themselves against death and accident. These provide for the welfare of their loved ones.

15. There is a sandwich shop by the police station, and we phone them when we get hungry.

16. Coaches sometimes ignore the best interests of their players for the sake of winning games, and they are angry if they lose them because of bad grades, after working them too hard.

17. When he had his last heart attack, it almost stopped beating.

18. A governor should know a little about law and a lot about people, and apply them diplomatically.

Modifiers Misused and Misplaced

Learn the difference between adjectives and adverbs.

Adjectives describe nouns; adverbs describe verbs, adjectives, or other adverbs ("He *very shrewdly* played a *really* conservative game"). But the adjective sometimes wrongly crowds out the adverb ("He played *real* well"). And the adverb sometimes steals the adjective's place, especially when the linking verb looks transitive but isn't (*feels, looks, tastes, smells*), making the sense wrong. "He feels *badly*" means incompetence, not misery. "It tastes *wonderfully*" means skill in the taster. And certain adjectives ending in *-ly* (*lonely, lovely, leisurely*) tend to masquerade as adverbs:

Wrong: **She swam lovely.**
Doubtful: **They walked leisurely.**
Wrong: **He brooded lonely.**

But notice how quickly you can restore the adjective if you press your words for their meanings:

She swam, lovely as a swan.
They walked, leisurely and thoughtful.
I wandered lonely as a cloud.

Or you can simply assert the adverbial:

She swam beautifully.
They strolled slowly.
He brooded solitarily.

Some words serve both as adjectives and adverbs: *early, late, near, far, only, little, right, wrong, straight, well, better, best, fast,* for example.

He waited *late* for the *late* train.
Think *little* of *little* things.
Go *straight* up the *straight* and narrow path.

Near is both an adverb of place (*near to it, near the barn*) and an adjective (*the near hill, the near future*); and *near,* the adverb of place, is often confused with *nearly,* the adverb of degree, which means "almost."

Right: It was *near* Toledo. [adverb of place]
Right: It was *nearly* perfect. [adverb of degree]

To avoid confusing the two, substitute *almost* or *nearly* for the *near* of degree that tends to slip wrongly into your prose, or convert it into a proper *near* of place, actual or figurative:

Faulty: He was near exhausted.
Revised: He was nearly exhausted.
Revised: He was near exhaustion.

Faulty: It was a near treasonous statement.
Revised: It was a nearly treasonous statement.

Faulty: We are nowhere near knowledgeable enough.
Revised: We are not nearly knowledgeable enough.

Faulty: With Dodge, he has a tie of near-filial rapport.
Revised: With Dodge, he has a nearly filial rapport.
Revised: With Dodge, he has an almost filial rapport.

Slow has a long history as an adverb, encouraged by its crisp antithesis to *fast* (and its convenience for street-signs), but *slowly* keeps the upper hand in print. Notice that adverbs usually go after and adjectives before:

The *slow* freight went *slowly.*

Don't let your modifiers squint.

Some modifiers squint in two directions at once. Put them in their proper places. Make clear which way you want them to face.

Ambiguous: She said on Friday to phone him.
Revised: On Friday, she said to phone him.

Ambiguous: They agreed when both sides ceased fire to open negotiations.
Revised: They agreed to open negotiations when both sides ceased fire.

Ambiguous: Several delegations we know have failed.
Revised: We know that several delegations have failed.

Ambiguous: They hoped to try thoroughly to understand.
Revised: They hoped to try to understand thoroughly.

Ambiguous: He resolved to dependably develop plans.
Revised: He resolved to develop dependable plans. [See "Split infinitives," pp. 370–371.]

Ambiguous: Prices moved upward sufficiently to virtually wipe out the loss.
Revised: Prices rose almost enough to wipe out the loss.

Make your comparisons complete.

Both adjectives and adverbs have "comparative" and "superlative" forms:

Adjective: green, green*er*, green*est*
Adverb: smoothly, *more* smoothly, *most* smoothly

All comparatives demand some completion of thought, some answer to the question *than what?*—"Greener than what?"; "More smoothly than what?"

Faulty: The western plains are flatter.
Revised: The western plains are flatter than those east of the Mississippi.

Faulty: He plays more skillfully.
Revised: He plays more skillfully than most boys his age.

Faulty: He was as tall if not taller than his sister.
Revised: He was as tall as his sister, if not taller.

Faulty: Jane told her more than Ellen.
Revised: Jane told her more than she told Ellen.

Faulty: His income is lower than a busboy.
Revised: His income is lower than a busboy's.

Faulty: The pack of a paratrooper is lighter than a soldier.
Revised: A paratrooper's pack is lighter than a soldier's.

Superlatives also need completion:

Faulty: This is the best painting.
Revised: This is the best painting in the exhibit.

Faulty: Here was the prettiest if not the fastest car in the show.
Revised: Here was the prettiest car in the show, if not the fastest.

Practice F

Cure the faulty modifiers:

1. They asked after ten days to be notified.
2. We wanted to win enough to cry.
3. Everyone feels badly about it.
4. She sang melancholy.
5. The bidding began quietly and leisurely.
6. The work of a student is more intense than his parents.
7. It was a near perfect shot.
8. Some girls have expectations beyond a husband.
9. The party planned to completely attempt reform.
10. Industry is as strong if not stronger than before the depression.

Dangling Constructions

Connect a modifier clearly to what it modifies.

Verbals are those *-ing* words, the gerunds (verbal nouns) and participles (verbal adjectives): *laughing, cooking, concentrating.* The phrases and clauses growing out of these words have a tendency to slip loose from the main sentence and dangle. Make sure your modifying verbals connect firmly with some other word in the sentence.

Faulty: **Going home, the walk was slippery.**
Revised: **Going home, I found the walk slippery.**

Faulty: **When getting out of bed, his toe hit the dresser.**
Revised: **When getting out of bed, he hit his toe on the dresser.**

Infinitive phrases also can dangle badly:

Faulty: **To work well, keep your scooter oiled.**
Revised: **To work well, your scooter needs frequent oiling.**

Faulty: **To think clearly, some logic is important.**
Revised: **To think clearly, you should learn some logic.**

Any clause or phrase may dangle:

Faulty: **When only a freshman, Jim's history teacher inspired him.**
Revised: **When Jim was only a freshman, his history teacher inspired him.**

Faulty: **After he had lectured thirty years, the average student still seemed average.**

Revised: **After he had lectured thirty years, he found the average student still average.**

Practice G

Mend these dangling constructions:

1. What we need is a file of engineers broken down by their specialties.
2. Following the games on television, the batting average of every player was at his fingertips.
3. When entering the door, the lamp fell over.
4. To study well, a quiet room helps.
5. After he arrived at the dorm, the dean phoned.

The Healthy English Sentence

If you have been actively speaking and reading and writing these many years since your first step, your prose is probably in good grammatical health. But you do need to exercise to keep it vigorous. Slips in grammar can only distract your reader from what you are saying, and start him thinking, unflatteringly, about you. Keep your mind and your language alert, and you will retain his attention and respect. Keep the parts of your sentence well fitted; your prose active and spare; your meanings clearly working together. Keep trimly to the essential structure of the simple active sentence. Rid yourself of all inconsistencies in tense, voice, and mood. Above all, make your thoughts complete, with every noun and pronoun and verb in proper form, with no limbs dangling, and with your meaning unmistakable. Good grammatical prose takes exercise, but nothing can make you feel so thoroughly on top of the world.

Practice H

Turn to the fifteen ailing sentences on pages 321–322, and bring them back to health.

A Glossary of Usage

Appendix B

Speech keeps a daily pressure on writing, and writing returns the compliment, exacting sense from new twists in the spoken language and keeping old senses straight. "Usage," generally, is "the way they say it." Usage is the current in the living stream of language; it keeps us afloat, it keeps us fresh—as it sweeps us along. But to distinguish himself the writer must always battle it, must always swim upstream. He may say, "Hooja-eatwith?"; but he will write: "With whom did they compare themselves? With the best, with whoever seemed admirable." Usage is, primarily, talk; and talk year by year gives words differing social approval, and differing meanings. Words move from the gutter to the penthouse, and back down the elevator shaft. *Bull,* a four-letter Anglo-Saxon word, was unmentionable in Victorian circles. One had to use *he-cow,* if at all. Phrases and syntactical patterns also have their fashions, mostly bad. *Like unto me* changes to *like me* to *like I do; this type of thing* becomes *this type thing; -wise,* after centuries of dormancy in only a few words (*likewise, clockwise, otherwise*), suddenly sprouts out the end of everything: *budgetwise, personalitywise, beautywise, prestigewise.* Suddenly, everyone is saying *hopefully.* As usual, the marketplace changes more than your money.

But the written language has always refined the language of the marketplace. The Attic Greek of Plato and Aristotle (as Aristotle's remarks about local usages show) was distilled from commercial exchange. Cicero and Catullus and Horace polished their currency against the archaic and the Greek. Mallarmé claimed that Poe had given *un sens plus pur aux mots de la tribu*—which Eliot rephrases for himself: "to purify the dialect of the tribe." It is the very nature of writing so to do; it is the writer's illusion that he has done so:

> **I have laboured to refine our language to grammatical purity, and to clear it from colloquial barbarisms, licentious idioms, and irregular combinations. Something, perhaps, I have added to the elegance of its construction, and something to the harmony of its cadence.**

—wrote Samuel Johnson as he closed his *Rambler* papers. And he had almost done what he hoped. He was to shape English writing for the next hundred years, until it was ready for another dip in the stream and another purification. His work, moreover, lasts. We would not imitate it now; but we can read it with pleasure, and imitate its enduring drive for excellence.

Johnson goes on to say that he has "rarely admitted any word not authorized by former writers." Writers provide the second level of usage, the paper money. But even this usage requires principle. If we accept "what the best writers use," we still cannot tell whether it is sound: we may be aping their bad habits. John F. Kennedy's inaugural address, carefully polished by Harvard's best, contains this oddity (my italics): "For man holds in his mortal hands the power to abolish *all form* of human poverty and *all form* of human life."* Clearly, he meant either *all forms* or *every form*—or *all* human poverty and *all* human life. This mixing of choices, this coupling of the collective *all* with singular *form,* can mean only something like "all traces of form," as if the President were melting a statue. Most singular indeed! Even the best go wrong.

So we cannot depend on usage for our rules. Usage is only a court of first appeal, where we can say little more than "He said it." Beyond that helpless litigation, we can test our writing by reason, and by simple principles: clarity is good, economy is good, ease is good, gracefulness is good, fullness is good, forcefulness is good. As with all predicaments on earth, we judge by appeal to principles, and we often find principles in conflict. Is it economical but unclear? Is it full but cumbersome? Is it clear but too colloquial for grace? Careful judgment will give the ruling.

* As delivered, and as given in the official press release, Jan. 21, 1961 (New York *Herald Tribune,* Late City Edition, p. 1; Chicago *Daily Tribune,* p. 4). *Form* was corrected to *forms* by the New York *Times,* Jan. 21, 1961, p. 4, and read as *forms* into the *Congressional Record,* Doc. No. 9, 87th Cong., 1st sess.

Which is right, "I feel *bad*" or "I feel *badly*"? "The dress looks *good* on her" or "The dress looks *well* on her"? The man on the street would say, "I feel *bad*" and "The dress looks *good*," and he would be right: not because of "usage," but because *badly* would indicate shaky fingers and *well* a dress with good eyes. "Tie it tight" means "Tie it so that it is tight." Unfortunately, people trying to be proper follow the pattern of "He writes badly" and fall into the errors of "I feel badly" and "Tie it tightly." But *writes badly* is a verb with an adverb telling how the action is done, and *feel bad* is a verb with a predicate adjective modifying the subject and telling how the subject *is*. The predicate adjective describes existences, as in *ring true* and *come thick:* "they ring, and they are true"; "they come, and they are thick." So it is with other verbs pointing to states of being—*seem, appear, become, grow, sound, smell, taste*—on which "good usage" might rule the wrong way. Just remember that you don't say "I feel goodly." Let reason be your guide.

Likewise with *the reason . . . is because*. You can find this colloquial redundancy on many a distinguished page. But everything a good writer writes is not necessarily good. The phrase is a collision between two choices, as the mind rushes after its meaning: between (1) *the reason is that* . . . and (2) *it is . . . because*. Delete *the reason . . . is*, the colloquial pump-primer, and you save three words, sometimes four (the following eminent sentence, in which I have bracketed the surplus words, also suffers some redundancy of the *be*'s):

> **In general it may be said that [the reason why] scholasticism was held to be an obstacle to truth [was] because it seemed to discourage further inquiry along experimental lines.**

And so, usage is perhaps where we begin; but if we end there, we may end in wordiness and mediocrity. The following prescriptions are just about what the doctor ordered to keep you ticking, and in good company. They summarize the practices of the most careful writers—those who constantly attend to what words mean. They provide tips on avoiding wordiness, and avoiding those slips in diction that sometimes turn your reception a little chilly.

Practical Prescriptions for Good Writing

A, an. Use *a* before *h* sounded in a first syllable: *a hospital, a hamburger*. Use *an* before a silent *h: an honor, heir, hour*.

Above. For naturalness and effectiveness, avoid such references as "The above statistics are . . . ," and "The above speaks for itself." Simply use "These" or "This."

Aesthetic. An adjective: *an aesthetic judgment, his aesthetic viewpoint. Aesthetics* is singular for the science of beauty: "Santayana's *aesthetics* agrees with his metaphysics."

Affect. *Affect* means "to produce an *effect*." Don't use it as a noun; just say *feeling* or *emotion. Affective* is jargon for *emotional* or *emotive.*

Aggravate. Means to add gravity to something already bad enough. Avoid using it to mean "irritate."

WRONG	RIGHT
He aggravated his mother.	**The rum aggravated his mother's fever.**

All ready, already. Two different meanings. *All ready* means that everything is ready; *already* means "by this time."

All right, alright. *Alright* is not all right; you are confusing it with the spelling of *already.*

Alot. You mean *a lot,* not *allot.*

Also. Do not use for *and,* especially to start a sentence; not "*Also,* it failed," but simply "And it failed."

And/or. An ungainly hair-splitter and thought-stopper. You never *say* it. Don't write "for stage and/or screen"; write "for stage or screen, or both."

Ante-, anti. *Ante-* means "before": *an antebellum house* (a house built before the [Civil] War); *antedate* (to date before). *Anti-* means "against": *antifeminine, antiseptic.* Hyphenate before capitals, and before *i: anti-American, anti-intellectual.*

Anxious Use to indicate *Angst,* agony, and anxiety. Does not mean cheerful expectation: "He was *anxious* to get started." Use *eager* instead.

Any. Do not overuse as a modifier:

POOR	GOOD
He was the best of any senior in the class.	**He was the best senior in the class.**
If any people know the answer, they aren't talking.	**If anyone knows the answer, he's not talking.**

Anybody. Don't write it as two words—*any body*—unless you mean "any corpse," or other inanimate object (stellar body, body of water).

Any more. Always written as two words.

Anyone. Don't write it as two words—*any one*—unless you mean "any one thing."

Anyplace, someplace. Use *anywhere* and *somewhere* (adverbs), unless you mean "any *place*" and "some *place*."

Appearing. Don't write "an expensive appearing house." "An expensive-looking house" is not much better. Write "an expensive house," or "the house looked expensive."

Appreciate. Means "recognize the worth of." Do not use to mean simply "understand."

LOOSE	CAREFUL
I appreciate your position.	**I understand your position.**
I appreciate that your position is grotesque.	**I realize that your position is grotesque.**

Around. Do not use for *about:* it will seem to mean "surrounding."

POOR	GOOD
Around thirty people came.	**About thirty people came.**
He sang at around ten o'clock.	**He sang at about ten o'clock.**

As. Use where the cigarette people have *like:* "It tastes good, *as* a goody should." (See also *like.*)

Do not use for *such as:* "Many things, *as* nails, hats, toothpicks . . . ." Write "Many things, *such as* nails . . . ."

Do not use for *because* or *since;* it is ambiguous:

AMBIGUOUS	PRECISE
As I was walking, I had time to think.	***Since* I was walking, I had time to think.**

Do not use *as* to mean "that" or "whether" (as in "I don't know *as* he would like her").

As . . . as. Use positively, not forgetting the second *as:*

WRONG	RIGHT
***as* long if not longer than the other.**	***as* long *as* the other, if not longer.**

Negatively, use *not so . . . as:*

It is *not so* long *as the* other.
His argument is *not so* clear *as* it ought to be.
His argument is *neither so* clear *nor so* thorough *as* it ought to be.

As if. Takes the subjunctive:

as if he *were* cold

As of, as of now. Avoid, except for humor. Use *at,* or delete entirely.

POOR	IMPROVED
He left as of ten o'clock.	He left at ten o'clock.
As of now, I've sworn off.	I've sworn off.
	I've just sworn off.

As to. Use only at the beginning of a sentence: "As to his first allegation, I can only say . . . ." Change it to *about,* or omit it, within a sentence: "He knows nothing *about* the details"; "He is not sure [as to] [whether] they are right."

At. Do not use after *where.* "Where is it *at*?" means "Where is it?"

Back of, in back of. *Behind* says it more smoothly.

Balance, bulk. Make them mean business, as in "he deposited the balance of his allowance" and "the bulk of the crop was ruined." Do not use them for people.

POOR	IMPROVED
The balance of the class went home.	The rest of the class went home.
The bulk of the crowd was indifferent.	Most of the crowd was indifferent.

Behalf—in your behalf, on your behalf. A nice distinction. "He did it *in your behalf*" means he did it in your interest. "He did it *on your behalf*" means he was representing you, speaking for you.

Besides. Means "in addition to," not "other than."

POOR	IMPROVED
Something besides smog was the cause. [unless smog was also a cause]	Something other than smog was the cause.

Better than. Unless you really mean *better than,* use *more than.*

POOR	IMPROVED
The lake was better than two miles across.	The lake was more than two miles across.

Between, among. *Between* ("by twain") has *two* in mind; *among* has several. *Between,* a preposition, takes an object; *between us, between you and me.* ("Between you and I" is sheer embarrassment; see *me,* below.) But words sometimes fail us. "Between you and me and the gatepost" cannot conform to the rule and become "among you and me and the gatepost." *Between* connotes an intimate sharing *among* all concerned, each to each. *Between* also indicates geographical placing: "It is midway between Chicago, Detroit, and Toledo." "The grenade fell between Jones and me and the gatepost"; but "The grenade fell among the fruit stands." Keep *between* for two and *among* for three or more—unless sense forces a compromise. "Between every building was a plot of petunias" conveys the idea as nothing else will, however nonsensical "between a building" is.

Bimonthly, biweekly. Careless usage has damaged these almost beyond recognition, confusing them with *semimonthly* and *semiweekly.* For clarity, better say "every two months" and "every two weeks."

But, cannot but. "He can but fail" is old but usable. After a negative, however, the natural turn in *but* causes confusion:

POOR	IMPROVED
He cannot *but* fail.	**He can only fail.**
He could not doubt but that it	**He could not doubt that it . . . .**
He could not help but take	**He could not help taking . . . .**

Similarly, *but's* too close or frequent keep your reader spinning:

POOR	IMPROVED
The campaign was successful *but* costly. *But* the victory was sweet.	**The campaign was costly, but victory was sweet.**

When *but* means *except,* it is a preposition.

WRONG	RIGHT
Everybody laughed but I.	**Everybody laughed but me.**

But that, but what. Colloquial redundancies.

POOR	IMPROVED
There is no doubt but that John's is the best steer.	**There is no doubt that John's is the best steer.** **John's is clearly the best steer.**
There is no one but what would enjoy it.	**Anyone would enjoy it.**

Can, may (could, might). Do not use *can* for permission, or possibility: "Can I see it?" means "Have I the physical capacity to see it?"

Use *may*. In assertions, the distinction is clear: " He can do it." "He may do it." "If he can, he may."

Could and *might* are the past tenses, but when used in the present time they are subjunctive, with shades of possibility, and hence politeness: "*Could* you come next Tuesday?" "*Might* I inquire about your plans?" *Could* may mean ability almost as strongly as *can:* "I'm sure he could do it." But *could* and *might* are usually subjunctives, expressing doubt:

Perhaps he could make it, if he tries.
I might be able to go, but I doubt it.

Can't hardly, couldn't hardly. Use *can hardly, could hardly.*

Case. Chop out this deadwood:

POOR	IMPROVED
In many cases, ants survive	Ants often . . . .
In such a case, surgery is recommended.	Then surgery is recommended.
In case he goes	If he goes . . . .
Everyone enjoyed himself, except in a few scattered cases.	Almost everyone enjoyed himself.

Cause-and-effect relationship. Verbal adhesive tape. Recast the sentence, with some verb other than the wordy *cause:*

POOR	IMPROVED
Othello's jealousy rises in a cause-and-effect relationship when he sees the handkerchief.	Seeing the handkerchief arouses Othello's jealousy.

Center around. A physical impossibility. Make it: *centers on,* or *revolves around,* or *concerns,* or *is about.*

Circumstances. *In these circumstances* makes more sense than *under these circumstances,* since the stances are standing around (*circum*), not standing under.

Clichés. Don't use unwittingly. But they can be effective. There are two kinds: (1) the rhetorical—*tried and true, the not too distant future, sadder but wiser, in the style to which she had become accustomed;* (2) the proverbial—*apple of his eye, skin of your teeth, sharp as a tack, quick as a flash, twinkling of an eye.* The rhetorical ones are clinched by sound alone; the proverbial are metaphors caught in the popular fancy.

Proverbial clichés can lighten a dull passage. You may even revitalize them, since they are frequently dead metaphors (see pp. 185–186). Avoid the rhetorical clichés unless you turn them to your advantage: *tried and untrue, gladder and wiser, a future not too distant.*

Compare to, compare with. To compare *to* is to show similarities (and differences) between different kinds; to compare *with* is to show differences (and similarities) between like kinds.

> **Composition has been compared *to* architecture.**
> **He compares favorably *with* Mickey Spillane.**
> **Compare Shakespeare *with* Ben Jonson.**

Comparisons. Make them complete; add a *than:*

> **It is more like a jigsaw puzzle *than a rational plan.***
> **They are more thoughtful *than the others.***
> **The first is better *than the second.* (Or "The first is *the* better.")**

Connected with, in connection with. Always wordy. Say *about, with,* or *in.*

POOR	IMPROVED
They discussed several things connected with history.	They discussed several historical questions.
They liked everything in connection with the university.	They liked everything about the university.
He is connected with the Smith Corporation.	He is with the Smith Corporation.

Consider, consider as. The first means "believe to be"; the second, "think about" or "speak about": "I consider him excellent." "I consider him first as a student, then as a man."

Contact. Don't *contact* anyone: get in touch with him, call him, write him, find him, tell him. Don't make a good *contact,* make a helpful friend.

Continual, continuous. You can improve your writing by *continual* practice, but the effort cannot be *continuous.* The first means "frequently repeated"; the second, "without interruption."

> **It requires continual practice.**
> **There was a continuous line of clouds.**

Couple. Use *two, a few,* or *several.* Only the breeziest occasions will allow *a couple of.*

Curriculum. The plural is *curricula;* the adjective, *curricular.*

> **The school offers three separate curricula.**
> **Extracurricular activities also count.**

Data. A plural, like *curricula, strata, phenomena:*

> **The data are inconclusive.**

Definitely. A high-school favorite. Cut it out.

Different than. Never use it. Things differ *from* each other. Only in comparing differences could *than* be used: "All three of his copies differ from the original, but his last one is *more* different *than* the others." But here *than* is controlled by *more,* not by *different.*

WRONG	RIGHT
It is different *than* I expected.	**It is different *from* what I expected.**
	It is not what I expected.
This is different *than* all the others.	**This is different *from* all the others.**

Disinterested. Does not mean "uninterested" nor "indifferent." *Disinterested* means impartial, without private interests in the issue.

WRONG	RIGHT
You seem disinterested in the case.	**You seem uninterested in the case.**
	The judge was disinterested and perfectly fair.
He was disinterested in it.	**He was indifferent to it.**

Due to. Never begin a sentence with "*Due* to circumstances beyond his control, he . . . ." *Due* is an adjective and must always relate to a noun or pronoun: "The castastrophe *due to* circumstances beyond his control was unavoidable," or "The catastrophe was *due to* circumstances beyond his control" (predicate adjective). But you are still better off with *because of, through, by,* or *owing to. Due to* is usually a symptom of wordiness, especially when it leads to *due to the fact that.*

WRONG	RIGHT
He resigned due to sickness.	**He resigned because of sickness.**
He succeeded due to hard work.	**He succeeded through hard work.**
He lost his shirt due to leaving it in the locker room.	**He lost his shirt by leaving it in the locker room.**
The Far East will continue to worry the West, due to a general social upheaval.	**The Far East will continue to worry the West, owing to a general social upheaval.**

Due to the fact that. A venerable piece of plumbing meaning *because.*

JARGON	IMPROVED
The program failed due to the fact that a recession had set in.	**The program failed because a recession had set in.**

Effect. As a noun, it means *result;* as a verb, *to bring about* (not to be confused with *to affect,* meaning "to concern, impress, touch, move" —or "to pretend").

What was the effect?
He effected a thorough change.
How did it affect you?

Enormity. Means "atrociousness"; does not mean "enormousness."

the enormity of the crime
the enormousness of the mountain

Enthuse. Don't use it; it coos and gushes:

WRONG	RIGHT
She *enthused* over her new dress.	**She gushed on and on about her new dress.**
He was *enthused.*	**He was enthusiastic.**

Equally as good. A redundant mixture of two choices, *as good as* and *equally good.* Use only one of these at a time.

Etc. Substitute something specific for it, or drop it, or use something like "and so forth":

POOR	IMPROVED
She served fruit, cheese, candies, etc.	**She served fruit, cheese, candies, and little sweet pickles.** **She served fruit, cheese, candies, and the like.**

Ethic. A mannered rendition of *ethics,* the singular and plural noun meaning a system or science of moral principles. Even poorer as an adjective for *ethical.*

Exists. Another symptom of wordiness.

POOR	IMPROVED
a system like that which exists at the university	**a system like that at the university**

The fact that. Deadly with *due to,* often sickening by itself.

POOR	IMPROVED
The fact that Rome fell due to moral decay is clear.	**That Rome fell through moral decay is clear.**
This disparity is in part a result of the fact that some of the best indicators make their best showings in an expanding market.	**This disparity arises in part because some of the best indicators . . . .**

Factor. Avoid it. We've used it to death. Try *element* when you mean "element." Look for an accurate verb when you mean "cause."

POOR	IMPROVED
The increase in female employment is a factor in juvenile delinquency.	The increase in female employment has contributed to juvenile delinquency.
Puritan self-sufficiency was an important factor in the rise of capitalism.	Puritan self-sufficiency favored the rise of capitalism.

Farther, further. The first means distance; the second means time or figurative distance. You look *farther* and consider *further.*

The field of. Try to omit it—you usually can—or bring the metaphor to life.

POOR	IMPROVED
He is studying in the field of geology.	He is studying geology.
He changed from the field of science to fine arts.	He moved from the field of science to the green pasture of fine arts.

Firstly. Archaic. Trim all such terms to *first, second, third,* and so on.

Fix. The word means *to establish in place;* it means "to repair" only in speech or colloquial writing.

Flaunt, flout. *Flaunt* means to parade, to wave impudently; *flout* means to scoff at. The first is metaphorical; the second, not: "She *flaunted* her wickedness and *flouted* the police."

Folks. Use *parents, mother and father,* or *family* instead.

Former, latter. Passable, but they often make the reader look back. It is better simply to repeat the antecedents.

POOR	IMPROVED
The Athenians and Spartans were always in conflict. *The former* had a better civilization; *the latter* had a better army.	The Athenians and Spartans were always in conflict. Athens had the better culture; Sparta, the better army.

Gray. America prefers *gray;* England, *grey*—matching our initials.

Hanged, hung. *Hanged* is the past of *hang* only for the death penalty.

They hung the rope and hanged the man.
The rope was hung; the man was hanged.

Hardly. Watch the negative here. "I can't *hardly*" means "I *can* easily." Write: "One can hardly conceive the vastness."

Hopefully. An inaccurate dangler, a cliché. "Hopefully, they are at work" does not mean that they are working hopefully. Simply use "I hope." Not "They are a symbol of idealism, and, hopefully, are representative," but "They are a symbol of idealism and are, I hope, representative."

However. Bury it between commas, or replace it with *but* or *nevertheless.*

POOR	IMPROVED
However, the day had not been entirely lost.	**_But_ the day had not been entirely lost.**
However, the script that Alcuin invented became the forerunner of modern handwriting.	**The script that Alcuin invented, _however,_ became the forerunner of modern handwriting.**

Initial *however* should be an adverb:

However **long it takes, it will be done.**
However **she did it, she did it well.**

The idea that. Like *the fact that*—and the cure is the same.

POOR	IMPROVED
He liked the idea that she was going.	**He was pleased she was going.**
The idea that space is infinite is difficult to grasp.	**That space is infinite is difficult to grasp.**

Identify. Give it an object:

He _identified the wallet._
He _identified himself_ with the hero. (_Not_ "He identified with the hero.")

Image. Resist its popularity, make it mean what it says, and never make it a verb. Do NOT say, "The university should *image* the handsome intellectual."

Imply, infer. The author *implies;* you *infer* ("carry in") what you think he means.

He _implied_ that all women were hypocrites.
From the ending, we _infer_ that tragedy ennobles as it kills.

Importantly. Often an inaccurate (and popular) adverb, like *hopefully.*

INACCURATE	IMPROVED
More importantly, he walked home.	**More important, he walked home.**

He did not walk home importantly, nor more importantly.

Individual. Write *person,* unless you really mean someone separate and unique.

Inside of, outside of. "They painted the *outside of* the house" is sound usage; but these expressions can be redundant and inaccurate.

POOR	IMPROVED
inside of half an hour	**within half an hour**
He had nothing for dinner outside of a few potato chips.	**He had nothing for dinner but a few potato chips.**

Instances. Redundant. *In many instances* means "often," "frequently."

Interesting. Make what you say interesting, but never tell the reader *it is interesting:* he may not believe you. *It is interesting* is merely a lazy preamble:

POOR	IMPROVED
It is interesting to note that nicotine is named for Jean Nicot, who introduced tobacco into France in 1560.	**Nicotine is named for Jean Nicot, who introduced tobacco into France in 1560.**

Irony. Not the same as *sarcasm* (which see). A clash between appearance and reality. Irony may be either comic or tragic, depending on your view. But, comic or tragic, irony is of three essential kinds:

Verbal irony. You say the opposite of what you mean: "It's a *great* day," appearing to mean "great" but really meaning "terrible."

Dramatic irony. Someone unwittingly states, or acts upon, a contrariety to the truth. A character in a play, for example, might say "This is my great day," and dance a jig, when the audience has just seen his daughter abducted and the mortgage foreclosed.

Irony of circumstance. The opposite of what ought to happen happens (it rains on the day of the Weather Bureau's picnic; the best man of all is killed); and we are sharply aware of the contrast.

Irregardless. No such word. The *ir-* (meaning *not*) is doing what the *-less* already does. You are thinking of *irrespective,* and trying to say *regardless.*

Is when, is where. Avoid these loose attempts.

LOOSE	SPECIFIC
Combustion is when oxidation bursts into flame.	**Combustion is oxidation bursting into flame.**
"Trivia" is where three roads meet.	**"Trivia" is the place where three roads meet.**

-ize. A handy way to make verbs from nouns and adjectives (*patron-ize, civil-ize*). But handle with care. Manufacture new *-izes* only with a sense of humor and daring ("they Harvardized the party"). Business overdoes the trick: *finalize,* a relative newcomer, has provoked strong disapproval from writers not commercially familiarized.

Kind of, sort of. Colloquialisms for *somewhat, rather, something,* and the like. "It is *kind of* odd" will not get by. But "It is a *kind of* academic hippopotamus" will get by nicely, because *a kind of* means *a species of.* Change "a kind of a poor sport" to "a kind of poor sport," and you will seem as knowledgeable as a scientist.

Lay. Don't use *lay* to mean *lie. Lay* means "to put" and needs an object; *lie* means "to recline." Memorize both their present and past tenses, which are frequently confused:

I *lie* down when I can; I *lay* down yesterday; I have *lain* down often. [Intransitive, no object.]

The hen *lays* an egg; *she* laid *one* yesterday; she has *laid* four this week. [Transitive, *lays* an object.]

Now I *lay* the book on the table; I *laid* it there yesterday; I have *laid* it there many times.

Lend, loan. Don't use *loan* for *lend. Lend* is the verb; *loan,* the noun: "Please *lend* me a five; I need a *loan* badly." Remember the line from the song: "I'll *send* you to a *friend* who'll be willing to *lend.*"

Less, few. Do not use one for the other. *Less* answers "How much?" *Few* answers "How many?"

WRONG	RIGHT
We had *less* people than last time.	**We had *fewer* people this time than last.**

Like, as, as if. Learn to distinguish these three. *Like* is a preposition, taking an object; when a verb follows, use *as* or *as if:*

He looks *like* me.
He dresses *as* I do.
He acts *as if* he *were* mad.

Note that *like* takes the objective case, and that *as*, being a conjunction, is followed by the nominative:

She looks like *her*.
He is as tall as *I* [am].
He is tall, like *me*.

The pattern of the prepositional phrase (*like me, like a house, like a river*) has caused *like* to replace *as* where no verb follows in phrases other than comparisons (*as . . . as*):

It works *like* a charm. (. . . *as* a charm *works*.)
It went over *like* a lead balloon. (. . . *as* a lead balloon *does*.)
They worked *like* beavers. (. . . *as* beavers *do*.)

Notice that *as* would give these three statements a meaning of substitution or disguise: "It works as a charm" (but it really isn't a charm); "It went over as a lead balloon" (disguised as a lead balloon).

Manner. Drop this from your working vocabulary. *In a . . . manner* is a favorite redundancy. Replace it with an adverb: *in a clever manner* means "cleverly"; *in an awkward manner* means "awkwardly."

Me. Use *me* boldly. It is the proper object of verbs and prepositions. Nothing is sadder than faulty propriety: "between you and *I*," or "They gave it to John and *I*," or "They invited my wife and *I*." Test yourself by dropping the first member: "between I" (*no*), "gave it to I" (*no*), "invited I" (*no*). And do NOT substitute *myself*.

Medium, media. The singular and the plural. Avoid *medias*, and you will distinguish yourself from the masses.

Most. Does not mean *almost*.

WRONG	RIGHT
Most everyone knows.	Almost everyone knows.

Myself. Use it only reflexively ("I hurt *myself*"), or intensively ("I *myself* often have trouble"). Fear of *me* leads to the incorrect "They gave it to John and *myself*." Do not use *myself, himself, herself, themselves* for *me, him, her, them*.

Nature. Avoid this padding. Do not write *moderate in nature, moderate by nature, of a moderate nature;* simply write *moderate*.

Near. Avoid using it for degree:

POOR	IMPROVED
a near perfect orbit	a nearly perfect orbit
	an almost perfect orbit

We are nowhere near knowledgeable enough.	**We are not nearly knowledgeable enough.**
It was a near disaster.	**It was nearly a disaster [or "nearly disastrous"].**

None. This pronoun means "no one" and takes a singular verb, as do *each, every, everyone, nobody,* and other distributives. *None are* has been common and admissible for centuries, but *none is* holds its own, with a certain prestige, even in the daily newspaper. Another pronoun referring back to any of these must also be singular.

POOR	IMPROVED
None of them *are* perfect.	**None of them *is* perfect.**
Every one of the men *eat* a big breakfast.	**Every one of the men *eats* a big breakfast.**
Everybody thinks *they have* the worst of it.	**Everybody thinks *he has* the worst of it.**

No one. Always two words, not *noone,* nor *no-one.*

Off of. Write *from:* "He jumped *from* his horse."

One. Avoid this common redundancy.

POOR	IMPROVED
One of the most effective ways of writing is rewriting.	**The best writing is rewriting.**
***The Ambassadors* is one of the most interesting of James's books.**	***The Ambassadors* is James at his best.**
The meeting was obviously a poor one.	**The meeting was obviously poor.**

In constructions such as "one of the best that . . ." and "one of the worst who . . . ," the relative pronouns often are mistakenly considered singular. The plural noun of the prepositional phrase (*the best, worst*), not *the one,* is the antecedent, and the verb must be plural too:

WRONG	RIGHT
one of the best (*players*) who *has* ever swung a bat	**one of the best (*players*) who *have* ever swung a bat**

Only. Don't put it in too soon; you will say what you do not mean.

WRONG	RIGHT
He *only liked* mystery stories.	**He liked *only mystery stories.***

Participle for gerund. Avoid this frequent confusion of the *-ing*'s. The participle works as an adjective; the gerund, as a noun. You want gerunds in the following constructions, and you can get them by changing the misleading noun or pronoun to the possessive case:

WRONG	RIGHT
Washington commended *him passing* through the British lines.	**Washington commended *his passing* through the British lines.**
Do you mind *me staying* late?	**Do you mind *my staying* late?**
She disliked *Bill smoking.*	**She disliked *Bill's smoking.***
We all enjoyed *them singing* songs and *having* a good time.	**We all enjoyed *their singing* songs and *having* a good time.**

You can catch these errors by asking yourself if you mean that "Washington commended *him,*" or that "She disliked *Bill*" (which you do not).

Per. Use *a:* "He worked ten hours *a* day." *Per* is jargonish.

Perfect. Not "more perfect," but "more nearly perfect."

Personal. Change "personal friend" to "good friend," and protect him from seeming too personal.

Personally. Always superfluous.

POOR	IMPROVED
I want to welcome them *personally.*	**I want to welcome them [myself].**
***Personally,* I like it.**	**I like it.**

Phase. *Phase* is not *faze* ("daunt"), nor does it mean *aspect* or *part;* it is a stage in a familiar cycle, like that of the moon or the caterpillar.

Picket. A pointed fence-post, or a person so staked. *To picket* is to deploy people as pickets, or to join with others as a protesting fence against wrongs.

POOR	IMPROVED
They began a picket of	**They began to picket . . . .**
They began their picket	**They began picketing . . . .**
Until they withdraw their picket	**Until they withdraw their pickets . . . .**

Plan on. Use *plan to.*

WRONG	RIGHT
He planned on going.	**He planned to go.**

Power vacuum. A physical contradiction. Delete the *power,* or put it where it belongs, and your phrase will be accurate.

Prejudice. The illiterate are beginning to write "He was *prejudice.*" Their readers are outrage.

Proof, evidence. *Proof* results from enough *evidence* to establish a point beyond doubt. Be modest about claiming proof:

POOR	IMPROVED
This *proves* that Fielding was in Bath at the time.	Evidently, Fielding was in Bath at the time.

Proved, proven. *Proved* is the past participle, which may serve as an adjective meaning "successfully tested or demonstrated"; *proven* is an adjective only, and means "tested by time":

WRONG	RIGHT
It has proven true. [past part.]	It has proved true.
a proven theory [past part. as adj.]	a proved theory
The theory was proven. [same]	The theory was proved.
a proved remedy [pure adj.]	a proven remedy

Quality. Keep it as a noun. Too many *professional quality writers* are already cluttering our prose, and "poor in quality" means *poor.*

Quote, quotation. Quote your quotations, and put them in quotation marks. Distinguish the verb from the noun. The best solution is to use *quote* as a verb and to find synonyms for the noun: *passage, remark, assertion.*

WRONG	RIGHT
As the following quote from Milton shows:	As the following passage from Milton shows: . . . .

Real. Do not use for *very. Real* is an adjective meaning "actual":

WRONG	RIGHT
It was *real* good.	It was *very* good. It was *really* good.

Reason . . . is because. Knock out *the reason . . . is,* and you will have a good sentence.

[The reason] they have difficulty with languages [is] because they have no interest in them.

Regarding, in regard to. Redundant or inaccurate.

POOR	IMPROVED
Regarding the banknote, Jones was perplexed. [Was he *looking* at it?]	Jones was perplexed by the banknote.

He knew nothing *regarding* money.	**He knew nothing about money.**
She was careful *in regard to* the facts.	**She respected the facts.**

Respective, respectively. Redundant.

POOR	IMPROVED
The armies retreated to their *respective* trenches.	**The armies retreated to their trenches.**
Smith and Jones won the first and second prize *respectively.*	**Smith won the first prize; Jones, the second.**

Round. British for *around.*

Sanction. Beatifically ambiguous, now meaning both "to approve" and "to penalize." But why contribute to confusion? Stick to the root; use it only "to bless," "to sanctify," "to approve," "to permit." Use *penalize* or *prohibit* when you mean just that.

POOR	IMPROVED
They exacted sanctions.	**They exacted penalties.**

Sarcasm. The student's word for irony. Sarcasm intends personal hurt. It may also be ironic, but need not be. "Well, little man, what now?" is pure sarcasm when a dwarf interrupts the class; it is ironic sarcasm when a seven-footer bursts in. See *Irony.*

Shall, will; should, would. The older distinctions—*shall* and *should* for *I* and *we*—have faded; *will* and *would* are usual: "I will go; I would if I could; he will try; they all would." *Shall* in the third person expresses determination: "they shall not pass."

Similar to. Use *like:*

POOR	IMPROVED
This is *similar to* that.	**This is *like* that.**

Slow. GO SLOW is what the street signs and the men on the street all say, but write "go slowly."

So. Should be followed by *that* in describing extent: "It was *so* foggy *that* traffic almost stopped." Avoid its incomplete form, the school girl's intensive—*so nice, so wonderful, so pretty*—though occasionally this is effective.

Split infinitives. Improve them. They are cliché traps: *to really know, to really like, to better understand.* They are misleaders: *to better . . . , to further . . . , to well . . . , to even . . . ,* all look and sound like complete infinitives: *to further investigate* starts out like *to further our investigation,* throwing the reader momentarily off the track. *To better know* is to make *know* better, *to even like* is to make *like* even, all of which is nonsense. Indeed, in perverse moments *to eventually go* seems to say that *go* is being "eventualied." Finally, they are usually redundant: *to really understand* is *to understand.* The quickest cure for split infinitives is to drop the adverb.

Even the splitters do not recommend splitting as a rule. The rule remains DON'T SPLIT; and if you must, learn what you are doing—a little deviltry is better for the soul than ignorance. But I am convinced that you can always mend the split for a gain in grace, and often for a saving of words. You can sometimes change the adverb to an adjective: "to adequately think out solutions" can become "to think out adequate solutions." Or you can drop the adverb—often exuberant—or bring it forward, or move it along:

POOR	IMPROVED
I cannot bring myself to really like the fellow.	**I cannot bring myself to like the fellow.**
	I cannot bring myself really to like the fellow.
	I really cannot bring myself to like the fellow.

George O. Curme gives the following examples from eminent splitters, arguing that usage makes them right.* But each of them can be improved:

POOR	IMPROVED
I wish the reader to clearly understand this. (Ruskin)	**I wish the reader to understand this.**
	I wish the reader to understand this clearly.
It would have overburdened the text to there incorporate many details. (Hempl, *Mod. Lang. Notes*)	**Details there would have overburdened the text.**
. . . without permitting himself to actually mention the name. (Arnold)	**. . . without permitting himself to mention the name.**
. . . of a kind to directly stimulate curiosity. (Pater)	**. . . of a kind to stimulate curiosity.**

* *English Grammar* (New York: Barnes and Noble, 1947).

POOR	IMPROVED
	. . . of a kind to stimulate curiosity directly.
. . . things which few except parents can be expected to really understand. (Oliver Wendell Holmes)	. . . things only parents can understand.
. . . to bravely disbelieve (Browning, *The Ring and the Book*, Cambridge ed., p. 570)	. . . bravely to disbelieve

Browning's full line, in fact, would have thumped somewhat less if he had dared bravely to vary his meter and mend his infinitive:

Whence need bravely to disbelieve report.

Structure. A darling of the jargoneer, often meaning nothing more framelike than "unity" or "coherence." *Plot structure* usually means "plot," with little idea of beams and girders. Use it only for something you could diagram, like the ribs of a snake, and never use it as a verb.

POOR	IMPROVED
He structured the meeting.	He organized (planned, arranged) the meeting.

That, which, who. *That* defines and restricts; *which* is explanatory and nonrestrictive; *who* stands for people, and may be restrictive or nonrestrictive. (See pp. 136 and 154–155.)

The faucet *that* drips is in the basement.
The faucet, *which* drips badly, needs attention.
Of all the Democrats *who* supported him at first, none was more ardent than Jones.
Of all the Democrats, *who* supported him at first, none was more ardent than Jones.

There is, there are, it is. *C'est dangereusement verbeux.* In French, it is almost as necessary as breathing. In English, it is natural, convenient—AND WORDY. Notice that *it* has here been referring to something specific, differing distinctly from the *it* in *It is easy to write badly.* This indefinite subject, as also do *there is* and *there are,* gives the trouble. Of course, you will occasionally need an *it* or a *there* to assert existences:

There are ants in the cupboard.
There is only one Kenneth.
There are craters on the moon.
It is too bad.

But avoid *there is* and *it is,* and you will avoid some sludgy traps. They are part of the spoken language, like clearing the throat, and they frequently add just as little, especially when entailing a *that* or a *which:*

There are three men on duty.
[Three men are on duty—5 words for 6.]

There is nothing wrong with this.
[Nothing is wrong with this—5 words for 6.]

There are two things which are important here.
[Two things are important here—5 words for 8.]

It is a habit which few can break.
[Few can break this habit—5 words for 8.]

It is a shame that they had no lawyer.
[Unfortunately, they had no lawyer—5 words for 9.]

They. A loose indefinite pronoun; tighten it:

POOR	IMPROVED
***They* are all against us, you know.**	***Everyone* is against us, you know.**
***They* launch our rockets at Cape Kennedy.**	**The *United States* launches its rockets from Cape Kennedy.**

Do not use *they* with a singular antecedent.

WRONG	RIGHT
***Everyone* knows *they* should write correctly.**	***Everyone* knows *he* should write correctly.**
***Every one* of the students assumes *they* will pass.**	***Every one* of the students assumes *he* will pass.**

Till, until. Both are respectable. Note the spelling. Do not use *'til.*

Too. Awful as a conjunctive adverb: "Too, it was unjust." Also poor as an intensive: "They did not do too well" (note the difference in Shakespeare's "not wisely but too well"—he really means it). Use *very;* or (better) nothing: "They did not do well."

Trite. From Latin *tritus:* "worn out." Many words get temporarily worn out and unusable: *emasculated, viable, situation,* to name a few. And many phrases are permanently frayed; see *Clichés.*

Try and. Write *try to. To try and do* means "to try and to do," which is probably not what you mean.

Type. Banish it, abolish it. If you must use it, insert *of:* not *that type person* but *that type OF person,* though even this is really jargon for *that kind of person, a person like that.* The newspapers have succumbed, and we hear of *commando-type forces* for *commando forces,* of *a Castro-type dictator* for *another Castro.* The most accurate translations of *-type* are *-like, -ish, -esque,* and *-ate,* depending on sense and euphony: *Castro-like, Castro-ish, Russianesque, Italianate.* English has many ways of saying it:

WRONG	RIGHT
essay-type question	essay question
Mondrian's checkerboard-type painting	Mondrian's checkerboard of a painting.
	Mondrian's checkerboardish painting
	Mondrian's checkerboard-like painting
French-type dressing	French dressing
Italian-type spaghetti	Italian spaghetti [Be bold!—we neither know nor care whether it's imported.]
atomic-type submarine	atomic submarine
She was a Brigitte Bardot-type girl.	She was like Brigitte Bardot.
	She was a Brigitte Bardot.
	She was a Brigitte Bardot kind of girl.
	She was a Brigitte Bardot type.
an apprentice-type situation	apprenticeship
a string-type playpen	a string playpen
a Puck-type person	a Puckish person, a Puck-like person

Unique. Something *unique* has nothing in the world like it.

WRONG	RIGHT
The more unique the organization	The more nearly unique . . . .
the most unique man I know	the most unusual man I know
a very unique personality	a unique personality

Use, use of. A dangerously wordy word. "Through [the use of] personification, he asserts a theme." "In this sense, [the use of] physical detail is significant."

POOR	IMPROVED
He uses personification	He personifies . . . .
He uses inductive reasoning	He reasons inductively . . . .

Utilize, utilization Wordy. *Utilize* means "use" (verb). *Utilization* means *the use* (noun). And the whole idea of *using*—a basic, universal concept—is frequently contained in the other words of your sentence.

POOR	IMPROVED
He *utilizes* frequent dialogue to enliven his stories.	**Frequent dialogue enlivens his stories.**
The *utilization* of a scapegoat eases their guilt.	**A scapegoat eases their guilt.**

Very. Spare the *very* and the *quite, rather, pretty,* and *little.* I would hate to admit (and don't care to know) how many of these qualifiers I have cut from this text. You can do without them entirely.

Ways. Means *way:* "He went a short *way* into the woods."

While. Reserve for time only, as in "*While* I was talking, she smoked constantly."

WRONG	RIGHT
***While* I like her, I don't admire her.**	***Although* I like her, I don't admire her.**
The side roads were impassable, *while* the highways were clear.	**The side roads were impassable, *but* the highways were clear.**
The seniors eat in clubs, *while* the freshmen eat in their dormitories.	**The seniors eat in clubs, *and* the freshmen eat in their dormitories.**

Whom, whomever. The objective forms, after verbs and prepositions; but each is often wrongly put as the subject of a clause.

WRONG	RIGHT
Give the ticket to *whomever* wants it.	**Give the ticket to *whoever wants it.* [The whole clause is the object of *to*; *whoever* is the subject of *wants.*]**
The president, *whom* he said would be late	**The president, *who* he said *would be late* . . . . [Commas around *he said* would clear the confusion.]**
***Whom* shall I say called?**	***Who* shall I say called?**

BUT:

They did not know *whom* to elect. [The infinitive takes the objective case.]

-wise. Avoid all confections like *marketwise, customerwise, pricewise, gradewise, confectionwise*—except for humor.

Would. For habitual acts, the simple past is more economical:

POOR	IMPROVED
The parliament *would meet* only when called by the king.	The parliament *met* only when called by the king.
Every hour, the watchman *would make* his round.	Every hour, the watchman *made* his round.

Would sometimes seeps into the premise of a supposition. Rule: Don't use *would* in an *if* clause.

WRONG	RIGHT
If he *would have* gone, he would have succeeded.	If he *had* gone, he would have succeeded. *Had* he gone, he would have succeeded [more economical].
I wish I *would have* learned it.	I wish I *had* learned it.

Rhetorical Devices

Appendix C

The Greeks had words for them, and the Romans improved the supply. We still run into the words from time to time; we still fall into the rhetorical patterns even when unaware of the terms. Sooner or later, the natural dynamics of expression will get you to many of the rhetorical devices the Greeks long ago discovered and named. But the terms, commonplace during ancient times, are today difficult to find listed in one place; and the devices, still more common than one might think, are such pleasant exercisers of the verbal torso, such excellent invigorators of the linguistic circulation, that it seems good to have them grouped and handy. I have had great pleasure in seeing the rhetorical modes as active in modern English as in ancient Greek and Latin, and in trying them out in my own idiom. Here they are, arranged for your convenience within functional categories (by no means mutually exclusive), and with pronunciations suggested for those your desk dictionary may not include. You can indeed increase your power by making these venerable devices your own, by having them ready, by learning through them the fair and beautiful play of language.

Alluding to the Familiar

anamnesis (AN-am-NEE-sis). "A remembering." You remind your reader of former success or catastrophe to emphasize your point.

This is the very day on which we lost last year. Again we meet a stronger team in our own stadium. Again injuries have wiped out our strongest hope. Again the weather looks hopeless.

parachresis (para-KREE-sis). You bring another's words into your own context, with new emphasis or effect.

As Ovid says of the sun: Ann sees all things.

Bill constantly follows John around, like Plato's shadow of a shadow.

When Thoreau said that the mass of men lead lives of quiet desperation he must have had Butch in mind.

paradiorthosis (para-die-or-THO-sis). You quote famous words with your own twist and without identifying them: a witty, subtle, and learned game much played by the Greek poets and T. S. Eliot.

The boredom, the horror, and the glory of life [Eliot's allusive twisting of "the kingdom, the power, and the glory"].

paroemia (pa-REE-mi-a). You apply proverbs to a new situation.

Even the rose has thorns [when a plan has drawbacks, or a girl a temper].

Every dog has its day. [Your opponent has just won the election.]

Man shall not live by bread alone. [He has just ordered steak.]

Never look a gift-horse in the mouth. [Someone has criticized the doorway of a new building given the university.]

Building to Climax

asyndeton (a-SIN-de-ton). "Without joining." You rush a series of clauses together without conjunctions, as if tumbled together by emotional haste.

They tried, they fought, they did their best.

climax. You repeat the same word or sound in each succeeding phrase or clause—an intensified form of *anadiplosis* (see p. 384).

Knowing that tribulation works patience, and patience experience, and experience hope. (Rom. v.3–4)

incrementum (in-kre-MENT-um). You arrange items from lowest to highest.

The law will be kept in the shacks of the farms, in the tenements of the slums, in the bungalows and homes of the suburbs, and in the mansions of the countryside.

synonymy (si-NON-i-me). You repeat, by synonyms, for emphasis.

A miserable, wretched, depressed neighborhood.

Intensifying

anacoenosis (ana-see-NO-sis). You heighten your style as if in urgent consultation with your audience, and with frequent rhetorical questions. You gain an urgent mixture of intimacy and elegance.

If I be a father, where is mine honor? If I be a master, where is my fear? (Mal. i.6)

Would we really want freedom? Would we really want liberty of all kinds? Would we really want anarchy more than peace of mind? We would, I think you will agree, gladly accept a restricted peace for some measure of quiet.

apodioxis (apo-die-OX-is). You reject an idea emphatically.

Absurd! Now really! Well, after all!

Can anything be less practical?

aposiopesis (apo-sigh-o-PE-sis). "A silence." You stop suddenly in midsentence, as if words fail, or as if a word to your wise reader has been completely sufficient.

But the cat . . . .

Do you believe that he can cope . . . ?

And in the name of common sense—!

apostrophe (a-POS-tro-fee). "A turning away." You "turn away" from your audience to address someone new—God, the angels, heaven, the dead, or anyone not present.

Hear, O heavens.

Death, where is thy sting?

Blush, America, for this stupidity.

ecphonesis (ek-fo-NEE-sis). Also called **exclamatio.** You cry out against something—usually in an apostrophe.

O wicked speed, to post with such dexterity to incestuous sheets.

erotesis (ero-TEE-sis). This is what we know as the rhetorical question.

Is this the best course? Will this pave the streets?

Irony

antonomasia (antono-MAY-zhia). You substitute an epithet, a label, for a person's real name, usually with ironic emphasis.

The Philosopher. The Blowhard. A Solomon. A Castro. A Mickey Mouse. The Swede.

apophasis (a-POF-a-sis). Also called **paralepsis** or **preteritio.** "A passing over." You pretend not to mention something in the very act of mentioning it. The effect is strongly, and sometimes hilariously, ironic. It was a favorite of Cicero's.

I shall not mention the time he failed to come home at all, or his somewhat wobbly condition at breakfast.

I shall not go into all his broken promises, his campaign speeches, or his scandalous treatment of his aged mother.

I pass over . . . .

We had perhaps better forget . . . .

I shall not mention . . . .

aporia (a-POR-i-a). "Doubting." You hesitate ironically between alternatives.

Whether he is more stupid than negligent, I hesitate to guess.

One hardly knows what to call it, folly or forgetfulness, ignorance or ignominy.

epitrope (e-PIT-ro-pe). You ironically grant permission.

Let her go, let her go, God bless her!

All right, go on, have a good time, kill yourself.

euphemism (YOU-fe-mizm). You substitute less pungent words for harsh ones, with excellent ironic effect.

The schoolmaster corrected the slightest fault with his birch reminder.

After a gallon of whiskey, he was slightly indisposed.

ironia (eye-RO-ni-a). Also called **antiphrasis** (an-TIF-ra-sis). You say the contrary of what you mean, in what is usually designated "verbal irony" (see p. 200).

He was a beauty.

She is so kind to her friends.

How thoughtful!

litotes (LIE-toh-teez). "Simplifying." You assert something by denying its opposite.

Not bad.
This is no small matter.
My house is not large.
She was not supremely happy.
He is not the wisest man in the world.

oxymoron (ox-i-MOR-on). "Pointed stupidity." You emphasize your point by the irony of an apparent contradiction or inconsistency.

A wise fool, a fearful joy, a sweet sadness, a quiet orgy.
Their silence is eloquent.
This somebody is nobody.

paralepsis (or **preteritio**). *See* **apothasis,** page 380.

zeugma (ZYEWG-ma). "Yoking." You yoke two words so that one is accurate and the other an ironic misfit (a favorite irony of Edward Gibbon's in *The Decline and Fall of the Roman Empire*).

Waging *war* and *peace*.
Laws the wily tyrant *dictated* and *obeyed*.
Pacified by *gifts* and *threats*.
A position they *enjoyed* and *feared*.

Overstating, Understating

auxesis (awk-SEE-sis). You ironically use an overly weighty or exaggerated term for the accurate one.

She is an angel.
He is a devil.
That pig ate all the olives.

hyperbole (high-PER-bo-lee). You exaggerate for emphasis, humorous or serious.

She cried like a banshee.

hypothesis. You illustrate with an impossible supposition.

If salt lose its savor, wherewith shall it be salted?
Even if he had a million dollars, he would be unhappy.
I'll come to thee by moonlight, though Hell should bar the way.

meiosis (my-o-sis). You make big things seem trifles, or substitute a lighter word for ironic effect. The opposite of **auxesis** (see above).

> **He had three sandwiches and a quart of milk for his *snack*.**
> **It was *nothing;* a *pinprick*.**
> **He had a mansion in the country and another *little place* in town.**

Posing Contrasts

antithesis. You strongly and closely contrast your ideas.

> **From rags to riches, from beans to beef, from water to wine.**
> **Man proposes, God disposes.**
> **A world in a grain of sand, a heaven in a wild flower.**
> **The world will *little note nor long remember* what *we say* here, but it can *never forget* what *they did* here.**
> **It was the best of times; it was the worst of times.**

chiasmus (ky-AZ-mus). "A crossing"—from the Greek letter *chi*, χ, a cross. (Also called **antimitabole.**) You "cross" the terms of one clause by reversing their order in the next.

> **Ask not what your country can do for you: ask what you can do for your country.**

comparison. In an extended and balanced comparison, you match your clauses almost syllable for syllable.

> **My years are not so many, but that one death may conclude them, nor my faults so many, but that one death may satisfy them.**
> **He who loves pleasure shall be a poor man; he who loves wine and oil shall not be rich.**

dilemma. You catch the argument both ways, in a pair of opposing suppositions.

> **If you're so smart, why aren't you rich? If you're rich, why act so smart?**
> **If he is right, why disparage him? If he is wrong, why pay attention to him at all?**

dissimile. You emphasize the condition of something by saying how dissimilar it is from the usual run of things.

> **The foxes have holes, and the fowls of the air their nests, but the son of man has nowhere to lay his head. (Luke ix.58)**
> **A woman is only a woman, but a good cigar is a smoke.**

One generation passeth away, and another generation cometh; but the earth abideth forever.

enantiosis (en-AN-ti-o-sis). Also called **contentio.** You emphasize contraries, often with chiasmus.

One wouldn't hurt her; the other couldn't help her.
Could not go on, would not go back.
Serious in silly things, and silly in serious.

Refining, Elaborating

epanorthosis (EP-an-or-THO-sis). "A correction." You seem to "correct" yourself to reinforce your idea.

Written not in tables of stone but in the fleshy tables of the heart. (II Cor. iii.3.)
He asks, or rather demands, an answer.
A gift-horse—no, a white elephant.

exegesis (ek-suh-JEE-sis). Also called **explicatio.** You clarify a thought in the same sentence.

Time is both short and long, short when you are happy, long when in pain.

exergasia (eks-er-GAY-zhia). "A polishing." You put the same thing several ways.

A beauty, a dream, a vision, a phantom of delight.

hirmos (HEAR-mos). "A series." You heap appositives together.

All men, rich, poor, tall, short, young, old, love it.

horismos (ho-RIZ-mos). You elaborate a concept by defining it.

Beauty is transitory, a snare for the unwary, an invitation to disaster.

Repeating

alliteration. You repeat the initial letter or sound in two or more nearby words.

The morning air was *c*ool and *c*risp.
They have *b*ribed us with promises, *bl*ackmailed us with threats, *bl*udgeoned us with prohibitions, and *bl*ed us with taxes.

Speak the *s*peech, I *p*ray you, as I *p*ronounc'd it to you, *t*rippingly on the *t*ongue . . . .

anadiplosis (ana-di-PLO-sis). You repeat early in a clause a significant word from the end of the preceding clause.

They rode in on a *wave* of fear, but the *wave* took them up the beach.
Learn as though you would *live* forever; *live* as though you would die tomorrow.

anaphora (a-NAF-or-a). "A bringing again." You begin successive sentences or clauses with the same word or sound.

The voice of the Lord is powerful. The voice of the Lord is full of majestie. The voice of the Lord breaks the cedars. (Psa. xxix.4–5)
The game is lost. The game was finished before it began. The game was a farce of sportsmanship.

antanaclasis (anta-NAK-la-sis). You repeat the same word in a different sense, punning on it to drive home your point.

Learn a *craft* so you may live without *craft.*
Care* in your youth so you may live without *care.

epanalepsis (EP-ana-LEP-sis). You end your second clause with the same word or sound that began your first clause.

A fool with his friends, with his wife a fool.
In sorrow was I born, and will die in sorrow.

epistrophe (e-PIS-tro-fee). You end several sentences alike for emphasis.

They loved football. They ate football. They slept football.

epizeuxis (EP-i-ZYEWK-sis). You double the same word for emphasis.

Romeo, Romeo, wherefore art thou Romeo?
Oh, John, John.
It is not, believe me, it is not.
War, war after war.

homeoteleuton (homeo-TEL-yu-ton). You end successive clauses or phrases with the same sound.

In activity commendable, in commonwealth formidable, in war terrible.
He spoke wittily, praised the principal mightily, and ended happily.

paregmenon (pa-REG-meh-non). You play upon derivatives of a word.

A discrete discretion.
A marvel of the marvelous.
The humble are proud of humility.

paronomasia (parono-MAY-zhia). You pun by changing a letter or syllable.

His *sword* is better than his *word*.
***Errors* cause *terrors*.**
Bolder in the *buttery* than in the *battery*.
***Friends* turned *fiends*.**
***Repining* but not *repenting*.**

ploce (PLO-see). You repeat a word emphatically to bring out its literal meaning.

A *man's* a *man*, for a' that.
A *player* who is really a *player*.
In that battle *Caesar* was *Caesar*.

Substituting

hendiadys (hen-DIE-a-dis). "One through two." You divide what would be an adjective-and-noun into two nouns connected by *and*.

We drank from cups and gold [golden cups].
He looked with eyes and anger [angry eyes].

metaphor. "A carrying across." You describe something as if it were something else (see pp. 183–186).

All flesh is grass.
She was a horse.
She preened her feathers.

metonymy (meh-TON-i-me). A kind of metaphor, in which you substitute an associated item for the thing itself.

The *White House* declares [for "the *President* declares"].
The *crown* decides [for "the *king* decides"].
The *hot rod* is here [for "the young man who drives a car in which the piston rods run at high temperatures is here"—*hot rod* is already a synecdoche for *car*].

parabola (pa-RAB-o-la). You illustrate with a slight narrative touch, or "parable." This is a **hypothesis** (see p. 381) somewhat nearer the possible.

It is as if a man were to hit the bull's eye without aiming, or indeed without even seeing the target.
But this is to count your chickens before they hatch.

paradiastole (para-die-ASS-to-lee). In a kind of euphemism, you substitute a term remotely similar to the real idea, as in calling a reckless driver "playful" to underline his recklessness ironically.

The *generous* Mr. Smith [actually improvident].
The general's tactics were *cautious* [downright timid or cowardly].
Bill played a *conservative* game [obviously stupid].
She is *considerate* of her appearance [does nothing but work on it].

prosopopoeia (pro-so-po-PE-ya). You personify an inanimate object. Originally, the idea was pretending that an inanimate thing, an imaginary being, or an absent person (especially the illustrious dead) was speaking; now, more broadly, it is the general endowing of inanimate objects with human attributes.

Thou still unravished bride of quietness.
The stadium settled back for a lonely week.
This car is a sweetheart in every line.

synecdoche (si-NEK-do-kee). You put (a) the part for the whole, (b) the whole for the part, (c) the species for the genus, (d) the genus for the species, (e) the material for the object it constitutes.

(a) **He is a good *hand*.**
(b) **Here comes *Michigan* [for only the football team of one university within the state].**
(c) **a *cutthroat* [for any kind of murderer].**
(d) **the *felines* [for lions].**
(e) **He handles his *woods* well [for golf clubs made of wood].**

Miscellaneous

hyperbaton (high-PER-ba-ton). You transpose the normal order of words for elegance.

That the lady will surely enjoy.
Him the crowd adores.

martyria (mar-TIR-i-a). "Witnessing." You confirm something from your own experience.

> I have seen thousands standing with their rice bowls.
>
> Many times I have found the stadium only half filled.

metabasis (meh-TAB-a-sis). "Transition." Briefly reminding the reader where you and he are, where you have been, and where you are going.

> We have just seen some of radiation's immediate effects; now let us consider the long-term effects.
>
> I have already mentioned property taxes; now I shall consider those that hit everybody.

mimesis (mi-MEE-sis). "Imitation." You imitate the language of others.

> The cracker-barrel politician is just about *done gone* from the Southern scene.
>
> Try *to never split* your infinitives, if you wish *to further improve* your diction and *to really understand* good writing.

synchoresis (SIN-ko-REE-sis). You concede something, usually ironically, in order to retort with greater force.

> I admit that we have no business in their affairs, except the business of helping them, at their request, toward freedom and justice.
>
> They are surly, unmanageable, ungrateful. I admit it. But I deny that society can afford not to help them.

Index

Symbols for Common Errors

( )	Misspelling.
[ ]	This should be cut.
___	Something wrong here; diction too high; too low; word misused.
,	Put in a comma! (See pp. 147–156.)
(,)	This punctuation is wrong: usually a run-on sentence, a comma where a period or semicolon should be. (See Ch. 10.)
/M	Make this letter lower case. (The opposite would be: Matthew.)
^	Something omitted.
?	Not clear.
∽	Transpose.
¶	Paragraph. Or you may find No ¶
//st	Parallel construction. (See pp. 121–125.)
agr	Agreement of subject and verb. (See pp. 329–331.)
ambig	Ambiguous: clarify.
awk	Awkward.
DM	Dangling or squinting modifier. (See pp. 119, 347–350.)
Frag	Fragmentary sentence. (See pp. 144–145.)
gr	Bad grammar in the underlined pronoun, verb, adjective, or adverb. (See Appendix A.)
ref	Bad reference; it doesn't match, or have, an antecedent. (See pp. 343–345.)
S	Bad sentence: reconstruct.
tense	Your verbs have slipped in tense, voice, or mood. (See pp. 333–335.)
trite	Worn-out words.
usage	Not standard; check your levels.
wordy	Words, words, words: recast, condense. (See pp. 132–140, 189–191.)

THOMAS Y. CROWELL COMPANY
New York Established 1834